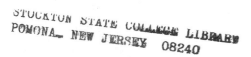

SIR WILLIAM GREGORY OF COOLE

SIR WILLIAM GREGORY OF COOLE
THE BIOGRAPHY
OF AN ANGLO-IRISHMAN

Brian Jenkins

COLIN SMYTHE
Gerrards Cross 1986

U.S. DISTRIBUTOR
DUFOUR EDITIONS
CHESTER SPRINGS,
PA 19425-0449
(215) 458-5005

Copyright © 1986 Brian Jenkins

First published in Great Britain in 1986 by Colin Smythe Limited
Gerrards Cross, Buckinghamshire

British Library Cataloguing in Publication Data
Jenkins, Brian
Sir William Gregory of Coole: the biography of
an Anglo-Irishman
1. Gregory, *Sir* William 2. Politicians—Great
Britain—Biography 3. Sri Lanka—Governors
—Biography 4. Politicians—Irish—Biography
I. Title
325'.341'09549'3 DA565.G8
ISBN 0-86140-175-1

Produced in Great Britain
Set by Action Typesetting, Gloucester
and printed and bound by Billing & Sons Ltd, Worcester

for
Jean Jenkins

CONTENTS

ILLUSTRATIONS

ACKNOWLEDGEMENTS

It was a dozen years ago that I discovered, quite by chance, the common interest I shared with a friend and colleague at the University of Saskatchewan, Edward McCourt, in the career of Sir William Gregory. Edward, a distinguished Canadian author, was preparing a biography of Gregory while I was at work on the first of a pair of volumes on Britain and the American Civil War and was naturally intrigued by the leading partisan of the Confederate cause in the House of Commons. Following Edward McCourt's untimely death, and with the encouragement of his widow Margaret, I agreed to complete what he had begun. However, I quickly realized that I could neither match Edward McCourt's style nor continue a biography that was informed by his deep knowledge of English literature. Instead, I decided to start afresh on an historical analysis of Gregory's life though I did profit enormously from my reading of the four chapters Edward McCourt wrote and which are now to be found among his papers held in the Archives of the University of Saskatchewan. Although I was unable to devote myself to this project until I had completed in 1979 the second volume of my diplomatic history, I received every cooperation from Sir William's grandson, the late Major Richard Gregory. He permitted me to carry off to Canada his grandfather's papers and never for one moment revealed any impatience with my slow progress. It was a remarkable act of trust and generosity for which I remain deeply grateful. I was also assisted by the many kindnesses and suggestions of Colin Smythe who possesses a matchless knowledge of the Gregory family. Finally, I owe a debt of gratitude to my wife. In an important respect this book is as much her work as it is my own. She read through the Gregory Papers and provided me with a guide to their contents; she encouraged me to write biography; and she read every page of the manuscript.

BRIAN JENKINS

Bishop's University,
Lennoxville, Canada.
May, 1983

1

THE FAMILY FORTUNE
AND A FAMILY TRADITION

They arrived with Cromwell and came to exemplify, even to epitomise, the Ascendancy. They were Irishmen but remained faithful to the British connection, and just as that loyalty was their making so eventually it was to prove their undoing. The Gregorys traced their lineage to the Twelfth Century, to John Gregory, Lord of Freseley and Asfordby in Leicestershire. Branches of the family tree soon extended to the counties of Lincoln, Warwick and Hereford, but if their pedigree was long, and the multiple quarterings of the family arms were a testimony to astute marriages, few Gregorys had by the Seventeenth Century emerged from the mists of historical obscurity. One had fallen with Simon de Montford at the Battle of Evesham, being the Earl's standard bearer, while another was slain at Bannockburn. A third lived to enjoy his distinction. Law and politics are natural bedfellows and William Gregory, of the Hereford branch, having been appointed Recorder of Gloucester in 1672 entered Parliament six years later and was elected Speaker in 1679. A knighthood and appointment as a Baron of the Exchequer quickly followed, but he was stripped of his offices in 1685. Of course, to have run afoul of James II soon became a recommendation and in 1689 William Gregory was elevated to the august solitude of the King's Bench. That same year saw the first generation of Irish Gregorys make their mark in their native land.

Thomas Gregory, and his cousin Giles, members of the Puritan squirearchy, served with Cromwell in Ireland and in the settlement following that savage campaign Giles 'obtained a grant of lands in Tipperary and a house in the "Citty" of Cashel'. Giles died without a male heir so it was left to Thomas to root the family in Irish soil. Settling in Londonderry, he married there, and fathered two sons, Robert and George. They were to be found among the many Protestants who with their families and belongings took refuge behind Derry's walls early in 1689.[1]

The Jacobite years were a difficult period for the dominant Protestant minority in Ireland, as James II implemented his 'Catholic design' for the kingdom. They watched fearfully as the army expanded rapidly in size and became as exclusively Catholic as formerly it had been Protestant. They saw their fellow religionists purged from office, the Protestant charters of the larger towns revoked, and the corporations

1

opened to Catholics. Nor did the landing of William of Orange in England in 1688 immediately lighten the mood of grim foreboding. Catholic Ireland declared for Catholic James. In Dublin, the 'Patriot' Parliament zealously bent to the task of undoing the Restoration land settlement which had modified the Cromwellian but had fallen far short of the expectations of the Catholic Irish who had suffered for their loyalty to the Crown. Consequently, the advance of the King's Catholic army on Protestant Ulster caused panic among people who had either survived or been raised on the legendary atrocities of 1641. Protestants feared that their lands would be reclaimed by those Catholics who had been dispossessed three decades earlier; they were alarmed by the act of attainder directed against supporters of William but seemingly readily adaptable as a weapon of religious extirpation; they were incensed and frightened by the seizure of many of their churches. In panic, Protestants sought refuge in the fortified city which had proven a haven in 1641 and had withstood a siege of twenty weeks eight years later.[2]

By April of 1689 those within Derry's walls had closed the gates of the city in the face of the King's troops and uttered the immortal cry of 'No Surrender'. The decision of the reinforcements from Britain to withdraw without even attempting to land, and the desertion of their governor and the departure of the leading officers, obliged the defenders to look to themselves and it was at this crucial moment that the Gregorys stepped forward from the ranks to play important roles in this great Protestant drama. The brothers, together with two of Robert's sons, repaired gun carriages, they 'performed the office of Guners during the seige (*sic*), all day in the City, and did their duty at the Windmill at night', and it was they who mounted the famous gun on the Cathedral steeple which did so much to sustain the morale of the beleagured citizens. When it opened fire the defenders took heart from the sight of the besiegers on the opposite bank of the River Foyle rushing from their positions in disorder and throwing themselves face down on the ground for cover. Also, Robert Gregory 'built a horse-mill that went with Double Harness at his own expense for the use of the Army, and ground all the graine for the whole garrison during the Seige, maintaining men and horses to perform the said work'. He fed the men who built the mill, dividing among them the eighteen large oxen, the twenty-two cows, the twenty barrels of meal and the horse load of cheese which he had brought with him into the city. 'When they had eaten that he gave them two large horses which they also eat.' His had been a significant contribution to the city's triumphant resistance, Robert Gregory submitted, for had he 'not built the said mill, the whole garrison must have perished for want of bread, the Enemy having got possession of all the mills abt the City'.[3]

Although they saw the campaign through to its end and were among William's victorious troops at the Boyne, the Gregorys in common with so many of Derry's courageous citizen soldiers were subsequently treated with rank ingratitude. Robert Gregory calculated that the value of the 'goods and money' he had laid out during the siege came to £258 but that when he added his pay as 'one of the Chief Guners' — pay promised but not received — the total he was owed by the Crown exceeded £700. Yet by 1712 a mere pittance of £50 had been forthcoming, and he had been obliged to beg for that in order 'to prevent himself and family from perishing'. 1716 found him still petitioning for recovery of his due. 'Your Petr and his great family, he having a wife and fifteen children, whereof ten are unprovided for, most humbly pray your Excies and Lordships to take his miserable circumstances into your serious consideration, and grant him some Releife out of the Concordatum otherwise they must unavoidably starve for want of bread.' This pathetic appeal failed to move a thankless government to generosity, and two years later Robert Gregory renewed his entreaty. Meanwhile, George Gregory and his numerous progeny had fared rather better. Perhaps they had sacrificed less, or had husbanded more, but with the fall of Jacobite Ireland they quickly dispersed across the island. As befitted gentlemen they usually held either commissions or benefices. The seventh of George's sons, Henry, settled first in Limerick, where he leased a farm of some 800 acres, but following a dispute with the landowner he moved on to the town of Galway.[4]

The Galway to which Henry Gregory came, and with his marriage to Mary Shawe he connected himself to one of its leading families, was something of an anomaly. Despite an overwhelmingly Catholic population it had been less than full-hearted in its commitment to the cause of James II. The heart of 'that province which rock and morass have doomed to a perpetual poverty', and to which Cromwell had banished those Irish he dispossessed, Galway had survived and even prospered under the terms of the settlement imposed with the restoration of Charles II in 1660. By the time of James's accession not only did Catholics own the greater part of the county, but in the port Catholic merchants had recovered the bulk of their trade. Galway landowners therefore responded with some alacrity to peace overtures from the Williamite forces during the winter of 1690–91, and the town willingly capitulated on handsome terms in July 1691. In short, the revolution had been a comparatively painless experience for Galway, and most of the merchants and other inhabitants of the town were 'well pleased that English Government is again restored among them'. As for the accompanying penal laws, such as the provision that after March 1703, 'no person of the Popish religion except seamen, fishermen, and day labourers, who do not pay upwards of 40s a year rent, should come to live within its walls; that no Papist should purchase any house or tenement in the city or in its suburbs, and that those who were living there at the date of the enactment should be compelled to find Protestant sureties for their good behaviour', they effected little change. By the middle of the Eighteenth Century only 350 of the town's 14,000 residents were Protestants.[5]

No doubt Henry Gregory, like his wife's brothers, made his living through trade. Galway merchants owned more than a dozen ships in the 1730s, though as a port and a commercial centre the town was already slowly declining. And it is family legend that Henry's only son, Robert (b. 1727) stowed away as a youth on one of the vessels of his maternal uncles trading to East India, worked his passage as a cabin boy and secured on his arrival in Calcutta a Writership in the East India Company's service. The truth is just a little less romantic, for at the age of nineteen Robert Gregory was a young man rather than an adventurous boy and he may have travelled as a supercargo. Nor did he enter the service of the Company. Instead, he went to India as a free merchant, one of that group of men who 'goes out to all places to the Eastward of the Cape of Good Hope, with leave of the Company under a Bond not to Trade with Europe, except in Diamonds nor from Europe but with coral'.

When he finally set sail for home in February 1766, along with his wife and children, and accompanied by a retinue of 'black servants', Robert Gregory could afford to travel in style. If the actual size of his fortune is unknown he soon gave every evidence that it was substantial. 'In those days the pagoda tree had not shed all its golden fruit', his great-grandson wrote more than a century later, 'and my relative was undoubtedly not behind his neighbours in gathering it'. Certainly on arrival in England Robert Gregory's behaviour did not differ markedly from that of the returning 'nabobs'. He acquired a London residence, in Upper Brook Street, off Grosvenor Square, but then moved to Berners Street, which runs north from Oxford Street. He purchased country estates, at Valence, Kent; Chigwell, Essex; and a third in his native Galway. The dream of joining the landed gentry, membership of which guaranteed status and respect and promised to open doors to a society which valued its exclusivity, had sustained many an expatriate during the years of steamy heat and tedium in India. Gregory had his portrait painted by the fashionable Nathanial Dance, who also captured Robert Clive. If there was a roundness to his features which gave them a youthfulness even in middle age, they, together with the whig and the stock, and the characteristic contrast between the pale forehead and the suntanned and ruddy lower half of the face, all suggest the working squirearchy. Yet there is also more than a hint of the nabob. The eyes are dark and kindly, but the lips are too full, their sensuality heightened by the shadow of a heavy beard, and the chin recedes into the folds of a neck that betrays over-indulgence.

In common with other nabobs Gregory sought a seat in Parliament and played an active role in the affairs of the East India Company, disdaining to sink down into 'curry, mulligatawny and indolence'. Indeed, the former involvement was often no more than an extension of the latter, and India dominated Gregory's life for as many years after his return to Britain as he had spent in Bengal. Not that he was merely another nabob. While his behaviour conformed to the pattern, even to his custom of travelling between his estates in ostentatious magnificence, attended by a small army of liveried flunkeys decked out in black breeches, black silk stockings and gold garters, he escaped the hostility encountered by so many of those who returned from India laden with riches. Scorn for their meretricious style of living was mixed with envy of the size of their fortunes and contempt for the means by which they had been made. But Gregory had not been a Company servant who had sacrificed his employer's interests in the service of his own, nor had he oppressed the native population. On the contrary, he impressed as 'a gentleman of good Fortune, acquired really in a very honourable manner in the East Indies'. Moreover, if Gregory's motives in entering Parliament were little different from those of other nabobs — status, prestige, and the power to protect and advance his commercial interest in the East India Company — he carefully avoided the pitfall into which so many of them stumbled. Elections and thus parliamentary seats were commonly purchased but the nabobs offended both because of the sums they were able to lay out and the crudity with which they did so. Richard Smith, having been defeated at Rochester in 1771, announced his candidacy for Hinden in 1774 from the Market Cross and promised five guineas to every elector who voted for him. Angered and alarmed by such profligacy, the elder Pitt railed against those who had 'forced their way into Parliament by such a torrent of private corruption as no private hereditary fortune can resist'. When Gregory successfully sought a seat in 1768 as a supporter of the Earl of Rockingham he 'particularly desired that where he stood — It might be with the Countenance of the Neighbouring gentlemen and some old and known interest as thinking that ground was better and freer from the accusation of coming as an Adventurer'.[6]

Explaining the respect Gregory soon enjoyed in the House, one contemporary attributed it to the fact that he was 'a very honourable, incorrupt, independent man; simple, or rather shy and repulsive, in his manners, unadorned by any accomplishment of mind, but laborious, attentive to business, and possessing very extensive local information on East Indian concerns'. He was also a powerful figure within the East India Company, serving for many years as a Director and very briefly as Chairman. Yet, unlike those many other nabobs whose concern was exclusively with the profits, prestige and patronage of their investment and the byzantine politics of the Court of Directors, Robert Gregory always kept larger objects in mind. He certainly defended stoutly the Company and its interests in the House but not to the exclusion of the public interest. When the fear was voiced that significant documents would be withheld by the Directors from the Secret Committee of inquiry elected in 1781 'He pledged himself to the House, that if any such circumstance should occur, he would move in his place for the most exemplary punishment that could be inflicted on the man, or set of men, that should be guilty of this offence. . . .'[7]

The Robert Gregory who emerges from his correspondence, as from his speeches, is a man of studied formality (by no means unusual in that age) and unaffected humility. However, he was proud of his rectitude. Following his resignation as Chairman of the East India Company he drafted a formal deposition listing the sixteen appointments he had made to the Company's civil service during his membership of the Direction and solemnly denied 'that During that Time or after Did I ever recieve (*sic*) Directly or Indirectly any Sum or Sums of Money or otherwise for any Nomination or Service that I ever Tendered to any Person or Persons'. He remained confident to the end that his interest in India was public spirited. His concerns were national and humanitarian — to preserve India for Britain by protecting it from ruin and to promote the welfare of the natives. In 1786 he was still offering moral support, somewhat tinged with pessimism, to his friend Edmund Burke in the battle for reform. 'I most truly wish you every success', he wrote, 'but I fear the country is too languid to give you the support they ought to a business where the honour and interest of this country is so materially concerned'. Indeed, he was evidently thinking of his own career and composing its epitaph when he declared that Burke's efforts would prove that there had been men who in the worst of times had laboured to save the innocent, to punish the guilty, and to 'preserve an extensive advantageous Dominion at the extremity of the Globe to Great Britain'. And he reaffirmed his faith in a progressive policy in the last letter of his life.[8]

By 1784 Robert Gregory's public career was behind him. Slowly, he began to put his private affairs in order. His life style had been an expensive one. He had surely sunk a substantial portion of his fortune in the purchase of three country estates and a house in a fashionable section of the capital, while his expenditure in politics had also been 'very great'. His investment in the East India Company had not always been profitable, and examination of stock ledgers suggests that he was not among those Directors who capitalized upon their inside information to unload holdings early in the 1770s before word of the Company's distress leaked out. Anxiety about his own financial position may well explain Gregory's later sale of two of his estates, and if it was the Irish property he retained that choice was not governed simply by sentiment. The large sprawling estate in his native Galway was worth £7,000 a year. Nor was he any more sentimental or less businesslike when he turned to the task of appointing an heir.

Three of the children his wife bore him survived, all sons and all born in India. The eldest, Robert, was twelve when the family returned to Britain in 1766. Entering Harrow with his brothers in 1770, he was appointed to a Writership in the East India Company in 1772. However, as a result of his father's influence, he was permitted to delay his departure for India until 1775 without any loss of seniority. He steadily advanced through the various grades of Company servants — factor, Junior Merchant and Senior Merchant. Then, in 1782, he was appointed Assistant Resident at Lucknow. If this was a peace overture by Governor-General Hastings to an old foe who was the new chairman of the Company it served the younger Robert Gregory ill. All residencies were valuable, being regarded as 'the most lucrative posts' in the Company's service, and Gregory had already earmarked his son for Patna, but Lucknow was without doubt the most prized. The Europeans 'lived in a style far exceeding even the expense and luxuriousness of Calcutta', one writer noted. They were also notoriously corrupt and Hastings described Lucknow after his visit in 1781 as 'a Sink of Iniquity, the School of Rapacity'. The spendthrift Nawab of Oudh, Asaf-ud-daulah, maintained a score of palaces and employed thousands of domestic servants. He lavished money on his 'pigeon-house, cockpits, sheep-folds, deer park, monkey, snake, scorpion and spiderhouses', money he had wrung from his subjects or had borrowed. He in turn was victimised by the Europeans, including the officials of the Residency, who extorted 'presents' from the Nawab, loaned him money at unconscionable rates of interest, and imported goods for him from Europe which they marked up by as much as 500 per cent.[9]

That a son of his was a party to the misrule against which he had always fought must have come as a hard blow to Gregory. Equally unpleasant was the evidence not only that his son had remained in this depraved environment after the Residency was temporarily withdrawn but that he had succumbed to one of its most expensive temptations. The perils of gambling must have been all too obvious to the senior Gregory. Bored East India Company servants had traditionally squandered time and money in this way and the efforts of the Directors to lessen 'the itch of gaming' (they did not attempt to cure it) had not been effective during his time in Bengal. Further, he had returned to Britain at a time when gaming clubs were growing in popularity and number in the capital. Among those who fell prey to this vice was his friend Charles James Fox. By the age of twenty five, an anniversary he celebrated in 1774, Fox had lost £140,000, most of it at the tables. As one lampoonist observed:

> No doubt such behaviour exceedingly shocks
> All the friends and acquaintances of this Mr. Fox.

All the reports from Lucknow were of acts of dissipation rivalling those of Fox, of men frittering away £25,000 at a sitting. As for Gregory's eldest son, there was startling visual proof of his prodigality.[10]

In 1783, having fallen on hard times after a period of astonishing success, the artist John Zoffany had travelled to India in a desperate attempt to restore his fortunes. There, as he had hoped, his talents as a portrait painter were well rewarded. Inevitably, he was attracted to the opulence of Lucknow, its racy and free-spending society, and among the works his residence inspired was 'Colonel Mordaunt's Cock Match'. Prominent among the sporting gentlemen captured by Zoffany, and detailed likenesses were one of his great strengths, was the younger Robert Gregory. Unfortunately for the son the picture was exhibited in the window of a firm of frame makers located in the Strand and there it was spotted by the father. This graphic evidence, which was confirmed by additional enquiries in India, that his son had continued to gamble despite repeated warnings to desist, appears to have been the last straw for the elder Robert Gregory. Alarmed for the security of what remained of the fortune he had so laboriously amassed in Bengal, hopeful that it would still be sufficient to increase the family's influence and significance, he now disinherited his eldest son 'because of his propensity for gambling, and his continued neglect of me'. Under the terms of his father's will Robert Gregory received £300 a year for life, which was sufficient, together with his pay as a Senior Merchant, to ensure that he lived in relative comfort. He 'died unmarried at Calcutta in December, 1814'.[11]

If his eldest son was profligate, Robert Gregory's second child appears to have been one of those men marked by fate for misfortune. Richard had been born in India in 1761 and the family's return to England saw him both educated and employed in the manner befitting a gentleman — Harrow School, Trinity College, Cambridge, the Army. Robert Gregory purchased a commission for this son in one of the prestigious regiments of Guards, but Richard's military career came to an abrupt, sad and humiliating end in 1793. The abandonment of an outpost by troops under his direct command, during the Valenciennes campaign, led to a court-martial. Acquitted of the most serious charge, that of cowardice, he was convicted of misconduct and sentenced 'to be reprimanded by the President in the presence of the Courtmartial only'. Smarting from this indignity and the accompanying shame, convinced that he had been unfairly condemned, Richard Gregory soon resigned his commission and then launched a somewhat quixotic defence of his conduct by publishing the proceedings of the court-martial for circulation among friends. He also withdrew from 'general society', and the strain of this self-imposed isolation — for he had been the most gregarious of men — and the festering sense of grievance he harboured over his disgrace, may well have contributed to the 'severe paralytic stroke' he suffered, 'which ruined his previous good looks and twisted his head on one side'. Disfigured, Richard Gregory retreated 'into complete misanthropy'.[12]

For Robert Gregory, who had guarded his public reputation and the family name so jealously and so successfully, the stain on his second son's honour must have been a doubly cruel blow. And while he did not entirely disinherit Richard, his was to be a life interest only in the Irish estate.[13] No matter the number of children Richard might father, the Irish lands were left 'in Trust' for Robert Gregory's third son,

William, who had married well, was raising a family, and gave every sign of upholding the family tradition of public service.

William Gregory had been born in India in February, 1762. He, like his brother Richard, was educated in Harrow before also going up to Trinity College, Cambridge, 'where he graduated B.A. in 1783 and M.A. in 1787'. With one younger son already destined for the Army, Robert Gregory appears initially to have earmarked William for the Bar and he was admitted a student of the Inner Temple in May, 1781. Although called to the Bar in 1788, he does not appear to have practised his profession. No doubt William was employed for a time administering his father's vast Galway estate, for in 1789 he married Anne Trench and thus joined a local family of resident gentry which was not only one of the most powerful in the county but was emerging as one of Ireland's most influential. It was also a family of diehard Tories, but to attribute to this alliance William Gregory's subsequent career as an unrelenting opponent of Catholic claims, and his abandonment of the liberal opinions on which his father had raised him, is too simplistic.

The late Eighteenth Century had brought Irish Catholics relief from many of the penal laws under which they had laboured. In these years of Enlightenment and Revolution, measures of religious discrimination directed against the great majority of the population appeared to be both benighted and foolishly provocative. Among the obsolete laws swept away were those closing the town of Galway to Catholic residents, but Catholics continued to be barred from Parliament, from the highest offices of state, from the bench, and from the office of High Sheriff. Yet they were permitted, after 1793, to exercise the franchise on the same terms as Protestants. It was to these decisions — 'giving full political power to the Catholic democracy, and at the same time withholding political power and influence from the Catholic gentry' — that W. E. H. Lecky traced the origins of much of the ensuing political turbulence. [14]

The Rockingham Whigs had long espoused a liberal policy towards Ireland, supporting its demands for commercial freedom and during their brief tenure of power in 1782 negotiating its legislative independence. The outbreak of the French Revolution and the eruption of fresh disorders in Ireland, disorders excited by a variety of economic grievances including the tithing of Catholics for the support of the Established Church, had prompted Edmund Burke to advocate concessions. Convinced of the inherent conservatism of the Catholic population, he argued that if dealt with justly it would loyally defend an existing order which included the Establishment. Then, in 1795, the Whigs having entered into a coalition with Pitt, Lord Fitzwilliam was sent to Ireland as Viceroy. A well meaning man and a pupil of Burke's, he was worried about the danger of a French invasion and sought to win the loyalty of Catholics by removing their remaining disabilities. But he travelled too fast for the cabinet in London and within a few weeks had been recalled. [15]

Robert Gregory, sharing Burke's view of the problems of their native land, had been one of those who had supported Fitzwilliam and who believed that an upsurge of rural violence by Catholic 'Defenders' was one consequence of his dismissal. Writing from Galway in September 1795, Gregory deplored the 'corruption' in Ireland. Too many men entered the exclusively Protestant Parliament for the same reason others joined a commercial house in London — to profit. There was an absence of a sense of public duty, he complained. This contrasted sharply with the behaviour of those country gentlemen who co-operated with the military to hold the troublesome 'Defenders' in check, and in Galway none did so with greater zeal than Roman Catholic gentlemen. 'I have no particular connection with them', he wrote, 'but I believe them to be as good subjects as His Majesty has in Ireland'. The gentlemen of Galway, he added, were fully convinced that Fitzwilliam's measures would have soon checked 'the corruption and abuses that prevails (*sic*) so openly in this country and that had your lordship been permitted, that you would have soon united the People in perfect confidence of a just Government'.

Two years later the sense of an opportunity missed was even stronger, for by then the radical and dissident United Irishmen were much in evidence throughout the island. Making his annual journey to Galway, Gregory reported to Fitzwilliam on the state of the country. Dublin's streets were constantly patrolled, he noted, and its jails filled with persons taken up on information or suspicion. As he continued west, through Kildare, Meath and Westmeath, he found troops everywhere, and learned that they had to be dispatched each night to protect the homes of magistrates and country gentlemen. Nevertheless, they were unable to prevent attacks by United Irishmen on people or stock. Across the Shannon conditions were calmer, but there were disturbing reports of the spread of violence. All of this might have been avoided, he believed, had remedial measures been adopted in time.[16]

There had always been powerful voices raised in opposition to the policy of concessions Robert Gregory endorsed. To remove the remaining disabilities and open Parliament to Catholics would merely clear the way for their recovery of power, conservatives warned, and they considered themselves vindicated by the rebellion in 1798. Although savagery was common to both sides, as the Irish cycle of reciprocal atrocities gained new momentum, the barbarism in Wexford, which took on the colour at times of a priest-led war of religious extermination, 'made a profound and indelible impression' on the mind of the Protestant minority. The ' "bloodhounds of Enniscorthy and Wexford" by the horrors they had committed, had "added new disgrace to a religion whose former enormities it would have been infinitely better to have expatiated than revived".' If some Protestants interpreted the uprising as a Catholic conspiracy, others saw it as the work of Jacobins whose inspiration was the French Revolution and whose objective was the founding of a democratic republic that would confiscate property, abolish ranks and eradicate church establishments. Nor were these two explanations incompatible. Had republicanism and Catholic bigotry joined hands 'in a deadly league'?[17]

The British Government concluded that union was the best solution for the problems of Ireland, and it gave to Lord Castlereagh the formidable task of persuading the members of the Irish Parliament to vote their legislature's extinction. Initially, the Trenches, to whom William Gregory was allied by marriage, were numbered among the opponents of this act of political suicide. In 1799 William Power Keating Trench, Gregory's father-in-law, having been created an Irish peer two years earlier, wrote to Castlereagh to complain that he had been passed over for promotion even though his family (sons Richard and Charles sat in the Irish Parliament, as later did his son-in-law briefly) had supported the government on every major issue bar that of union. A change of heart on this measure saw Trench advanced as Earl of Clancarty in 1801 and his sons, and son-in-law, rewarded with new positions within the Irish administration. Yet it would be unfair to charge that they had simply bartered their support, that they had grasped the plums Castlereagh dangled before influential figures as part of his campaign 'of bribing knaves into honesty and fools into Commonsense'. The Trench clan had shifted ground in order to remain aligned with opinion in Galway, which had moved from opposition to support of union.[18]

William Gregory 'was originally a man of liberal opinions', and it was during the last days of the Fitzwilliam Viceroyalty that his career in the Irish administration had been launched. Appointed Surveyor of Skerries, 1799 found him serving as High Sheriff of Galway and as a commissioner examining the claims of loyalists who had suffered in the rebellion. The commission, of which his brother-in-law Charles was another member, sat until 1806, which ensured that Gregory did not quickly put behind him the terrible events of 1798. Trench influence may also explain his appointment in 1800 as Secretary to the Director General of Inland Navigation, and his brief career as a Member of the Irish Parliament. Nor did this family connection harm his prospects of further advancement. However, he earned promotion. Unhappily, his father did not live to see him selected as Ireland's senior 'civil servant'.

Robert Gregory died at his London home on 1 September 1810. On 6 September William set out from Ireland to attend the funeral. He sailed from Dublin aboard the *Uxbridge*, landing the following day at Holyhead, the Welsh port on the tip of Anglesey. The crossing, only some sixty miles as the crow flies, had been a long one of thirty hours. Taking the mail coach to Shrewsbury, he then turned south to Gloucester and Bath. Four days of hard travel at a cost of £17 had brought him from Dublin to the spa, and another two days of discomfort had yet to be endured, and £9 more paid out, before he finally reached London. His father was buried on 14 September in Marylebone Church Yard, which was only a short distance from the house on

Berners Street. Five days later, accompanied by his elder brother Richard, he went to Doctors Commons to prove his father's will.

Among the bequests were a number of annuities, which included the £300 for Robert Gregory's eldest son and lesser but generous settlements on a handful of servants. There was also an annuity of £225 for Anne Maria Frances Rees, whom Gregory recognized as his granddaughter. This provision lends some substance to the sad tale recounted by William Hickey in his memoirs. Hickey secured, with Gregory's help, an appointment in India, and there he met a former schoolfellow, Nathaniel Penry Rees. The son of an eminent scholar and leading Dissenting Minister, Rees appears to have rebelled against his father's sobriety and self-discipline. His life, in fact, serves to illustrate the accuracy of the statement which the American humorist Finley Peter Dunne put into the mouth of his creation Mr. Dooley a century later, that vice is indeed a heinous thing because the more you see of it the better you like it. Packed off to India, young Rees was given an appointment on the Supreme Court, which carried a generous salary, but the heavy expenses of dissipation soon prompted him as an attractive and engaging young man to seek the traditional relief — a good marriage. The lady of his choice was inaccurately described by Hickey as the 'natural daughter of the famous Mr. Gregory, by a Hindustanee woman, a well educated and handsome body whom everyone respected, receiving a handsome fortune with her, the principal of which was luckily settled on her and any issue she might bear'. If the terms of Robert Gregory's will suggest the settlement was not as large as was popularly believed, that may also account for Rees's careless alienation of his wife's affections soon after the birth of their daughter. His seduction of an English friend of hers, who had come out to stay with them, saw Margaret leave their house for that of her father's agent. Presumably she died soon afterwards (as did Rees, quitting life in the style he had lived it and carried to his grave in a puncheon of rum) and the child was sent to England were she lived with the nabob. Robert Gregory provided in his will not only for her support but also for the employment of a servant of his late wife to be her companion. [19]

Two years after his father's death William Gregory was plucked from obscurity within the Irish administration and appointed Civil Under Secretary. An Irish Executive had survived the Union. At its head there remained the viceregal representative, the Lord Lieutenant, complete with his Privy Council and Household, but the location of power soon began to shift. The fact that the Chief Secretary divided his time between London and Dublin, that he defended Irish policy in the Commons and directed its application from Dublin Castle, increased the significance of his office while the Viceroy was slowly relegated to the role of a figurehead. The administrative work of the Chief Secretary's office was managed by two departments, the Civil and the Military, each headed by an Under Secretary. In 1812 a young politician of promise, Robert Peel, was appointed Chief Secretary, having occupied an Irish

seat in the Commons for three years, although 'he had found no
occasion to visit his constituents or to hold communication with them'.
Shortly after his arrival in Dublin Peel was seeking an Under Secretary
of the Civil Department, for the occupant resigned to enter Parliament.
He offered the post to a friend in the Home Office, but the generous
salary of £2,500 and the handsome residence in Phoenix Park failed to
tempt this Englishman across the Irish Sea. The knowledge that Peel
held no strong opinion on any alternative candidate saw the Lord
Lieutenant, the Duke of Richmond, intervene to secure the
appointment of Gregory. Obliged to meet frequently with the Under
Secretary during the Chief Secretary's long absences, attending the
parliamentary sessions in London, Richmond was determined to deal
only with a gentleman and William Gregory impressed on this and
several other scores. Here was 'a perfect gentleman' and 'an excellent
man of business' who possessed extensive knowledge of both the
country and its gentry. In 1819 the retirement of the Military Under
Secretary saw the two departments merged under a single head —
William Gregory.[20]

Throughout the seventeen years of his tenure of the office of Under
Secretary Gregory showed himself to be an able administrator,
handling duties and superiors alike with intelligence, skill and
decision. He proved to be calm in emergencies. So impressed was Peel
by his subordinate that he soon granted him the widest latitude in the
exercise of his initiative. 'You will have no scruple in acting upon
everything of a public nature that occurs without reference to me', he
wrote in 1815 on the eve of a trip to the Continent, 'and you may be
quite sure of my approbation'. Thus did Gregory become, during those
long periods when the Chief Secretary was of necessity absent in
London, 'master of the whole machine of Government'. 'The petitioner
at the Castle did not ask what the Lord Lieutenant thought but what
the Lord Lieutenant's secretary thought, or rather what his Secretary's
secretary thought', one observer complained. It was Gregory, he went
on, 'who held in his hands the destinies of Ireland'. And the ends to
which he employed the influence he exerted and the power he wielded
saw Gregory denounced by some contemporaries as 'A violent anti-
Catholic — a furious Tory' who had vitiated the liberal tendencies of
several Chief Secretaries and Viceroys.[21]

Gregory brought to his office conservative attitudes characteristic of
many members of the Protestant Ascendancy who had lived through
the rebellion of 1798. This cast of mind did not always preclude
recognition of the genuine grievances of the poor, and Gregory freely
admitted that it was 'quite impossible for any man with commonsense
and common Feelings not to see and to bitterly deplore the lamentable
poverty of the Irish peasants, and none but a Brute or an Absentee
would refuse his money, his labour and his time to promote any rational
System for their amelioration'. Certainly as Under Secretary he was, as
even enemies granted, 'a sincere and active friend and promoter of the

physical interests of Ireland'. By the same token, the existence of wide-spread disaffection necessitated greater efforts to protect the minds of the public from the contagion of radicalism, and Gregory diligently supervised Peel's campaign to manipulate opinion both by stifling newspapers which opposed the government and rewarding those which offered it support. Nor did sympathy for the impoverished masses ever overcome the conservative's fundamental concern to uphold the law and maintain order. The 'ferocity' of a destitute and desperate peasantry, who were organized in a number of secret agrarian societies and subjected persons they regarded as enemies to punishment that was all too often horrifyingly brutal, was always in the forefront of Gregory's mind. It was nonsense, he insisted, to engage in 'sympathizing, philosophizing Prancing, when Insurrection of the most sanguinary spirit has manifested itself in so many acts of Outrage and is nightly and rapidly encreasing'. He resisted proposals to treat with lenity those whose activities were 'conducted with an impenetrable Secrecy and unrelenting cruelty', and was a champion of the salutary effect of 'severe' examples. More constructively, he supported Peel's efforts to reform the inadequate system of law enforcement in Ireland. An efficient police force and an active and effective magistracy would make it 'easier for the Irish peasant to look to the government instead of to the secret societies for protection and justice'.[22]

The long and intimate collaboration of Robert Peel and William Gregory in the government of Ireland, a partnership which extended beyond Peel's service as Chief Secretary to embrace his years as Home Secretary, was anchored in personal warmth and political compatibility. Although more than a score of years separated them in age, they had much in common. Both came from mercantile families; both had been fashionably educated, Peel going up to Christ Church, Oxford, from Harrow; both exhibited the industry common to their backgrounds; both shared a respect for time proven, even time worn, institutions. Peel described the Irishman simply as 'My friend'. But their friendship was fed by and in turn sustained an ideological harmony, for after only a brief residence in Ireland Peel was reciting the creed of Gregory's Irish conservatism. 'It is quite impossible for anyone to witness the remorselessness with which crimes are committed here, the almost total annihilation of the agency of conscience as a preventive of crime, and the universal contempt in which the obligation of any but an illegal oath is held by the mass of the people', he declared in 1816, 'without being satisfied that the prevailing religion of Ireland operates as an impediment rather than an aid to the ends of the civil government'. Consequently, Peel was an unswerving opponent of Catholic claims.[23]

Gregory's own unyielding opposition to Catholic emancipation was not merely an expression of simple if ugly Protestant bigotry. Rather, it reflected a 'domino theory' of Irish history. For him, as for other members of the Ascendancy, the removal of the remaining Catholic disabilities would set in motion a train of events that would end only with the fall of the British Empire. An 'equal division of power between rival parties who have so long been opposed, hating each other, is contrary to human nature', Gregory believed, thus either Protestant or Catholic 'must have the ascendancy'. [24] To fulfill the undertaking given to Catholics in 1800, that union would be followed by emancipation, would set them on the road to domination. Aware of their insignificance in Britain, but alive to how great they might be in Ireland, constituting as they did 80% of the population, Catholics would soon begin to agitate for the restoration of the Irish Parliament. Fearing this, most of those members of the Ascendancy who had opposed union, seeing a Protestant Parliament of Ireland as a bulwark, now clung to the connection to the rest of Britain as a 'guarantee of stability' and of their 'position'.

A successful attack on the union seemed certain to be followed by an assault on the Established Church. That these were the twin immediate objectives of organized Catholic agitation Gregory never for one moment doubted, thus he argued that 'concession in its most unqualified signification is vain, so long as the connexion with England is presumed to be maintained, or the protestant Establishment preserved so long will the same Body continue its hostility'. Further, he saw no room for Protestants in an Ireland governed by Catholics. 'Every Irish Protestant who has property he can remove, must look for some other Country; the young will emigrate; the hapless residue, whose ages or circumstances compel them to remain, must await their fate'. It was not a fate to be contemplated with equanimity a later and distinguished foreign visitor to Ireland admitted. The members of the Ascendancy would receive 'such treatment by the masses as was a few years ago, in Spain, experienced by the convents'. And where would this chain reaction of emancipation, repeal of the union, disestablishment, and emigration end but in the founding of a separate and independent Ireland which 'would lead to the speedy dismemberment of the Empire'. [25]

The emergence of Daniel O'Connell as the dominant figure in the struggle for Catholic emancipation, and the nature of the campaign of agitation he directed, merely strengthened Gregory's resolve to resist this fatal first concession. Born in 1775, chosen by his uncle to inherit the family's extensive lands in Kerry, educated in France, but fleeing from there to England to escape the Revolution, opting for law as his profession, O'Connell first attracted attention as an opponent of union and then played a prominent role in a succession of organizations pressing for emancipation. Significantly, Gregory was describing him as early as 1815 as 'this Jacobin Hero of the Catholic Faith'. By the 1820s he was welding the turbulent and disorganized peasantry into a disciplined political movement, the Catholic Association, through the inspired device of having them contribute a penny a month to the cause, and by the employment of the Catholic clergy as collectors of this 'Catholic Rent'. Priests did not scruple to resort to intimidation, physical and spiritual, in order to collect the dues which converted this association into a truly mass one. No less alarming was the skill with which the Association avoided contravening a 1793 statute prohibiting representative organizations and yet behaved like one. Gregory was quick to grasp that the real significance of the 'Rent' was less the money it put into the Association's coffers (essential though the funds were) than the direct communication it established between 'Popish people' and 'Popish Parliament'. Finally, the agitation was marked by demagogic attacks upon opponents of the Catholic cause, among them the royal heir, and by implied threats to let loose the 'desperate peasantry'; and by oratorical references to American independence, to the possibility of French and American aid and to Ireland's need for a Simon Bolivar. Hence Gregory's dismay in 1825 when he heard that Catholic relief was about to be taken up by Parliament and stood a fair chance of being enacted. He protested 'that when such denunciations were held out against Protestant Churches, such threats of separation from England by means of foreign aid, such foul calumny uttered against the Heir Apparent to the throne; the whole country organized by the agency of a bigotted and relentless Priesthood; it was natural to conclude that the Catholic Cause could not have gained supporters under such circumstances'. [26]

Many of those Members of Parliament ready to concede Catholic claims also favoured the offering of 'securities' to the Ascendancy. Gregory gloomily dismissed the guarantees as 'downright nonsense' because they were certain to be removed one day for exactly the same reason as emancipation would be granted — 'to satisfy Catholics'. One proposal was for state payment of the Catholic clergy. To free the priests of their financial dependence on parishioners would help keep them loyal, it was argued, while to make them pensioners of the state would lessen the influence they now exercised over their flocks. Gregory was not convinced by either argument and warned that 'the Popish Priesthood' would become more formidable not less 'when paid and acknowledged by the state, without their acknowledging the state by whom they are paid'. He was somewhat less dismissive of a scheme to diminish the political power of Catholics by disenfranchising the forty shilling freeholders. Catholic freeholders had been granted the franchise in 1793. At that time there was a broad measure of confidence that these new voters would be controlled by their landlords, who qualified them as electors by granting them leases and expected to be able to marshal them through a combination of inducements and threats. But the explosion in the size of the electorate — in Gregory's Galway it increased over a few years from a mere 700 to some 13,000 — saw a weakening of landlord control and the growth of a Catholic interest. In the emerging struggle between Protestant landowners and Catholic priests to influence the Catholic voter the latter had a priceless advantage. It was illustrated by the tenant who explained to his inquiring landlord 'That I could injure them in this world; but that they believed that the Priest could injure them in the next'. Contemplating the 'depravity' of the electoral system and the need for its reform, Gregory concluded that this issue ought to be exploited as a weapon to defeat not to facilitate Catholic relief. He urged friends to 'support, or oppose, the abolition of the 40s. freeholders, as may best serve the Protestant cause, by dividing the ranks of the enemy on the question'. [27]

Opposed to concessions even with 'securities' attached, Gregory gave thought to the desperate problem of how to maintain the Ascendancy in the face of widespread disaffection. One traditional ally — the Orange Lodges — had been reduced to ineffectiveness as a result of a determined effort begun in 1823 to dissolve these bodies of militant Protestants. Gregory's attitude towards them was ambivalent. Their unsavoury reputation for violence was offset in his mind by the knowledge that they admitted no man unless he had sworn oaths of allegiance and supremacy. He worried that to disband the Orangemen was to alienate the loyal without encouraging loyalty among the alienated. Therefore, he saw no immediate alternative to the suppression of organized Catholic agitation. Ineffectual efforts to repress the Catholic Association between 1825 and 1827 notwithstanding, he was still insisting in 1828 that it was 'vain to think of restoring vigour or power to the Executive Government of Ireland until the Popish Parliament is effectually put down'. Perhaps he agreed with his friend Peel that the best solution for Ireland was an honest despotic form of government — the benevolent autocracy so beloved of generations of political elitists of various stripes. Yet repression was not a permanent solution for the Ascendancy's problems, and in the long term a devout Gregory looked hopefully to the remedial influence of Protestantism. The 1820s found a band of evangelical clerics attempting to rouse the Established Church from its complacency and inertia. They undertook a 'Protestant Crusade' and in the vanguard of these proselytizers were several of Gregory's relations. One brother-in-law, Power le Poer Trench, directed the mission throughout Connaught from his archdiocese of Tuam. Another, the ubiquitous Charles, who had forsaken civil administration for ecclesiastical, becoming Rector of Athenry and Archdeacon of Ardagh, had taught himself to preach in Irish. Both were accused of exploiting the peasantry's poverty to coerce them into sending their children to Protestant Bible Schools. No doubt Gregory agreed with the Archdeacon that 'Wherever there is a good land-lord, and a good Protestant clergyman, the influence of the Romish priest will diminish'. Equally, he may have been impressed by Charles's boast that in his area priests were rapidly losing their authority over the people. But the evangelicals quickly aroused cultural as well as religious animosities that ultimately doomed their mission to failure. [28]

The totality of the proselytizers' defeat was not to become apparent for some time but William Gregory's hope in 1825 that the tide of emancipation could be held back until Protestantism worked its therapeutic effect upon Irish minds was dashed almost immediately. The elections of 1826 saw the Catholic Association successfully challenge the political influence of landlords in several constituencies. The most dramatic result came in Waterford. There, with the local Association's support, a liberal Protestant candidate defeated Lord George Beresford — the epitome of the Ascendancy. The campaign had been marked by small provocations — the wife of a leading light of the Association walked through the streets with orange ribbons tied to the soles of her shoes — and a great effort by the Catholic clergy. Their encouraging, chiding and threatening of Catholic voters served to heighten all of Gregory's fears that the 'popish Supremacy' was at hand, but it was the by-election in County Clare in 1828 that proved to be the climactic event.

Vesey Fitzgerald, a popular landlord in Clare and long a supporter of Catholic emancipation, had been promoted to the Cabinet. As the law dictated, this liberal Protestant resigned his seat and stood for reelection. After some indecision, O'Connell, a Catholic and thus legally excluded from Parliament, decided to stand against him. He was assisted by scores of priests whose speeches to the faithful often took on the colour of invitations to engage in a holy war. Addressing Fitzgerald's tenants before they entered the polling place, one of these clerical election agents declared: 'You have heard the tones of the tempter and the charmer whose confederates have through all ages joined the descendants of the Dane, the Norman, and the Saxon, in burning your churches, in levelling your altars, in slaughtering your clergy, in stamping out your religion. Let every renegade to God and his country follow Vesey Fitzgerald, and every true Catholic Irishman follow me'. O'Connell's triumphant return for the constituency compelled the British Government to confront the Catholic issue.[29]

Simply to prevent O'Connell from taking his seat would solve nothing, for he would surely stand again, and be re-elected, and who could foretell the extent of the turbulence that would follow his continued exclusion from Parliament. Futhermore, the issue of emancipation was not one on which members of successive governments had been able to present a united front, and it had divided the two Houses of Parliament. The Commons had several times voted for relief only for the Lords to vote it down. The sentiment in the lower House precluded the formation of an exclusively Protestant government, while to dissolve Parliament in search of such a majority would give the Catholic Association an opportunity to elect, as O'Connell boasted, dozens of Catholics. Yet Gregory was confident that this crisis would pass without surrender, for the government was led by those stalwart Protestants the Duke of Wellington and Robert Peel. He continued to look to Peel for leadership of the defence of the Ascendancy, having detected not a hint of a change of policy or a weakening of his friend's resolve during a visit to London to discuss Irish affairs. Consequently, he was overwhelmed with 'surprise' and 'dismay' by the news which reached him only on the eve of the King's Speech opening Parliament in February 1829, that emancipation was going to be introduced. His friendship with Peel suffered a blow from which it never fully recovered.[30]

The relief bill was accompanied by one of the 'securities' that had been under discussion since 1825. The franchise in Ireland was raised from forty shillings to ten pounds and this reduced the electorate from one of more than 100,000 to a mere 16,000. But this effort to combine a concession to Catholic opinion with a limitation of Catholic political power did not restore order in Ireland. When the Whigs replaced the Tories in 1830 they inherited chronic Irish unrest, and the fact that the agrarian violence was now associated with demands for an end of the union and with attacks on the Established Church (O'Connell was calling for the former and the tithe war was a manifestation of the latter) must have been morbidly greeted by Gregory as fulfilment of his dire predictions concerning the ultimate objective of the earlier agitation.

The passage of emancipation and the fall of the Tories effectively marked the end of Gregory's long public career. His position had been an extremely difficult one for a number of years. The departure of Peel in 1818 had seen either the office of Chief Secretary or that of Lord Lieutenant filled by a supporter of Catholic claims. The situation became especially tense with the appointment of the Marquis of Wellesley as Viceroy in 1821, and he invited Gregory to resign if he could not support the policy of the new administration. The Under Secretary did briefly consider surrendering his office in the spring of 1823, but was persuaded by friends to hold on to it in the interests of the Protestant cause. In 1827, when George Canning, a supporter of Catholic claims, was called on to form a government, one in which Peel declined to serve, a dispirited Gregory did announce his resignation to the Lord Lieutenant. Once again friends persuaded him, with the Viceroy's consent, to withdraw it. A few months later the Marquis of Anglesey was appointed Lord Lieutenant and he wanted to remove Gregory, for the Under Secretary was widely credited with having successfully frustrated previous liberals. However, it was the Viceroy who was subsequently dismissed and by his old commander at Waterloo, Wellington. The Marquis only agreed to return to Ireland in 1830, when the Whigs took office, on condition that Gregory was finally ousted.

To dismiss Gregory was one further way to conciliate Daniel O'Connell. The leader of the struggle for emancipation had long demanded that Catholic 'securities' be attached to that measure, and the first of these was a reorganization of the Irish Executive which included the dropping of Gregory — 'the very demon of Orangeism'. O'Connell could not accept a situation in which Gregory remained 'in full power at the Castle' and 'The Trenches in full pay and patronage at the Custom House (another of Gregory's many brothers-in-law was on the Board of Customs) as well as in Connaught'. Thus enactment of emancipation brought no relaxation of his pressure for the removal of Gregory 'and other firebrands' from 'working the government machine'. This step was 'indispensable' for the pacification of Ireland. Yet, as the obliging and disappointed Anglesey was quick to note, Gregory's ousting passed largely 'unnoticed' by Catholics but provided 'a rallying point for the ill-humour and disgust of the Protestants'.[31]

Among the members of William Gregory's household during these tension filled years, who watched him fight and lose the battle against Catholic emancipation, with all that he believed to be at stake for Protestant Ireland, was his young grandson William Henry.

2
FORMATIVE YEARS

William and Anne Gregory had three children. The first born they dutifully christened Robert, no doubt in honour of his paternal grandfather,
while to their younger son and his sister they gave the names of Anne's
parents which were also their own. Daughter Anne proved to be a
devoted child, remaining at the family home until the death of both her
parents and being rescued only in middle age from spinsterhood. The
two boys were sent off to England for their education, entering their
father's old school of Harrow together in 1804 when Robert was
fourteen. The French savant Alexis de Tocqueville later attributed this
growing migration (the last half of the Eighteenth Century had seen
more than 200 Irish boys despatched to Eton or Harrow) to the fear of
Ascendancy parents 'that a vague instinct of patriotism and youthful
memories' might otherwise attract their children to Ireland.[1] The
Gregorys appear to have been motivated by nothing more sinister or
ulterior than the normal desire to provide their sons with the most
fashionable of schooling. In 1808 they withdrew young William from
Harrow, bringing him home to Dublin to attend Trinity College. From
there he graduated M.A. and found a living in the Established Church.
It was a natural and predictable choice, for Richard's miserable experience in the Army discouraged any thought of a military career while two
of William's maternal uncles had emerged as influential clerics. Thus did
the younger William Gregory become the incumbent of Fiddown,
Kilkenny, and he was to live well beyond the biblical span of years.

Robert, having remained one year longer at Harrow than his brother,
went up to Trinity College, Oxford. The choice of university reflected his
father's conversion to Toryism. Robert did not distinguish himself
academically but was hailed as 'the fastest runner of his day at Oxford'.
His return home raised the problem of an occupation, one that would
provide him with an adequate income until he succeeded to the Galway
estates. An obvious haven was the Irish administration and his father
secured a post for him at the Board of Works. The undemanding nature
of the work soon attracted the attention of another of the Trenches. He
had discovered that to be a Commissioner of Stamps interfered with his
various private pursuits and not the least of these was his service as
Lord Drogheda's land agent. This Trench proposed a simple exchange
of places with Robert Gregory. The Under Secretary enthusiastically
endorsed the proposal when he forwarded it to Chief Secretary Peel for

approval, explaining frankly that it would mean an additional annual income of £100 for his son and that Robert could not make a worse Commissioner than his relation who spent too much of his time away from his duties anyway. Unexpectedly, the request was denied on the grounds that the young Gregory's good fortune would look a little too much like 'jobbing'.[2]

On Wednesday 5 July 1815 Robert married Elizabeth 'Bess' O'Hara of Raheen. Only sixteen, she was a stunningly attractive girl. The two families were already distantly connected, having turned to the House of Shawe for wives a century earlier, and an O'Hara had commanded the vessel on which the nabob first sailed to India. It was a sound match, for the O'Haras were also a family of some local prominence in Galway and the owners of 'considerable estates in that county'. Indeed, Elizabeth's father settled £4,000 upon her and in return William Gregory provided for Robert's direct succession to the Coole estates on the death of Richard. The young couple made their home with Robert's parents and sister. Inevitably there was tension, at least between the women. Mother and sister were a little resentful of this girl who had supplanted them in Robert's affections, even a little jealous of her beauty. Nor were relations improved by Bess Gregory's provocative sympathy for Catholic claims and her inviting of fellow liberals to the Under Secretary's residence. If this suggests a girl of spirit as well as of beauty, Robert's mother remained the dominating figure and personality in the household. With her strong sense of propriety, and by no means inconsiderable estimate of her family's importance and her own position, Lady Anne (she acquired the courtesy title with her father's promotion to an earldom) had by her conduct widened the breach between her husband and his increasingly reclusive and misanthropic brother. Shortly after the military disgrace which surely did not endear him to his proud sister-in-law, Richard had fallen in love with a very young girl. He first persuaded her to run away from the London boarding school she was attending and then to accompany him to Ireland. There, he had hidden her in a steward's house on the estate and disguised her as a boy. It was not until his father's death — whose response to a second scrape he had feared — that Richard married Isabella Nimmo. But Lady Anne refused to acknowledge either a woman or a wife who had for so long been known among the good natured tenants on the estate, and no doubt throughout Galway, as 'Jack the Sailor'. The result was a 'total separation between the brothers', which Richard's subsequent behaviour in no way lessened. The death of his wife saw him quickly remarry, choosing Jack the Sailor's maid as his bride. Within two years she also was in her grave and it required the intervention of fate, in the form of an accident, and the protective activities of an Italian attendant, to save Richard from the designs of a public singer. The artiste in question later became Lady Molesworth.

On 13 July 1816, a year almost to the day after her wedding, Bess Gregory was 'brought to bed of a son'. There were to be two other children of the marriage, another boy born the following year and a daughter several years later, but the former lived for only an hour and the latter died in infancy. On 20 August this first born child, and heir, was baptised William Henry Gregory, the service being conducted by Samuel Slade, the first Chaplain to the Lord Lieutenant, 'according to the due and prescribed Order of the Church' and 'before divers witnesses' at Ashtown Lodge, Phoenix Park. [3]

William Henry Gregory was born into a society which had undergone something of a transformation during the decade and a half since the union. Dublin still boasted a population of 175,000 and remained Britain's second city, but it had lost some of the social brilliance and intellectual excitement associated with a true seat of government. Visitors continued to marvel at the graceful Georgian appearance of large sections of the city, for the Wide Streets Commission appointed in 1757 had carefully laid out the streets and squares, and Merrion Square had no equal even in London 'for beauty and uniformity of appearance'. There remained also the magnificent public buildings — the Bank (formerly the Parliament building), the Custom House, the Exchange, the Lying-in Hospital, the Four Courts. The Post Office was under construction. Trinity College was 'a very extensive pile of buildings, of heavy masonry, sombre features, and for its purpose a proud national monument'. Yet it was the very fact that such buildings were monuments to a past splendour which explained much of the adverse comment. Unquestionably, there had been a deterioration in the artistic and cultural life of a capital which had seen the first performance of Handel's 'Messiah'. Dublin had been reduced to a mere provincial centre and some visitors complained of the absence of places of public amusement, finding 'but one theatre, not very large, nor in general well filled. . . .' There were also fewer newspapers, fewer booksellers, fewer books, fewer publishers and fewer printers than of old. All of this appeared to be the inevitable consequence of the extinction of the Parliament and the resulting departure of the members of the Irish nobility and gentry who in the Eighteenth Century had built the elegant town houses. 'Three hundred Bacchanals, whose sun daily set in claret, spending six months every year with their wives and children in Dublin must have been of infinite service' in sustaining prosperity and creating social excitement, one temporary resident mused in 1810. Union had seen society's natural leaders desert Dublin for the social whirl of England. Like swallows, they 'take an annual flight to England, where they hop about from London to Weymouth, from Bath to Cheltenham, till their purses are as empty as their heads; when they return to wring further sums from the hard hands of their wretched tenants, who seldom see them but on such occasion'.

If union did tend to hasten the spread of the cancer of absenteeism, to lay at this door the many other ills of Dublin was harsh if not unjust. Rags, filth, misery, intoxication, these were some of the darker memories the city's more sensititve visitors carried away, and the suffering had certainly not been eased by 'the retreat of the most noble and most opulent inhabitants'. However, Dublin had long been infamous for poverty and disease far in excess of that customarily found in Eighteenth Century cities and towns. Moreover, the years following union saw important improvements in the quality of life. William Gregory patiently supervised the negotiations between the Paving Board and the Gas Light Company which before the end of his tenure had resulted in a city 'better paved and drained', one in which new sewers had been laid, an adequate supply of water assured, and oil lamps replaced by those which used gas. Further, if Dublin society, unlike the capital's streets, was now dimmer than it had been before the union, it had not been extinguished nor was it devoid of attraction and excitement.

The Viceregal court, invariably presided over by a British landed magnate, had a season of balls and presentations at that jumble of buildings called Dublin Castle. It still drew the resident Irish gentry from their country seats, while the large military establishment ensured that there was never any shortage of officers to add colour to gatherings or of troops to give pageantry to the proceedings. And if the balance of the attendant society was composed of members of the professions and wealthy merchants, thus the whole was more bourgeois than aristocratic in complexion, this was not without its advantages. Strangers were greeted with a refreshing hospitality by men who could afford to entertain sumptuously; they discovered that 'talkers were many, and listeners were few', and that wit held pride of place in conversation. 'It animates the man and sharpens his faculties, and makes him alive to the approbation of those about him; — his is the complete reverse, therefore, of the lazy, lounging man of fashion in London; who holds it the essence of ton to be haughty, silent, supercilious, and indifferent. . . .' Not that Irishmen were any slower to take offence or to take to the duelling ground to settle questions of honour. 'Hairspring Harrison' and 'Clickety Oily' (the latter so called because he spent so much time "cleaning, oiling and clicking his pistols") may have faded from the Dublin scene, or have fallen, but men were still to be found early of a morning pacing, turning and firing at a celebrated spot not far from the Under Secretary's lodge in Phoenix Park. Amidst this society and in these surroundings the youngest Gregory spent much of his childhood.[4]

The lodge was a 'lovely place' for a young boy. Dubbed the Trench Hotel, and William later admitted that it was 'a very excellent title, considering how many members of that branch of the family was ever quartering themselves upon it', the house was spacious with many attractive rooms to explore. On one side of the 'very pretty' entrance hall was a large drawing room with a handsome bow and three French windows opening onto a lawn 'beautifully diversified with shrubs and flower beds'. A similar bow offered the same view from the neighbouring dining room, the two rooms being divided by a double door. The major rooms on the second floor included a study/library, where the Under Secretary worked when not at his office in the Castle. There was also a 'noble bedroom' above the dining room, and a dressing room where a fascinated young William often watched his grandfather perform the daily labour of shaving. A second large bedroom on this same floor was where his parents slept during their extended visits. No less exciting than the house were the forty-two acres in which it was set, and the child quickly made friends with the gardener. Their friendship survived his theft of the peaches the poor man had so carefully raised in the greenhouses for exhibition at the Dublin Flower Show. Beyond the grounds there lay the vast expanse of the Park which one admirer described as 'the finest national playground in Europe, and I believe in the world'. The 1700 acres were 'more or less covered with trees and shrubs growing as wild as in any uncultivated region of the globe', but there was also a great clear expanse of grass ringed by fir and larch plantations from which in the distance could be seen the Dublin mountains. In this glorious setting military reviews were frequently held, and William surely had an excellent vantage point from which to watch the troops parade for George IV in 1821. No doubt he was also on hand to witness the King's speech from the steps of the Viceregal Lodge, at the end of a triumphal entrance into Dublin, which the monarch concluded in characteristic style: 'Go, and do by me as I shall do by you — drink my health in a bumper. I shall drink yours in a bumper of Irish Whiskey.'[5]

William frequently left these idyllic surroundings to visit his maternal grandmother in Mountjoy Square. There he encountered the other members of his mother's family, for she was the seventh of twelve children. Two of her brothers were heroes of the Peninsular war, two others engaging scamps, though one of these 'made a bad fight in the battle of life — He got into trouble about a girl, married her very foolishly, and became an exile'. The eldest brother, James, went into voluntary exile. 'He became quite Italianised early in life, bought property at Florence, and lived and died there bequeathing everything away from his own family to an Italian sycophant who had certainly earned the bequest by a life of obsequious toadying.' Of course, not a few families were surprised during the course of the century when one of their number who had expired in Italy bequeathed his estate to a devoted manservant. At a time when homosexual activities were far from safe in Britain, Italy offered opportunity and security. However, it was with his mother's youngest brother, also named William and only a handful of years older than himself, that young Gregory struck up a friendship. They were to remain close friends for the length of their lives.[6]

Privileged from birth, the only child, surrounded by doting relations, his grandmothers engaged in the traditional competition for his affection, mothered by two of his maternal aunts, William Gregory developed a common failing. Self-indulgence was a danger from which his mother's sensible efforts 'to counteract the spoiling process' did not entirely save him. Significantly, his father does not appear to have played the dominant or even a major role in his upbringing being somewhat 'timid'. Instead, to the extent that he absorbed the goals, values and assumptions of an elder, they were those of his grandfather. It was to his grandfather's dinner table that he was summoned and would climb upon a chair to drink a toast to the glorious memory of William III. An impressionable child, perhaps a little heady with wine and excitement, he then listened to the conversation of a company that was likely to include Lord Norbury, 'the hanging judge', William Saurin, the Attorney-General, Surgeon-General Sir Philip Crampton, and Chief Justice Burke. Having eaten well and freely sampled the Under Secretary's fine cellar, they would discuss the iniquitites of the Roman Catholic religion and the treason of Daniel O'Connell. The guests' views of the great mass of the Catholic population were better natured if condescending. Few of them would have challenged Dr. Crampton's diagnosis of the chief features of the Irish character as 'a morbid excitability' and an impetuosity which inclined them to 'rush upon any action without due consideration of the consequences'.[7]

The boy was also introduced by his proud grandfather to the great men who came from England to occupy the office of Lord Lieutenant or that of Chief Secretary. Years later he recalled a conversation with William Lamb, the future Lord Melbourne. ' "Now, my boy, is there anything here you would like", the Chief Secretary asked. "Yes", I answered, pointing to a very large stick of sealing-wax. "That's right", said Lord Melbourne, pressing on me a bundle of pens, "begin life early. All these things belong to the public, and your business must always be to get out of the public as much as you can." ' It was William's pursuit of his grandfather's favourite pastime — angling — that helped to thaw the icy relationship which had long existed between the Under Secretary and Lord Wellesley. Determined to conciliate the Catholic majority, this Viceroy had dismissed Saurin and replaced him with a distinguished advocate of emancipation. He had removed the commander of the Irish forces in order to give 'an intelligible notice that the sword of the executive was no longer to be unsheathed from its scabbard at the mere requisition of the ascendant party'. He banned the provocative decoration of William III's statue in College Green on the anniversary of the Protestant hero's birth, when by tradition it was festooned with orange ribbons while a bow of green ribbon was symbolically placed beneath the uplifted hoof of the monarch's horse. In 1823 Wellesley struck against the Orange Order. Nor were his relations with Orangemen and Ascendancy improved by his marriage to an American Catholic, by the officious behaviour of the natural son whom he appointed his secretary, and by the creation of a 'corps d'espionage' which encouraged the servants of families suspected of opposing the Viceroy's policies 'to betray the conversations held at their masters' tables'. Contemplating Wellesley's courting of Catholic opinion, Gregory sourly remarked that flattery 'is a food in as much use amongst all classes of the Irish Population as potatoes, and is cheaper, costing nothing but loss of character'. Yet the Under Secretary could not have failed to be touched by the kind attention Wellesly gave to 'Little Will', the grandson upon whom he himself lavished so much love and for whom he had such high hopes.[8]

Child and Viceroy first encountered one another at the pond in the grounds of the Lord Lieutenant's Lodge, when the boy was busy landing a roach, and Wellesley was clearly much taken with him and his young and ravishing mother. A few days later he presented him 'with a remarkable fine edition' of Izaak Walton's *Compleat Angler*, but this classic was followed by others. Wellesley encouraged the boy, now eight, to begin his classical studies, and it was before this august master that William declined nouns and conjugated verbs. To encourage him in his labours there were gifts, among them editions of Ovid, Livy and Homer. The Viceroy's influence, Gregory later wrote, 'I really think brought me to a love of classic literature, and thereby tinged my whole after-life'. Indeed, Wellesley remained an interested observer of the boy's progress throughout his school years, and they continued an intermittent correspondence until the Marquis's death in 1842. Bess Gregory also took a hand in her son's education, for she was determined that it would not be exclusively classical. Convinced of the value of modern languages, she insisted on the employment of her former French governess and by the age of twelve William spoke 'both French and Italian with the greatest fluency'. No less important was the decision to send him off to a boarding school in England as preparation for entering Harrow.[9] On 10 April 1826, Robert Gregory and 'his dear Boy' sailed from Dublin.

Separation from his family, for on their arrival his father immediately returned home, and an abrupt end to the extraordinary attention of which he had been the centre, must have been a cruel moment in William's young life. Nor was the blow made any easier to bear by the fact that he was often obliged to remain in England throughout the school holidays. Trips to Dublin, whether to the Under Secretary's Lodge or to the 'spacious and well-proportioned' house in elegant Merrion Square which his grandfather leased following his removal from office, were tediously long. They were also expensive and the crossing from Holyhead was often unpleasant and frequently dangerous.[10] Most holidays tended to be spent, therefore, either at Styvechall Hall just outside the medieval city of Coventry, the home of the senior English branch of the Gregory family, or at Ingestre in the rolling Staffordshire countryside. The latter was the residence of Lord Talbot, a former Viceroy with whom William's grandfather had established a friendship even more intimate than that with Peel. The Jacobean house was a magnificent building set in grounds that Capability Brown had landscaped, and alongside it sat St. Mary's Church. Reputedly the only Wren church outside of London, the classical simplicity of its style prevents it being dwarfed by the large and ornate Hall. Close by, in the neighbouring village of Tixall, there stood the ruins of the mansion in which, or so locals insisted, Mary Queen of Scots had been held. To the northwest lay Houghton Heath, the scene in 1643 of a victory by the forces of Parliament over those of the King. If none of these historic sites fired the imagination of a youth he could while away the hours fishing the Trent. William was also sure of company. The kindly Talbot had a son just three years his guest's junior. Moreover, the former Under Secretary was another frequent guest at Ingestre.

In the development of any individual's personality — his distinctive traits, attitudes, interests, values and ideals — environment evidently plays a major role. And while the quality of the home, and of the family, are of prime importance, the school is not without significance. There a child is often instructed in prevalent values, acquires a clearer understanding of acceptable forms of behaviour and is thrust into a competitive society. Gregory's preparatory school was at Iver, a picturesque Buckinghamshire village some seventeen miles west of London. Its two old inns were a reminder that it had once boasted an important market, and if its most impressive structure was the large and ancient church of St. Peter's, around which the houses were clustered, a nearby 'trouty' tributary of the Thames probably proved a stronger attraction for the young angler. William failed to warm to the school's head, Mr. Ward, and thought little of his scholarship, though neither reaction was surprising in a young boy who had been separated from his family for the first time and had been coached in classics by a marquis. Yet he acquired a solid grounding in arithmetic, for this was a school run by a former naval chaplain, and was encouraged to take an interest in at least one natural science — entomology. In short, his time at Iver was neither unpleasant nor was it entirely wasted and his memories of his years there were sufficiently pleasant for him to return to the village fifty years later to discover to what extent it had changed.[11]

On 7 October 1830 Robert Gregory and his son set out from Dublin for Harrow. As they approached their destination William's attention would have been fixed on the church spire which crowns the hill at Harrow. As they drew nearer so the tall brick buildings grouped around the church would have become more distinct. Some were modern, having been erected only a decade earlier, but it was the old school that housed the lower forms. Built in 1595 the original schoolhouse continued to stand, 'a substantial but not very elegant structure of brick, forming the western portion' of the block of buildings. Inside, the somewhat forbidding air was maintained by 'gloomy old windows and oaken wainscot.' No doubt William was repelled by his first glimpse of 'the bare and dirty roughcast corridors, the ill-drained latrines, the stuffy studies with wired windows, the cheerless refectory', but this was to be his home for the next five years.[12]

Gregory entered Harrow at a time of crisis for the seven great public schools, of which it and Eton were the foremost. The schools were regarded as an integral part of a gentleman's education. The English youths who attended them were of that class 'whose birth and fortune place them above professional ambition'. Here they would acquire 'the capacity to govern others while controlling themselves', thus would social responsibility be allied to a fitness to command. Few critics challenged the need for a heavy emphasis upon mental discipline and manliness as the essential preparation for a life of social and political leadership but there was growing disenchantment with the means employed by the public schools. Reliance upon rote and the rod seemed inappropriate in the Nineteenth Century. 'My master whipped me very well', Dr. Samuel Johnson had said to Boswell. 'Without that, Sir, I should have done nothing.' The tradition of flogging for the slightest infraction lived on. So too did the obsession with classical literature. The analysis of the grammar and rhetoric of classics was considered the best training for a mind. It was the strength of this conviction that led to the charge that the schools were failing in their purpose of providing the nation's born leaders with effective intellectual training. A boy emerged from school virtually if not 'utterly ignorant of mathematical or physical science, and even of arithmetic; — the very names of logical, moral, or political science, are unknown to him. Modern history and modern languages are, of course, out of the question.' As a result, 'the most precious years of youth are spent, not in filling the mind with solid knowledge, — not in training it to habits of correct and patient thought, — but in a course of half studious idleness, of which the only lasting trace is the bitter recollection of misspent time'.

There was criticism of the brevity of the normal school week, which in some instances amounted to no more than eleven hours. The dangers of so much liberty and too few teachers were 'that a considerable laxity of conduct may exist in the youths of older standing, without being restrained or detected; and the smaller and weaker boys are exposed, without hope of redress, to the merciless tyranny of their superiors in age and strength'. The practice of fagging, which saw junior boys perform a variety of menial tasks for the most senior, was damned as 'the only regular institution of slave-labour, enforced by brute violence, which now exists in these islands'. Sydney Smith, best remembered as a divine wit, had long drawn attention to the wider implications of this system. 'Reasonable obedience is extremely useful in forming disposition', he had written in 1810. 'Submission to tyranny lays the foundation of hatred, suspicion, cunning, and a variety of odious passions.' Finally, there was growing talk if not mounting concern that the schools were the sources of moral corruption. If 'they only prevent men from being corrupted by the world, by corrupting them before their entry into the world,' Smith observed, 'they can only be looked upon as evils of the greatest magnitude.' Was it true, as William Thackeray charged, having survived Charterhouse, that 'all the world is improving except the gentlemen'?

Harrow had acquired notoriety even among public schools. From humble beginnings in the Sixteenth Century it had by the opening of the Nineteenth emerged as a rival to Eton in the education of nobility and gentry. Yet its rise had been marked by extraordinary disorders. The decision of the Governors in 1771 to appoint an Eton undermaster to the position of head, instead of a popular Harrow one, led to a rebellion. Prominent among the rebels was young Richard Wellesley, who was pulled around the town in the splendour of a ramshackle cart his fellows had knocked together. When order was finally restored, after three weeks, the future Viceroy was packed off to Eton. There was another uprising in 1805, at which time both William's father and his uncle were at the school, and the cause was the same. Three years later, when the new and still unpopular headmaster, George Butler, sought to exercise more control over the monitors, another rebellion flared into life during the week of the traditional Guy Fawkes celebrations. For five days, beginning on 3 November 1808, the boys refused to attend school or chapel, paraded through the streets chanting 'No Butler' and 'Liberty or Rebellion', and blocked the London road in order to prevent the headmaster from sending for the assistance of their parents. The experience left poor Butler ever fearful of 5 November. 'Great was my anxiety, and restless my vigilance, and most fidgety my feelings', he later admitted, 'during that session of temptation'. Nor did the school's reputation improve during the 1820s. In 1826 a dispute between some of the boys and the children of a local blacksmith ended with the destruction of the blacksmith's house and the summoning of police from London to quell the disorder.

It was not merely the well deserved reputation for unruliness that prompted observers, such as the Irish authoress Maria Edgeworth, to declare that Harrow was a place where the home influence was soon shattered because of the quite different and questionable tone set there. The school was notorious for drunkenness and dissipation, and the 'Red Nightcap' Club was its own 'Hell-fire' association. However, the unspoken corruption of homosexuality does not appear to have been a serious problem during these years, for the very slackness of discipline permitted boys to find more natural outlets for sexual desires. (The senior boys at Eton had their own brothel.) But fagging and bullying were common and the quality of education was no better than many critics of the schools in general averred. Mathematics and French were not allowed, even though there was a French master who 'lived the life of a dog', and whenever the Arithmetic and Writing masters appeared they were greeted with 'hallowing and hooting'. As for the dominant Classics, an important part of schoolwork involved the submission of exercises in Latin and Greek to form masters, but by long tradition the boys submitted them first to private tutors for correction. Thus such exercises scarcely provided a guide to a pupil's progress.

The need for reform was obvious and Butler made an attempt to effect it. He took steps to tighten discipline but at the same time sought to establish a closer relationship between himself and the senior boys. He began to entertain the entire fifth and sixth forms to supper 'with good Madeira'. However, they continued 'to play pranks' at his expense. Among Butler's academic improvements were his introduction of annual prizes for Greek verse, Latin Hexameters and Latin Lyrics, and in 1826 Robert Peel founded the award of an annual gold medal for Latin prose. Nevertheless, when Butler resigned in 1829 to accept the deanery of Peterborough the school's Governors must have given a collective sigh of relief. There had been a sharp fall in the school's population, from a high of 345 boys in 1803 to a low of 115 in 1829, and the appointment of a new head offered an opportunity to reverse this worrying decline. [13]

Charles Longley arrived in Harrow to take up the headship in April 1829, travelling from West Tytherley in Hampshire where for the past nine months he had been Rector. Chosen over two internal candidates, he came highly recommended. 'As a firm and quiet disciplinarian Mr. Longley is conspicuously pre-eminent', wrote one of his notable supporters to a Governor of the school. As 'a religious and gentlemanly man, I know not his superior, and his attainments in Classical Literature have been such as to distinguish him at School and College [Westminster and Christ Church], and to enable him to fill with great credit the situations of Tutor of Christ Church and Public Examiner of the University.' This was the man the Governors expected to rescue the school, and the importance they attached to its survival was expressed by Lord Aberdeen, a future Prime Minister, when he wrote to Longley: 'I will only now say that I consider it as a most fortunate circumstance for the School, and from the importance of the situation, I may add, to the country, that you have been pursuaded to go to Harrow.' [14]

Anxious, no doubt, to head off any danger of a repetition of past up-heavals, Longley assiduously cultivated the stronger of the unsuccessful internal candidates for the post of headmaster. He indicated to his defeated rival that they shared a common desire to 'get rid of flogging, at least above the fourth form', and to encourage some study of 'modern literature' among the senior boys, but that he would 'alter nothing of the basis of the system'. Longley's commitment, then, was to moderate and cautious reform. From Thomas Arnold, whom he had known at Oxford as a fellow member of 'A Club of Young Masters of Arts', and who had recently been appointed headmaster of Rugby, Longley received advice and an invitation to the midlands school. Spare the rod as much as possible, Arnold recommended, and establish an ascending scale of punishments for obstinate offenders. No less important, at least in Arnold's opinion, was the avoidance of a 'school manner' in speaking to boys. 'They mind the usual tone and manner just as much if they know they cannot presume upon it,' he continued, 'and you thus diminish something their notion of your acting from fudge: a belief which as far as it prevails renders all moral influence in a master out of the question.' Anthony Trollope later attested to Longley's success in avoiding his predecessor's mistake of using a 'school manner'. But it was to Samuel Butler of Shrewsbury that Longley looked most often for guidance in shaping his own course at Harrow. After all Arnold had yet to establish his reputation whereas Butler had saved Shrewsbury from collapse (there had been only 18 boys there when he was appointed in 1798) and was highly regarded as an educational reformer. He urged the lowering of barriers between master and boys, and although he was a traditionalist in matters of curriculum, holding fast to his faith in the Classics, he had instituted at Shrewsbury a regular system of written examinations (unseen before they were sat) to test the progress of boys and determine their place in the school.

At Harrow Longley established new half-yearly examinations, dubbed 'Trials', at all levels including the sixth form. He sought to make the school work as regular as possible by designating Tuesday the only holiday. Thus no matter the day on which 5 November fell the Guy Fawkes celebrations were always to be held on a Tuesday. He broadened, if somewhat hesitantly, the curriculum. French and Mathematics were first added to it and then eventually made compulsory. He acted to prevent boys from running up huge debts with local traders, by persuading the merchants to sign an agreement not to extend credit to Harrow boys. His natural persuasiveness was reinforced during these negotiations by a threat to cut off all school business. He discouraged parents from sending game to their children, for that provided them with a reasonable excuse to go into town to have it prepared for 'feastings'. At the same time he denied boys permission to go shopping for tea, coffee and sugar. Instead, the school began to supply these provisions. If the intent of these restrictions was to prevent indebtedness and improve discipline they also served to make the boys greater captives of the school's kitchens. Breakfast was at 9:00 a.m., following the first school of an hour or so, and the respective houses provided the main fare of tea or coffee, milk, bread and butter, but the boys had to purchase whatever relishes they wanted from the pastry cooks. The main meal, dinner, was at 1:00 p.m., following second school between 11:00 a.m. and noon. There were different joints and pudding for each day of the week, thus roast mutton was invariably followed by a baked rice pudding. So few of these uninteresting and often tasteless dishes were eaten that the cooks soon cut the number, only for the boys to conspire to demand their dessert. Meals would be enlivened by chants of 'not pudding enough' and 'more pudding'. Tea was taken soon after 6:00 p.m., and there was a supper of cold meat before the boys were sent off to bed at 10:00 p.m.

Longley's reforms did encourage a belief that the situation and the atmosphere at Harrow were improving and there was a sharp increase in the school's population. By 1833 it numbered 259 boys, though by the time Longley resigned in 1836 to accept a bishopric (he went on to become Archbishop of Canterbury) a decline had again set in. He failed to solve the school's fundamental problems. He did not entirely realize his ambition to institute a regime of moral influence, thus flogging was not abandoned. Indeed, he proved to be a quiet but not a firm disciplinarian. He was to be seen at his best 'when ruling over those of mature age'. Boys took advantage of his good nature, and this knowledge discouraged monitors from attempting to enforce discipline. Under Longley 'skylarking continued to be the order of the day', as did fagging, fighting and bullying. Boys 'were called out of their beds at night to have cold water poured down their backs, — for no special reason, but as part of the hardening process considered good for fags generally. . . .' Nor were Longley's efforts to raise the school's academic standards particularly successful. The examiners, in their report for the year 1832–33, expressed dissatisfaction with the proficiency of the candidates. Senior boys who had been before them the preceding year offered little evidence of progress. 'They had evidently been idle or careless, and it was this conviction which induced the Examiners to recommend only one candidate for a [University] scholarship.'[15]

Later in life Gregory was to repeat, in Parliament and in his *Autobiography*, the familiar criticisms of public school education. Speaking and writing of his own experiences at Harrow, he deplored the narrowness of the curriculum and, with one notable exception, the inadequacy of his teachers. He knew 'how often it is that boys from indisposition to Classical Studies and especially to verse making, lose all heart and all hope of distinction — If they had an opening to something else they would often work, as it is they now entirely despair and get over their weary and distasteful duties as best they can.' He complained that 'There was hardly any attempt to make a boy think. A Latin essay or theme was written once a week; but far more attention was paid to the grammatical accuracy than to the thoughtfulness of the production. History was little more to us than a collection of dry facts and dates; it was anything but philosophy teaching by example.' He grumbled that the store of knowledge in French, Italian and Arithmetic he brought with him to the school had actually dwindled during his years there. Yet he was careful to defend Harrow against charges of 'corruption'. In his day, he insisted, it had been 'a fine, manly place'. There had been little bullying, while fagging 'was a salutary discipline for young gentlemen who had been made much of at home'. Although Gregory was just such a boy he escaped, significantly, this form of therapy. Moreover, for all his later criticisms, it is clear that at the time he relished his experiences at Harrow, which was not surprising given the somewhat special circumstances and the triumph of his school career.

Entering Harrow at the age he did — fourteen — Gregory went to the 'shell,' 'a kind of limbo between the fourth and fifth forms, between the fagged and the faggers'. His master, the Rev. W. Oxenham, was a clever and a gentle man, and the other boys in his form were small and some of them were also 'very clever and well educated'. Thus Gregory not only avoided much if not all of the bullying and flogging associated with school life but found himself in an environment characterized by healthy academic competition. Equally important and fortunate was the house in which he was placed and the tutor to whom he was assigned. From the day of his admission he was a member of Longley's house, whose 'handsome face and winning manner' helped to make him a popular figure. He gained and kept the respect of those boys who appreciated being treated as 'gentlemen'. Gregory grew to love him 'dearly'. His weaknesses were not only his failure to maintain discipline but also his inability to inspire boys with enthusiasm for their studies. However, it was Gregory's good luck to find a tutor who compensated for this latter deficiency. Benjamin Hall Kennedy was young, had been a brilliant pupil of Samuel Butler at Shrewsbury (whom he was to succeed as headmaster in 1836, having turned down the Harrow headship out of a distaste for the fagging that was so deeply imbedded there) and had gone on to a no less successful career at Cambridge. As a freshman he had been one of the original members in 1824 of the Athenaeum Club, and beyond his mastery of Classics 'he revelled over a wide range of modern literature, especially poetry and history, which was always a favourite topic'. Fired by Kennedy's enthusiasm 'and having my studies rendered easy by his constant readiness to explain and illustrate every passage that barred my way', Gregory later wrote, 'I soon began to love my classics with all my heart.' It was also a profitable and ultimately an egotistical passion.[16]

In 1833 Gregory won the prize for Latin Lyrics and placed third in that for Greek verse. He had been somewhat fortunate, as Longley informed his father, because one or two boys who were 'decidedly his superior' had not entered. 'However he really deserves encouragement', the headmaster reported, 'for he has been doing his utmost to improve himself this quarter, and really gives promise of becoming a very good scholar.' William's natural excitement was heightened by his family's pride in his achievement, by the pleasure his success gave to his tutor, and by the added distinction of being the first member of Longley's house to carry off a prize. There were other rewards. A proud grandfather sent him £10, while a letter to that recluse, great uncle Richard, brought a brief reply and a cheque for £25. Each subsequent prize was to earn the same recognition and William was eventually admitted to the house on Berners Street, becoming a regular if not a frequent visitor. It was William who confirmed the rumour that Richard had married his housemaid, though he depended on a local grocer for the information that she was a respectable, elderly woman in very bad health who always conducted herself with great propriety.

Excited by his success and flush with its rewards, Gregory signalled his determination to persevere in the quest for academic distinction by purchasing a ten volume edition of Euripides. Not even an accident in which he narrowly escaped death could dampen his high spirits. While out riding he had fallen from a gig, striking his head. Confined to bed for a considerable period and unable to pursue his studies, because he had been ordered to rest his eyes, indeed they were covered with shades, he was comforted by the knowledge that he would be fit enough to read his Lyrics on Speech Day. The following year he entered for the most prestigious of prizes, the Peel. He placed second, and in one of the competition's three parts his work had been superior to that of the winner. It was Longley's opinion that the honour would surely be his the next year. He was soon roused from daydreams of future glory by a present disaster. Longley disqualified his prize winning Lyrics. In showing his work to Kennedy before the competition Gregory had contravened the rules. Although the tutor assured Longley that not a word had been altered the headmaster decided that no violation of the regulations could or should be tolerated. The harsh decision embittered Gregory at the time and continued to rankle for the rest of his long life, but he did have the satisfaction of bringing his school career to a glorious conclusion. In 1835 he captured the prize for Latin verse and then topped this success by winning the Peel. The crowning glory in this succession of academic triumphs was the announcement that he had been awarded the only Harrow scholarship to Oxford. 'You have no idea of the kind of delight I am in', he wrote joyfully to his grandfather, 'so were both Longley and Kennedy, as I was very ill during the scholarship owing to a rush of blood to the head which very nearly obliged me to leave off. My hand is nearly wrung off by congratulations and my ears dinned by the cheers of the fellows of my house.'

The young man who left Harrow in 1835 was evidently more mature than the youth who had entered the school five years earlier. A small child, he had grown 'tremendously' and was to exceed average height. Although Longley had described him in 1833 as 'a wild colt to be sure', and reported that he had been obliged to rap 'his knuckles rather sharply for a prank or two', William had shunned the company of those whose talk was of cricket, football, drinking and cigars. Academic success and good sense helped steer him well away from the vices of drunkenness and dissipation. By 1834 Longley could describe his conduct as generally 'very good' and he predicted that he would make 'a valuable head' of his house. Together with a small group of friends, who had dubbed him 'Pope' following the enthronement of Gregory XVI in 1831, he established a debating society in Longley's house which met every Monday evening. After a hearty supper of lamb chops and green peas they would turn to such pressing issues of the day as the advisability of admitting dissenters to the Universities. 'Pope's' position was suitably conservative. Cambridge might fall but 'I hope and trust not Oxford, that there may be something left to the Established Church unplucked', he announced. He also played a leading role in founding a *Harrow Magazine*, of which he was 'unanimously elected president'. 'A great number of clever articles have been written, and we are confident that it will be of the greatest advantage to the school, without in the least interrupting the studies', he assured his grandfather. 'Do make *all* and *every* friend of yours buy it, as nobody in Dublin will refuse you except Dan O'Connell.' Yet Gregory's school years are also significant for the evidence they provide of the awakening of a sense of personal identity which was not merely a reflection of his grandfather's personality.[17]

For the first time in his life Gregory now lived with his parents alone. In 1829 the Under Secretary had attempted to protect his elder son's immediate future by securing for him a better paid position in the Irish administration, but he had been frustrated by an unsympathetic Chief Secretary. As a result, Robert retired from the Irish service at much the same time his father was removed from office.[18] His life for the next few years was an itinerant one, travelling and residing first in England and then abroad. And it was with his parents that William spent the burning summer of 1833. They were then staying at Southampton. He sailed a great deal with a friend, attended the Portsmouth and Cowes regattas, and crossed to Cherbourg to attend the grand fête staged in honour of King Louis Philippe, whose twenty cooks ensured 'good eating for the bon vivants'. Robert and Bess Gregory remained at Southampton after their son returned to Harrow, and they were still there when word came in November of the death of Lady Anne. She had been ill for a number of years and had lived for the past three in great pain despite the ministrations of Philip Crampton, who ranked 'among the greatest of English-speaking surgeons and scientists' of his day. On 18 November she had developed a high fever, following a violent shivering fit, had clung to life for two days, and briefly rallied before dying in her sleep on the morning of 21 November.

Robert did not return to Dublin for his mother's internment, but wrote in his large and painfully ill-formed hand a touching and pious letter to his desolate father. Then, in 1834, he and Bess crossed the Channel and took up residence in Paris. At first, he did not like the French capital. Nor was their life one of great ease, for his principal source of income was his retirement allowance from the Irish administration. Later he wrote to a friend: 'We are quite well and like Paris much better than when we first arrived, but are too poor to enjoy the many amusements of this gay and frivolous city.' William spent another wonderful summer vacation with his parents, though it almost came to a disagreeable end. Neither he nor his father thought to procure him a passport, despite a crisis in Franco-Spanish relations, and at Boulogne he was briefly held by nervous and suspicious police. Fortunately, the British consul there knew his family and was able to vouch for him. He returned to Paris for the Christmas vacation and found his parents somewhat happier, having moved to the Hotel de l'Europe in the Rue Rivoli, which was more comfortable and less out of the way than their earlier accommodation. William's holiday was even more enjoyable than that of the previous summer, and it culminated in a magnificent Christmas dinner, English style — roast beef, plum pudding and foaming ale, all consumed before a roaring fire.

It was at this time in his life that the young man first ceased to style himself 'William Gregory', and began to include the distinguishing "H" in his signature. Not that there was any weakening of his affection for or attachment to his grandfather. They corresponded frequently, whereas William's father proved to be a poor correspondent and it was old William Gregory who financed his grandson's education at England's most expensive school. Nor was there any reason for the former Under Secretary to be disturbed by his young namesake's lively interest in current political events. Like the heroes of Disraeli's *Coningsby,* he was growing up 'Amid the contentions of party, the fierce struggles of ambition, and the intricacies of political intrigue ... from the failure of the Duke of Wellington to form a government in 1832, to the failure of Sir Robert Peel to carry a government in 1835. ...'

Peel's short ministry saw a reconciliation with his old friend and loyal deputy in the Irish Executive. They had been fellow guests of Talbot at Ingestre earlier in 1834, and Peel had urged Gregory to contest Athlone. He refused to run for election but did accept appointment as an Irish Privy Councillor. And when O'Connell seized upon the announcement to denounce the government as one conducted on Orange principles, young William read the reports of the debate and applauded the defence of his grandfather in the Commons. He also voiced concern that Conservatives would be annihilated in the Irish constituencies by 'O'Connell's set', and queried his grandfather (whom he had hoped would run for Parliament because he was sure that he would have been of great assistance to Peel in settling Irish affairs) whether petitions might not be one way to overturn unfavourable election results. The young man responded enthusiastically to Peel's Tamworth speech, hailing its 'oratory', 'firmness', and 'reliance on the people of England'. Unlike Disraeli's Young Englanders, he did not interpret Peel's promise of sound conservative government to be one of 'Tory men and Whig measures' — 'The prerogatives of the Crown, provided they are not exercised; the independence of the House of Lords, provided it is not asserted; the Ecclesiastical estate, provided it is regulated by a commission of laymen.' In short, 'an attempt to construct a party without principles'. Thus William H. Gregory celebrated the initial failure of the Whigs and their O'Connellite allies to turn Peel out of office early in 1835, and like many a good Tory he was contemptuous of that 'horrid Lord John Russell' who reminded him 'of some little barking terrier which worries by its barking but does no good in the end'.

As he prepared in 1835 to go up to Oxford the example of Peel and the hope of a political career were firmly fixed in young William's mind. The greatest influence on his life so far had been his grandfather, once an intimate and now again a friend of Peel's. He had gone to Peel's school, and won Peel's medal, and his composition had contained a flattering allusion to him as the model modern statesman. He was destined for Peel's college and had every expectation of achieving a

distinction at Oxford which if it did not equal Peel's double first would
at least confirm that he was a young man of remarkable ability and
outstanding promise. He knew that Longley had described his Peel
essay as 'the best ever sent in', and when he visited Oxford in June to
matriculate, his fame had preceded him. Dean Gaisford of Christ
Church opened their interview with the statement: 'Well you have got
Peel's medal — Only taking up your time examining you — quite useless
— sure to pass.' The Dean had then enrolled Gregory on his books.
There was a flattering report circulating in Oxford that one of its
legendary scholars had pronounced Gregory's essay 'the best School
exercise and the most spirited production he had seen, save one which
came once from Winchester'. None of this diminished the young man's
growing self-esteem. [19]

Spoilt at home Gregory had now been spoilt by success at school.
'What fame of other days equals the rapture of celebrity that thrills the
youthful poet, as in tones of rare emotion he recites his triumphant
verses amid the devoted plaudits of the flower of England?' an ironic
Disraeli later asked. Among those who attended Speech Day and
flattered Gregory with attention was his hero and model — Peel.
However, academic achievement had gone hand in hand with his
selection as head boy, and Sydney Smith's generalizations a quarter of
a century earlier had particular application to Gregory. 'The *head* of a
public school is generally a very conceited young man, utterly ignorant
of his own dimensions and losing all that habit of conciliation towards
others, and all that anxiety for self-improvement, which result from the
natural modesty of youth,' Smith declared. Sensing the danger ahead
a proud but prescient old man confided in his friend Peel. 'I hope the
scholastic prizes my dear boy has gained, and the consequent applause
bestowed upon him, will not turn his head, as they nearly have his
Grandfather's — he has three critical years before him at College, at
present he has not any expensive habits, yet they are easily acquired.
I trust however that his ambition for literary distinction will keep him
from intimacy with those who might lead him into expense.' [20]

Unable to obtain rooms at Christ Church before Christmas, Gregory
persuaded his grandfather to place him with a private tutor for the
period of the Michaelmas term. They settled upon the Rev. Nutcombe
Oxenham, Vicar of Modbury, Devon. Related, no doubt, to William's
former form master, Oxenham was 'perfectly well qualified'. He had
himself gained almost everything at Harrow before going up to Oxford,
where he had been elected to an Exeter fellowship. Gregory found him
to be 'a nice gentlemanly fellow, and a capital scholar', and he remained
with him at Modbury for three months bar four days. The village itself
straggled either side of a coach road linking Plymouth and Exeter, and
at a point where the road was joined by a smaller one running cross
country from Dartmouth. The setting was attractive, the centre of the
village being in the dip of one of the many steep sided little defiles of
the region. The houses were large and some were elegant, while the

inhabitants were well supplied with inns and even had Assembly Rooms. The church and the vicarage sat on the side of the hill at the western end of the village, huddled down beneath the crown as if to shelter from the prevailing winds. There, Gregory read as 'honestly' as his tutor could wish and his scholarship improved 'considerably'. He also found time to pursue 'a small love affair'. Writing to his grandfather just before his departure for Oxford, he expressed his gratitude for an opportunity 'which will enable me in after life to appear even if a poor gentleman, at all events a well educated one'.

Gregory left Modbury on 18 January 1836, spending the first night of his journey at Exeter and the second at Cheltenham before reaching Oxford on the afternoon of 21 January. He arrived at a time when the University was under attack, accused of many of the same failings as the public schools. A satire written by George Cox, of New College, entitled *Black Gowns and Red Coats*, and published posthumously in 1834, gave a picture of Oxford that all too many critics regarded as accurate — 'the teaching barren, the teachers sunk in crapulence and sloth, the taught licentious, extravagant, idle'. To the familiar charge, that study was almost exclusively of classical antiquity, the President of Trinity College offered the equally familiar reply. 'The very object of selecting ancient, and particularly Greek writers', he wrote in the *Quarterly Review*, 'is to accustom the mind to think, and reason, and judge for itself, so far as judging for itself is not folly — by familiarizing it with the highest and most perfect forms of human rationalism, thrown out boldly, and almost recklessly, in an age when man had contrived to cast off every check of authority, and by intellects full of energy and power.' The accusations of indolence levelled at the occupants of the twenty-seven endowed chairs moved him to point to their annual salaries, which in many cases fell between £30 and £100. Therefore, 'If not many lectures were delivered, there could be no cause for complaint'. Anyway, the instruction of students was 'carried on far better by tutors'.

There was a tendency to interpret the attacks on Oxford as being motivated less by a wish to improve the University than by a desire 'to revolutionize a system of education which, more than anything, has tended to form young men of this country to sound, sober, loyal, and religious habits; and which, therefore, must be destroyed if the institutions of the nation are to be overturned'. This High Toryism was yet another source of criticism and controversy. The University had opposed to the last the repeal of the Test Act, the enactment of Catholic Emancipation (Peel had been obliged to relinquish his Oxford seat), the passage of the Reform Bill of 1832, and the admission of Dissenters. Then, in 1835, Lord Melbourne had as a Whig Prime Minister offered to a fellow Whig, Dr. Renn Hampden, but one identified with Low Church sentiments, the Regius Professorship of Divinity. The result was the unedifying spectacle of internecine warfare waged by High Churchmen against Hampden, for these were years when the Oxford Movement of Anglo-Catholicism was gaining momentum, and it was not long before charges of bigotry and popery were being hurled at the University. The fact that Hampden's professorship entitled him to a canonry at Christ Church, which was cathedral as well as college, ensured that its members were touched by the controversy. Gregory, for one, deplored the violence and abuse of both sides, especially in a community where people were obliged to live so close together and had the time to dwell upon and foster real and imaginary wrongs.

Although the largest, the wealthiest, the most aristocratic and one of the most successful of colleges, whether success was measured in honours won or the number of statesmen and scholars contributed to society, Christ Church was already in a period of decline when Gregory finally took up residence in January 1836. The elite of society still came there, and among its tutors was to be found the University's greatest snob, but its reputation in matters educational and moral was slipping.[21]

William liked his rooms, for they were 'much better than those of any freshman of my acquaintance'. However, he was soon complaining that 'Everything is exorbitantly dear, and not very good for the price'. He had to pay £21 for entering his rooms, and another £2 for 'bedroom things'. An additional £2 went to the ironmonger for coal scuttle, bellows and irons, while there was a bill for £12 for tutorage and other fees during the period since matriculation when he had not even been in residence. These expenses, together with those for his washing, exhausted the £40 his grandfather had forwarded, and Gregory was soon sending home for £20 of great uncle Richard's money. And it was as a 'great beggarman' that he requested some wine from his grandfather's 'famous cellar'. Oxford wine merchants, he explained, were 'dear' and 'bad'.

When he left Modbury Gregory had been determined to try 'to pick up anything' that he might be fortunate enough to have a chance for at Oxford. Interest as well as honour demanded it. Yet Dean Gaisford prevented him from going immediately for a University prize, he being opposed to first term men entering the competition. However, his tutor (and a future Dean), Henry Liddell, encouraged him to try for the Craven in his second term, and suggested that he remain at Oxford throughout the vacation to prepare for it. He wrote to his grandfather to explain why he would not be returning home to Ireland as planned. 'I think I ought to leave nothing undone, and make every sacrifice to gain honours at Oxford, particularly as I must make up by application the superiority of many others in talent.'

His first few months at Oxford had been a humbling experience for the somewhat conceited Harrow scholar who had matriculated in such style the previous June. There was the dawn of the realization that he was neither as well prepared academically nor as clever as he and others had thought. He discovered that the reputation of Harrow boys had sunk very low at Christ Church, for tutors complained that it was necessary to teach them Greek, Latin and English. Liddell urged him 'to read

Dryden's Prose Works, and to write English composition twice a week, for he said "Except in the case of the Rugby boys, slovenliness of style and incorrectness in writing English were characteristics of public schoolboys".' Indeed, exposure to some of Arnold's pupils left Gregory with a growing and frightening sense of his own inadequacy. When 'questions arose of historical deductions, when the trains of thought of the great classical writers were discussed, when the spirit of ancient literature rather than the words of writers was appealed to, and when the wide and novel field of German criticism was traversed, I felt I had come across men of a different calibre and that they had regarded the ancient world with a broad glass while I examined it with a microscope.' Significantly, he resolved to use the long vacation of 1836 to learn German and do a great deal of Latin and Greek.

It was Gregory's double misfortune at this time of acute anxiety and erosion of self-confidence to find himself competing with a truly out-standing classical scholar. William Linwood seemed curiously out of place at Christ Church. He was the nephew of 'the once celebrated Miss Linwood, whose needlework imitation of great paintings drew crowds to her Exhibition Rooms in Leicester Square'. If this was an unlikely social background for a Christ Church man, Linwood was also 'a rough, shabby fellow' in appearance. However, he was to go on to win a double first and to compile the *Anthologia Oxeniesis*. In a series of competitions, including the Craven, he defeated Gregory. The following year an even greater humiliation befell the former Peel medallist. He placed second to a fellow pupil of Liddell's whom he had been widely expected to best. [22]

Weaknesses of temperament and character rather than intellectual and educational deficiencies explain, however, the disastrous end to Gregory's undergraduate career. Men of far less ability than he had done well at University. He wanted to succeed, both for his own sake and for that of his family, and not least for the grandfather who had such high hopes for him. He had grown used to success and applause at Harrow, but even there he had shown ominous signs of an emotional inability to confront the possibility of failure. He had worked himself into a state of near nervous exhaustion preparing for the Harrow scholarship, and as the date of the Craven neared in the spring of 1836 he complained of 'quite a prostration of mental exertion'. The end of his vacation of study found him in 'a dreadful state from continued solitariness, which I think did away with much of the good effects produced from reading', and he likened the mind 'to a bow which if continually kept to the point of tention (*sic*) becomes in the end weak and unprofitable inasmuch as it derives its chief strength from being only strong at and for the time required'. Yet by May he was studying night and day, fortified only by soda water, but it was to no avail in the contest with Linwood. Application did not triumph over superiority. Evidently he had failed to achieve the Homeric ideal, 'Always to be champion and to excel over others'.

The young W. H. Gregory, a watercolour probably painted during his under-graduate days at Cambridge.

Gregory's emotional weakness was compounded by the somewhat more simple character defect of any spoilt child. The loss of the Latin Lyrics prize at Harrow in 1834 had sent him into a prolonged sulk. Privately, he condemned Longley of partiality for the boy who had been declared the winner with his disqualification. Publicly, he abandoned books and reading for his favourite pastimes of shooting and angling 'and there was not a field within miles of Harrow in which [he] had not poached by day, or a pond [he] had not dragged at night with a celebrated loose character, Billy Warner by name'. Unfortunately, his setbacks at Oxford coincided with his exposure to a new and more exhilarating distraction. A visit during the Easter vacation of 1837 to his Harrow friends at Cambridge brought him into contact with under-graduates 'who were bitten with the love of racing'. They took him the short distance to Newmarket, 'the centre of the English horse-racing world'. He saw the famous course on which races had been run since 1619; the headquarters of the Jockey Club; he was introduced to a number of jockeys and he watched the training of the horses. Perhaps, as Gregory suggests in his *Autobiography*, he was instantly captivated by this new world of excitement. Of course, gaming was in his blood and had already cost one of his forbears the inheritance. William had himself been an enthusiastic participant in the annual breaking up race at Harrow. Small groups of boys hired postchaises and raced the eleven miles up the London road to the Marble Arch at the northern end of Hyde Park. In 1835 his party had won the race, a race that was to be abandoned the following year when the leading chaise hit a covered cart and the post boy died from the injuries he suffered in the collision.[23]

Returning to Christ Church from Cambridge, and Newmarket, Gregory increasingly sought refuge from his academic disappointments in this new pastime. He also took up the art of self defence, 'being knocked about by Mr. Sambo Sutton', a black prize fighter. In short, he deserted his 'studious friends' and began to mix with the more 'uproarious set' in the college. Many of these men kept horses and lived extravagantly. Thirty years later a prominent Tory was moved to complain of Christ Church: 'Thus reading and a quiet life are dis-couraged, debts incurred, and even wealthy families crippled, while the college is discredited. We are in England too tolerant of such scandals.'[24] If Gregory did not as yet accumulate heavy debts, he had found a diversion which consumed time and ultimately invariably con-sumed income. He acquired a dubious form of distinction by riding with his new friends, among them the future Earl of Winchelsea, 'from Oxford to Epsom and back on relays of hacks, cantering all the way', and had the fatal good fortune to win £300 on the Derby.

In 1838 he had travelled with a friend to Germany to spend the long vacation reading 'with Mr. Massey, fellow of Wadham, and sub-sequently head of Durham College'. But he was all too easily distracted from study, first by one of the nieces of the owner of the *gasthof* where they put up in Nassau, from whom at least he did learn some German, and then by the gaming tables of nearby Ems. He also allowed himself to be drawn into a brawl with a handful of intoxicated young Germans. However successful as a vacation, the trip had done little to prepare him for the approaching examinations. Moreover, having already out-stayed the normal number of terms at the college he moved out to New Inn Hall, where 'no discipline was observed'. He lived in the town and had the freedom to do as he wished, which meant visiting taverns such as that just across the Magdalen Bridge where the landlord was a store of racing knowledge.

Gregory was now trapped in a vicious circle of his own making. A defect of character saw him hide from his academic disappointments by indulging his growing appetite for racing, but this merely served to heighten all of his anxiety about academic success. In one sense he had already failed, because he had not captured the distinctions both he and his family had confidently expected him to take. Yet he might still redeem himself and rescue his reputation as a scholar if he graduated first class. As that last hope receded so Gregory fell prey to his old nervous disorder. Taken 'violently ill by a rush of blood to the head' (presumably the pounding of incessant headaches), he was ordered to rest for six months. In October, 1839, he returned briefly to Oxford, going into residence at St. Mary's Hall, but left 'in broken spirits, and did not go in even for a common degree'.

Gregory had withdrawn from Oxford without obtaining 'the credentials ... for the start of an ambitious young man in life'. Hopes that he would uphold the family tradition of public service by entering politics must have dimmed in the aftermath of this 'unfortunate fiasco'. He could dream of his inheritance but in 1840 it was too distant a vision to be enervating. Although great uncle Richard had died and the grandfather whom he had so grievously disappointed was approaching his seventy-eighth year, his father was only just entering middle age and, like all Gregorys, would surely enjoy long life. In short, William had scant reason to contemplate with enthusiasm or equanimity his immediate future.

3

The Peelite Member for Dublin

The summer of 1841 brought a general election to Britain, but there were contests in only half of the constituencies. Peel's Conservatives made striking gains, capturing almost fifty additional seats, and when Parliament met in August the Melbourne Government was promptly defeated in both Houses and it resigned. Before year's end one of the pair of Tory Members returned for Dublin, John Beatty West, was dead. His 'spirit took its flight from earth, leaving a family of eight children to deplore his loss.' The Whigs quickly settled upon a popular and liberal former Chief Secretary, Lord Morpeth, as their candidate in the by-election and he was promised the support of the late government's recent Irish allies. Daniel O'Connell informed the members of the Repeal Association that he intended to canvass the city, ward by ward, for Morpeth. Yet, for a man who usually gave careful attention to political matters, O'Connell's endeavours on Morpeth's behalf soon seemed surprisingly slipshod and gave rise to the suspicion that having been defeated himself at Dublin in the general election 'Dan' had no wish for Morpeth to succeed where he had failed. [1]

However half-hearted Repealer support for Morpeth appeared to be — some nationalists were demanding an Irish candidate — his 'personal popularity, agreeable manners and noble birth' made him in the eyes of a number of conservatives a formidable opponent. This insight imposed upon them an obligation 'to themselves and the empire to oppose him in the person of a candidate of equal, if not higher personal qualifications, in addition to sounder principles'. Indeed, few men who were not Repealers could have been more of anathema to the Ascendancy than was Morpeth. As Chief Secretary he had finally cleared the 'Old gang' out of the Castle, weeded Orangemen out of the police, appointed many Catholics to posts in the Irish administration and introduced measures which strengthened, or promised to increase, Catholic political influence. Therefore, a deputation of Dublin Tories went off to England in search of an impressive figure to run against him. But this 'hawking about the offer of the city' did not sit well with everyone, and few tears were shed when the itinerants returned empty-handed. Already, that powerful voice of Irish Toryism, the *Dublin Evening Mail*, had described the kind of candidate local conservatives sought. He ought to be a person 'who possesses hereditary claims upon the consideration and respect of the citizens of Dublin — who would appear before them with the prestige of an honoured name — the fame of literary triumphs — with talents, wealth, station — all that could render him worthy to take the place of him who is no more'.[2]

Of course, the *Evening Mail* had someone in mind. The newspaper's proprietor-editor, Remigius (Remmy) Sheehan, 'a funny looking little man, like a peg-top, full of self-conceit and pomposity, but of considerable ability and vigour' and influence, had been induced to endorse William H. Gregory. Here was a young man who not only had the backing of the powerful Clancarty family, and through whose veins there flowed the blood of 'uncompromising' Protestants, but who bore the name of an illustrious defender of the Ascendancy. Clearly, William's principal political asset was his grandfather's reputation. He was hailed, accurately enough, as 'the heir of his virtues and the inheritor of his name — as he will ultimately be of his fortune also'. Not that the *Evening Mail* was wedded to accuracy. It sought to head off the charge that this Gregory was too young by claiming that he was 'old enough to have taken the highest honours which the University of Oxford could confer upon a course of ardent and successful study'.[3]

Since fleeing from Oxford Gregory had made little effort to put his life in order. His father had succeeded directly to the family's estates in 1839, with the death of Richard, and in accordance with the marriage contract of 1815, while his grandfather had died in April 1840. For much of this period William H. Gregory lived in Galway, where he devoted himself to field sports. Moreover, far from abandoning the Turf, he expanded his racing interests, indulged as he was by a father who was now a man of considerable wealth. Robert paid his son £500 a year and gave additional sums whenever they were requested, for he no longer had to count his money carefully. When the family journeyed to Italy during the winter of 1840–1841 they travelled and lived in style — 'two carriages, two maids, two manservants, and a courier'; apartments in Rome's Piazza d'Espagna; and they practised hospitality 'on a liberal scale'. Yet the trip was not without unpleasant incident, for William fell seriously ill. Throughout his childhood and youth he appears to have enjoyed good health, but there had been an unnerving experience at Modbury. One day while returning from a shoot blood had suddenly started to spurt from his mouth. He staggered back to the vicarage and a physician was summoned. The doctor diagnosed a burst blood vessel and ordered the patient to encase himself in flannel, abstain from wine and meat, and eat only vegetables. Despite the remedy William had recovered. Now, in Italy, he succumbed to a 'gastric fever', and suffered a serious relapse when he attempted to return too quickly to active pursuits. His chest seemed to be bursting with pain and his joints were painfully swollen, and in desperation the attending physician decided to bleed him. Once again he survived the cure, and his faith in bleeding as a treatment for this particular malady was confirmed two years later. A recurrence of the fever during a visit to Paris saw him insist over his doctor's protests that he be bled, and within a few days he was on the road to a complete recovery.

William was staying with the Clancartys at Garbally in Galway when the news came of John West's death, and it was there that the decision was taken to advertise his availability as a Conservative candidate. By 8 January 1842 the field had been reduced to Gregory and the son of a prominent Dublin merchant, but the latter was 'unceremoniously' cast aside by the local Tories and when William arrived in Dublin four days later the nomination was safely his. The city had changed little since his grandfather's days of power, and his own childhood there. It remained one of some elegance and much poverty, the architectural splendour of Merrion Square still standing in cruel contrast to the 'Liberties' beyond nearby Grafton Street where thousands lived in hovels. It remained a capital, and still boasted a viceregal court, but visiting English sophisticates continued to mock its provincialism. The leaves might be green not black as in sooty London, but Dublin's streets lacked the bustle and the throngs of people and carriages so characteristic of the metropolis. There was still no true aristocracy in the Irish capital, for tradesmen remained its only magnates and 'brass plates' were their titles of honour. In short, the Dublin of 1841 was depicted as a sleepy backwater. Summarizing his impressions, William Makepeace Thackeray remarked that at the door of the Kildare Street Club — the exclusive preserve of the gentry and men of influence — he saw 'eight gentlemen looking at two boys playing leapfrog. . . .'[4]

Langour did not envelop the parliamentary politics of Dublin. The Reform Bill of 1832 had necessarily modified that 'security' attached to Catholic Emancipation and designed to restrict the franchise. If the establishment of the £10 householder suffrage failed to enlarge significantly the electorate in most Irish boroughs, in Dublin the number of voters (among them the freemen) exceeded 8,000. Not all of these were properly qualified, for it was by no means unusual for persons who paid less than £10 a year in rent to find their way onto the electoral register. There was, however, an additional test of 'respectability'. Payment of local taxes was in many instances a prerequisite for exercising the franchise, and this requirement provided a rich source of controversy. In Dublin, partisan tax collectors effectively disenfranchised supporters of the opposition by hiding from them when they came to make payment. The non-payment of taxes by a number of voters might also lead to the overturning of an election result. O'Connell had been unseated in Dublin in 1835 because of the neglect of many of his supporters to pay 'the miserable pipe-water rent'.[5]

The nature of the electorate and the ever-present opportunities for its manipulation ensured that politics was an expensive business. Candidates had to bear a number of regular expenses, such as those for the employment of returning officers and poll clerks; for the administration of the variety of oaths which could be demanded of voters, though the purpose was frequently to discourage opponents or prolong polling beyond the allotted time; and the even heavier charges which often resulted when objections were lodged against a particular voter, who then had to appear in person to establish his right to vote. Other expenses bordered upon or crossed the boundary of corruption. All too many boroughs resembled Charles Dickens's Eatanswill, for many voters did expect to do both. Plied with liquor, provided with food, entertained, they were also paid for coming to the poll. Nor were those practices discouraged by the difficulty of proving bribery to the satisfaction of a parliamentary committee of inquiry, and the frightening costs of contesting a result. In large and corrupt constituencies, and Dublin was both, candidates were expected to lay out small fortunes. With the backing of his indulgent father, Gregory agreed to contribute £4,000 towards his election expenses, but he also obtained a promise of assistance from the government.[6]

Peel and his colleagues had quickly concluded that to fight the Dublin election would strengthen the Conservative Party, 'for in Ireland either fighting or drinking together is the real bond of Union' and local Tories were already complaining of the new Irish Executive's lack of partisanship. By the same token, it was important that the government 'enter the Lists forcibly and give to the conservative Candidate the full manner of their support and influence'. Had the opposition's candidate been a repealer every voter who was in the Crown's employ would have been required to support the Conservative standard bearer, but once it was clear that Lord Morpeth would be the nominee the decision was taken to 'use against him exactly the same degree of pressure and influence, which he himself applied at the last Election in favour of O'Connell' and against the Tory candidates. Indeed, the desire to inflict another political reverse upon the Irish leader must have been in the back of the Peel Government's mind. The Repealer had been defeated at Dublin in the general election but Tory satisfaction at this setback had been shortlived. Not only was he promptly returned for Cork but the long campaign for municipal reform in Ireland had culminated in a measure which sounded the death knell of 'exclusive', and virtually 'self-elected', corporations and introduced more popularly elected bodies. In Dublin, as many Conservatives had feared, O'Connell rode the reform tide to a municipal victory and took office as Lord Mayor in November. His endorsement of Morpeth, no matter how tepid it proved to be, presented the government with an immediate opportunity to reemphasise the limits of the Liberator's electoral influence in the capital.[7]

From London the Gregory campaign received financial help. The candidate's personal contribution of £4,000 was matched. From Dublin Castle he received the sort of support Morpeth had extended in his own time there to the Whigs' Irish allies. Gregory and a group of his supporters were invited to dine with the Lord Lieutenant and a member of the Viceroy's household accompanied him on his canvass of the electorate. And prominent among his earliest supporters were the

Aldermen of Skinners Alley. On 12 January 1842 they met and unanimously endorsed him as the Tory nominee. This organization had its origins in an act of defiance by a group of Protestant Aldermen during the Jacobite years. They had been dismissed for their support of William of Orange but had continued to hold meetings, assembling in an ale house in an obscure part of the city called Skinners Alley. Although reinstated following the Protestant victory, they did not dissolve their association. Instead, meetings became regular, membership was enlarged by the simple device of accepting anyone proposed and seconded by aldermen, and all pledged to maintain the British Constitution as settled in 1688 'and consequently the ascendancy of Protestant truth, and the extirpation of Popish error'. Naturally, the anniversary of the battle of the Boyne was an annual celebration. William III's bust was placed on a table in the centre of the gathering, those in attendance ate their charter supper of sheep's trotters — an allusion to James's flight from Dublin — and they then toasted 'The glorious, pious, and immortal memory of the great and good King William — not forgetting Oliver Cromwell who assisted in redeeming us from popery, slavery, arbitrary power, brass money and wooden shoes'. In January 1842 they warned fellow Protestant electors: 'if you would have popery ascendant in the Castle, as well as in the Mansionhouse, and Mr. O'Connell master of Ireland, as well as Lord Mayor of the city, then permit through your inaction Lord Morpeth to be returned.'[8]

The nature of his support and of his upbringing inevitably shaped Gregory's campaign. He began to style himself William Gregory once again, and observed that 'The political opinions of my family have long been known in the city of Dublin'. He did announce a position on a number of specific issues, opposing repeal of the corn laws and such 'wild speculations' as repeal of the union, universal suffrage and vote by ballot. He did declare his support for the Peel Government, but his claim to be the truest of Conservatives was always overshadowed by the boast that he was the staunchest of Protestants. 'I offer myself as a firm and uncompromising supporter of our Protestant institutions both in church and state,' he proclaimed. On the sensitive question of Maynooth, the Catholic seminary which received state aid, he attacked the manner in which the grant was carried out and vowed that a rigorous and searching investigation would have to be conducted before he could support its continuance. When he spoke to the members of the Protestant Operative Association and Reformation Society he extended his criticisms to embrace the existing educational system. 'I object to a species of education that confers a degree of moral knowledge,' he informed his audience, 'and leaves men's minds open to imbibe the poison of sedition and blasphemy.'[9]

Popularizing the antidote to that poison was the life's work of the President of the Association, the Rev. Tresham Dames Gregg. An evangelical Protestant determined to arouse his fellow religionists to the dangers posed by the progress of popery since emancipation, 'Thrash em' (his enemies dubbed him 'Trashy') was an inspiring and a courageous demagogue (he had almost single-handedly disrupted the first election meeting held by Morpeth's supporters). He convinced large numbers of Protestant working people that the economic depression which had afflicted them and the municipal reform which had cost them as Protestants both influence and status, for the freemen had been deprived of the civic franchise and the householders to whom it had been given were overwhelmingly Catholic, were inextricably linked. The advance of Roman Catholicism and the suffering of the Protestant working class were part of the eternal struggle between the forces of light and those of darkness. However, if state concessions to Catholicism were halted, and the work of conversion was pressed, then popery would be overthrown and prosperity restored. 'My theory is,' he later explained to a no doubt bemused Benjamin Disraeli, 'that our Church is thoroughly apostolic, thoroughly Catholic, thoroughly sound in doctrine, and that if the Government made it its first object, to render it *thoroughly efficient*, Popery and Sectarianism would disappear, our National evils vanish, and happiness reign from the throne to the Cottage.' Significantly, at the meeting in the Fishamble Street Theatre which Gregory addressed, but only after a bust of his grandfather had with great ceremony been placed on an empty chair in the middle of the stage, Gregg first reminded the candidate that among the Association's members were 300 electors and then issued a warning to the Peel Government. The Association would never rest, he declared, until the concessions to papists which had brought such suffering to Protestants were reversed.[10]

The following evening, Wednesday 19 January, Gregory spoke to a gathering of Protestant freemen. His purpose, he informed them, was 'to fan the flame of the pure spirit of Protestantism'. As a Repeal organ, the *Dublin Monitor*, sardonically observed, 'the Protestant freeman knows only one test of his support to Protestant institutions: and this is a five or ten pound note — he would prefer the latter'. Ironically, it had been with O'Connell's backing that the notoriously venal freemen had retained the parliamentary franchise in the Reform Bill. Gregory purchased their votes at the flat rate of £3 each, for a total cost of £4,500.[11]

Accusations of bribery were not the only ones hurled at Gregory as the campaign 'progressed'. He was ridiculed as a 'thorough green horn', 'an inflated pompous prig, fresh from Oxford', and dismissed as a 'poor, silly, bigotted and brainless' young man. His failure at Oxford was quickly uncovered by the Repealer press as was his attachment to the Turf. Indeed, when his behaviour at a ball given by the Chief Secretary's wife suggested that he was under the influence of something even more intoxicating than political excitement, he was mocked as 'the tipsy boy from the Curragh'. No doubt he squirmed uncomfortably in his seat during the public meeting held on 24 January to nominate both candidates formally. In seconding the nomination of the absent Morpeth (he was a member of the deputation from the British and Foreign Anti–Slavery Society then lobbying in the American capital for abolition of slavery in the United States), O'Connell first upbraided the Conservative for the 'vituperative' assaults of his supporters on Roman Catholicism and then derided him as a callow politician. 'Mr. Gregory, whatever his age might be, his politics were certainly in their infancy,' O'Connell declared. 'He had not got out of his pops and lollypops yet.' Significantly, the nature of the Liberator's remarks had been disclosed beforehand to Remmy Sheehan. Thus Gregory was well prepared to answer the more serious charge, that of bigotry, by disassociating himself from any cry of 'to hell with the Pope and Popery'. Nor did he overlook O'Connell's inconsistency in supporting Morpeth, for the Whig had always stood behind the union. At the end of the meeting the Liberator leaned over and said to his young adversary, ' "May I shake you by the hand, young man? Your speech has gratified me so much, that if you will only whisper the little word repeal — only *whisper* it, mind you — I will be the first tomorrow at the polling booth to vote for you".'[12]

The polling was spread over the remaining five days of the week, ending on Saturday 29 January. The fact that under the terms of the Municipal Reform Act the appointment of Dublin's sheriff had been retained by the Crown gave Gregory an important electoral advantage, for the sheriff and his deputies supervised elections. The police were instructed to arrest those tally agents for Lord Morpeth seen sporting his card, though they claimed they advertised this allegiance simply to get through the crowds. There was also trouble about the location and number of polling booths. In Repealer/Whig areas they were often so situated as to cause difficulty, annoyance and delay in voting. The law permitted the erection of one booth for each 600 electors but the 1,900 whose surnames began with the letter 'M', and they tended to be Catholics and O'Connellites, were provided with 'one narrow crib' in the open street. Further, it was placed under the charge of 'an old mumbling Orange Deputy' who never polled more than 20 men in an hour. At other times the booths were closed prematurely. To add to the confusion and delay Gregory's agents 'unnecessarily and improperly' administered the bribery and qualification oaths to their own as well as to Morpeth's supporters. Finally, they lodged objections to many voters. The result, or so Morpeth claimed in a petition requesting that Gregory be unseated, was that at the end of the five days allowed for polling as many as 1,000 people had been unable to vote. Certainly in a constituency which numbered 8,600 voters only 7,260 had gone to the poll, and of the 3,825 who voted for Gregory only two, he later claimed, were Roman Catholics. He identified one of this fearless pair as a solicitor, 'Mr. Conservative Keogh', who had sought to strengthen his claim for preferment by dramatising his martyrdom. 'It was said at the time that he was recognized dressed as a shabby artisan, and busily

W. H. Gregory, a sketch of the young Member of Parliament in 1844 by
S. Wagner, reproduced as a lithograph.

engaged in breaking his own windows.' 'Whenever a clerkship of the Crown fell due,' Gregory recalled in his *Autobiography*, 'it became my duty to accompany [Keogh] to the Castle to enumerate his sufferings, and to impress on the Government the strong effect which would be produced on the Catholic mind of Ireland by his appointment.' On one occasion this indefatigable suppliant was nearly shot by Gregory during a shooting party at Coole 'when he lay in wait behind a thick brake of blackthorn'. Ironically, when eventually he secured a judicial appointment 'his native land knew him no more, as, owing to his pecuniary difficulties, he retired to France, and only appeared at the Assizes, when his person was safe from his creditors'. [13]

Gregory survived the challenge, for the petition was not prosecuted, and his victory by 390 votes stood. Yet the scandal was not forgotten and in 1846, as another general election neared, the Polling Places (Ireland) Act was passed. It sought to prevent in future the disenfranchisement of voters through the interlocking devices of an inadequate number of polling places and the lethargy of officials. Gregory's argument that this measure would facilitate fraud, by multiplying the opportunities for the unscrupulous to personate qualified voters (one of his own supporters claimed to have voted under thirteen different names, but he prudently witheld this information), was greeted with incredulity. It amounted, one Member observed, to an insistence that 'Because there might be an attempt on the part of some to personate the *bonâ fide* voter was not to have an opportunity of polling'. [14]

Election to Parliament dramatically rescued W.H. Gregory — for he now reverted to this form of signature — from the obscurity to which he had seemingly relegated himself by his conduct at Oxford. But the celebration of his good fortune, and of the revival of his prospects in public life, was interrupted by a severe bout of influenza which not only took him home to Galway for rest but delayed his departure for London to take his Commons seat. However, this was no ill-omen and the next five years proved to be one of the happiest periods of his entire life. He was young, strong in health, handsome, and well off through the generosity of a father 'who never denied me anything'. A pencil sketch, made in 1844, reveals a slight man, dapper, even a little dandified. His features had lost the puffiness and sullenness of the Harrow youth, though the lips were pursed beneath the thin moustache and the sparse and wispy beard added neither maturity nor masculinity to his appearance. In London Gregory was befriended by the Clanricardes — he Galway's Whig magnate and she a daughter of Canning. There he encountered 'a fat elderly parson' whom he assumed to be the domestic chaplain 'and with whom, to set him at his ease [he] entered at once into conversation with the most condescending affability'. 'To my amazement,' Gregory later recalled, 'my advances were met with something very like chaff, and in a few minutes I found myself an object of the broadest banter by the fat old parson. My dignity was a little rubbed, but he was so extremely droll that we were shortly in fits of laughter and excellent friends.' Only when they went in to dinner did the somewhat conceited young Member of Parliament discover his new friend's identity — Sydney Smith. 'I almost sunk into my evening boots', he remembered.

Gregory was taken up by all the great ladies who presided over salons and his good looks, quickness of wit, and fondness for the Turf saw him occasionally invited to that 'paradise of expiring dandies', Chesterfield House. Being a Tory he had joined the Carlton Club, and as a gaming man he secured election to Crockford's. As a fashionable young man he was elected also to the Coventry, 'a kind of expiring effort to lift old tottering, decrepit dandyism to a pedestal'. 'It is worth belonging to, besides the incomparable *cuisine,*' he wrote in his diary, 'if only to watch the last death struggle of these priests of that foolish false god, before which simple and honest Englishmen so long submitted to bow down.' But these private protestations of sardonic detachment are not entirely convincing, for Gregory was drawn to that species of romantic nonsense termed Young England. Its members were a group of aristocrats of his own age who had gathered around the middle aged, and by no means aristocratic, Benjamin Disraeli. Gregory had taken up residence at No.14 Park Street, off Grosvenor Square. As Disraeli lived at nearby Grosvenor Gate, they often walked home together from Westminster and barely a week passed that Gregory 'did not dine with him in frock coat coming from the House of Commons'. Among the other regular guests were Monckton Milnes, who was already 'eaten up with conceit' and later succumbed to the more common form of gluttony; George Smythe, 'an ugly dirty little fellow,' hailed as a young man of great promise but to be lamented as one of greater indolence; and Lord John Manners. The company was gay and amusing, except for their host, who was 'generally disposed to be silent, though genial enough and often startling' [them] 'with some brilliant remark or sarcasm'. No less fascinating to observe was Disraeli's attitude towards his wife. He had married her to save himself from financial ruin, but no matter how she embarrassed him by her gaucheries 'he treated her with the deepest, most trusting affection; indeed with a chivalrous devotion'.

It was of chivalry and a form of mystical monarchy that the Young Englanders spoke. They would reverse the Whigs' policy of giving the people political power. Instead, they would prove to the lower orders that they were their true friends 'by voting money to build baths, to keep up, or rather restore, public games, to form public walks'. Later in life it all seemed more than a little ludicrous, 'a kind of High-Church-divine-right-of-Kings-philanthropic brothers, in which the working classes were to be looked after and elevated on the principle of everything for the people, but nothing by the people'. Perhaps the attraction of Young England for Gregory at the time was that it served to remind him of his grandfather's efforts to improve the material condition of the Catholic masses of Ireland while seeking to deny them political rights. [15]

Ireland dominated Gregory's early political career. He entered

Parliament at that moment when the Liberator's campaign to secure repeal of the union was gathering fresh momentum. O'Connell modeled the repeal organization upon the Association which had triumphed with the enactment of Catholic emancipation, and he again employed the Catholic clergy both as recruiters and rent collectors. Yet, as contemporaries noted, he was eager to win Protestant support and when the young Protestant barrister Thomas Davis joined the Repeal Association he was promptly elevated to its executive board. In the words of the Tory *Quarterly Review,* 'any hybrid Protestant who will countenance Mr. O'Connell becomes at once a respectable authority'. How much more telling and satisfying would have been the capture of the grandson of the former Under Secretary? Thus no sooner had the Dublin election been decided than O'Connell began assiduously to court young Gregory. Frequent notice, personal flattery, praise of the Gregorys as enlightened landlords, invitations to visit O'Connell's Kerry estate at Darrynane, these the artful old politician mixed with appeals to a sense of Irish nationality and grievance. O'Connell sought to tap any feelings of resentment Gregory shared either at the superior attitude adopted by so many in England to all Irishmen or their disregard of the island's interests. ' "If you could only see yourself in the glass my dear boy, how much better you look than over the way," ' the Liberator remarked after the young man had crossed the chamber one evening to talk to him, ' "You would never go back to those fellows".' There could never be perfect equality without repeal of the union, he argued.[16]

Many years later, and confronted by far more radical Irish nationalists, Gregory drew an admiring portrait of O'Connell, generously describing him as 'the most powerful popular leader whom perhaps the world has ever seen'. No doubt he was captivated by O'Connell's charm and personality, and would have been less than human had he not basked in the attention the Irish leader lavished upon him. If his personal opinion of O'Connell changed he did not waver in his opposition to the nationalist's objective. He had been raised by his grandfather on the necessity of the 'connection' with England, and while still at Oxford had written of waiting patiently 'for the hanging of O'Connell, as the happy day of deliverance from civic revolution'. Even the more liberal opinions of his mother had not embraced O'Connell. There were many reform minded Protestants who had sympathized with the Catholics' claim to equal rights but had insisted that they not be permitted to establish a religious dominance. Such liberals had also expected the Protestant gentry to continue to control the country. Consequently, they had quickly grown to distrust and dislike O'Connell with an intensity which matched that of the old conservatives, for his incremental demands threatened the Established Church and beyond that the security of the gentry. As fast as one was granted another was insisted upon, William later asserted in the Commons, 'that were the Protestant Church swept away tomorrow,

something new would be required, as little contemplated at present, as
the right of the Catholics to sit in that House was expected by the
Petitioners for the free exercise of their religious worship.'[17]

True to his upbringing and class Gregory continued to regard union
as the cornerstone of a Protestant and prosperous Ireland, but he was
slowly being weaned from the political and religious intransigence on
which he had been nourished since infancy and it was Robert Peel not
Daniel O'Connell who served as his ideological wet-nurse. That
'portly, fair-haired gentleman, with a smiling and somewhat cat-like
expression' replaced William's dead grandfather as his mentor. Of
course, he had long idolized the Prime Minister from afar. Now, the
worshipper was invited to his hero's home and treated with familial
intimacy. Peel encouraged him to come to lunch whenever he pleased
and Gregory frequently called at his house and if the first minister was
not engaged they would talk. Behind the 'cold and haughty'
demeanour which Peel showed to so many of his world there was a
warmth and even a raciness, and with young men in particular 'he
became almost a boy again and was full of jokes and stories and
nonsense.' 'I loved and revered him, and used to run in and out of
Whitehall Place like a tame rabbit', Gregory recalled at the end of his
own life. Perhaps it was Peel's obvious fondness for the boyish
Member for Dublin that prompted several of the other young men
whom he had pushed to the front — Lord Lincoln (the future Duke of
Newcastle), Edward Cardwell, Sidney Herbert — to be so 'civil' to
Gregory. Certainly it was the Prime Minister who prevented him from
immediately making a fool of himself in the House, for he dissuaded
the freshman member from presenting the petitions of his more rabid
constituents. One group demanded 'a measure to prevent Roman
Catholics from using bells at their chapels, which, as being summonses
to idol worship, greatly distressed the ears of the petitioners.' Another
sought repeal of the Municipal Corporation Act, at least as it applied
to Dublin. But that reform had been passed only after years of acrid
debate and frustration, thus there was little likelihood of Parliament
undoing its work simply to drive O'Connell from the Dublin Mansion
House. 'Neither on public grounds, nor, allow me to say, on grounds
of private regard for yourself could I advise you to come prominently
forward,' Peel cautioned. Gregory did present a petition protesting
O'Connell's admission of 1,400 freemen since taking office as mayor in
November, and several years later he was to be found opposing a
Dublin Improvement Bill which would invest the corporation with the
same powers as those enjoyed by the governments of English cities.
'The corporation of Dublin had performed its duties in a sectarian
spirit, and ought not to be trusted with the vast powers granted by the
Bill,' he protested.[18]

Peel had faced a daunting list of problems when he took office in
1841. He inherited an economy in the grips of a depression and a

nation cursed with the manifold miseries of 'stagflation' — idle industries and declining trade; mounting government deficits; soaring prices and rising unemployment; social distress and unrest; political agitation. The working class Chartists were demanding democratic reform while the middle class Anti-Corn Law League buttressed its demands for an end to protective duties on this vital commodity with rhetorical assaults upon the landed classes. Leading a party that was pre-eminently English in its composition, Peel's overriding concern was England's economic recovery. The restoration of prosperity, the growth of employment, the availability of inexpensive food, these would surely re-establish social and even political stability. But measures lowering the duties on agricultural products which were included in the 1842 Budget provoked the ominous opposition of a substantial minority of the Prime Minister's own party. [19]

Confronted by difficulties enough in England, Peel naturally hoped that the tranquillity the Whigs had at least bequeathed to him in Ireland would last. As the *Edinburgh Review* observed, though it was not given to understating Whig achievements, 'Not only has political discontent ceased to exhibit itself in armed resistance to authority; but the ordinary and unceasing outrages against individuals and private property, which have for centuries been the main obstacles to the improvement of Ireland, have been in great measure repressed by the growing influence of orderly feelings among the people.' In an effort to preserve this peaceful state of affairs Peel appointed a moderate, Lord Eliot, as Chief Secretary. The government 'were resolved to act upon liberal and impartial principles,' one of its senior members remarked.

Eliot arrived in Dublin confident that through such 'contrivances' as an increased grant to Maynooth 'a commanding influence' might be gained over the powerful Roman Catholic priesthood. He expected to win the support of an important section of lay Catholic opinion by showing an unexpected impartiality in making appointments to the Irish administration. However, his initial optimism soon evaporated. A staunchly Protestant Lord Lieutenant successfully frustrated the policy of moderation, much to Peel's as well as Eliot's irritation. The religious prejudice released and exploited during the Dublin by-election depressed the Chief Secretary and he came to regard West's death as one of the greatest misfortunes that could have befallen Peel's Government. 'The proceedings at this Election will I am afraid alienate many of the Catholics who were gradually drawing near us and they will strengthen and encourage the Ascendancy party which was beginning to see the necessity of moderation. We shall carry this election,' he predicted, 'but we shall pay dearly for the triumph.' Nor did the petitions drafted by Gregory's constituents dispel this pessimism. Year's end found the Home Secretary, Sir James Graham, bluntly refusing to lay before the Queen an address from Gregg's Operative Association which declared that 'a handful of Englishmen, when the blessing of God is on the cause, in which they are engaged, are more than a match for millions of factious idolators.' Finally, Peel's hopes of tranquillity were dashed by his old nemesis O'Connell. [20]

The poor showing made by Repealers in the general election and luke-warm response to a repeal meeting and dinner held in County Meath later in 1841 had encouraged Peel to believe that the movement was expiring. He was determined not to resuscitate it by launching prosecutions and thus creating martyrs. To the Viceroy, Lord DeGrey, an uncomplicated Protestant, he patiently explained that 'neglect and contempt are more formidable than vigorous interference on the part of the Executive Government'. But the Repeal Association gathered support and strength as the year progressed, and among its adherents were a few Protestants with nationalist sympathies such as the landlord William Smith O'Brien. Moreover, most members of the Ascendancy were alarmed if not unnerved by the evidence that among the great mass of Irishmen repeal was 'the common topic, morning and night, at work and at rest, at table and even at altar'. Conscious of their vulnerability as a minority, they began to exert pressure on the government to halt the spread of repeal sympathies and thereby reverse the accompanying 'discouragement of Protestantism'. The Protestant gentry of Galway, led by their High Sheriff, Robert Gregory, protested in 1843 against the 'ruinous agitation' of this question and urged the government to act decisively 'to put, as speedily as possible, a termination to a state of affairs so fraught with injury to all classes of society'. The Earl of Clancarty was in the van of the great Tory landowners in the Lords who demanded action. Nor were these insistent and increasingly strident calls for the silencing of O'Connell and his associates easily ignored by the leaders of the new conservatism. Conservatives defined themselves as supporters of law and order, of strong executive government, of the Establishment and of property, and many of them interpreted repeal as a challenge, immediate or eventual, on all four grounds. In such circumstances talk of concessions was anathema, for they likened concession to 'a Welch pedigree, in which Owen Griffith begets Griffith Owen, and Griffith Owen begets another Owen Griffith, and so on alternately to the end of the chapter'. Convinced that agitation and concession would follow one another until there was nothing left to concede, Tories saw in firm and decisive action the validation of their principles and the end of this demoralizing alternation. [21]

The despatch to Ireland of more than 30,000 troops, and the removal from the Bench of more than 30 repealer magistrates, won the approval of the Ascendancy without silencing its criticism of the government, for these measures did not check the repeal agitation. Thus when O'Connell overstepped the boundaries of wisdom and propriety — he made a virulent attack in August 1843 on the Queen's speech proroguing Parliament, and then employed military terminology in convening a monster repeal rally at Clontarf, Dublin, in October — the government struck. First, the meeting was proclaimed. Then, when this ban was meekly obeyed, Peel conquered his fear of creating martyrs. O'Connell, along with other leaders of the Association, was arrested on a charge of treasonable conspiracy and put on trial. The Liberator's conviction by a jury from which Catholics had been systematically excluded excited considerable criticism, but he was subsequently released from the martyrdom of imprisonment by the House of Lords which in September 1844 overturned the conviction on appeal. By that time Peel had put on show the obverse side of his Irish policy. Being both a sophisticated and pragmatic politician the Prime Minister had never intended to resort simply to coercion as he struggled to guard imperial security, separate the priests from O'Connell and defend the Established Church. Once 'the great end of arresting agitation' had been accomplished he turned to the equally important and more demanding task of convincing the priesthood and moderate lay Catholics that reform was possible within a union which would never be repealed. He was still seeking the cooperation of those Irishmen Eliot had gone to Ireland in 1841 resolved to court, and was aided by the timely resignation of DeGrey who as Lord Lieutenant had found himself consistently out of step with the government. Peel's investment in conciliation offered a double political return. The repeal movement would be weakened and the cause of law and order strengthened.[22]

The ministry's initial proposals were modest enough. A commission, chaired by the liberal Lord Devon, was named to investigate the relationship between landlords and tenants in Ireland, for the treatment of the latter by the former provided a rich treasury of grievances. Reform of the county franchise was also proposed and Catholics were appointed to minor offices. Of course, far more sweeping measures would clearly be required if those Irishmen the Prime Minister was looking to conciliate were to be persuaded of his government's commitment to their religious, political and cultural equality. By the time Parliament assembled in February, therefore, Peel was describing far more ambitious proposals to his cabinet. To ensure that the hand of cooperation he intended to extend to the Catholic clergy was grasped, Peel wanted to facilitate the voluntary endowment of the Roman Catholic Church and to do what Eliot had long urged — increase the grant to the seminary at Maynooth. Meanwhile, lay Catholics were to be wooed with improved educational facilities and further reforms to the municipal and parliamentary franchises which would more nearly equalize the voting qualifications in the two kingdoms. Even as the Prime Minister's stunned colleagues privately discussed his far reaching programme the parliamentary opposition launched an attack on the government's Irish policy. For nine evenings in February 1844 the debate continued, prompting an irritated Disraeli to observe that the Irish question was 'the Pope one day, potatoes the next', but it provided the appropriate setting for Gregory's first major speech.[23]

The young Member's approach to the art of speech-making allowed little leeway for improvisation and inspiration. Invariably, he would visit the Parliamentary Library to research his topic. He jotted down ideas and quotations and then worked these into the text which he wrote out in full in his small, neat handwriting on paper carefully folded in half. If this form of methodical preparation was natural in a young man anxious to demonstrate the clarity of his thought, the fact that he continued it throughout his parliamentary life suggests, perhaps, that he never entirely conquered the nervousness he experienced when he first stood up in the chamber to speak at length. 'Unfortunately, my memory is defective as regards retention,' he acknowledged subsequently. 'I can get up for the moment any amount of matter, but after a time only a hazy remembrance remains.' So, in the Commons, he exchanged spontaneity for the assurance only a detailed draft of his remarks gave that he would not stumble. As a result, he soon earned a reputation as a ponderous speaker.

When he rose in his place on the eighth night of debate Gregory had one eye on the Treasury bench and the other on his constituency. He launched a spirited attack on the opposition. In turn sarcastic and indignant, he protested its efforts to depict the ministry and its supporters as the inveterate enemies of the Roman Catholic population of Ireland. He defended the government for its conduct in putting O'Connell on trial and disputed accusations of partiality in the matter of jury selection. Despite this predictably partisan line Gregory did voice sentiments and opinions which suggested the extent to which Peel and time had tempered his Ascendancy convictions. He was quick to deny that he was an 'advocate for a Government of the sword', and demanded 'liberal and generous measures' for Ireland's benefit. The idea of repeal, he explained to his English listeners, was not inspired by an 'absolute love of a Parliament in College-green'. It was less 'a single and individual abstraction' than the 'great focus to which determine all the complaints, murmurs, the grievances of Ireland.' It was the murmur of the Irish priesthood against the Established Church, a church which Gregory, of course, was determined to defend. It was the murmur of the agitator, whom Gregory insisted be ignored. However, it was also the murmur of the tradesman ruined by the agitation; of the man taxed to support paupers 'not one whit worse off' than himself; of the unfortunate father who saw his child dying of fever in a ditch while the Commons squabbled about the system of medical relief; of the tenant 'who, because he can minister no longer to the political ambition of his master or the extortion of the middleman, is driven out roofless and homeless on the wide world, to swell the lists of those to whom any change must be a God-send'. 'Let no country such as Ireland, an anomaly among civilised states, be treated by the niggardly and exact rule of political economy,' he declared. 'She wants assistance for the creation of commerce, the revival of trade, the employment of her poor.'

Gregory's espousal of practical measures to quieten political and social unrest seemed fully consistent with his admiration for the Prime Minister. Equally, his advocacy of an Irish policy of 'firmness and impartiality' sounded no less Peelite. Nor did such statements imply any abandonment of his grandfather's remedies for Ireland's ills. Further, Gregory's declaration of support for Peel's policy came at a time when only the more modest proposals had been disclosed. Even so, his backing was far from unqualified. Although he had, by implication, endorsed the Devon Commission's inquiry, he remained very much a representative of the landed interest. He attributed the restriction of the county franchise in Ireland to a reluctance on the part of the peasantry to be registered rather than that of their landlords to grant them the qualifying leases. 'Naturally induced to rally round his landlord, proud of his success, and grieving in his failure, perhaps occasionally influenced by other and less elevated motives', the peasant who exercised the franchise was all too likely to collide with that power before which even the bravest trembled — the Roman Catholic clergy. Confronted by the unenviable choice of offending the landlord 'at whose hands he has received kindness, or on whose will all his future is dependent,' or of being branded an apostate to his faith, was it any wonder, Gregory asked, that the Irish peasant declined 'to exercise so dangerous a privilege?'

The issue of parliamentary reform was evidently one on which Gregory did not follow his leader. His reply to those Englishmen who waxed indignant over the discrepancies between the voting qualifications in the two kingdoms was to point to those which existed within England. How was it that Thetford's 160 electors balanced Birmingham's 5,000 or Tamworth's 300 equalled Manchester's 12,000, he queried? However, the main thrust of his argument was that the situation in Ireland was unique and could not be properly compared to that in England. 'The more extensive the augmentation of these (Irish) constituencies, the greater powers are you lodging,' he warned, 'not in the friends of Ireland, but in the hands of those who are determined enemies of the British connexion, and of the re-establishment of tranquillity in that country.'[24] Gregory's opposition to franchise reform, together with his denunciation during the Dublin election campaign of the 'wild speculations' of universal suffrage and vote by ballot, also reflected a profound distrust of democracy. That hostility, later fortified by a journey to the United States, was ultimately to carry him into the Cave of Adullam.

There was one other ground of difference between Peel and his young acolyte. Gregory's religious convictions do not at this time appear to have been especially deep but he was wedded to the Established Church. It was an attachment of class and interest, for as a member of the Ascendancy he had been raised to regard the fate of the Church as indissoluble from that of the union and thus of the Protestant gentry. Nor could he ever forget who his supporters were in Dublin. Peel's efforts to conciliate Ireland and separate the Catholic Church from the

Repealers stopped well short of any tampering with the union or weakening of the Established Church, but the increase in the Maynooth grant was central to his policy. Yet for many Protestants this measure was pregnant with mischief and it aroused both a storm of controversy and passionate opposition.

The Charitable Bequests Act, encouraging the voluntary endowment of the Roman Catholic Church, did not meet an unfriendly reception in the House. Outside, the loudest objections came from those members of the Catholic hierarchy, led by Archbishop MacHale, who claimed that the measure would bring the property of the church under the control of the state. The same scenario was to be followed later, when the Academical Institutions Bill establishing three provincial university colleges was introduced, though in this instance MacHale deplored the dangers to the faithful inherent in non-sectarian colleges which he denounced as 'Godless'. However, the county franchise bill had been withdrawn in the face of prolonged parliamentary resistance, and a measure to give effect to the modest recommendations of the Devon Commission was eventually to be dropped for the same reason. Then, in February 1845, one of Peel's youngish men, William Ewart Gladstone, resigned from the government with the novel explanation that although he now supported the Prime Minister's plan to increase the Maynooth grant it was contrary to his former opinions. Immediately, the opponents to this measure began to gather.

Conditions at the seminary were deplorable. After a visit to the College, Thackeray remarked that an 'Irish union-house [workhouse] is a palace to it. Ruin so needless, filth so disgusting, such a look of lazy squalor, no Englishman who has not seen can conceive. Lecture-room and dining-hall, kitchen and students'-room, were all the same.' The crumbling buildings and lamentable conditions had prompted the Irish bishops to seek government help in 1842, and again in 1844. Peel's response was to propose that the annual subsidy be tripled and to recommend that a single grant of £30,000 be made for the construction of new buildings. The reaction in the House and in the country suggested that the cracks which had already appeared in the dykes holding back criticism of the Irish policy of conciliation and generosity had finally burst open and that the Conservative party was in danger of being engulfed by the flood.[25]

The College had been founded in 1795 to train in Ireland priests who had traditionally gone to Europe for their education. The government of William Pitt had supported it because the Catholic Church was an ally in the struggle against revolutionary France. However, the later involvement of Maynooth clergy in political issues saw the wisdom of the decision questioned. 'This was a piece of Pitt's handiwork, to have these chaps educated in a Catholic college at home, to escape foreign contagion, and they turn out the lowest and the most perfidious villains going,' one choleric observer spluttered indignantly. Not surprisingly, the annual vote of the Maynooth grant sparked controversy and this was why Peel wanted to place it on a statutory basis. But the virulent assaults on Peel's proposals drew on a more inspirational source of strength. The celebrations in 1835 of the tercentenary of the introduction of the Protestant Bible to England had given a fillip to anti-Catholic sentiment, and this the Conservatives had earlier both exploited and fostered. While in opposition, they had castigated the Whigs for their alliance with the Irish papists led by O'Connell. The Orange Order, which had been formally dissolved in 1836, now began to reappear. Indeed, the religious arguments against the Maynooth grant had an orange hue for they 'varied from crude hatred of Catholicism on doctrinal grounds to crude distrust of Catholicism on historical'. Catholicism was assailed as 'repugnant to protestant truth and morality', and dangerous 'to civil liberty'. There was fear that the increase in the grant was the first step toward concurrent endowment of the Churches, perhaps even a long stride toward the disestablishment of the Protestant and the establishment of the Catholic. Finally, the proposal provoked the Dissenters who opposed all state endowments and every connection of church and state. The Anti-Maynooth alliance was centred on Exeter Hall, London, but Irish evangelicals formed their own committee and a united conference was subsequently held in Dublin at the beginning of June.[26]

In his *Autobiography*, written four decades later, Gregory claimed that only under pressure from the Dublin Tory press had he been driven from a moderate to a more extreme position on the grant. The Maynooth bill did excite Dublin Protestants to a frenzy of denunciation. The *Dublin University Magazine*, a journal of some intellectual influence, conceded that an increased grant would improve the quality of student life. 'They will no longer be obliged to sleep three in a bed; and they will be provided with table-cloths, so that they may take their meals like other Christians,' it remarked with undergraduate humour. It found the larger consequence less comical. This reinforcement of the Papists' stronghold had come just at the moment when their power was almost gone, it protested. The same thought moved Tresham Gregg to fury. At meetings of the Operative Association he excoriated the Prime Minister as an apostate to Protestantism and railed against this 'grand experimental step towards the incorporation of popery with the state, and its certain ulterior granding ascendancy, if once so incorporated.' The *Dublin Evening Mail*, perhaps the most powerful Tory organ, asked: 'Is England to remain a Protestant nation?' And if England fell what future was there for Protestantism in Ireland? But Gregory's initial comments on the Maynooth grant were greeted not with criticism but unqualified praise. His speech was hailed as 'clever', 'witty', 'well-arranged', 'modestly but admirably delivered', 'full of point and humour', 'and replete with sound constitutional illustrations'. 'We are glad to see the Member for Dublin, thus distinguishing himself in the great political arena of the world,' the *Evening Mail* announced, 'and bearing the fruit of that promise which his first appearance on our hustings led his friends and supporters to hope for.' The conclusion fairly drawn from this is that Gregory's immediate reaction to the Maynooth grant, embarrassing as it proved to be forty years on, found him in harmony with his most extreme constituents.[27]

When he spoke in the House on 3 April Gregory was as ever well prepared. He had read 'all the former debates on the subject — weary work enough.' His fear was that criticism would be 'disgraced' by the 'abominable fanaticism' of some of the other opponents of the measure. Thus he disclaimed any intention to give offence to the Irish Roman Catholics on the benches opposite. Moreover, he was evidently just as anxious not to alienate those occupying the Treasury bench. His main argument was the familar one, that Maynooth had failed to produce a Catholic clergy which was well-instructed, loyal and peaceful; therefore, to reward it with an increased grant was to employ 'the argument of the drunkard, after his debauch! He endeavoured to cure the effects of his intemperance by having recourse to fresh and more copious draughts.' What Ireland required, he went on, was a Catholic clergy acquainted with the world. The seclusion and exclusiveness of Maynooth had prevented many priests from divesting their minds of prejudice and error. The best solution was to do away with the seminary and apply the funds to the other and non-sectarian colleges Peel was about to establish. For in these institutions Irishmen would meet and mingle with fellow Irishmen, differences of religion would not produce hostility, kindly feelings might be extended from the individual to the class, and those dedicated to the holy calling would acquire the necessary prior knowledge of mankind. Clearly, thoughts of conciliating Catholic opinion were not in the forefront of Gregory's mind.

Throughout his speech Gregory mocked the idea that by pacifying Catholics this action would strengthen Protestantism. Instead, it ought to be seen as a boon to the Roman Catholic clergy, 'a great concession, a concession of principle; an acknowledgment of their Church by the State — a union commenced by the Bequests Act, consummated by the present Bill'. And this was the point he developed more forcefully on 14 April. Assailed by her enemies, the Established Church was being weakened by the 'irresoluteness and false position of her friends'. The fact that some supporters of the measure, such as Lord John Russell, had advocated concurrent endowment, while others had suggested that the Catholic clergy be paid out of the present revenues of the Established Church, had convinced him that endowment of the Catholic priesthood would inevitably follow this measure. In words reminiscent of those used by his late grandfather twenty years earlier, when objecting to any state payment of the Catholic clergy, Gregory asked whether 'the people of England consent to pay the ministers of a religion who would grant to the state no concession, and be bound by no tie, and who were to be seen ever aiding those who endeavoured to disjoin the two countries'.[28]

The safeguarding of the union remained Gregory's fundamental concern. To him, far reaching concessions to Catholics posed twin threats to this vital shield of his class — an accretion of power to its enemies and the alienation of its allies. Many Protestants had been discouraged from agitating for repeal, he warned the House, 'solely by their veneration for the Established Church' which they feared would be swept away in a Repealer triumph. Now the government appeared to be cutting the institution adrift. Recalling O'Connell's efforts to attract the support of Protestant operatives Gregory could not ignore the warnings issued by Joseph Le Fanu's *Warder*, an organ for Protestant working class opinion in Dublin. 'The government are wrong then in supposing that the Irish Protestant people, on whose subservient zeal they rely with such supercilious confidence are attached to (the) British connection by no motives higher in the scale of human feeling and intelligence than the blind obstinacy of a ferocious bigotry unsupported by reason and inaccessible to argument,' the newspaper protested. The value of the connection had been 'the assured enjoyment of the privileges and security of the British constitution'; the protection it afforded 'the Protestantism and loyalty of the country from the proscription under which, they feared, the numerically predominant party here would have laid them'; and the supposed 'firm security for the recognition of Protestantism, and of the Bible, as the organ of Protestant truth in every religious and educational institution in the country'. In the opinion of the *Warder* all of these advantages had been imperilled by Peel's policies. [29]

Although the Maynooth bill passed the House it did so only because of the overwhelming support of the opposition Whig-Liberals. Peel's own party had been riven, with a majority of Conservatives entering the lobby for the nays. 'Everybody knows that the Tory party has ceased to exist as a party,' wrote one observer, and 'that Peel's unpopularity is at this moment so great and so general that there is no knowing where to find any interest friendly to him, scarcely any individual.' [30] To his credit Gregory was not one of those who deserted the Prime Minister. On the contrary, he courageously came to his aid when Peel responded to the Irish Famine with another controversial measure.

The failure of the potato crop upon which the people in large areas of the overpopulated island were so heavily dependent saw Peel act with energy and imagination. Although he did not believe it to be the duty of government to feed those in need, relief measures designed to ensure that the needy at least did not starve and that profiteers did not exploit the unhappy situation were introduced. Moreover, the Prime Minister sought to provide the sufferers with employment on such 'reproductive' works as land drainage and the construction of piers and harbours. But as Gregory pointed out in the House, good intentions were liable to be thwarted by vested interests. The bill encouraging the construction of small piers and harbours, and intended to promote the fisheries as a source of employment and of food, did not allow for the obstructionism of those corporations which had gained control of fishing in certain areas, such as Galway Bay, and insisted that locals use only a hook and prohibited any resort to trawls. 'The Irish fishermen ought to have the opportunity of using the trawl on their own coasts,' he observed, 'and not be compelled to stay at home while the fishermen from Torbay came round with the trawl, and swept the fish into English boats.'[31] However, attention quickly concentrated on one specific proposal.

The suspicion some observers had harboured from the moment the serious nature of the Irish crisis became evident, that Peel would grasp this opportunity to do away with the protective corn laws, was promptly confirmed. For him, it was less a question of pushing down dramatically the price of bread — a succession of good harvests had already done that by 1846 — than of pulling the teeth of the well organized Anti-Corn Law League. It would surely exploit the possibilities for class antagonism inherent in Englishmen being taxed to aid and feed Ireland at a time they were also subsidizing the large landowners through the corn laws. Equally, the repeal of these laws would serve to reassure the unenfranchised lower orders that their intersts were protected by a Parliament dominated by the representatives of the gentry and aristocracy. Finally, Peel had long since ceased to believe that protection from foreign competition profited British agriculture. Unfortunately, many of his party's landed supporters in the country had not reached that advanced position, and few of them grasped its paradoxical conservatism. With this reform Peel expected to relieve the pressure 'for democratic change in the constitution of the House of Commons.' His failure to convince his own followers of this benefit and the other advantages ensured that repeal of the corn laws, as the opposition to the more modest proposals introduced in 1842 had indicated, would prove divisive. The gulf which had separated Peel from a large section of his party since the Maynooth debate was certain to be deepened and broadened, perhaps to the point of being unbridgeable.[32]

The successful repeal of the corn laws plainly indicates that a majority of the representatives of the landed interest, who dominated Parliament, acquiesced in the reform. Of course, in reaching his decision on how to vote, each individual Member of the Commons had to consider not merely his interest but the danger of his being 'diselected' by infuriated constituents. For Gregory this was, as he well knew, a real peril. In 1842, when Peel had proposed reductions in the tariff on food-stuffs, the young Member had returned to his constituency to discuss the merits and disadvantages of the Prime Minister's course with corn factors, cattle dealers and the Chamber of Commerce. Eventually, even the *Evening Mail* had rallied to the support of the sliding scale of duties, accepting that lower prices for Irish produce would be offset by decreases in the costs Irishmen paid for manufactures on which the duty was also to be lowered. However, it was not long before the *Mail* was complaining of the consequences for Irish farmers and graziers of this economic policy, and in January, 1843, the newspaper informed Irish

Members of Parliament that their first duty was to prevent Peel heading farther along this path. 'One step more in that direction and Ireland is bankrupt — her landlords without rents, and her labourers no employment.' Gregory's vote later that year for the free importation of colonial grain caused scarcely a ripple but a rumour in February 1846 that he intended to back Peel's 'measures of destruction towards this country', prompted the *Evening Mail* to observe that in that eventuality he ought to resign.

Gregory's speech on 10 February 1846 was the longest he had yet made in the House and the disapproving *Mail* conceded that it proved his ability. Skilfully planned, his remarks moved from a general statement of faith in the efficacy of free trade to a particular rejection of the charge that this policy would work hardship in Ireland. He had painstakingly worked his way through consular reports as well as trade and navigation accounts in order to add the authority of statistics to the argument that the initial changes in 1842 had either not damaged or had benefited Irish agriculture. Further, in the expansion of British trade and the consequent increase in English demand for Irish produce, and thus of Irish prosperity, Gregory envisaged a growth of commerce which would at last transform Dublin into a great city. An Irishman who crossed from Liverpool to his capital could not fail to note the contrast and be pained by the sight of 'the most noble bay in our possessions, free from shifting sands and natural obstructions, and yet only dotted by the sail of the fishermen or the pleasure boat'. If this was an appeal to the mercantile interests in his constituency he knew that many other traditional supporters would look askance at his association with O'Connell on this issue. Gregory was quick to defend the Liberator, therefore, against the charge that he supported repeal of the corn laws in order to promote repeal of the union. If O'Connell was guided exclusively by this ambition, he reasoned, the Repealer would have played upon the fears of all sorts of Irishmen that this measure would bring about their ruin. Instead, on this occasion, he and his followers had acted 'from humane and enlightened considerations'.[33]

Gregory's hope that reason would vanquish 'groundless fear' was quickly dashed. His political allies in Dublin turned on him, recalling his statement during the by-election that repeal of the corn laws would be 'peculiarly detrimental to the best interests of this portion of the United Kingdom'. Examining his parliamentary record, the *Evening Mail* concluded that with the single exception of the Maynooth Grant he had 'given his unqualified support to a Minister and a Government who have rendered life and prosperity insecure in this country'.[34]

Gregory was accurately described as the 'Peelite Representative of Dublin'. One of the recurrent themes of his speech on 10 February had been admiration of Peel. The Prime Minister's unmatched grasp of financial and commercial problems, his rescuing of the nation from the crises of 1842, his disinterested sense of public duty, all of these attainments and achievements the young follower had stopped to salute. Two days later the beleagured Peel offered Gregory the Irish Lordship of the Treasury. Although a minor position it promised to be of unusual if temporary significance. As there was at that moment no Chief Secretary in the House the conduct of Irish business would have been placed in Gregory's hands. Consequently, he came to regard his refusal of the office as a decisive mistake in his career. Peel had advanced many young men to the front of political life and he would 'have done the same for me, but for my perversities', Gregory sadly asserted at the end of his life. 'It would have put me fairly in the political groove,' he wrote in his *Autobiography*, 'and would have enrolled me in the corps of those famous young men whom Sir Robert had selected, and had shown his eminent sagacity in so doing — Mr. Gladstone, Lord Dalhousie, Lord Elgin, Lord Canning, Mr. Cardwell, Lord Lincoln, Sidney Herbert.'

Yet this was a less momentous episode in his life than Gregory later imagined. Had he joined the government and served temporarily as its spokesman on Irish affairs he would have had little time in which to make his mark for Peel's ministry was defeated four months later. Further, Gregory's performance might well have reflected his lack of confidence when it came to facing Repealers in debate. Fear of 'unpleasant discussions' with 'O'Connell's friends' discouraged him from voicing some of his opinions on Irish questions in the House and he may not have been entirely reassured by the Prime Minister's confidence that he would do well enough after a few encounters. An even greater fear was for the safety of his seat. In order to accept a position in the government he was required to resign from Parliament and seek re-election. Despite his later recollection of having informed Peel that his seat in Dublin was safe, Gregory would have been hard pressed to retain it in the spring of 1846. His stand on the corn laws had cost him much of his electoral support. The *Evening Mail* had broken with him while the *Warder*, an organ of the influential Tresham Gregg, accused him of betraying his principles and baldly declared that it would be impossible to return him for the constituency again. There was a suggestion, in the *Evening Packet*, that his change of views would be rewarded with 'a place and salary sauce'. These stories William's father drew to his attention when they discussed Peel's offer. No doubt Gregory touched upon all these problems when he refused the proffered appointment. Disappointed as he may have been, Peel surely recognized the soundness of the decision. Indeed, he agreed to keep the offer secret so that Gregory could use the refusal to his advantage at the general election Peel expected to call later in the year. It would be a 'most valuable weapon' in his battle to convince his constituents that he remained a man of principle. Hence his dismay when word of it leaked out. [35]

Peelite that he was, and persistent opponent of parliamentary reform that he proved to be, Gregory had naturally endorsed the conservative intent of the repeal of the corn laws. 'Remember 1842,' he had urged the House. Should a disaster of the same order as that now visiting

Ireland strike England, would it be accepted with the meekness and resignation of the Irish? He thought not. 'Could the starving operative be told that all that a wise, enlightened, and humane Legislature could effect had been done?' he asked. 'Preserve their restriction upon the people's food, and then preach resignation, if they dared, to an angry and terrified nation.' Enlightened class interest had clearly played its part in determining his conduct.[36]

That the defence of the landed interest, especially the Irish, was the very heart of Gregory's politics had long been evident. He had not supported Peel on Maynooth because he saw that measure as a threat to the position of the Established Church and thus to the union which the Protestant gentry regarded as essential to their security. But the preeminence of class interest was to emerge all too starkly, and crudely, during the profound crisis into which Ireland soon sank.

Peel's government could not survive the division of the Conservative party. 'The sacriligious hand that touched the altar and remained unscathed has assailed the wheatsheaf and been withered up,' Gregory sardonically observed. He listened to Peel's final speech as Prime Minister and remarked that 'He seemed happy enough, and sang his death dirge with the complacency of undoubted euthanasia'. Sadly, the return of the Whig-Liberals to office was followed by a grave deterioration of conditions in Ireland. Nor was this entirely coincidental, for in its response to the total failure of the potato crop the government of Lord John Russell proved to be more doctrinaire and less imaginative and less energetic than that of his predecessor. Within a year the *Freeman's Journal*, an organ of O'Connell and thus no admirer of the former Prime Minister, was freely conceding that 'No man died of famine during his [Peel's] administration, and it is a boast of which he might be proud'. O'Connell's rapid disillusionment with the harsh workings of Russell's particularly dismal economic theories was matched by the growing dismay of Irish landowners at the new government's grim determination to force them to shoulder a larger share of the burden of relief. They did not refuse to vote higher relief expenditures in their localities but they were frightened that the government's policy would result in their impoverishment and insisted that the monies be employed on 'reproductive' works. In short, they demanded that the relief funds be used as much needed capital investment which would increase agricultural productivity. By December 1846, the landowners had created a 'Reproductive Works Committee' and it summoned the landed interests and Irish Members of Parliament to meet in Dublin in mid-January 1847, to develop a coherent policy to meet the crisis. For a brief, bright moment during that dark winter it seemed that the magnitude of the disaster which had befallen Ireland had at last convinced Irishmen to put aside their religious and political differences and unite to rescue their island.

The *Dublin Evening Mail* and the *Freeman's Journal*, poles apart politically, had been as one for more than a year in their call for the formation of an 'Irish Party' at Westminster. Repealers must have rubbed their eyes in astonishment, and then licked their lips in expectation of Protestant conversions, when they read in the *Mail*: 'We want, in fact, from the United Parliament such legislation as we should have for ourselves, if we had an honest, as well affected, and an understanding Parliament of our own.' Then, in January 1847, seventy-eight Peers and Members of Parliament repeated the call, among them William Gregory. Although he did not attend the meeting held in Dublin on January 14, which brought together Tories and Repealers, gentry and professional men, and adopted unanimously thirty-six resolutions demanding prompt and extensive measures of redress, Gregory was present at the group's subsequent meetings at the rooms it had rented in the Palace Yard, Westminster. But once Parliament reassembled the precious Irish unity, which might have compelled Russell to make concessions, collapsed. [37]

At their meeting in the Westminster rooms the Irish members had appeared to give unanimous approval to a scheme of Lord George Bentinck. He was a great friend of George Hudson, the former linen draper who had been crowned king of the railroad craze. Bentinck was impressed both with the numbers of labourers employed on railroad construction and the wages they earned. Therefore, his uncomplicated mind fastened upon massive investment in railroad development as the solution to Ireland's immediate social problems and an instrument of enduring economic growth. He proposed that the Treasury advance £16 million to companies for that purpose. Long a friend of Bentinck's, though their relations had cooled with Lord George's emergence as a leader of the Tory Protectionists, and responding to the estimate that more than 100,000 men would find work, Gregory was a passionate supporter of the railway scheme. He voted for it even though Peel and most of his other personal followers in the Commons opposed the measure. Yet his confidence in this instrument for promoting 'the prompt and profitable employment' of the people of Ireland seems to have been misplaced. Few men were more knowledgeable on the subject of railways than Isambard Kingdom Brunel. He had been the engineer on the broad gauge Great Western Railway, dubbed Brunel's billiard table, and was in 1847 the engineer to the company building the Oxford, Worcester, and Wolverhampton line. Brunel was skeptical of the value of this labour-intensive industry as the answer to Ireland's troubles. It was his experience that railroads conferred little immediate benefit on a neighbourhood. He estimated that no more than one quarter of the total cash expenditures was spent on the employment of unskilled labour. Almost a third went on the purchase of manufactured items, which would have to be imported by Ireland, and the largest share of the remainder financed land purchases. Of the 25 per cent which did provide work for labourers, and Brunel suggested that each mile of track would employ no more than sixty men a year, even that sum was spread over a considerable period of time and little of it was expended during the first six months. [38]

Brunel's pessimistic analysis was forwarded to Lord John Russell and it may have influenced his decision to oppose Bentinck's scheme. Of course, the Tory's repudiation of economic orthodoxy and implied criticism of the government's response to the Famine probably guaranteed the ministry's opposition from the outset, and when Russell threatened to resign if defeated on this question a number of Repealers, alarmed at the prospect of the Tories returning to office, either voted against the measure or abstained. These defections fostered disunity within the ranks of the 'Irish Party' which was finally split asunder by the government's revision of the Irish Poor Law.

Proposals to extend to Ireland the system of outdoor relief that was in operation in England, thus abandoning the workhouse test, excited in Gregory fears for the survival of his class. The cost of providing work for all those who could labour would amount to double the real income of Ireland, he calculated, yet landlords had long since been reported 'done up' by the fatal combination of increased expenditures on relief and loss of revenue from rents. Many tenants could not make their payments to landlords and it was believed that others were using the crisis as an excuse not to do so. While in certain cases landowners were not to be pitied, it was 'painful to contemplate the destruction and misery that will be entailed on the country' should they be driven to the wall. Instinctively, Gregory rounded on those English critics who had 'attempted to fix on the landlords of Ireland all the social evils which afflicted that country'. He reminded them that English commercial jealousy had prevented the development in Ireland of industries, such as woollens, which would have produced a healthier economy and a more prosperous society. Beyond this refutation of the blanket condemnation of Irish landowners, he demanded policies that distinguished between the good and the bad among them. 'The great principle on which an enlightened Legislature should proceed,' he argued, 'should be to give encouragement to those who had made the best use of the advantages attached to their position, and, while imposing taxation on the lazy and improvident, to hold out every practical exemption to the man who was desirous of ameliorating the condition of the country.' Do not ride the willing horse to death, he implored.

One of the obvious attractions of Bentinck's scheme had been its promise of unburdening landlords of the growing weight of relief. Gregory also regretted the government's lack of interest in the funding of agricultural schools, at which a new generation of Irish farmers might learn the improved methods their fathers had declined to adopt at the suggestion of landlords. One million pounds applied to this purpose, he declared, 'would have been far more serviceable and more profitable to all parties, than if lavished, as proposed to be, in futile speculations to reclaim irreclaimably waste lands.'[39]

Gregory did not wage his campaign for reproductive works — those which would be of permanent benefit to Ireland and landowners — in ignorance of the appalling condition of the great mass of the population. He deplored the government's doctrinaire adherence to 'the science of political economy', and pointed to the arrival of starvation along the Galway coast. There, people were attempting to subsist on mussels but that diet led to dysentery and death. But when the peasants' immediate needs came into conflict with the future interests of his own and already hard pressed class Gregory's overriding concern was to protect the latter. He had allied with Galway's most powerful Whig, and greatest landowner, Lord Clanricarde, who believed that the 'root of most of our incapacity to act is the disorganized state of society', to seek firm government action to check disorders as a desperate peasantry fought for survival. 1847 saw the passage of a crime and outrage bill. Both men had also convinced themselves, and sought to persuade others, that 'hundreds of thousands who are not proper objects of charity, or famine works, are receiving Government pay, and leaving legitimate free labour'. That conviction rendered much easier their decision, amid the human calamity of the Famine, to fight the proposal for outdoor relief. The stakes were high. In the opinion of a somewhat more dispassionate observer, the revised Irish Poor Law would effect a complete revolution of property, ruin the landed proprietors, and bring down the Protestant Ascendancy and the Church.

When it became clear during the debate on the government's measure that outright opposition to outdoor relief would fail, and that demands for increased workhouse accommodation would not be heeded, Gregory moved two amendments to the bill. They were clearly intended to compensate landlords. Many a landowner's ambition to work his estates more profitably, by changing from tillage to livestock or dairy farming, had been frustrated by the presence of a mass of tenants holding small plots of land. Further, such small tenants were a double financial liability. Not only were they often unable to pay their rents but the landlord was responsible for the payment of the poor rate on such small holdings. If they could be cleared from the soil, perhaps even from Ireland, the ultimate savings would more than balance the immediate additional costs. To effect this, Gregory proposed a resort to the proverbial carrot and stick. Smallholders should be induced to give up their land and leave Ireland with an offer of assistance to emigrate and settle in the colonies, the landlords bearing two thirds of the expenses and the boards of guardians charged with administering the poor law finding the balance. Individual landowners had already resorted to schemes of assisted emigration as a means of clearing their estates, thus Gregory's plan was merely an effort to develop a more comprehensive programme which landlords would not have to finance alone. As for the goad, that was the brutal dilemma in which all occupiers of more than one quarter of an acre were to be placed. He moved that boards of guardians be prohibited from granting relief, either in or out of the workhouse, to these smallholders, their wives or their children. To save himself and his family from starvation a cottier would have to relinquish his plot. Thirty years later Gregory attempted to defend these provisions as measures of far sighted statesmanship, as attempts to solve Ireland's chronic problems arising out of overpopulation. Too many people were miserable squatters trying to eke out an existence on plots that could not support them, he argued correctly; but he was less than frank when he implied that his motive had been their welfare. The government made no bones about the reason for its acceptance of the second of Gregory's amendments. These 'smallholdings were the bane of Ireland', the Home Secretary explained. And when Smith O'Brien and Sharman Crawford appealed for a more generous and sympathetic response to the cottiers' plight Gregory cavalierly dismissed the argument that his amendment would destroy all the small farmers. 'If it could have such an effect,' he replied, 'he did not see of what use such small farmers could possibly be.'[40]

The opposition of Irish landlords to the principle of outdoor relief had destroyed the fragile unity of the Irish Members even before Gregory's amendment of the Poor Relief Bill. By 1847 O'Connell was spent, physically and politically, and he died in May while on his way to Rome. It was left to his son and political heir to lead his followers out of the 'Irish Party' meetings. However, the Liberator's nephew, Morgan John O'Connell, had supported Gregory in the House and co-operated with him outside Parliament to promote schemes of state assisted emigration. As cottiers lost their plots and the demand for labour decreased on improved estates so the able-bodied unemployed were certain to rise in number. Was not the settlement of this surplus population overseas one way, Gregory asked the House, 'to give security to life and property in Ireland, to promote the introduction of capital into that country, raise the Irish peasant to a level with the English agricultural labourer, and do away with the party feuds and religious animosities which distracted that portion of the United Kingdom?'[41]

Together with Morgan John O'Connell, and John Robert Godley, Gregory served on a committee which a group of interested landlords had struck to lobby for a massive state assisted exodus from Ireland. Theirs was a distant echo of a suggestion Gregory's mentor Robert Peel had made more than thirty years earlier. They proposed that the government provide the transportation for as many as 1,500,000 emigrants to Canada. The costs, which they estimated at £9 million, would be advanced by the government on the security of an escalating tax on Irish property. When they circulated this proposal to the Catholic Bishops of Ireland, seeking their support, they received a stinging reply from Edward McGinn, Bishop of Derry. He damned the scheme as one motivated by hatred both of the mass of the Irish people and of their religion. The members of the committee, with the exception of O'Connell, were denounced as the descendants of those who had abetted Cromwell in removing 70,000 Irishmen to the Indies to die like dogs. Finally, the Bishop saw no just reason for Irishmen to quit their

native land when 'the laws of God and of nature had given them just
title to the soil' — an assertion no Ascendancy landlord could accept. [42]
    Attacks on the plan, as a device to remove 'injured millions to some
untrodden region far west of the horizon', and to pack off the Roman
Catholic Church with them, were unceasing. Critics pointed to the
many thousands who had died in the Famine, or had already left the
country, to seek work in England or to settle in Australia, America or
Canada (more than 100,000 had emigrated in 1846 and the total for 1847
was more than double that number), and argued that a state sponsored
scheme would denude the country of inhabitants. Alternatively, fears
were expressed that emigration would take away the best of the
population, or that it would not have any significant economic impact
unless a third of the population quit the island. Any notion of a
migration on that scale was regarded as 'preposterous'. Indeed, a
campaign to dissuade Irishmen from emigrating voluntarily, for the
government saw no reason to intervene while thousands were paying
their own way or took up the offers of landlords to pay their passage,
was waged by the Catholic press. Canada's discomforts and dangers, its
'ague-breeding fens' and woods of 'the cat-o-mountain', were well
advertised as was the opposition in the colony to the scheme. The
hostility that greeted the unprecedented numbers of Irish immigrants to
the United States also received extensive coverage in popular
newspapers. From the hour the Irish land to the hour they expire, the
Tuam Herald was still warning years later, 'they are despised and spit
upon, and in thousands of cases they die without the last rites of the
Church'. For a devout people, this was a terrifying prospect. The
answer to the suffering and misery of Ireland was not to emigrate, and
risk evils of soul and body in some distant land, but to stay at home and
struggle 'to rectify the vicious system of legislation' which discouraged
the investment of labour or capital in the soil. [43]
    By his conduct throughout the spring of 1847 Gregory had made his
name one of the most detested in Ireland. The allegations of bigotry and
selfishness excited by the emigration scheme were overshadowed by the
bitter accusations that his quarter acre test for relief was 'an instrument
for the "clearance" of Irish estates, and for the utter pauperization of
the humbler classes of agriculturalists'. If the charge of facilitating
clearances was by no means unfounded, Gregory was not entirely
responsible for the stringency of the test. In the Lords, Irish landowners
had considered his amendment a 'most useful and valuable provision'
but had concluded that it contained a loophole. They disliked the
requirement that relief be withheld until the occupier had 'satisfied' the
guardians that he had surrended his plot of land. Sympathetic
guardians might declare themselves satisfied 'tho' there was neither
moral, nor legal proof, of the fact of the surrender of the land — and,
by consequence, of granting outdoor relief to persons who ought not to
obtain it.' Therefore, the Lords established a more stringent condition.
To obtain relief the cottier had to surrender his plot to his immediate

landlord. By 1851 a combination of famine deaths and the Gregory clause had greatly eased the landlords' problem of 'redundant population', for many of the tiny smallholdings had disappeared. It was not an achievement Gregory cared to claim, or long savoured, for the image of human misery found on the other side of this legislative coin was to dog his political career for years.[44]

In January 1846, as he prepared his speech on the corn laws, which was certain to alienate many of his supporters in Dublin, Gregory had sulkily dallied with the notion of retiring from politics. The news from the constituency was already depressing. His organizers warned that disillusionment with the Peel Government had fostered apathy or had tightened purse strings. In Ireland voters were required to register and a certificate of registry was valid for eight years, but the task of identifying and re-registering those whose certificates had expired, or registering new claimaints, was an expensive one. However, in December 1845, Fred Jackson, a prominent Dublin merchant and Gregory's election agent, reported to the Member that he and his fellow workers had been able to raise only a paltry 10/- during an entire week despite the 'utmost exertion'. By dint of hard work, and with judicious use of patronage and the argument that what was at stake was the holding of the city or its abandonment to O'Connell, Fred Jackson and Remmy Sheehan, together with another prominent local Tory and the other member for the city, Edward Grogan, eventually persuaded a group of leading merchants and bankers to open their pocket books and find the £663 that was required. Then came the shock of Gregory's support of the repeal of the corn laws, which saw him repudiated by many of his supporters. Yet as the year wore on, and a general election neared, Gregory had reason for renewed optimism about his political future.[45]

First, the Rev. Tresham Gregg volunteered his electoral services. Although Gregory had irritated Gregg and the Operative Association by his equivocal response to a factory bill introduced by Lord Ashley in 1844, which attacked the monstrous abuse of child and female labour by employers, the Member had been careful to maintain his connection to them. Gregory continued to be one of the Association's most generous subscribers and to serve as one of its patrons. Then, at the end of May 1846, only fourteen weeks after the *Warder*'s repudiation of him for his stand on the corn laws, Gregory received a letter from Gregg which, for all its insufferable arrogance, must have encouraged him to believe that he might yet hold his seat at the next election. 'I am quite disposed to allow you to do as you please about the Corn bill and I can secure you against the malignity of the miserable scribblers who on this ground would run a muck against you,' Gregg wrote. 'You have been as faithful against popery as any man. You have stood by the Protestant (cause) thus showing that your heart is right on the Grand point and I think I could on this ground carry your election if there be a dissolution tomorrow.' A second encouraging sign was that of failing enthusiasm among Repealers, Gregory's most likely opponents. By mid-October

Fred Jackson was able to report that the Repeal rent in Dublin was down to £47 a week and that almost the entire Repeal staff had in consequence been disbanded. A third fillip came from the Aldermen of Skinners Alley, who again endorsed Gregory's nomination. Finally, Remmy Sheehan and the *Evening Mail* rallied to him in the spring of 1847. Gregory had been diligent throughout his first three years as a Member of Parliament finding positions for those men the proprietor-editor recommended. 'You are one of the few public men I have ever met who bears a lively recollection of a political service rendered,' Sheehan had remarked. Alienated by Gregory's support of the repeal of the corn laws the newspaperman was now reconciled by rememberance of these earlier favours and his introduction of the 'two important checks upon the destructive power of the outdoor relief scheme'.[46]

Gregory's position in 1847 was not as strong as he imagined. Lord Clanricarde attempted to initiate in March a detailed Whig analysis of the political situation in Ireland, but not all of his proposals were taken seriously by his associates. He advised Dublin Castle to resort to the Kildare Street Club as 'the real place in which knowledge of every landlord's estate, and his influence, derived from either personal character, or from property, and of the general state of almost every constituency, and of the bias of persons of almost every class may be learned.' However, Lord John Russell, to whom Clanricarde's suggestions were forwarded, had a lower opinion of the Club's value as a source of intelligence. 'The consumption of claret at Kildare Street has, I hear, been so little,' he observed with characteristic superciliousness, 'that really there must be distress in Ireland.' Similarly, while all could agree with Clanricarde that the party should pursue a pragmatic policy of working in the forthcoming election with whoever would support the government afterwards, he failed to convince fellow Whigs that Gregory was a man of much ability who might 'easily be got to our side upon all important questions'. Describing the Peelite as a free trader, perhaps favourably disposed to state payment of the Roman Catholic clergy but 'certainly inclined to be liberal', he recommended him to the Lord Lieutenant, the Earl of Bessborough, as one of two men who might be profitably consulted on Irish problems. The other was Clanricarde's uncle, Sir John Burke. The Viceroy declined to place his trust in either man and the Under Secretary was reported to have said that the Castle would accept 'anything but Gregory' in Dublin.[47]

There was evidence by June that the Repealers, contrary to earlier indications, intended to mount a serious challenge to the Tories. They had formed an election committee, composed of respected local figures, and had launched a fund to pay clerks who would make copies of ward books and lists as preparation for a detailed canvass. The treasurer of the fund was John Reynolds, 'a great spouter at Repeal meetings', and when he emerged as the Repeal candidate Gregory's friends 'laughed at his pretensions' and insisted that he would never go to the poll. However, the dangers of over-confidence ought to have been obvious to Gregory and his backers and in this respect the death in May of the artful and knowledgeable Sheehan may have been significant. He would not have forgotten that host of freemen O'Connell had admitted as mayor, and few of them were likely to give their political allegiance to either of the Tory candidates. The passage of the Polling Places Act had also limited the possibilities of electoral manipulation. Moreover, Gregory decided to discontinue 'the vile system of bribery heretofore carried on'. It was a pragmatic rather than a high minded decision. Gregory's campaign suffered from a want of ready money and an excess of confidence. This time there would not be any contributions from England and it had been difficult to raise large sums within the constituency. Gregory had paid £750 out of his own pocket to meet the regular expenses and confident of being returned he probably saw no reason to dip any deeper to pay those that were irregular. Thus 'the hush money was not given to that religious Patriot Mr. T. Greg[g] on this as on former occasions.'[48]

Gregory returned to Dublin at the beginning of August to be nominated formally at a meeting held at the Court House in Green Street. To this date he had shunned the tiresome duties of candidacy, such as holding meetings with the city's Protestant electors, in favour of the excitement of the Goodward race meeting. But the consequences of his 'overweening confidence' were soon apparent, for when Gregory's name was placed in nomination at the crowded Court House on 2 August Gregg leapt to his feet and launched a diatribe of more than two hours duration against Peel and his loyal local ally whom he indicted and convicted of 'the foulest treachery'. In a desperate effort to save the situation Gregory represented his votes on the corn laws and the Poor Relief Bill as having been determined by the interests of his constituents, particularly those for whom Gregg so often spoke. The repeal of the corn laws had ensured that the artisan could buy his American loaf without paying a toll to the landowning class to which he belonged himself, Gregory declared. His fight against outdoor relief had been spurred by a determination to prevent a rise in the poor rate — the taxation for relief — which by taking more money out of the pockets of landlords and tenants would lessen their demand for the goods whose manufacture gave employment to the city's operatives, and the trade in which brought profit to its merchants. The confusion at the Court House, as cheers for Gregory were answered with hisses, extended to the polling. On the single day set aside for voting Gregory's election agent got drunk and an opportunity to bribe 150 freemen, whose votes would have saved the Tory seat, was missed. Reynolds pushed Gregory into third place.

An analysis of the poll revealed that Gregory had attracted 700 votes fewer than he had accumulated in 1842 and had captured 228 less than his fellow Tory, Grogan. The conclusion most observers drew from these figures was that Gregory owed his defeat to Gregg and his followers, who had 'plumped' for Grogan. They had voted for only

one candidate though two Members were to be returned, and by so
doing had let in the Repealer. Fellow Tories quickly brought this bill of
recriminations against Gregg and taking advantage of this sudden
unpopularity, the Archbishop of Dublin, who had long detested the
firebrand and had unsuccessfully sought to deny him a living, now
restrained him from officiating at his chapel of St. Mary in the parish
church of St. Nicholas Within. Next, Gregg was expelled from the
Aldermen of Skinners Alley and declared forever ineligible for membership. When in October a Greggist, and grand master of the local Orange
Lodge, was nominated for Governor of the Protestant body he was
defeated by Gregory's former election agent, Fred Jackson. The following January saw Gregg's supporters make another attempt to rescue
him. They introduced a resolution legitimising his opposition to
Gregory, only to have the debate end in a repudiation of Gregg and all
his works. The Aldermen congratulated 'each other in having expelled
one who has inflicted so much injury on civil and religious liberty by his
bigotry and intolerance, such a line of policy as this being (in our
opinion) the bane and ruin of Ireland and whilst we shall maintain and
uphold our own religious and political faith, we will as firmly condemn
the conduct pursued by this Rev. Gentleman in creating disunion and
ill will amongst his already too much divided countrymen.'[49]

Ironically, this welcome triumph of moderate conservatism, with its
promise of a movement 'towards a more liberal and enlightened view
which if only guided in a right course would be the foundation of a party
stronger and more effective than any yet formed to arrest the downward
career the country is running', ill-served Gregory's immediate political
interest. A group of his supporters had decided to challenge the election
result. They feared that if Reynolds was allowed to hold the seat
undisturbed it would be the end of the Tory party in Dublin and the ruin
of the country. Already, Reynolds's success had encouraged Repealers
in other constituencies, whose polls took place later, to try and upset
Tories and Whigs alike. An angry and sullen Gregory, still smarting
from his defeat, was at first reluctant to agree to accept renomination in
the event that the election was overturned. But pressed by his fellow
Peelite, Lord Lincoln, he quickly relented. The petition would go ahead
anyway and if Gregory refused to run again Dubliners would be
reduced to a choice between a demagogue (Repealer) and a bigot,
Lincoln warned. Nor should Gregory ignore the likelihood that he
would be unable to find another seat, at least for the life of the newly
elected Parliament. Finally, the Peelites offered some assistance in
meeting the heavy costs of a petition.[50]

With Fred Jackson in command, the movement to contest the election
result gathered momentum. Lawyers were retained, advertisements
were placed in the press requesting information about Reynolds's
'fictitious majority', and a small army of clerks was set to work checking
the lists of voters against those of taxpayers in default. By 20 August the
investigation of six wards had turned up among Reynolds's voters the

names of eleven men who had exercised the franchise from the grave; seven persons who had not been registered for the required six months; forty nine persons who had 'removed' from Dublin; five persons disqualified for reasons of insolvency or bankruptcy; and one proven case of personation of a sick elector. By early October there was optimistic talk, based upon the examination of the tax lists, of at least 700 valid objections.

It was the intention of the Tories to publish their findings, thinking that this would discourage the Repealers from contesting the petition. For this strategy to succeed it seemed important that Reynolds not be given the glimmer of hope that disunity among the Conservatives would provide. And it was against the background of the bill of recriminations brought by fellow Tories against Gregg, and of the conflict between his admirers and detractors, that Reynolds obtained a warrant to inspect and make copies of all the poll books, and his supporters summoned subscription meetings to finance the fighting of the petition. The expenses for both sides were frightening. Gregory's lawyer, and later judge of the Court of Common Pleas, Michael Morris, put the total cost of the two days he appeared before the House Committee at £1,100 or £100 an hour. The petition lasted six weeks. As a gaming man, Gregory was initially willing to offer odds of 7 to 4 in his favour that he would regain the seat. In February 1848 he was still 'certain' of emerging victorious. With his eye fixed firmly on a fresh contest in Dublin, and anxious to burnish his image as a liberal who had fallen victim to bigotry the year before, Gregory counselled his supporters to oppose 'a lay T. Gregg' in the election held that month for a third Dublin seat, that of the College. The successful moderate subsequently wrote to express his thanks for these 'kind exertions' on his behalf. A similar success did not accompany Gregory's expensive election petition, however. Efforts to invalidate many of Reynolds's votes on the ground that those who had cast them had failed to pay their taxes encountered in John Bright a formidable adversary on the Commons committee, and the petition was eventually abandoned. William H. Gregory had been returned to private life.[51]

4
Coole

'Still it is a great bore to be out of Parliament,' one of Gregory's friends remarked, 'half your occupation is gone.' The natural reluctance to yield the distinction which belonged to him as a member of the world's most famous legislature; the thought of ceasing to enjoy the same measure of deference; of losing that sense of power and responsibility the position carried; of abandoning the excitement of London society, all spurred Gregory to sanction the effort to overturn the Dublin result and sent him hurrying home to Galway when he received word that the county election had suddenly been thrown open. Galway's two most powerful political factions had earlier reached a far from uncommon under-standing — labelled the 'two donkey system' by a later gentlemanly nationalist — which averted the expense of a contested election by dividing the representation between them. The Tories, dominated by the Clancarty and Daly families, had agreed to nominate Denis Daly for one seat and Clanricarde had been content with the guarantee that his cousin, Thomas Burke, would be returned for the other. After all, the Whig magnate reported to Dublin Castle, Daly was a Peelite and therefore could be relied upon to support the government on all matters of real importance.[1]

This convenient arrangement was disrupted by the unexpected death of the Tory candidate's father. The new Lord Dunsandle withdrew from the contest, being ineligible to sit for an Irish constituency. Three men quickly stepped forward to volunteer to replace him, among them William Gregory. When the four candidates, accompanied by their supporters, gathered on 10 August to be nominated, Gregory was still thinking primarily of Dublin and of the likelihood that a fresh contest would be ordered there. 'Gregory, without demanding a poll, will make a very liberal speech on the Hustings at Galway,' Clanricarde explained to the Viceroy. 'It is certain the Repealers cannot carry a really contested Dublin Election; neither can Ultra-Tories, and I think Gregory will have great support from the liberals of both sides.' Certainly, when he spoke to the assembled electors in this most Catholic of counties Gregory portrayed himself as a victim of Parson Gregg and those 'who pander to the worst, most odious, and most contemptible of human passions'. This repudiation of bigotry was accompanied by a gentle expression of support for tenant rights, or 'a fair and equitable adjustment between the tillers and the owners of the soil,' and an affirmation of a moderate nationalism. Recalling the ill-fated 'Irish Party', he urged that Ireland cease to be a battlefield for English party warfare and that its representatives procure justice for their countrymen. Apart from one mischievous call for three cheers for John Reynolds, the speech was greeted with great enthusiasm and when the Sheriff demanded a show of hands for the rival candidates Gregory and Denis Kirwan, Tories both, were clearly the victors. However, the supporters of Thomas Burke and of the remaining Tory hopeful, Christopher St. George, promptly demanded a poll which was set for Wednesday 12 August.[2]

The prospect of a lively and expensive election was not one many of the gentry welcomed and at a metting held that same evening they persuaded Gregory and Kirwan to withdraw, thereby enabling Burke and St. George to be declared elected. For Gregory, this was a disappointing turn of events. Admittedly, he had achieved all that he had originally set out to do by entering the contest. His liberal speech would surely impress many of Dublin's voters. Yet he had won on a show of hands at the nomination meeting and he knew that neither Burke nor St. George were popular figures, at least with the vast majority of the county's electorate. Burke had won few friends among the £10 leaseholders by his opposition to tenant rights while St. George was 'hated by the peasantry'. Moreover, friends might regard him as a 'funker of the 1st water not to have fought the battle'. On the other hand there were good reasons to withdraw from the contest. Clanricarde, a powerful friend, would be 'provoked' if put to trouble and expense to secure the return of his cousin. Clancarty was not at home, thus there was no chance of Gregory obtaining strong support from that family quarter in time for the poll. Nor could he expect any assistance from the Catholic clergy. As unpopular as St. George was, a glance at the *Tuam Herald* disclosed that the bitter prefix 'Quarteracre' had been attached to Gregory's name by this organ of the local hierarchy. Finally, it was known that St. George, in the best Eatanswill tradition, had locked up a body of his voters in a stable so that they could not be tampered with before the poll. In short, Gregory elected to ruffle the fewest feathers. Even should he fail to regain his Dublin seat, he would by retiring gracefully from the Galway contest at least position himself well for the next Parliamentary election in the county. For it was in Galway that he would now make his home. The death of his father during the spring had seen William Gregory inherit the family's estates.[3]

The gentry Gregory had joined treasured their hard won reputation as a race apart. Jonah Barrington's memoirs, Charles Lever's novels and William Maxwell's *Wild Sports of the West* had fixed the stereotype. 'Careless of the present, reckless of the future', the 'hard-going sportsmen' of Galway 'acted from momentary impulse, and seemed indifferent whether the result was right or wrong. The women rode, visited, dressed, flirted, danced, and married. The men hunted, shot, played, drank, quarrelled, fought, and made friends again.' It had been one of William's female Trench cousins, 'a peculiarly ill-favoured maiden, with the sweetest voice, the kindest manner, and a very apparent desire for a little dissipation', who had introduced him in 1836 to Galway's heroic revels. They had left the proper Clancartys at Garbally ostensibly to visit Archbishop Trench at Tuam but with permission to dine at Carantrila, the home of the Handcocks. There a saturnalia, presided over by Clanricarde, was well under way when they arrived and it provided Gregory with a rich source of anecdotes. Here he encountered a servant stationed beneath the table, charged with the onerous duty of ensuring that those guests who drank themselves insensible and slipped from their chairs did not choke on their stocks. Rising somewhat shamefaced at noon the following morning he hurried downstairs only to be informed by an aged domestic: ' "The divil a mouthful you'll get before three o'clock, so you had much better go to bed again." ' After three o'clock 'by degrees the party dropped in for breakfast'. An enormous appetite if not capacity for liquor was much admired, as was fearlessness in the saddle. 'In person Lord Clanricarde was the thinnest and sparest of men, and his head resembled that of a corpse' but he was 'the best man to hounds they ever saw.' One Master of the Galway Blazers, famed as the most reckless of hunts, had achieved immortality by riding his favourite horse over a steeplechase course which included ten stone walls as well as twenty-five other fences, 'without saddle or bridle, whip or spur, and accomplished the feat without balk or fall'. Loud were the complaints when Galway rabbit hunters resorted to steel traps, for these snares conjured up in huntsmen's minds the nightmare vision of three-legged foxes. Like his father, William was an enthusiastic hunter. He was also an excellent shot. Yet if he possessed many of the attributes Galway society esteemed Gregory must surely have sensed in 1847 that he was entering an alien world. Although no stranger to the county it had never been the focus of his life, a point one of his rivals in the parliamentary contest had made in an unpleasant way when he charged Gregory with absenteeism. Galway and Gort were a far cry from Harrow and Oxford, Paris and Rome, Dublin and London.[4]

Galway 'is the dirtiest town I ever saw, and the most desolate and idle-looking', the novelist Maria Edgeworth had written in 1834. A group of energetic residents did initiate a number of 'improvements'. Streets were paved, a gas house was built to light the town, and a fine dock was constructed which could admit vessels of fourteen feet draught. Despite these efforts, and the presence of breweries, distilleries, flour mills, a paper mill, a foundry and a tan yard, Galway had continued to bear 'all the evidence of a decayed town'. Even the old Spanish-style houses with their projecting roofs sheltering piazza walks seemed no more than relics of a lost stateliness. Along the banks of the waters of Lough Corrib, which rushed and roared under bridges to the bay, were to be seen strange figures washing all sorts of rags. Pigs ran loose in the street, indeed 'the whole town shrieks with them'. In short, it was a 'large, poor, bustling, rough-and-ready looking town' of some 20,000 souls. And if the visitor's inability to obtain a cigar which cost more than two pence was one illustration of Galway's 'strangeness and remoteness', this impression was confirmed by the fortress-like character of the homes on the most fashionable streets and the Irish to be heard everywhere.[5]

Seventeen miles to the south of Galway, on the road to Ennis and Limerick, and standing in a gap between the Slieve Aughty mountains and the Burren, stands the town of Gort. The journey took the traveller through 'little but the most woeful country'. Stone was everywhere, and it gave a grey aspect to the entire area. There were stone-strewn fields, stone walls and fences, a few old stone castles and a number of stone houses, but even the mud hovels were constructed of a greyish mud, while off in the distance were grey mountains and usually a leaden sky overhead. Gort 'looked as if it wondered how the deuce it got into the midst of such a desolate country, and seemed to bore itself there considerably,' Thackeray observed. 'It had nothing to do, and no society.' That was a harsh judgment. In the middle of the Eighteenth Century Gort had been a 'very poor towne, like a village', but under the patronage of Lord Gort it had grown rapidly at the beginning of the Nineteenth and acquired some commercial importance. By 1837 it boasted more than 3,500 inhabitants and close to 600 houses. There was a symmetry to the broad streets, while both the tall business premises and the houses added to the pleasant and well-ordered appearance, and an air of prosperity prevailed in the years before the famine. A tan yard, a brewery, and a large flour mill which was able to produce 7,000 barrels annually, created wealth and employment, while the merchants served farmers from a large surrounding area. First and foremost Gort was a market town. The weekly market was held every Saturday but cattle and sheep fairs took place in May, August and November, and there was a very large pig fair each St. Patrick's Day. However, it was also an administrative centre of some importance. A courthouse had been erected in 1815 and the Quarter Sessions for the county were held there in October. Petty Sessions were held every Saturday. And there was not only a Revenue and Constabulary station but also a military barracks, which provided accommodation for eight officers and eighty-eight men and stables for more than one hundred and sixty horses. As for transportation, the Dublin-Galway and Galway-Limerick mail coaches ran through the town.[6]

A few miles to the south of Gort, on the shore of Lough Cutra, stood the Tudor-style, castellated mansion of the Gorts, which had been built early in the Nineteenth Century to a design of John Nash. Much the same distance to the north of the town, and lying west of the Galway road, was the older but more modest Gregory home — Coole. Robert Gregory had 'purchased from Oliver Martynn of Tullyra the extensive estates of Coole and Kiltartan' on 18 June 1768. To these he added the

Ballylee estate, obtained from a Clanricarde family heavily in his debt, and then greatly extended his holdings in and around the port of Kinvara which lay only eight miles to the west of the Coole lands and at the head of an inlet on the southern shore of Galway Bay. These acquisitions, together with the smaller Clooniffe estate beside Lough Corrib, brought the total area in Gregory's hands to more than 15,000 acres and made him one of the county's largest landowners. Moreover, he was fully imbued with the spirit of an age which regarded agricultural improvement as 'fashionable, patriotic and profitable'. That peripatetic agricultural writer Arthur Young visited Coole during his *Tour in Ireland* and he wrote admiringly of Robert Gregory. He discovered that Gregory had appointed two English bailiffs to oversee work on the 600 acres he kept in his own hands. One of them supervised the miles of perfect walling which Gregory erected around the demesne while the other, a Norfolk man, introduced 'the turnip husbandry'. Gregory also made full use of the local limestone quarried on his estate. It provided the stone for the walls and the buildings, among them the handsome stable, and when processed in a kiln also provided fertiliser for the lands. Nor had the nabob overlooked the need for trees in this windswept district so close to the Atlantic ocean. 'Mr. Gregory has a very noble nursery,' Young noted, 'from which he is making plantations, which will soon be a great ornament to the country.'[7]

It was on the original Coole estate that the nabob built 'a large house with numerous offices.' Yet the house was not a pretentious one, being no more than a three-storied rectangle with six bays, 'the centre bay having the customary Venetian window on the first floor and the Diocletian window above.' Such simplicity of design not only reflected the neoclassical style popularized in James Gibb's manuals but was eminently practical, for it permitted the employment of local craftsmen on the construction. The residence was beautifully sited, commanding from its rear a view of the Burren in the distance and of Coole lake in the foreground. A turlough rather than a true lake, thus the water level fluctuated dramatically, it did provide abundant fresh water which was drawn off by a horse powered pump and conveyed to the house by underground pipes. And as Richard Gregory discovered the house had taken its name, at least indirectly, from that body of water. His curiosity aroused by his own fleeting and his first wife's deeper interest in the Irish language, he enquired into the derivation of the name. The scholar he approached drew his attention to the description of one of the parcels of land purchased by the nabob, Coole/Cool Insher or Inshie, and explained that it was identified by its relation to the turlough.

The misanthropic Richard behaved somewhat more in character when he resisted the claims of a Seneschal, appointed by the Anglican Bishop of Clonfert for the manors of Clonfert and Kilmacduagh, to collect chief rents from and hold manor courts on the Gregory lands. The Seneschal's letters were left at the gatehouse but went unanswered and Gregory's arrears of chief rent, totalling £36-13s-4d, remained unpaid.

Furthermore, his tenantry were instructed not to obey any summons from the Seneschal and he forbade the holding of manor courts on his property because the Bishop 'had No Right or any claim over any part of my Estate'.

Richard followed in his father's improving footsteps at Coole. He pressed ahead with the planting of trees, for their value was aesthetic as well as functional. He changed the approach to the house, replacing the straight avenue with two great sweeping arcs. He made structural changes to the west side of the residence. The drawing room and the dining room were enlarged with large bow windows which broadened the vista of the distant hills behind which the sun went down. Richard — recluse, aesthete and bibliophile — filled the shelves of the library which linked those two rooms. To the books, mainly on the East, which his father had collected, Richard added editions of the Greek and Roman classics whose bindings gave him as much visual pleasure as their contents did intellectual. From Italy he imported a marble copy of the Venus de' Medici. Indeed, a variety of marbles and bronzes soon adorned the house which had to that time been decorated primarily with a number of Persian and Mogul paintings. In short, Richard established at Coole a tradition of refinement.[8]

None of its initial owners had settled at Coole. The nabob and his son Richard had kept the house in London and there they had lived the greater part of their lives, and there they had died and were buried. For William Gregory the Galway residence had briefly served as a retreat from Dublin where he had his elegant townhouse in Merrion Square. It was his son Robert who made Coole his home. If he added little by way of adornment — he did hang the engravings of public figures with whom his family had been involved, such as Fox, Wellesley and Peel — Robert Gregory ensured that life at Coole would be comfortable. The sunny breakfast room and those three magnificent rooms on the ground floor which caught the setting sun were refurnished, as were the seven bedrooms and guestrooms, and the small study, on the second floor. Between 1841 and 1843 Robert spent £1000 on new furniture and the reupholstering of old, on curtains and carpets. New plate, coffee and tea services, glass and china cost another £500. He even replaced the equipment of the household staff, six of whom had rooms on the third floor while the servants' hall, the kitchen, pantry, storerooms, and the housekeeper's room were located on the north side of the house.

In addition to a large and well furnished house and vast estates, Robert Gregory bequeathed to his son an enviable reputation as a landlord. The chronic problems of Irish agriculture and land tenure were evident throughout the 100,000 acres of the Gort Poor Law Union, within which the greater part of the Gregory lands were located. Much of the area was ill suited to farming, being hilly bog or coarse pasture, yet men sought to subsist on smallholdings. Some 60 per cent of the Union's landholders occupied less than 10 acres whereas between 10 and 15 acres were necessary in order to support a family on this poor

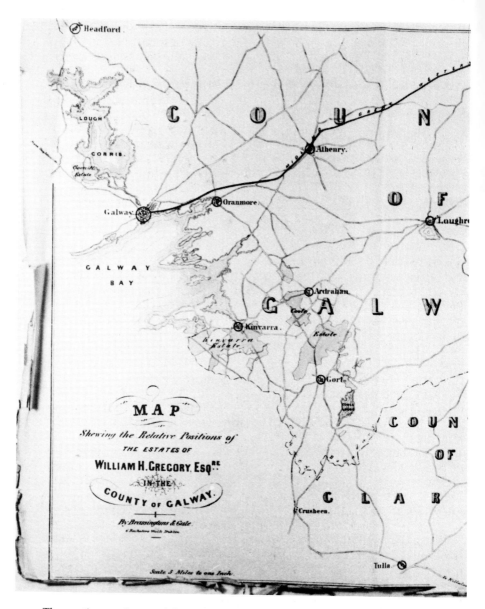

The auctioneers' map of the Gregory estates in the catalogue of the land sale that took place on 13 January 1857. The positioning of certain geographical details is rather imaginative on occasion.

western soil. But just as landlords often let land to a 'middleman' who divided and sublet the farm to poorer tenants instead of working it himself, so these tenants in turn continued the disastrous process of subdivision by letting out parcels of their small farms in conacre. The shortage and the uncertainty of employment as a labourer obliged many peasants to till a tiny plot of land, usually raising potatoes but occasionally sowing a crop of oats. Indeed, within the Gort Union some of these cottiers had entered into partnership agreements which resulted in the absurdity of one half acre being held by twenty-six different people. A man 'destitute of all knowledge and of all capital', the cottier 'found the land the only thing that remained between himself and starvation'. In this condition of utter dependence he was willing to do anything, or to pay almost any price, to avoid being deprived of his plot. Inevitably, the combination of increasing population and exhausted land drove up rents and left the cottier even more vulnerable to the danger that his crop would not cover the rent. Of course, disaster resulted whenever the crop failed.[9]

The cabins of the small tenants and the mud hovels of the cottiers were a constant reminder to visitors of the island's unromantic poverty. Perhaps these conditions were no worse, as the special correspondent of *The Times* wrote, than those to be seen in Sutherland and Ross in Scotland, but that knowledge did not lessen the shock of some travellers. Anthony Trollope, who had found employment in the Irish Post Office, described in his first published novel, *The Macdermots of Ballycloran*, the 'hovels without chimneys, windows, door, or signs of humanity, except the children playing in the collected filth in front of them. The very scraughs of which the roofs are composed are germinating afresh, and, sickly green with a new growth, look more like the tops of long neglected dungheaps, than the only protection over Christian beings from the winds of heaven.' 'Can that be the habitation of any of the human race,' he asked? The bureaucratic prose of the administrators of the Gort Poor Law Union may have been less evocative but their dispassionate tone was not without effect. The desolate appearance of the dwellings of the small farmers was not the result of indifference to comfort and carelessness of appearance but of poverty, they admitted. 'The cottages and farm-houses partake alike of the same dilapidated impoverished appearance, forming a striking contrast to the generally well-planted, well-fenced, and improved extensive sheep walks and grass farms of the occupying proprietary.'[10]

Robert Gregory was one of the occupying proprietary, and when the members of the Devon Commission, appointed by Sir Robert Peel to inquire 'into the state of the Law and Practice in respect to the Occupation of Land in Ireland', took evidence in Gort on 7 August 1844, Gregory's agent, Robert Bell, appeared before them. The Commission was soon to be assailed by that intellectual organ of the Ascendancy the *Dublin University Magazine* as 'one by which the landlords are put upon their trial, and which opens its ears to every imputation which, by envy, hatred, malice, or uncharitableness, has, at any time, been alleged against them'. However, the Commissioners heard only praise of Robert Gregory. [11]

On his estates Gregory had acted to correct many of the evils of Irish agriculture. As large farms formerly held by middlemen fell in he had rented them directly to the occupying tenants. He had attempted to promote the consolidation of holdings but had taken care to dispossess only non-residents and had given the land to occupiers. He had made clear his disapproval of subletting and subdivision, but it had been a passive disapproval for he had not forbidden practices that many smallholders regarded as a matter of survival. He had been more active in his discouragement of joint tenancies, and where the plots of land were large enough had encouraged tenants to divide their farms with walls allowing them 8d a perch against their rents. Gregory had shown himself to be no less enlightened on the question of leases. Although many of his tenants held their land from year to year, he had always been willing to convert such tenancies at will into two or three year leaseholds. And it was with some pride that his son declared during his election campaigns in 1847 that no man who wished a lease was refused one on the Gregory estates. Moreover, Robert Gregory even tolerated the custom of tenants selling their interest in tenancies, though he naturally preferred that the land be surrendered to him and that he deal directly and exclusively with the new occupier.

There were two other examples of Gregory's refreshingly progressive attitude towards the obligations of land ownership. First, he encouraged his tenants to improve their sorry dwellings. Alone among the landlords of the immediate neighbourhood, he allowed tenants to charge the costs of improving their cabins and houses against their rents. In his testimony before the Devon Commission, Robert Bell declared: 'I know that Mr. Gregory has paid for some houses, and I know that some of the large farmers who have agreed to build houses, he has given them slates and timber.' Second, Robert Gregory was careful to set reasonable rents. The rule of thumb on his lands was that a tenant's crop should be worth two or two and one half years rents. And when at the end of a tenancy the land was relet by 'proposal' — bids were invited — the sitting tenant was invariably given preference. Indeed, not only did Gregory often pass over the highest proposal and accept a lower one submitted by a man who had been or whom he thought would be a better tenant, but when the highest proposal came from a good tenant he would occasionally reduce it by as much as three shillings an acre. Rents on the estate varied from a low of five shillings an acre to a high of thirty-five shillings for excellent tillage which would produce about eight barrels of wheat. The rents were collected in two installments, in May and November, and some tenants were obliged to borrow money to make their payments. The bank in Gort did advance short term loans to tenants who found themselves short of cash on rent day, but the compound interest often worked out to an usurious annual rate of almost 30 per cent. Of course, the tenant who fell in arrears was likely to have his stock distrained. It was seized, taken to the pound and advertised for sale. But Bell was able to testify: 'I have never sold any cattle since I have been agent to Mr. Gregory. In other cases we must be a little lenient and give them a little time. They may have something to come in and be able to meet the rent, which is better than using severity.' That such tolerance did indeed mark Gregory's behaviour was confirmed by a former tenant on the estate who also gave evidence before the Commission. He criticised, by implication, Richard Gregory as an absentee landlord, for in his absence a corrupt bailiff had conspired with the keeper of the Kiltartan pound to extort money from those tenants unable to pay their rents on time. Their stock was driven to the pound and in order to recover it they had both to bribe the bailiff and pay fees to the driver and the poundkeeper. But he testified that this practice had been stopped 'Because there is a good landlord upon the estate, and he would not let him put a beast into the pound'. In fact, Robert Gregory had ordered the pound to be pulled down.[12]

Robert Gregory was a prominent participant at the meeting of proprietors, clergy and gentry of 'the improving town of Gort and its neighbourhood', summoned to establish an Agricultural Society. Such societies had proved to be 'of much practical advantage, encouraging those who cultivate the soil to the use of a better system, by which they will be enabled to obtain what the land is capable of yielding, a much larger amount of produce'. Yet successive years of low corn prices found many tenants in difficulty as 1845 opened. The small peasantry had 'a little more cleanliness and neatness about their houses' but they were not getting 'much more wealthy'. As for the labouring class, its members were still in 'a bad state, from want of employment — those who depend upon employment — and the wages are very small'. Thus all were vulnerable when the potato blight struck in 1845, and the people of Gort suffered grievously during the Famine.[13]

The destruction of the potato crop was 'so sudden and universal,' Robert Gregory observed, 'that the fields flourising today with all the appearance of a healthy and luxuriant crop, were, before tomorrow's sun, reduced to a heap of weeds.' He attempted, in vain, to persuade the 'bewildered peasantry' to take precautions against the disease. He put drains beneath his own potato pits, made holes to ensure adequate ventilation and then covered them with turf, mould and lime. In this way, he believed, the potatoes could be protected. As the crisis and the suffering deepened so Gregory performed what he understood to be his duty as a resident proprietor. He served as chairman of the Kinvara Relief Committee and headed the list of donors with a contribution of £25. His name also led the list of contributors to the Gort Relief Fund, and he sat on that relief committee as well. 'The time is come when every man must put his hand to the work, for the people should be fed, and unless they were, they would feed themselves,' he declared at a county meeting held in October 1846. Nor was this simply the voice of enlightened self interest speaking, for Gregory noted that those who plundered stock often failed to discriminate between the small farmer with his two or three sheep and the wealthiest grazier.[14]

As hard as he believed individual landlords ought to work, Robert Gregory did not overlook the need for greater action by the Russell Ministry. The people could not exist unless the government 'instantaneously established depots for the sale of provisions', he had warned at the county meeting, and they required provisions which were simple to prepare. There was no point in sending tons of corn to his neighbourhood because the people did not have the means to grind it. Why not provide rice, he asked, for this 'wholesome food' could be prepared for consumption 'with little trouble'. One activity of which Gregory did not approve was 'unproductive' public works. Instead of making roads that would rarely if ever be travelled, or levelling hills, men should be set to work on constructive labour. The tenant or cottier ought to be employed draining land, or clearing it of rocks, he argued, not on roads that would only become a burden to the county and would oblige tenants to neglect their farms or smallholdings in order to help maintain them. Evidently, Gregory sought to limit waste as well as promote works that would be of mutual benefit to tenant and landlord.[15]

The increasing weight of the financial burden of relief, which he agreed ought to fall most heavily on landlords, alarmed Gregory. A demonstration in Gort did nothing to relieve his anxiety. Encouraged by the local priest, almost one third of a workforce of seven hundred labourers employed on public works went on strike to support a demand for a guaranteed daily rate of one shilling. Only when threatened with a discontinuance of all works, and assured that it would be possible to earn one shilling and sixpence a day on task work, did the dissidents call off the protest. Moreover, as a member of several local relief committees, Gregory was aware of the evidence that a substantial number of ineligible persons had found their way onto the lists of labourers to be employed on public works. A 'committee of scrutiny' at Galway had struck off more than one hundred men found working on two roads and replaced them with 'genuine paupers'. For their failure to root out this problem some beleagured administrators held the Roman Catholic clergy responsible. Dependent upon parishioners for their stipends, and recognizing that for many small farmers public works were the only source of cash, priests were suspected of recommending men whom they knew ought not to be listed.[16]

Robert Gregory's financial anxiety had already led him into a fatal economy. At a meeting in January 1846, of the Board of Guardians of the Gort Poor Law Union, he had strenuously and successfully opposed the construction of a fever hospital, arguing that the precautionary scheme proposed by the Poor Law Commissioners in Dublin was too expensive. No doubt he was also influenced by the fact that few cases of fever had been reported in 1845 and only one death had been attributed to it. The number of cases, whether of typhus or relapsing fever, did increase slightly during 1846, but only to a total of fourteen and not a single loss of life was recorded. However, just how false the earlier economy had been became horrifyingly evident early in 1847. Suddenly the incidence of these diseases began to climb as dramatically as did the victims' temperatures, but there was no adequate facility in which to isolate and treat the sufferers. One result was a sharp rise in the death rate, and among those who died of fever, contracted while ministering to the poor, was Robert Gregory. The *Tuam Herald* was moved to observe that 'the loss of such gentlemen cannot be speedily supplied'.[17]

William Gregory succeeded his father at a time when the horrors of the Famine had reduced the strongest of men to tears of frustration and rage. Only a month earlier, and shortly after his success in writing the quarter-acre clause into the poor law bill, Gregory had received a sombre description of the plight of the peasantry from an acquaintance then serving as an agent of the British Relief Association in Ireland. The poor had already pawned their clothes to raise money to purchase food, Lord Robert Clinton reported, and they had nothing left to sell. Many were too weak to labour even if employment on public works was offered to them. 'In addition to this,' he went on, 'there is now to be a reduction of 20 per cent from the lists of the Public Works, now one half of these men will be unemployed, some from idleness, some from the impossibility of obtaining employment in their neighbourhood, and others from the determination of their former masters not to employ them, because they preferred the Public Works to their wages. I do not think that I overstate the calamity, when I say that I can-not see the alternative for these poor creatures unless it be gradual starvation.' Not surprisingly, 4,000 destitute labourers gathered in Gort on 5 April 1847 and demanded work from the officers of the Board of Works, and when they were informed that no employment was available they raided a local estate and slaughtered one hundred and fifty sheep. By mid-summer a fresh epidemic of disease had heightened the terror and multiplied the suffering within the county. The Gort Workhouse alone housed two hundred and forty fever cases, which was three times the number of patients its infirmary was designed to accommodate. There were stories of guardians sending fever stricken persons off their own estates with tickets of admission to the workhouse, and of these victims being placed alongside people who were still free of infection. Terrified inmates then fled the workhouse, carrying the fever to all parts of the Union. Yet none of these reports, which he received in London, could have prepared William Gregory for the human tragedy he witnessed when he returned to Galway in the autumn and settled at Coole. Certainly it had been easier to oppose the granting of outdoor relief, and to defend the validity of the workhouse test, from the distant capital.[18]

Sitting on a rise on the southern outskirts of the town, the Gort Workhouse was well built 'and even handsome in outward appearance'.

But a Poor Law inspector who visited it in February 1848, could scarcely 'conceive a house in a worse state, or in greater disorder'. Over-crowding had created a host of problems. The week prior to the inspector's arrival had seen the Board of Guardians consider more than three thousand applications for relief. Four hundred applicants had been marked for indoor relief, yet that number was two hundred more than the workhouse could receive. Another seventeen hundred persons had been accepted for outdoor relief, but one thousand and seventeen applications had been rejected. For those admitted to the workhouse there was little clothing available, which resulted in inmates being left for days without shirts or shifts. One visitor described the scene in the yard at the front of the building, where some two hundred unfortunates were taking the air. 'They were in a shameful state of neglect as to cleanliness and clothing,' he wrote; 'they were sitting, or squatting here and there, though not a cold day, still shivering; many were only clothed in such rags as I could conceive a beggar would consider as the cast clothing of his order; some actually, for want of anything better, were in pettycoats.' The quality of the food served was inferior even though the price paid by the staff to local merchants was excessively high, which suggested corruption. Because of the serious overcrowding meals had to be organized in relays, and some inmates had to wait until midnight to obtain their evening meal of stirabout. It was brought in by men carrying thick sticks which they wielded brutally to halt the rush of the ravenous for this unappetizing brew. Miserably clad and poorly fed the residents of the workhouse were breathing air that was foul. Many of the building's windows could not be opened and several of the wall ventilators did not function. In these filthy and fetid conditions the diseases that made life in the Gort Workhouse even more terrifying continued to thrive.[19]

The workhouse was 'the cesspool of contagion for the entire Union'. The inadequate accommodation for the sick, and the absence of a matron or 'respectable person' in charge of the infirmary, had brought suffering enough. However, an earlier decision to bury deceased inmates within the workhouse grounds, and over the previous six years more than one thousand bodies had been interred in shallow graves only eighteen inches deep, now returned to haunt residents. Indeed, bodies were occasionally left in an outhouse for several days before burial. Open sewers ran from the workhouse, and close to the infirmary was 'a very large heap of manure, the fetid exhalations from which must certainly be injurious to the occupants of that portion of the institution'. Few Unions, one inspector observed in March, 'can be in a more deplorable state — fever and dysentery raging in every quarter, and a distressing appeal to provide coffins meets you at every point.' Attempts to ease the problems within the workhouse by ordering officers not to send the sick there but to provide them with relief in their own homes had failed because there were simply too many cases of people 'found lying sick on the streets or on the road side'. No one would admit these victims to their homes, even for payment, thus the authorities were 'reluctantly compelled to receive them into the workhouse'.

The Gort Board of Guardians was indicted and convicted of negligence. Inspectors charged that the Board's administration of the workhouse had been ineffective and its supervision of the staff virtually non-existent. Not a single guardian had visited the building since the epidemic of fever in March 1847. Nor had the guardians levied a poor rate sufficient to cover the escalating costs of relief, and they had compounded this folly by their failure to collect even the sum set. As a result, the Union had fallen heavily into debt. With more than one thousand paupers within the workhouse and at times over ten thousand in receipt of outdoor relief, which meant that one quarter of the Union's entire population had been granted assistance, the landlords who served as guardians believed that they were involved in their own struggle for survival. However, early in 1848 the administration of the Union was taken out of the hands of the guardians and given to vice-guardians appointed by the Poor Law Commission. Workhouse over-crowding was relieved by the discharge of many of the inmates, who were now granted outdoor relief. Bedding, clothing, furniture and utensils were purchased for those who remained. Sheds to house the sick were erected on three acres of land obtained from Lord Gort. Of course, these measures and those to discharge the debt were expensive, and they led to resistance by the rate-payers. The response of the vice-guardians was to summon the civil and military authorities to assist in the collection of the poor rate, though the inevitable delay allowed many of those in arrears to dispose of crops which would otherwise have been seized.

By 1849 the town of Gort was no longer prosperous or pleasant, and to its accumulated miseries there was added during that spring and summer a cholera epidemic which claimed another four hundred lives. Entering the town in July, Thomas Carlyle noted the 'Sour milk firkins' and 'sordid garbage of vegetables' in the market square, and the 'blue cloaks on women, greasy looking rags on most of the men, defacing the summer sun' on a fine morning. Exposure to the human suffering influenced Gregory deeply. He never forgot either the taut skin over skeletal features or the hollow voices of those wasting away from hunger and disease, nor the sight of 'poor wretches' who had built 'wigwams of fir branches' against his desmesne wall. Yet he was unable to suppress entirely his longstanding aversion for or fear of massive outdoor relief. Like other landlords, he reacted angrily when tenants abandoned the task work he provided on the estate — he employed them for one day of each week at a rate of one shilling and fourpence and fed them soup twice a week — to find employment on public works at a daily rate of ten pence. Moreover, he feared that this system of outdoor relief was eroding the proprietors' local influence. It would, he believed, lead to 'jobbing' of the worst kind and thus result eventually in the selection of Poor Law Guardians from 'amongst the lowest and most reckless class of persons'. Of course, his underlying concern remained the crushing expense. 'The rates on the division of Kinvara were eighteen shillings in the pound,' Gregory recalled in his *Autobiography,* 'and that a fictitious pound, for it was never paid.' In many instances the poor rate was so heavy 'it exceeded the amount of the yearly rent of the land.'[20]

Appeals to the government in England for financial assistance evoked little sympathy, let alone loosened the Treasury's purse strings. The Lord Lieutenant informed Clanricarde that the appalling conditions in Galway notwithstanding, he was sure that the people of England would refuse, 'whatever may be the consequences', to relieve those who would not assist themselves. When it was known in the Commons that the West-port Union had collected in three full months a mere £111; that in areas of the county some people refused to seed their land; that bands of pirates had been organized to plunder provisions vessels; that the Enniskillen Union had repudiated 'on principle' the repayment of advances; would it be prudent, the Viceroy asked thetorically, for any Minister to propose taxes on the 'hardworking English' to assist such people? And when Gregory suggested to Clanricarde that he make one more attempt to call upon his influence with the Whig Government to secure additional help from England, he received the discouraging reply that not another farthing could be squeezed out of Parliament for Irish pauperism. 'Sow potatos (*sic*),' Clanricarde advised. 'I hear pigs are to be had. Sow all the potatos you can. They alone can enable us to live.'[21]

As he turned to the task of aiding and sustaining his own tenants, for his father had taught by example the precept: 'Property has its duties as well as its rights', Gregory was surely aware of the extent to which his name had become a synonym for misery, cruelty and starvation. 'It is a notorious fact that, at this moment, there are hundreds of families in this Union,' the *Tuam Herald* observed, 'pallid with hunger, and wasted away to mere skeletons, who cling with morbid and undying tenacity to the little spot, which alone on earth they can yet call their own, in dread of the results of becoming homeless and shelterless for ever.' Confronted by this desperate resistance to 'The Gregory Exterminator Clause' the Poor Law Commission issued a circular in May 1848 permitting guardians to give relief to the families of those men who clung to their plots of land. However, the boards were subsequently informed that 'it would be an entire perversion of the meaning of the law, and of the language and meaning of the circular, to give relief systematically and discriminately to the wives and children of persons occupying more than a quarter of an acre of land'. Moreover, the Irish Vagrants Act provided for the prosecution of any such occupier 'for wilfully neglecting to maintain his wife or child, and he "shall, on conviction therof, before any justice of the peace, be committed to the common gaol, or house of correction, there to be kept to hard labour for any time not exceeding three months"'.[22]

The ravages of the Gregory clause could be seen by any traveller. 'The startling evidence of the reality will meet his eye, everywhere in the shape of the roofless cottages, and the blackened walls, and the desolate hearths which were once the humble and happy homes of a peaceable and contented peasantry.' If such comments tended to romanticize living conditions which had always been squalid, there was no escaping the desolation justly attributed to a measure to which Gregory had given his name. But one landlord who did not resort to this instrument for clearing the land was its author. Charges that tenants had been ejected from Gregory's Kinvara property were immediately and publicly contradicted. Whenever a tenant was removed he was always paid, even though invariably he was simply being relocated on another part of the estate. Indeed, in practically every case the removal was effected with the consent or at the request of the occupier. It was to be Gregory's proud claim that he had never evicted a tenant. And he had held fast to this policy despite the fact that some tenants not only could not pay their rents but did not till the soil. Like many another landlord who was anxious not to lose his tenantry Gregory also reduced his rents, granting abatements of five shillings in the pound. He paid a substantial portion of the poor rates of his tenants, at a personal cost which exceeded £2,000. He borrowed heavily (£3,600) from the Commission of Public Works to provide his tenants with 'reproductive' employment — land drainage and reclamation, and the building of stone walls. He cut wood for fuel and gave it to those in need. In short, he managed to keep his own estate free from 'the worst symptoms of wretchedness'. 'If other landlords would treat their tenantry in this way,' declared one speaker at a public dinner held in May 1849, 'there would not be such a number of houses levelled between Gort and Galway, nor would the tenantry in many instances have run off with their rents.' This reputation for generosity soon spread. At the end of the year the *Limerick Examiner* singled Gregory out for special praise. 'Mr. Gregory is no longer to be classed among a hard-hearted or oppressive landocracy,' one of its correspondents reported. 'He has nobly eschewed their wicked counsels, and is resolved to enroll himself, in future, as a generous landlord and a friend of the poor. Mr. Gregory's demeanour convinces one that in his heart there are mercy, charity, and benevolence.' Of course, it was understood that he owed reparation to the poor for his 'unfortunate' connection with the dreaded quarter-acre test.[23]

Even as he endeavoured to perform his public duty to his tenants Gregory's private fortunes were sinking under a crushing burden of debt. His annual income when he succeeded his father was ostensibly in excess of £7,000, for to rents which totalled £6,786 he was able to add a variety of customs and tolls collected at the port of Kinvara. Yet the charges against these revenues were already heavy. There were interest payments to be made on the mortgages which financed earlier bequests to the nabob's granddaughter and the Under Secretary's younger children, and Robert's measures of relief when the Famine struck in 1845. Thus part of William's inheritance had been incumbrances to the amount of £50,000, and £1,500 was absorbed each year by his mother's jointure. When the human and economic crisis of the Famine deepened so William's financial position deteriorated, for his income was slashed. Unpaid rents and substantial abatements, assistance of tenants with their poor rates at a time when that rate reached astronomic levels, and the poor law valuation of his property (£6,200) which was not a great deal less than its nominal rental value, placed him in an economic vice. He would have had to borrow and borrow again in order to meet the old charges and the new at a time of plummeting revenues, securing his loans from individuals, institutions and the Commission of Public Works with additional mortgages. But his escalating interest payments were compounded by folly.

William Gregory proved to be a poor judge of character. His choice for the important position of land agent was Fred Jackson, his former election agent in Dublin. Within a short time he had misappropriated £6,000, a sum the hard pressed Gregory could ill-afford to lose. When the defalcations came to light Jackson did not attempt to deny them and offered his bond for their repayment, which Gregory angrily and foolishly refused. To replace the disgraced Jackson Gregory appointed a cousin, W. Stewart Maxwell. Unfortunately, this 'clever fellow' could not get along with Gregory's mother. The final straw for Bess Gregory was Maxwell's oversight in giving a ball at Coole, which was not his residence, without first consulting her. Their collision on this matter led to Maxwell's resignation. 'Though rough and somewhat uncouth he was an honourable straightforward man,' Gregory later attested, 'and I had great reason to regret (losing) him.' One immediate reason was the character of the neighbour whom his mother prevailed upon him to employ in Maxwell's stead. He had impressed Mrs. Gregory 'on account of his assumption of piety', but a 'more consummate rascal could not exist, and one detested by the tenants whom he tricked and fleeced.' Not only did he contrive to get his name into the wills of two old bachelors but it was rumoured that he had hurried one of these benefactors to his grave. Whatever the truth of this story, which amounted to a charge of murder, he did defraud Gregory. Hence William's pleasure at the man's misfortunes following his dismissal. He had purchased some bog land from the estate at a high price but was soon unable to meet his payments, with the result that he lost both his land and his home. He ended his days an itinerant, circulating religious begging letters and preaching from the top of a beer barrel on honesty, morality, and the world to come. Fortunately, Gregory's fourth agent, Henry Briscoe, whom he appointed on the recommendation of his uncle, Rev. William Gregory, proved to be a far happier choice. He managed the estates with skill and intelligence. Perhaps Briscoe would have dissuaded Gregory from his impulsive and expensive enthusiasm for 'a pinetum in the nut-wood of Coole', for more than half the conifers he planted died and very few of the survivors thrived in the region's limestone. Yet the master of Coole was indulging in wishful speculation when he wistfully argued that had he only appointed Briscoe earlier there would have been no necessity to sell off much of his inheritance.[24]

If the debts bequeathed by his father and those he saddled himself with as a landowner might have been managed, the sad truth was, as Gregory admitted elsewhere in his *Autobiography*, that his passion for the Turf completed his downfall. Perhaps the addiction was in his blood, or the mania was carried by his genes, for gambling had led to the disinheriting of great-uncle Robert. Even the sober Under Secretary had enjoyed race meetings. From his own father William had inherited an enthusiasm for hunting and a fondness for horses. But the allure of racing proved stronger than any fusion of these genetic strains could explain. There was, as he explained in his memoirs, the sheer physical exhilaration of rising early in the morning to watch the animals on their training gallops. There was that sense of belonging to the comparatively small and intimate set who exchanged information and discussed form, and who mixed with a frisky society of 'smart, good looking women' and 'fast young men of opulence'. Finally, there was the thrill of winning and the fear of losing, whether it be the race itself or the wagers riding on its outcome, even the secret shame of participation. 'It was a moment of excitement and joy when I won this fine piece of plate, in the midst of thousands of spectators,' one racing enthusiast wrote, 'but that past there returned the undying consciousness of the unworthiness of the pursuit, filling my thoughts, hopes, and wishes to the exclusion of all other objects and occupations, agitating me, rendering me incapable of application, thought, and reflection, and paralysing my power of reading, or busying myself with books of any kind.' These were the conflicting emotions William Gregory was ultimately to experience.[25]

The expenses of racing were considerable, for in addition to the purchase price of the animals there were training and jockey fees to be paid and the costs of feed, travel and stabling at the racecourse to be met. Irrespective of quality, a single racehorse required the outlay of £230 each year. While still at Oxford, his modest allowance then supplemented only by his early winnings, Gregory had instructed a noted trainer, William Trean, to purchase several yearlings for him. He adopted his own racing colours — a red shirt with a white stripe and a white cap — and soon enjoyed success. He had quickly found a useful three year old called 'Barrier' and a four year old named 'Una'. In all, his four horses won six races in 1842, including the Leamington Stakes at Warwick. The prize money exceeded £2,500, which was more than enough to cover the costs of maintaining his small string. The following year he was listed among 'the principal nobleman and gentry' to start horses, and sixteen entries resulted in seven victories. Once again, with prize money in excess of £2,000, racing had proven relatively profitable and Gregory had the pleasure of finding his name in the fifteenth position on a list of the year's twenty-nine principal winning owners. Beckoned by success he began to invest more heavily in thoroughbreds, yet it was one of his least expensive buys which brought him his greatest triumph. At a bloodstock sale in 1845, he bought for a mere fifteen guineas a scraggy-looking chestnut yearling whose weak ankles obviously would prevent him from racing whenever the going was heavy. Gregory named the horse 'Clermont', and in 1847 he gave his owner his most successful year on the Turf. 'Clermont' won the Newmarket Handicap and then the Great Metropolitan Stakes, the latter being a victory of sufficient note for the *Sportsman's Magazine* to devote a full page to an illustration of the horse. That year, which saw Gregory pocket almost £3,000 in prize money, was the summit of his racing career, although the tantalizing thought of discovering another 'Clermont' encouraged him to persist long after he ought to have quit the sport. In 1849 he thought he had found just such an animal in 'Loup-garou', a good—looking grey which attracted considerable attention and support. However, apart from a third place finish in the Chester Cup he proved to be a disappointment and from that year on Gregory's name was ominously absent from the annual lists of winning owners.[26]

That racing was corrupt as well as expensive was all too evident. One of Gregory's friends spoke no less than the truth when he warned 'that the views and the men, with which it [the Turf] brings its votary in contact, tend, instead of elevating, to contract and undermine the heart's best feelings'. Horses were still 'nobbled' before races, despite the execution in 1812 of Dan Dawson for poisoning four animals at Newmarket. The race officials who set the weights horses carried in handicaps were by no means immune to 'influence', a problem which the aristocratic ruling body of the sport, the Jockey Club, belatedly sought to resolve through the appointment of a public handicapper. He was Admiral Rous, who had performed a remarkable feat of sea-manship in sailing a rudderless frigate home from the Labrador coast in 1835. His new task proved no less demanding. He had to contend with owners who were not above running horses when they were not entirely fit in order to obtain a favourable handicap at some future event. The Jockey Club's earlier expression of 'extreme disapprobation' of the practice of starting animals in races they were intended to lose evidently had failed to persuade owners to mend their ways. As for fancied runners, it was not unknown for them to be victimized by unscrupulous race officials through a series of deliberately false starts or be deliberately obstructed by other horses. Also jockeys were paid 'to take a back seat'. Indeed, in one celebrated case, when the horse refused to be held back, his desperate rider threw himself off just before the post. An even greater scandal was that of personation, of entering over age horses for the most important races. The classic example of these various misdeeds was the 1844 Derby, for which one of Gregory's horses had been nominated but did not run. The first horse to pass the post, 'Running Rein', was subsequently disqualified for being a four year old substitute in a race for those of no more than three years. Another runner, 'Leander', injured during the race and put down, was later exhumed and an examination of the lower jaw (unaccountably the owners had destroyed only the upper) proved that this animal had also been over age. Meanwhile, the favourite, 'Ugly Bird', had been denied a chance of victory by foul riding, and a second widely fancied runner, 'Ratan', had been pulled up by his jockey who had backed one of the other entrants.

The vast sums staked on races provided ample incentive for such acts of dishonest ingenuity. It was rumoured, but never proven, that William Crockford, who had given his name to the famous club, had died before a running of The Oaks, for which he had backed on his own behalf and that of friends the filly 'Princess'. The understanding of the day was that death cancels all wagers. However, Crockford's associates recognized a riskless opportunity when it was presented to them. Allegedly, they sent one of their number to the racecourse with a homing pigeon and when it returned with the news that 'Princess' had won they propped Crockford up in the window of the club. Returning racegoers saw him sitting there and some commented that he looked 'rather lively'. Now he could die, while his sad death *before* the race would have been established had 'Princess' lost. When those who had suffered heavy losses threatened to renege on their debts the Jockey Club intervened to declare that as Crockford had died after the race all wagers had to be honoured. However, the problem of 'Levanters', that is of men defaulting, was a growing one. The *Sportsman's Magazine* was moved to complain: 'What with the fraudulent riding and bad paying, a man who acts fairly, has hard work enough to make the turf a profitable speculation.'[27]

Racing's disrepute was the background against which a legal action was launched in 1843 to curtail gambling, and Gregory found himself named as one of the principals in the suit. He had won £5,000 on the Derby that year, and had placed bets for the owner of the winning horse which returned to that fortunate friend the princely sum of £22,000. This windfall suddenly seemed less welcome when a 'rascally attorney' cited Gregory in a prosecution against excessive gambling which he intended to press under a statute of Queen Anne's reign. One of the other defendants, and the principal target, was Lord George Bentinck, with whom Gregory had established a friendly relationship. Bentinck was a striking figure, his erect bearing making him appear even taller than his six feet, while his taste in clothes was individual if not peculiar and might be described as exotic rusticity. 'His tight fitting buckskin trousers were in admirable contrast to a claret-coloured coat, with brass or gilt buttons. [A] massive gold chain shone brilliantly on a dark velvet waistcoat. His necktie was always of a spotless white or cream-coloured satin, and very long and full; and in it a neat pearl pin was always to be seen.' Bullheaded, his temper was appropriately short, his enmities long and his energy in pursuit of his many enemies seemingly inexhaustible. His own career on the Turf had not been entirely devoid of sharp practice — he had run horses when not entirely fit so as to mislead observers about their quality and had thus obtained better odds at some later date. More than one Bentinck horse ran last in its first race and finished first in its last. He had been quick to recognize the advantages of secretly transporting his animals in horse drawn vans to race meetings, while other runners walked, and such shrewdness had paid handsome dividends. By the 1840s Bentinck not only dominated the Jockey Club but had taken up the issue of reform, and he was the driving force behind the exposure of the 'Running Rein' fraud in 1844. He was already waging war on defaulters, and among those he had warned off the Turf was Charles Henry Russell. It was Russell who in revenge and on the advice of his solicitor-brother obtained the evidence on which the thirty actions against Bentinck and his racing associates were started. However, this blow against gambling was supported by worthier figures for more honourable reasons. Bentinck was not alone in suspecting that Prince Albert, the Queen's earnest consort, was implicated in what the infuriated Lord George termed 'the lewd and disorderly proceedings'.[28]

Bentinck warned Gregory that the act of Anne's reign, as invariably construed by judges, did embrace horse racing (there had been some doubt about this), thus it was vain for them to disguise from themselves 'that these vagabonds have prima facie the law on their side.' No less disturbing was his information that Gregory would be pursued for all of the money he had won for himself and others. This disagreeable and even frightening intelligence so unnerved Gregory that he remained in Galway, long a refuge for those anxious to avoid a bailiff bearing a summons. But this 'skulking' in Ireland irritated his quick tempered friend, who was diligently working to find a solution to their common predicament and wanted Gregory's assistance in London. To lessen the danger of a successful prosecution he recommended that the young Irishman follow his own example, and take the elementary precaution of retaining every leading counsel on the circuit where the action would be heard. In Gregory's case, arising as it did out of the Epsom Derby, this would be Surrey. For a trivial sum — each retainer would cost no more than £5-8-0 — their accusers could be denied the finest legal talent. More important, he wanted Gregory's aid in lobbying their fellow Members of Parliament for a change in the law. Indeed, the Duke of Richmond, a friend of Bentinck, introduced a measure on the first day of the parliamentary session in 1844. This 'bold, manly straightforward' bill as Bentinck described it, would legalize betting on horse races, foot races, sailing matches, cricket, coursing 'and all other manly and wholesome sports'.

Although rescued by the timely passage of the 'Manly Sports Bill', Gregory was slow to forgive at least one member of the Commons who had attempted to obstruct it. Rumour identified Gregory as the person who had called at a house of ill-repute to leave the name of this straightlaced colleague, who almost suffered a stroke when the madam subsequently contacted him and offered her services. Twenty years later Gregory was to deny that he was the author of this juvenile prank, but then added maliciously that whoever had given the Member's name evidently believed he was addicted to the society of disreputable women.[29]

This brush with financial disaster saw Gregory's devotion to the Turf waver, at least momentarily. He gave thought to withdrawing from racing. One friend whom he consulted urged him to make the break, arguing 'that the turf is not the theatre in which those talents with which you have been so largely gifted were destined to expand and flourish.' Had he been able to accept Peel's offer of office in 1846 he might then have called a halt to his sporting career, for the Prime Minister had attached just such a condition. Nor did Gregory want for timely reminders that the 'sport of kings' was also one of rogues. In 1850 he was obliged to dismiss his old trainer Trean when that poor man became involved in a scheme to arrange the result of the Ascot Stakes. A horse Gregory had once owned but had sold to Trean had been backed heavily by the former owner and his friends when it defeated the favourite for the Stakes in a private gallop. Unknown to Gregory the animal had already been secretly sold to a third party who withdrew it from the race, and the favourite won in a canter. Because of the system of 'Play or Pay', those who bet on horses that were scratched forfeited their wagers. Infuriated by this costly experience Gregory challenged one of the leading conspirators to a duel. Although duelling still enjoyed a measure of romantic glamour, and Gregory was a fine shot, practising regularly at a pistol gallery in Leicester Square, this gesture was doubly foolhardy. In the event of a death, the danger of being convicted by a jury was real enough to oblige the survivor to scurry into exile. Fortunately, neither Gregory nor his opponent was injured. As for the dubious distinction of fighting the last notable duel on English soil that belonged to George Smythe and Colonel Frederick Romilly who faced one another in 1852.[30]

Gregory wagered heavily and successfully on the Derby in 1851 but he could no longer afford the losses he suffered the following year. With the assistance of friends, such as Sir Robert Peel, the son of his former political mentor, he was able to borrow to meet his debts. However, this expedient eventually brought the chaotic state of his personal finances into the glare of humiliating publicity.

During his brief foray into County Galway politics in 1847 Gregory had met Edmund O'Flaherty of Knockbane. He was an engaging, intelligent rascal, but 'so open and candid' about his lack of scruples that this 'laxity' seemed forgivable. The two men struck up a friendship which soon blossomed into intimacy. Their shared interest in politics provided the immediate bond, and they would spend hours sitting beneath the spruce trees beside Coole lake framing ministries and constitutions. When Gregory planned a brief excursion to Paris it was O'Flaherty whom he urged to accompany him. Indeed, there was an increasingly feline if not effeminate quality to the relationship which culminated in an unsigned and rather pathetic letter to O'Flaherty when the latter broke off the friendship. 'I have always been ready to sacrifice myself for yr happiness and welfare,' he protested after the painful rejection. Certainly, he had clung to this friend in the face of his mother's disapproval and that of other intimates.

O'Flaherty, deploring Gregory's lack of financial system, had undertaken the difficult and distasteful task of juggling his debts. The number he sought to keep in the air multiplied dangerously. The tantalizing hope of recouping his fortunes on the Turf was one the master of Coole could never banish from his mind. 'I cd easily pay the interest [on some of his debts] by the results of one good autumn Newmarket meeting without touching Coole rents at all,' he wrote in the spring of 1852. 'It wd enable me moreover to take up some rascally bills and get clear of the synagogue.' Subsequently, he admitted lamely to O'Flaherty that 'The gentlemen have been terribly punished at Newmarket. I only lost £290 but in fact every one is a heavy loser. It was the worse (*sic*) meeting I ever saw except one so give myself great credit for getting out so cheap.' Yet even such trivial losses were disastrous for a man compelled to borrow in order to meet minor expenses, such as the purchase of household items, Christmas gifts and the settling of whist scores. Inevitably, the estate became ever more encumbered and by the summer of 1853 Gregory had resolved soon to follow the example of many landlords and increase his rents by as much as 20 per cent from the Famine levels, though less with the view of swelling his direct income than to use the higher rentals as collateral for additional loans. Nor was he unmindful of the extent to which financial need was driving him to be less than honest in some of his transactions. 'I am quite ready to assign the £8000 mortgage,' he informed O'Flaherty at one point, 'and hope that others may not perceive the *perjury* but I hear that they are not as good lawyers as we are.'

Eventually, the strain of this hand to mouth and sordid existence began to take its toll on his self-confidence. In January 1852, he was still able to discuss his troubles with humour and no more than a hint of bravado. 'I am quite flattered of the high terms in which the money lenders talk of me,' he remarked, 'it is reserved for me evidently to restore Irish credit in the financial world — I feel surprised and delighted with my prowess when I look on the number of bills taken up, and survey the broad sheet of the Derby book which is looking better every change — and which I trust on the 1st of June will realize in my person Grattan's description of the emancipated serf, his person proudly expanding and the fetters falling from his limbs. I must encircle myself with a fetter or two more, as I have some very urgent claims for the spring.' But a heavy loser at Epsom his mood darkened. The dishonouring of one of his cheques, news which reached him, appropriately, at the Doncaster meeting, provided an all too pointed reminder of the direction his life had been travelling. Writing to O'Flaherty, he admitted that 'in spite of the pressure I am subjected to I cannot forget the position I have held, and the mortifications which apparently pass unnoticed, sink more deeply than in the case of those who have no recollections of more prosperous times and seasons — It is very difficult to descend with equanimity.' By the end of 1853 he was in a 'funk' about his debts.

Perhaps alarmed both by the depth of the relationship with Edmund O'Flaherty and the utter dependence upon him for financial advice, first Gregory's mother, and then Lord Dunkellin, Clanricarde's heir, attempted to loosen the tie if not break the bond. Thus Gregory asked his intimate to be careful in handling his tangled affairs 'as people have been telling my mother that you have mentioned my being under pecuniary obligations to you and she is as sore and irritated about it as well can be conceived. This annoys me beyond measure, as I like my mother to like my friends as much as I do myself, more especially as she always lives with me.' However, when O'Flaherty resented the implied suggestion that he had been indiscreet and pointed to the problems of conducting in absolute secrecy borrowings that amounted to several thousands of pounds, Gregory hastily attributed the stories 'to the infernal system of backbiting and calumny rife in this country, which invents much and prevents still more'. 'I am as little sensitive of Galway gossip and tale-bearing as a Rhinoceros is of fleas,' he added colourfully when he repeated his desire that O'Flaherty be on terms of friendship with his mother, 'as I shd wish my mother who is the best and truest mother man ever had to share in every liking I have, for as you well know indifference to all but a few, is my predominant disposition.' Among that few was Dunkellin, who also detested O'Flaherty. Gregory attributed this hostility to a defect of character. 'He is one of the best hearted fellows alive, but singularly determined in disliking,' he assured O'Flaherty. 'I know many men whom he dislikes from no cause whatever, but for whom one of these days I dare say he will take a fancy as strong, and with as little reason.' Unfortunately, Dunkellin's instincts proved all too accurate.

By the summer of 1854 and shortly before O'Flaherty's abrupt termination of the relationship there was disturbing evidence that he was seeking to discount bills which had only been given for renewal. Gregory's solicitor drew his attention to a pair of bills which had been drawn by Dunkellin and accepted by the impecunious master of Coole. 'I think it madness your cashing those acceptances I gave you,' the already 'terror' struck debtor informed his financial confidant, 'as it will only add to the burden and prevent me from ultimately arranging everything.' But he seems to have attributed this inexplicable behaviour to the personal crisis which had followed O'Flaherty's desertion by his intended. She ran off with another suitor leaving him the butt of Dublin humour. Stories of his desolate friend wandering near Kingstown, unshaven, unkempt and unclean, prompted Gregory to exhort him to pull himself together. The lady had not been worth such misery, he added consolingly. Before long came the startling word that O'Flaherty had fled the country having been accused of forging the names on a number of bills he had passed, and Gregory was soon approached by a person named Henry Richardson who claimed to be holding two of his bills. His refusal to honour either of them, for they were forgeries, brought the final indignity — public scrutiny of his tangled finances.[31]

Richardson was a particularly unpleasant and unsavoury character, as enquiries conducted by Gregory's solicitors revealed. He and his brother had published a penny scandal sheet which they called *Paul Pry* and employed as a weapon of extortion. They would simply threaten to publish something infamous about a victim and then allow him to purchase their silence. Richardson had also run a gambling 'hell' in Jermyn Street, where he fleeced the unwary. One unfortunate provincial solicitor had lost £2,400 at the club, for which he gave bills and cheques, but when on reflection he balked at paying these 'debts' Richardson had sued for their prompt recovery. When the solicitor filed a counter suit to restrain Richardson from proceeding he tired of the legal process and resorted to extortion. He had handbills printed up detailing the poor man's 'debts' and threatened to post them throughout Lichfield where the solicitor practised and whose Bishop was one of his distinguished clients. Frightened, the man settled out of court. In Gregory's case Richardson's tactic was to launch an action for payment of the bills, hoping that he would also settle rather than submit to a public examination of the sorry mess he had made of his private income. Yet for Gregory there could be no withdrawal. To pay Richardson the £800 he claimed would have been an invitation to any number of other holders of forged bills to present them for payment.

Supported morally by O'Flaherty's brother, Anthony, the Member of Parliament for Galway borough, and evidentially by Dunkellin, who testified that his signature had been forged on one of the bills; appearing before a sympathetic judge whose family had long been friendly with the Gregorys and whose rulings were frequently helpful to the defence; represented by able counsel who made much of Richardson's disreputable character, Gregory won his case in the court of Queen's Bench at the end of June 1855. However, he must have squirmed with embarrassment throughout the proceedings. Richardson's counsel depicted the defendant not as a liar but as a man whose 'unfortunate speculations' on the Turf had obliged him to borrow so heavily that he could scarcely know just how many bills he had put his name on. He pointed to an earlier incident in which Gregory had labelled bills as forgeries only to pay up when friends examined them and concluded that they were genuine. When Gregory entered the witness box he admitted under cross examination that he had lost £5,000 on a single race in 1854 and that he did not know the extent of his liabilities on bills of exchange. 'Their name is legion,' he conceded. 'I cannot say now,' he replied when the question was repeated, 'there are a great many liabilities for which I am accountable for other parties.' And his imprudence in endorsing bills for friends had certainly compounded his own financial problems, for several of those friends defaulted or absconded leaving him responsible for their debts.[32]

The Hon. Francis Villiers, one of the stewards of the Jockey Club, had fled to Spain — a haven chosen for its lack of an extradition treaty with Britain — leaving a trail of forgeries and debts that amounted to £100,000. The disgrace of Frank Lawley had been even more sensational. The youngest son of Lord Wenlock, he had been elected to Parliament in 1852 and when William Gladstone entered the Aberdeen Coalition as Chancellor of the Exchequer he appointed Lawley, a cousin of his wife, as his private secretary. But political responsibility had not, as his family had hoped it would, cured Lawley of his addiction to the Turf. So, it was decided to send him out of the reach of temptation and of his creditors. He was offered the post of Governor of South Australia. However, in the face of accusations that he had abused his position close to Gladstone to speculate on the stock market in order to meet his racing debts, young Lawley, despite protestations of innocence of any wrong-doing, was forced to resign his office, his governorship and his seat in Parliament. Disgraced, he fled to America to begin life anew in the hope of making his fortune and ultimately returning home to redeem his good name. In a letter to Gregory he summarised the painful lesson they had both been taught. 'The Turf is a bitter schoolmaster, and heavy on the school-fees which it exacts.' 'It is not satisfied with having devoured the best years of one's life: with having dimmed the bright and shining sense of honour which is the birthright of an English gentleman, and which feels a stain like a wound. Slowly and insidiously it saps the energies of the mind and substitutes vague regrets, and uneasy longings for the long, strong, steady pull by which such as (Sir James) Graham and the last Sir R. Peel and Gladstone drag themselves up the hill.'[33]

By the mid 1850s Gregory had every reason to feel, like the hero of one of Anthony Trollope's Irish novels, (and Trollope, a schoolfellow at Harrow, was a frequent guest at Coole and hunting companion), 'that the kind of life he was leading — contracting debts which he could not pay, and spending his time in pursuits which were not really congenial to him, was unsatisfactory and discreditable.' He later described these years as a time of struggle and humiliation.

But if he was now ready to quit the Turf, Gregory found himself on the very brink of ruin. From his father he had inherited an estate with encumbrances which totalled £50,000, but the burden of relief during the Famine and the folly of horse racing had more than doubled that sum by 1855. One traditional refuge for the impecunious bachelor was a good marriage, and Dunkellin facetiously proposed Lady Molesworth. She was the same gentlewoman who had attempted to snare Gregory's great-uncle Richard twenty years earlier. Defeated in that enterprise she

Above: the entrance front of Coole, a photograph taken in 1887 by Mrs. Ernest Hart. Below: the library at Coole, taken some years after Sir William's death, but without significant change since the time he knew it.

had married Sir William Molesworth and with his death in October 1855 her life interest in his Devon and Cornwall estates was worth £12,000 a year and she 'knows her business.' If this was never a serious solution, William had been paying sufficient court to Clementina Villiers, Francis's sister, to excite comment and move her formidable mother, Lady Jersey, who 'had set her heart on her marrying some great magnate', to warn him off. In short, there was no alternative but for Gregory to sell off his property to settle up his debts.[34]

As he prepared for the sale Gregory provided an additional measure of security to his tenants, many of whom would soon have to deal with a different and perhaps less liberal landlord. The great majority were granted leases for a period of seven years. Of the remainder, about one hundred in number and a quarter of the total, half of them obtained leases for extended terms — either twenty-one or thirty-one years, or for the life of Clanricarde's younger son. Such lengthy agreements contained the standard prohibitions on subdivision, subletting or alienation of the tenancy without Gregory's prior consent, and committed the tenant to pay the entire poor rate levied on his land. Unaccountably, Gregory failed to urge the fifty-two tenants who continued to hold land at will, almost all of whom were to be found around Kinvara, to accept the protection of a lease.

For the purpose of the sale the estate was divided into forty-seven lots, but Bess Gregory's jointure protected a substantial portion of the property. Further, Gregory had already sold several lots by private treaty, to neighbours and relatives, such as Clancarty, before the public sale was held in the Encumbered Estates Court on 13 January 1857. The court had been established for the express purpose of facilitating the sale of the heavily encumbered estates of landlords who had collapsed under the weight of their debts, and it had been the hope of the framers of the act that the purchasers would provide Ireland with a new class of agricultural capitalists. Hence Gregory's delight in calling attention in his memoirs to one of the largest purchasers in the court sale, a former carpenter called Comerford who had certainly made money but who borrowed extensively to finance his investment of £16,250 in an estate. He bought the property around Kinvara and took immediate and full advantage of the tenancies at will to increase rents sharply and thereby 'killed the goose for the golden egg, the town of Kinvara was all but ruined, and all the best tenants ran away'.[35]

The court sale raised £35,590, and when the proceeds of the private sales were added the total exceeded £50,000. Moreover, the sale had been completed with great intelligence, for the land Gregory had been careful to reserve was that around the Coole demesne, thus consolidating his remaining holdings, and it was also the most productive. He had lost half the area of his enormous estate but at a sacrifice of only one third of his rents. Unhappily, the proceeds of the sale were insufficient to cover his accumulated debts. Before the year of 1857 was out another 600 acres had been sold, raising a further £2,300, although in this instance the purchaser of the greater portion of the land was his mother and thus it was not lost but was protected. However, over the next few years more of the estate was sold off and Gregory's holdings around the demesne continued to shrink in size, as did his income. In 1865 lawyers reported that the charges on the estate still exceeded its annual yield, and in this emergency Gregory's mother again came to the rescue. She had long been supplementing his income but in 1867 she bought out for the sum of £12,000 her son's life interest in what remained of the estate, some 5,000 acres of the more than 15,000 he had inherited. Happily, Gregory had long since recouped his political fortunes. [36]

In middle age he was finally to redeem the promise of youth, which had been misspent. The terrifying experience of the Famine and the bitter lessons of the Turf were in a real sense the making of William Gregory. For having lost or squandered so many of the advantages of his birth he rebuilt his life and emerged from that labour a man of greater strength, maturity and compassion. The clearly defined and independent personality he now revealed was his own. No longer could or would he be regarded merely as the Under Secretary's grandson or Peel's acolyte, and his authorship of the quarter-acre test was slowly forgiven if not forgotten, at least in Galway.

5
Member for Galway

The pivot on which all of William Gregory's hopes of rebuilding his life and fortunes turned was his recapture of a seat in Parliament. At least he would be safe from creditors during the parliamentary session. Yet his longing for Westminster had a worthier inspiration. As he sank into debt he saw in a return to public service the possibility of redemption. Moreover, like Trollope's Phineas Finn, he hankered for the 'lobbies, and the clubs, and the gossip of men in office, and the chance of promotion for himself'. 'It is dreadful my not being in the House of Commons', he admitted to one friend whose help he sought in advertising his availability as a candidate. 'It is no better than being a dead dog.' But for a considerable time this political ambition did indeed creep rather than soar. A willing and diligent performance of his local duties as a landowner served to emphasise that there had been no weakening of his sense of public responsibility. He now began his long years of service as chairman of the Gort Board of Guardians and throughout the 1850s became almost as permanent a fixture of the county Grand Jury. Among the Grand Jurors, who were charged with the administration of public works and institutions as well as attending the Assizes, Gregory quickly emerged as a dominant figure. When mounting concern at the increasing costs of the county prison, and a startling rise in the number of deaths there, led to the appointment of a committee of inquiry in 1849 Gregory was named to head it. Perhaps with an eye to the future he courted one of the most influential of the local newspapers, the *Galway Vindicator,* by providing it with a copy of his draft report. The committee had been able to correlate the shocking leap in mortalities — from a single case in 1844 to 485 in 1848 — to the numbers of persons jailed as vagrants. The destitute, it seemed, sought imprisonment rather than admission to the workhouse because both the food and the accommodation were superior in the county jail. Hence the committee recommended that this absurd anomaly be ended. In future the treatment of prisoners was to be no better than that of paupers. Gregory also took the lead in demanding action to stamp out the thefts of livestock. Such crimes had reached epidemic proportions. In 1849 the Grand Jury considered more than one hundred bills of indictment for sheep and cattle stealing and this was a mere fraction of the total, for many of the cases had been tried at the quarter sessions. Arguing that the extension of the poor law had removed starvation as a justification for these thefts, and that the victims (among them poor farmers who could not afford to maintain a constant watch over their animals) were already being taxed heavily for the relief of the impoverished, Gregory insisted that the existing law was too lax and proposed that Parliament be requested to reenact the 'mutton act' with all its harsh penalties. [1]

Gregory's call for the stern punishment of those who had been driven to crime — for it was nonsense to pretend, as he did, that the thieves were all men disinclined to work but determined to enjoy a luxurious diet — was offset by his support of constructive measures to promote the county's economic revival. The Gregorys had long been enthusiasts for railway development. Robert had been active in the pre-Famine campaign to secure an extension to Galway, linking that city with Dublin, and William had been an ardent supporter of Bentinck's grandiose scheme. So when in 1849 the agitation for a line to Galway was revived a Gregory was once again in the van. William seconded the resolutions moved at the meeting held in the County Courthouse in March and made quite the longest and best of the reported speeches. He invoked the name of O'Connell as a champion of this particular instrument of prosperity and employment for the poor, and appealed to his fellow landowners not to obstruct these boons by holding out for too high a price for the land required by the railway company. The Mullingar to Galway extension was opened to the public on 1 August 1851. [2]

One measure of Gregory's success in persuading his fellow landlords that he was a sound and trustworthy member of the gentry, and of the mark he had quickly made in the county, was his appointment as High Sheriff in the spring of 1850. Essentially an honorific position, although the sheriff's duties did include the selection of the Grand Jury, the supervision of parliamentary elections and the election of the coroner, and the service of writs for the superior and county courts, it carried a certain prestige. Locally, Gregory's term was uneventful but during his year of office he did lend his rank to the efforts of the families of a group of children at the centre of the Carshalton affair. A preparatory Ordnance School for the Woolwich military academy had been established at Carshalton in 1848, and some eighty boys had been admitted. Then in 1850 three of the boys who had gone on to the academy were dismissed for engaging in homosexual practices, but during their interrogation they had charged that such activities were 'commonly perpetrated at Carshalton'. A committee of inquiry promptly descended upon the school and questioned about forty boys, though Gregory later likened their questions to those 'framed for inmates of convents by the prurient imaginations of monkish visitors'. Nevertheless, the investigation resulted in the dismissal of the head-master, who was given six days to remove himself and his belongings from the premises, and saw the parents of a large group of boys (twenty three from the school and ten cadets who had moved on to the academy, among them one of Gregory's O'Hara relations) required to withdraw their sons immediately from these establishments. The children of those who balked were subjected to the humiliation of being 'marched off in the custody of non-commissioned officers to their homes, and duly paraded through their respective villages'. As a result, word of the expulsions soon reached the press as did a copy of the circular which had ordered them. It referred to 'practices of a distressing and disgusting nature'. Desperate parents feared that all doors of advancement, whether those at other public schools or the universities, the armed services or the Indian Service, would be forever closed to their children. Indeed, it was the crudity with which the Master General of the Ordnance — who was none other than the Marquis of Anglesey, the old nemesis of Gregory's grandfather — had handled the situation which so enraged William Gregory and the members of the other families involved.

Anglesey had decided to root out all those who might have been 'tainted' by 'corruption.' This meant not only the expulsion of boys who had gone to the beds of their fellows in the mornings, however innocent the purpose, whether to read a book or learn a lesson, perhaps even for warmth, but also that of those who had merely been present and had never left their own beds. To brand boys, some of whom were no more than eleven and twelve years of age, as homosexuals for this behaviour was a scandal. It was, Gregory justly complained in a letter to the *Morning Chronicle*, 'a sentence of intolerable cruelty and injustice'. Nor did the unfortunate headmaster and the frantic families fail to point out that Carshalton's cadets had all arrived there from other schools. 'If it were really the case that at a public School so lately organized from all the other Schools of England, the most hideous crime existed and had attained to such a height as to involve 33 out of 90 boys,' a spokesman for the parents observed, 'would it not be asked in what state can the Schools of England be; and is not every parent in England and Society at large interested in demanding that the falsity of this imputation be made known in such a way as to remove the doubts of the most unbelieving.' Finally, it was difficult for those aware of the misconduct long tolerated at Woolwich to treat seriously any suggestion that it was a place of innocence which needed to be protected from depravity originating in the Ordnance School. At the Academy senior cadets submitted junior boys to various forms of degradation and bullying, such as forcing them to fornicate with prostitutes before an audience. Those who resisted or retaliated — one boy washed the toothbrush of a tormentor in a dirty chamber pot — ran a brutal gauntlet. The victim was compelled to crawl beneath a long table on which as many as forty boys sat in order to kick him as he passed. Yet neither private nor public appeals for clemency for the Carshalton boys, or for a more discriminating measure of justice, could move the Master General. In November 1850 he informed the members of the distraught families, among them the High Sheriff of Galway, that his earlier decision stood and that he would not receive any further communication on the subject. [3]

Having cut quite a figure locally Gregory's thoughts turned confidently to national politics as his term as High Sheriff drew to a close in 1851. The turmoil and confusion resulting from the passage of the Ecclesiastical Titles Bill, together with the probable consequences of the Irish Reform Act, appeared to have thrown open the representation for the county. Certainly, both sitting MPs were vulnerable to a challenge.

The Pope had set an entirely unforseen but by no means unpredictable train of events in motion when in September 1850, he established an English hierarchy complete with territorial titles, and made Nicholas Wiseman a cardinal. None of this was likely to pass without comment or protest in a nation which had so recently been convulsed by Peel's proposal to increase the annual grant to Maynooth Seminary and where the dramatic growth in the size of the Catholic community, bolstered as it was by large numbers of Irish immigrants, had aroused deep popular concern. Nor were the suspicions that the Pope's action signalled a grab for power by the Roman Church allayed by an ineptly worded pastoral letter of the new cardinal. He appeared to be claiming an authority far more extensive than the private and spiritual government of Catholics. Less than three weeks later, on 4 November, the Prime Minister, Lord John Russell, replying to a letter from the Bishop of Durham, agreed that 'the late aggression of the Pope upon our Protestantism' was 'insolent and insidious'; asserted that it was a 'pretension to supremacy over the realm of England'; and concluded with a rousing if not hysterical statement of his personal resolution not to 'bate a jot of heart or hope, so long a the glorious principles and the immortal martyrs of the Reformation shall be held in reverence by the great mass of the nation which looks with contempt on the mummeries of superstition, and with scorn at the laborious endeavours which are now making to confine the intellect and enslave the soul'.[4]

The Durham letter to the contrary, Russell was not an impulsive Protestant zealot and had a praiseworthy record of redressing Catholic grievances. Moreover, his immediate target was less the Roman Church than the Tractarians within the Church of England whom he regarded as a fifth column. In this sense the provocative behaviour of one of the most illustrious Tractarian converts to Catholicism, John Henry Newman, may have acquired somewhat greater meaning than it deserved. Preaching the sermon at the enthronement of the Catholic Bishop of Birmingham on 27 October, Newman had declared that God was leading England back to the true church. However, if Russell saw the Pope's rescript primarily as an opportunity to focus attention on the 'evils' of Tractarianism, the knowledge that any legislative action would be directed against the newly announced hierarchy concerned him not at all. Relations with the Papacy had not developed as he had hoped. Efforts to establish closer diplomatic ties had come to naught, as had hopes of obtaining papal cooperation against nationalist clerics in Ireland. Instead, the Pope had encouraged the resistance of powerful members of the Irish hierarchy to the Queen's Colleges established by Peel and supported wholeheartedly by the Russell ministry. The appointment of Paul Cullen as Archbishop of Armagh and Primate of Ireland in 1849 had brought no improvement in the relationship, for the government's attempt to reach a compromise settlement of the differences over the Colleges was promptly rebuffed. Then at the Synod of Thurles, which had opened in August 1850, and was to commence Cullen's decade-long struggle to unite and dominate the Catholic Church in Ireland, the denunciation of the 'Godless' Colleges had been repeated. Perhaps, like his father-in-law, the Earl of Minto, a member of the Cabinet, Russell hoped that the 'no Popery' outcry in England would finally induce the Pope to be more helpful on the Colleges, even to the extent of endorsing the stand of that minority within the Irish hierarchy who supported them. But the publication of Russell's letter to the Bishop of Durham, with its offensive references to Catholicism, made difficult if not impossible any concession by the Pope.[5]

Unfortunately, the Prime Minister's remarks coincided with a fresh wave of anti-Catholicism. Many a bonfire the following evening — Guy Fawkes night — was adorned with an effigy of Cardinal Wiseman. There were disturbances in several cities and towns as the Anglican clergy mounted their pulpits to denounce 'Papal Aggression' and raise the ghosts of the Armada, 'Bloody Mary', the Inquisition and the St. Bartholomew's Day massacre. Some 800 clergy signed an Address to the Bishop of Norwich which deplored 'this daring attempt to convert a powerful and independent nation into a province of a foreign see.' Thomas Arnold's successor as headmaster of Rugby School petitioned the Postmaster General for the removal of a local letter carrier whom he had discovered was a Catholic. Surveying the reaction, one contemporary described it as a 'mass of impotent fury and revolting vulgarity and impertinence, without genius or argument or end and object — mere abuse in the coarsest and stupidest shape'. And when in February 1851 Russell introduced the Ecclesiastical Titles Bill, to counter the Pope's 'aggression', listeners to his speech quickly detected 'the disproportion between the indignation it expressed, and the measure to which it served as an introduction.' As finally enacted in August it prohibited Catholic clerics from assuming ecclesiastical titles on pain of a fine of £100 for disregarding the ban, but the restriction was ignored and the penalty was never enforced. The government's achievement, Charles Greville commented, was 'to conciliate nobody and offend everybody'.[6]

Among those most deeply offended were Irishmen, for in their country clerics had long taken territorial titles. Certainly, Russell's speech introducing the measure and the subsequent debate served to alienate the government's Irish supporters in the Commons. Provoked by some of the 'most offensive speeches ever heard in a British parliament', and one English Member likened nunneries to prisons and brothels, Irishmen threatened physical violence and practised retaliation on divisions. Defeated on another measure, Russell's ministry was briefly out of office in February 1851, but the Opposition was too weak to form a government and he returned to power after a fortnight. However, he had done irreparable damage to his position and his enfeebled administration finally collapsed one year later.[7]

The Tories took office in February 1852 and soon announced that there would be a general election in July. In Ireland there was abundant evidence that the Ecclesiastical Titles Bill had provided the perfect excuse for unprecedented clerical intervention in the campaign. The first of the 'Objects of the Catholic Defence Association', which had been launched by the hierarchy and leading members of the laity in August 1851, was repeal of the Bill. Another aim was to secure the return of representatives 'whose known integrity and talents best fit them to support in the Imperial Parliament our religious rights, to remove the many grievances under which the Catholics of the United Kingdom still continue to labour, and to carry out the objects of this Association.' And among the additional objects were the protection of the inmates of prisons and workhouses from proselytism, and provisions to ensure the spiritual welfare of Catholics in the armed forces.

If the intervention of the Catholic clergy in the election in Ireland was certain, it was no less obvious to some observers that one result of the Irish Reform Bill passed in 1850 would be to place the parliamentary representation of the country 'almost entirely in the hands of the priests.' By quadrupling the county electorate this measure had greatly increased the numbers of voters priests could influence, and thus seemed to have finally tipped the scales against landlords in the long struggle for political dominance. Not that the landlords were devoid of influence, for many could still command the 'unforced loyalty' of their enfranchised tenants. Others resorted to traditional forms of intimidation — threatening ejectment for non-payment of rents, distraining the cattle of those in arrears, instituting expensive proceedings for the recovery of debts and thereby confronting tenants with ruinous court expenses, and refusing to deal with traders who voted the wrong way. They also employed bribery. But those voters who through loyalty, fear or venality showed a disposition to follow their landlords' directions were subjected to intense popular pressure which was often organized by priests. There were accusations of the clergy abusing the confessional, of their haranguing mobs, or suggesting that large groups of parishioners visit individual Catholic voters to 'implore' support for popular candidates. There were expulsions from chapels and threats of excommunication, which often proved more frightening to Catholic voters than those of ejectment. It has been argued that the fervour of pre-Famine Catholics and the zeal of their clergy notwithstanding, the 1850s saw the beginning of a 'devotional revolution'. Compared to the previous decade the proportion of priests to population increased significantly, for the numbers of clergy rose but the ranks of those to whom they ministered declined as a result of the Famine. Moreover, this shrunken population possessed a 'stronger devotional nucleus' than the larger one of pre-Famine days. Then, many had been unable to attend services because of the relative shortage of both priests and chapels. Of course, political influence was a mark of the priest's dominance of his flocks as a man of education and one possessed of organizational skills. The clergy often played leading roles in the selection of popular candidates, spoke for them at or after mass and at public meetings, and even ensured that transportation was available to get voters to the poll. [8]

The importance of an understanding with the local hierarchy was apparent to any aspiring politician able to gauge the swelling political power of the priesthood from the greater frequency of communion and confession. In Galway, that most Catholic of counties, an arrangement was essential. The organ of the hierarchy there, the *Tuam Herald*, had made clear its displeasure with the conduct of the two county Members during the passage of the Ecclesiastical Titles Bill. 'The milk-and-water policy of one of [them] . . . was as destructive as the open absence of the other,' the *Herald* had charged in July 1851, before adding ominously: 'The day of reckoning will come round in due time; and if the constituents do not settle a clear account with both, we have no more to say on the matter.' [9]

Employing the slyly astute and responsive Edmund O'Flaherty as a political thermometer, Gregory began to test the temperature of the local water in preparation for another plunge into parliamentary politics. Initially, the reports were encouraging. Of the two likely Conservative candidates for the county, the sitting Member, Christopher St. George, had alienated 'the respectable portion of the community' as well as the Catholic hierarchy by his frequent absences from the Commons and general neglect of public business, while his reputation as an 'exterminator' guaranteed a lively agitation among the voting tenantry. The obvious Tory alternative to the unpopular St. George, Robert Daly, Lord Dunsandle's younger brother, was regarded as gentlemanly but inexperienced and lacking both ability and energy. Thus in seeking support for his candidacy among his fellow landlords Gregory emphasised the County's need for an experienced and 'efficient' representative. In a public letter he proclaimed 'the relief of the landed interest' as his principal objective, but was at pains to explain that by that expression he meant 'the occupier as well as the owner of the land, the tenant as well as the landlord'. The land had to be relieved of the burdens 'which so partially, unfairly, and ruinously depress it', and a settlement of the differences between landlord and tenant 'definitively effected'. In March there was promising talk of the seats again being shared by the two parties. 'Many here seem to be of the opinion that Sir Thomas Burke and Mr. Gregory would, if elected, prove efficient Representatives of the County,' one landlord informed Clanricarde. Meanwhile, O'Flaherty was taking the pulse of the Catholic electorate, paying especial attention to those who as a result of the decisions of the Encumbered Estates Court had acquired land and thus independence.

Their religion suggested that they would not be immune the 'influence' of their priests. [10]

Gregory's hope was that his rejection by Dublin in 1847, which was widely attributed to the hostility of Tresham Gregg; his liberal speech in the county election that year; the more recent evidence of his 'desire and ability to promote the great social improvements of which this country stands so much in need'; and his continuing association with the Peelites, who had supported the Irish Reform Act and had steadily opposed the Ecclesiastical Titles Bill, would make him acceptable to Catholics in general and the hierarchy in particular. It was a hope John Derry, Bishop of Clonfert, promptly extinguished.

Almost one third of the county fell within the boundaries of Derry's diocese, and although 'a very prudent man, and at the same time learned and pious', he was a loyal supporter of the most nationalistic and political of Irish clerics — his archbishop — John MacHale of Tuam. It had been Derry who had moved, at the launching of the Catholic Defence Association the previous August, the most important political resolution. The gathering had pledged 'to make every effort to strengthen the hands and increase the power of those faithful representatives who, in the last session of Parliament, so energetically devoted themselves to the formation of an independent party in the Legislature, having for its object the maintenance of Civil and Religious liberty in the British Empire. ...' Approached indirectly by Gregory, who sought an endorsement, Derry's reply was chilling. 'It would require indeed a very thorough renunciation of hereditary prejudices, and a total disruption of influential family ties to qualify Mr. Gregory as the candidate of the Catholic party,' he remarked. Not merely was Gregory connected to the proseltyzing Clancarty family but he was identified 'with a most disastrous clause' in the Poor Relief Act. Evidently, the welfare of the cottiers whose protection and encouragement Derry regarded as a special concern of the Catholic clergy, because of the smallholders' defencelessness and fidelity to their faith, had not been William Gregory's prime concern. Finally, the Bishop specified terms for Catholic electoral support which Gregory could not meet. A candidate would have to commit himself to work for the disestablishment of the Protestant Church; to vote for separate educational grants for Catholics and the transfer of the Queen's Colleges at Cork and Galway to Catholic management for the 'exclusive' education of Catholics; to exert himself in Parliament for the removal of all those other grievances of which Catholics had reason to complain; and to strive for a just and immediate settlement of the landlord-tenant question. [11]

Derry's response left Gregory in no doubt that the hierarchy's support would not be forthcoming, and within a few weeks both the Bishop and the Archbishop had settled on a much more suitable candidate. Captain Thomas Bellew was a close friend of Gregory's but the son of a Catholic landlord, and he willingly committed himself to work for civil and religious equality for his fellow religionists; for tenant rights; for the release of those nationalists transported for their participation in the pathetic skirmish which had taken place in 1848 and been dignified with the title of an uprising; and to associate with any truly Irish party in the Commons. All Gregory could think to do in an effort to undermine Bellew's clerical support was to employ Catholic friends to suggest to MacHale that the Captain was at heart a Whig, but this whispering campaign met with no success. Meanwhile, the Conservative landlords, led by Clancarty and Clonbrock, from both of whom Gregory might have expected support, for he was related to the former and the latter was a liberal Conservative, had decided to back Robert Daly. St. George withdrew from the contest and Gregory, denied both landlord and priestly influence, followed suit. However, as in 1847, he did so with an eye to the future.

Carefully, Gregory set about the task of cultivating the influential Derry. In a letter to the local Gort priest, which he knew would be forwarded, he described the Bishop flatteringly as 'the ablest ecclesiastic of your Church in this country'. He sought to convince Derry that a moderate policy — and thus one Gregory might avow — would ultimately be more advantageous both to Catholics and Ireland than persistence in the present radical demands of the hierarchy. Parliament was dominated by Protestants and Englishmen, he reminded the Bishop. 'Much caution, much knowledge of the prevalent opinions of those with whom you have to deal, step by step gradually and almost unapparently begun, tenderness for the strongly rooted sentiment or prejudices however much opposed to your own, these are the arms with which a hostile House of Commons may be rendered favourable to views which a less careful policy wd altogether frustrate.' In short, a policy of gradual reform immediately begun. A second requirement for success was the support of a powerful and united party whose members would be 'able to encounter and overcome by their reputation for honesty, ability and successful government' the unpopularity that measures of justice to Roman Catholics were certain to arouse. The Peelites were just such a party, Gregory claimed. As for Derry's charge that his authorship of the 'quarter-acre test' had demonstrated a want of sympathy for the poor, Gregory sought to meet it head on. He protested that the test had never been intended as an instrument for clearances and insisted that its object had been to preserve the ratepayers, 'the greater part hardly better off than the recipients of relief, from the total ruin which the absence of such checks wd have entailed'. Without some measure of this kind every class would have been reduced to 'hopeless pauperism', he argued. Nor did he overlook the fact that a motion to repeal the test had drawn only four Irish votes and a total of six. However, had he been present in the Commons at that time he would 'have unquestionably declared that its object was for the usual working of the poor law, and not an enactment fitted for the emergency of a famine'. His course would never be governed by the interests of 'the so called rich', Gregory added, but by the determination 'to relieve the misery that daily forces itself on the attention of every thinking man'. And the best pledge of his sincereity was his behaviour as a landlord. 'To my tenants and their pastors I can confidently appeal that the same just and impartial tenor of conduct I have ever endeavoured to pursue in my relations with them, I shall advocate if their Parliamentary Representative.'

Even as he was seeking to overcome Derry's hostility and to convince him that if ever returned to Parliament his voice and vote would not be wanting whenever there were injustices to be redressed and grievances to be remedied, Gregory won a not entirely deserved popularity for his actions during the election. He did not follow the lead of his Clancarty relations, who let it be known that recent remittances of between 10 per cent and 15 per cent in rents would be cancelled for those tenants who failed to vote for Daly. Instead, Gregory gave instructions that his tenants were not to be interfered with and were to vote as they thought proper. This rejection of intimidation brought cheers and applause for this 'staunch Protestant' at a rally of Bellew's Catholic supporters held in Gort on 4 July. Yet the decision was less a manifestation of Gregory's 'most liberal spirit', or a further effort to conciliate the hierarchy, than it was a mark of his anxiety to placate the powerful Clanricarde. [12]

Clanricarde may well have been a model for Trollope's Lord Cashel, 'a wealthy man and possessed of great influence — able to shower down . . . a degree of patronage'. As Postmaster General in Russell's ministry he had distributed patronage in Galway 'with little regard to local politics, and petty party-feelings'. Consequently, he had approached the election in confident mood, fully expecting to reach the traditional understanding with the Tories by which the spoils were divided. After all, his cousin Thomas Burke, 'personally objectionable to no man, and no class', would be seeking re-election as the Whig candidate. But the mutually beneficial arrangement to return Burke and Daly collapsed in the face of Bellew's challenge. The Tories, judging that the hierarchy's man would be more difficult to defeat than Clanricarde's, decided to 'plump' for their own man and thus withhold their second ballots from the Whig. And in an effort to prevent Clanricarde from retaliating they threatened to intervene in the borough election where his son Dunkellin was standing. Infuriated by this Tory strategy, and the treatment of Burke as if he was indistinguishable from Bellew, whereas in the mind of the Marquess the latter's 'extreme opinions' placed him in an entirely separate category, he declined to offer Clancarty, Clonbrock and Dunsandle the assurances they sought. They then did as they had threatened and meddled in the borough, trading votes they controlled there for the promise of those the weaker of Dunkellin's opponents commanded in the county. [13]

Dunkellin's chances of success had never been as good as he and his father imagined. Having sounded opinion in the borough, where his brother Anthony was the leading candidate, Edmund O'Flaherty informed Gregory that if he chose to stand there he would outpoll the Clanricarde heir. The electors, but especially the Catholic ones, would take Dunkellin's money and then vote against him, O'Flaherty predicted. They were certainly well 'treated' by Dunkellin's agents, who supplied the ever thirsty freemen with whisky in public houses and provisions for consumption at home. Then, on polling day, a Clanricarde friend stood beside each booth and gave a piece of paper, on which he penciled a figure before sealing it, to those who cast their ballot for the son. The voter then presented the paper at the special aperture which had been cut in the door of the Dunkellin committee rooms and received his money. Yet even the laying out of more than £2,000 could not ensure victory in the aftermath of another outburst of anti-Catholicism in England. Riots in Stockport at the end of June had resulted in acts of desecration. 'Blood has been shed in torrents — churches have been ransacked — Catholic clergymen openly insulted in the streets; the very tabernacle rifled and its contents scattered on the floor and trampled upon by an infuriated populace,' the outraged *Tuam Herald* reported. 'The clergy and honest Catholics of this vicinity look upon the present election struggle as a terrible crisis in the fate of Catholicity.' Not only was Dunkellin a Protestant but it was now recalled that his father had been one of the commissioners in the Lords who gave royal assent to the hated Ecclesiastical Titles Bill.[14]

Humiliated in the borough, Dunkellin attributed the defeat to his election agents' incompetence and 'the disgraceful and spiteful behaviour of the Daly family'. He had been opposed by Protestants as well as by priests, mob and sheriff. But the borough election had preceded that in the county and this order of events presented father and son with an opportunity to exact retribution. Dunkellin appealed to Gregory — a personal friend, 'a liberal friend to religion', and a liberal landlord — not to support the reactionary Dalys. 'Of course I do not and did not expect you to vote for Bellew but I hope and trust you will do what you can for Tom [Burke], and let all who feel inclined among your tenants [to] plump for him,' he concluded. Meanwhile, Clanricarde exerted additional pressure on Gregory through their common Peelite friends. The Duke of Newcastle (the former Lord Lincoln), who was working hard to hold the group together, wrote to inform Gregory that Clanricarde had complained that he was withholding support from Burke. He urged him to reconsider his position. Clanricarde had behaved 'very kindly' towards the Peelites in a couple of Irish elections, Newcastle observed. Moreover, Gregory's chances of securing a seat in Galway at the next election would be greatly strengthened by 'an amicable arrangement' with the Whig magnate. Thus did Gregory free his tenants to vote as they wished, which amounted to a withdrawal of support from Daly. With Burke now declaring himself both a good Catholic and a supporter of tenant right, it would have required the exertion of all of his influence for Gregory to have provided the Tory with votes. Daly did not even go to the poll, and Burke and Bellew were returned for the county.[15]

Pleased with Gregory's contribution to this satisfying outcome Clanricarde wrote to express his thanks and to ask if he would like Galway borough. 'We can knock up the election if we please,' he boasted. But this was not the moment for any Protestant to be standing there, as Gregory surely realized, so he made no move to grasp at this straw. However, by year's end, and with the Peelite dominated Aberdeen Coalition striving to strengthen its position in Ireland by appointing a number of Irish Members to minor offices in the government or the civil establishment, Galway borough appeared to be a somewhat more attractive proposition. Rumours were circulating at the beginning of the new year that Anthony O'Flaherty would soon be named to an office, and encouraged by Edmund O'Flaherty Gregory began to fancy his chances of filling the seat. A measure of his desperation to get back into Parliament was his willingness to challenge Dunkellin should he decide to contest the borough again. He recognized the political dangers in such a struggle. 'It will be repugnant to me for many reasons to stand against Dunkellin in the town, but my belief is that I shd beat him by a very large majority,' he confided to Edmund O'Flaherty. 'It would be nevertheless a triumph I shd greatly dislike — There must arise unpleasantness from it, and when the dissolution takes place, I shd have Clanricarde's interest dead against me in the County.' As for those bonds of friendship which ought to have impeded his intervention, Gregory had little difficulty arguing himself loose of them. He admitted that he knew few people 'so warm, well-meaning, honourable and agreeable as Dunkellin', but insisted that laziness would always prevent him achieving a truly prominent position. 'If I thought he really wd make Parliament the means of rising, my own private affection wd induce me to sacrifice the seat I look to, however all-essential to me,' he protested, 'but I am confident he wd not trouble his head once in beyond voting, and therefore I shall fairly tell him I stand in the gap.' Happily, Dunkellin had decided not to run in the event that the borough seat fell vacant. All that remained to be considered, therefore, was the cost of an election. A scrutiny of the registry disclosed an electorate of 687 freemen, 138 freeholders and 461 ratepayers. In short, the notoriously venal freemen constituted an absolute majority. 'There is of course always a difficulty dealing with venal people, and considerable risk,' Gregory observed to O'Flaherty, 'but if delicately managed the affair might be arranged at no great outlay. To get into the House I certainly shd not stick at a few hundred pounds, it is worth it any outlay.' There was also encouraging word from London. 'I am glad there is a prospect of your coming into Parliament again — the sooner the better,' one member of the governing Coalition wrote. However, the Anthony O'Flaherty appointment was not made and thus the opening in Galway did not materialize. No doubt it was the frustration of watching helplessly as yet another hope was snuffed out that induced Gregory to become a party to the machinations of the other O'Flaherty.[16]

Edmund O'Flaherty had stood at Dungarvan in the general election. Defeated by the popular proprietor of the *Cork Examiner*, John Maguire, he decided to challenge the result. Eventually, it was agreed that Maguire would resign the seat and the two men allow the voters to resolve the issue in a by-election. No sooner had Maguire fulfilled his side of the bargain than O'Flaherty withdrew from the contest to accept the position of commissioner of Income Tax. Gregory was nominated to run in his stead. To many it seemed that there was something distasteful if not dishonourable in this turn of events. 'It looks bad the whole business, the trying to get in by a ruse instead of openly coming forward as a candidate and fighting boldly from the first,' Dunkellin warned. Not only was the ploy a bad one but it was also unsuccessful. Maguire attracted more than double the number of the votes given to Gregory. For Gregory, his pressing task was now to disassociate himself from this 'murky business'. Fortunately, he had been abroad at the time of the election so he was able to plead innocence and convincingly attribute his nomination to the misguided enthusiasm of friends. Yet he was implicated in the affair. He had introduced O'Flaherty to Peelite friends seeking to build support in Ireland, and the result had been the appointment as an Income Tax commissioner. Further, Gregory had quietly raised several hundreds of pounds — money which at the time he could ill-afford — to cover the costs of the election.[17]

If his driving ambition to return to Parliament remained unrealized, Gregory's success in maintaining the most amicable of relations with the Clanricarde family promised to serve him well at the next opportunity. His friendship with Dunkellin was one of the closest of his life, and its foundation had been their common delight in the fast life. They both enjoyed horse racing, and they 'ratted', shot, drank, wenched and travelled together. Indeed, one reason young men of that rank journeyed to the continent was to enjoy a greater measure of sexual freedom. There, they could engage in amatory escapades without the dangerous necessity as at home of resorting to prostitutes or domestics. Gregory frequently accompanied Dunkellin on his European sorties, and if the former's references in his memoirs to his own 'love affairs' are predictably bland the latter's letters provide a rather different picture. Dunkellin's exuberant preoccuption with the pleasures of the flesh suggest that any companion of his would inevitably be drawn into the unflagging pursuit of the less chaste members of the fairer sex. Characteristically, the prurient Dunkellin quickly found himself in hot water when he went out to India to serve as military secretary to Lord Canning, the Viceroy and his uncle. He issued tickets to a ball to a pair of ladies of blemished reputation, and of whose notoriety he was well aware. The understanding had been, he lamely explained later, that they would not draw attention to themselves. Instead, they outraged the virtuous matrons present by cavorting with the attentive men. If Dunkellin's aura was the far from unappealing one of the roué, he was also 'witty', 'sweet-tempered', and unfailingly generous and honourable in all his dealing with his friends. He loaned money to the insolvent Gregory, endorsed many of his notes and loyally stood behind him during the unpleasant court battle with Henry Richardson. Nor was he a man devoid of public virtues. Mourning Dunkellin's premature death in 1867, a political opponent observed that he 'loved Ireland so truly, and understood her so well, that he would have done real good for us all some day'.[18]

Scandal followed the father even more closely than it did the son. The Clanricardes who in 1842 befriended the newly elected young Member for Dublin — he was the heir to a Galway estate which if dwarfed by the 50,000 acres of the Marquess was nevertheless of a size which ensured he would be a substantial local figure — were 'excellent members of society, both of them extremely clever, quick, light in hand.' He and Gregory had quickly hit it off, exchanging betting information and gossip both political and salacious. They often found themselves in agreement on the remedial measures necessary in Ireland, and after Gregory's setback at Dublin in 1847 Clanricarde had remained sympathetic to the younger man's political ambition. Consequently, friendship and interest combined to ensure that Gregory did not shun contact with the family when scandal finally overtook it.[19]

Gregory had first met Clanricarde in 1836, at the house party which served as the callow youth's introduction to Galway's revels. Although held at the Handcock home, Carantrila, the Marquess had presided and his intimate relationship with the hostess did not escape observant guests. It was a strange attraction, Gregory later recalled, for the lady's physical charms were less manifest than her disregard of personal hygiene. Known before her marriage as 'Dirty Kitty Kelly', she 'maintained during wedlock the characteristics of her maidenhood'. Catharine Handcock died in 1853, having survived her husband by a decade, and within a few months of her death the last of their three children, all girls, expired. There then ensued the all too familiar and unedifying squabble over the inheritance. The fortune had been bequeathed, via the mother and daughters, to John Delacour, whom Mrs. Handcock had described as her 'adopted son' but who was widely believed to be the fruit of her extra-marital union with Clanricarde during a period of separation from her husband. The settlement was contested by John Stratford Handcock, a scion of another branch of the family. At first, he sought to persuade Delacour — who was still a minor — to waive his claim to the estates in return for a settlement of £20,000. When this offer was refused Handcock brought an action in the Court of Chancery and Clanricarde suddenly found himself faced with social and political ruin, for the imputations made against him were many and serious. In effect, he was accused of having persuaded William Handcock to marry Catharine Kelly in 1824; of having caused the separation of the Handcocks in 1841 by his 'improper intimacy' with the wife; of siring John Delacour; of having assisted William Handcock to prepare a codicil to his will, after he and his wife were nominally reconciled, which appointed Mrs. Handcock as the guardian to the three daughters and Clanricarde as that of their fortunes; of being a party to Mrs. Handcock's 'cruel' treatment of her daughters 'whereby their health was injured and their lives shortened'; and of abusing his position as guardian to coerce the girls into leaving their fortunes to Delacour.

Clanricarde's tragedy was his failure to offer a truly convincing reply to these sensational charges, which were a finely spun web of truth and falsehood. His earlier and notorious liaison with Catharine Handcock created an obvious difficulty, as did the fact that Delacour had also been known as John de Burgh, and this was the Clanricarde family name. Yet he had not engineered the Handcocks' marriage, while their separation was not the result of his relations with the wife (indeed he vehemently denied that he had been intimate with her in 1840 or subsequently) but of the husband's infatuation with a French maid and his conviction that his wife was hiding his money for her own use. Clanricarde could not, therefore, have been the father of John Delacour who was born in 1841. The child's father was in fact, as Gregory later learned, another member of Clanricarde's family — Sir John Burke. Clanricarde's sense of personal honour would not allow him to bring forward this evidence, vital as it was. For had he been able to disprove paternity the charge that he had exerted undue influence on the girls in favour of his natural son would have collapsed. Nor was his explanation of their insistence on leaving the entire fortune to Delacour, thereby excluding other Handcocks, entirely unreasonable. The daughters, being devoted Catholics, had despised the 'very strong Protestant feelings' of their relations. Finally, the accusation that Clanricarde had helped Mrs. Handcock hurry her legitimate children to their graves was evidently malicious. All three girls had been victims of consumption and the mother had always obtained the best available medical advice and had taken them to a succession of resorts, such as Budleigh Salterton and St. Leonard's on Sea, in search of health.

The case was eventually settled on much the same terms as those Delacour had initially rejected, although in addition to the sum of £20,000 he was to receive at age 21 interest computed at an annual rate of 4 per cent. For Clanricarde, however, there was no end to the affair. When *The Times* had commented on the case in February 1855, demanding an explanation from Clanricarde or his withdrawal from the Lords, he had been dissuaded from issuing a writ by his counsel's discouraging opinion that the article did not constitute criminal libel. Yet he ignored the advice of friends and relations who urged him to write to the newspaper. 'People may not value the opinion of the *Times* as much as they did,' his brother-in-law observed, 'but they read it, and they remember its allegations of fact.' Perhaps too proud to respond to *The Times* directly, at least in such a feeble manner, he elected to write instead to the *Daily News*. He did file an affidavit in the Court of Chancery in March, contradicting the imputations made against him, and then in April circulated a pamphlet putting forth his denials. Nevertheless, when in December 1857, he accepted Palmerston's offer of the Privy Seal, the sordid episode was quickly revived. Desperately, Clanricarde sought to defend his reputation. He sent copies of his affidavit and the pamphlet to his Cabinet colleagues, but on the advice of the Lord Chancellor abandoned a promised declaration in the Lords. Such a statement would do little good, Lord Cranworth warned, 'for as there cannot from the nature of things be any discussion of the subject, the matter will after all rest only on your statement, incapable from the nature of the case of being confirmed.' Nor did the unfortunate Clanricarde receive the help he sought from fellow peers, several of whom he asked to assist him to withdraw gracefully. This he might have done had someone simply requested that he not go ahead, explaining to the House that a statement was both unnecessary and inappropriate. He approached Brougham, Lyndhurst, Grey and Stanhope in turn, but all offered excuses and the last being the most original — Stanhope had to go to Peterborough to observe the eclipse. Even before this embarrassment in the Lords Clanricarde had watched helplessly as a motion was put down in the Commons calling for the abolition of the Privy Seal. To the relief of almost everyone the government fell before the motion was debated. However, Palmerston's decision to bring Clanricarde into the ministry had contributed to the erosion of the government's support in Parliament and thus to its defeat. Himself the product of another era, the Prime Minister and former 'Prince Cupid' had misjudged the 'disgust and indignation' this appointment would arouse in the mid-Victorian age. Clanricarde was never to be reappointed to office. Delacour went on to become a close friend of the Prince of Wales.[20]

No doubt Gregory's own misery in 1855 encouraged him to be sympathetic toward Clanricarde. Admittedly more humdrum, his troubles were almost as hard to bear and gave every sign of dragging on for just as long. He suffered the humiliation not merely of listening in the Court of Queen's Bench as his defects of character and errors of judgment were argued, but of preparing for the sale of his estate while fending off or avoiding importunate creditors. Visits to London became difficult if not impossible and were devoid of dignity, involving either surreptitious entry and hasty flight or negotiations with his creditors for a short period of grace. Not surprisingly, the prospect of travel to places of interest which were also thankfully remote proved an increasingly attractive one. In the summer of 1854, seeking a respite from his accumulating financial worries, Gregory had contemplated visiting Dunkellin who was serving in the Crimea. But word soon arrived that his short-sighted friend had stumbled into a Russian outpost. Later released by the Tsar as a mark of respect for Clanricarde — a former British Ambassador to the Imperial Court — Dunkellin returned home and then rejoined his regiment during the autumn of 1855. By that time Gregory had planned a journey to Egypt, which held a powerful attraction for classicists and inquiring minds. The work of Jean-Francois Champollion in deciphering the hieroglyphs; Giovanni Belzoni's opening of the tombs in the Valley of the Kings and his initiating of the study of the pyramids; Auguste Mariette's excavation of the Sphinxes; all had surely helped to fire Gregory's imagination and interest.

In November he travelled through France to Marseilles, and remained in southern France for two weeks before embarking for Alexandria on what proved to be 'a most lovely passage'. Gentle winds made for a smooth sea and the weather was blissfully warm. Indeed, the sun was so strong that an awning had to be erected on the deck and Gregory enjoyed a daily cold bath. He also ate well, for the fare was excellent, while the congeniality of most of the other passengers minimized the friction which is ever likely to develop in cramped quarters. Gregory found particular delight in the company of three Americans, who seemed to be a cross section of their Republic's citizenry. They included Townshend Harris, a prominent New York merchant who was on his way to the East to take up the appointment as his nation's first Consul General to Japan. (According to legend, Madama Butterfly was to be inspired by the story of a geisha who entered his household only to commit suicide when subsequently ostracised by an outraged society.) Harris impressed Gregory with his knowledge of 'every corner of the world' and as the most agreeable companion he had ever met. The two other Americans were no less entertaining, being a merry Kentuckian 'fresh from the backwoods' and a Yankee sea captain who performed a vast repertoire of 'nigger songs'.

By mid-December Gregory was established in the small, clean, cool, comfortable and inexpensive Williams Hotel, Cairo. He had been carrying £150 when he set out from England, and although accompanied by a servant whom his mother had recommended, he had managed to live frugally, spending on average no more than £1-2s-6d each day. At Cairo he expected to meet his companion for an expedition up the Nile into Nubia — a friend, Sandford Graham — but there was no sign of him. Gregory had a pleasant enough time while he waited for Graham to arrive, basking in the warmth; communicating with a fellow resident, a Greek, in that man's classical language; showing himself to be a good sport by riding a dromedary while dressed in English clothes for the amusement of the locals; going each evening to the home of an English merchant to make up a four of whist and walking home every night through the narrow and eerily silent streets of the city; and dining with Lord and Lady Canning, and Lord Hubert de Burgh — Dunkellin's younger brother — who were travelling out to India. And when word finally arrived that Graham had been obliged to return to France, having forfeited his life insurance by visiting the Crimea, Gregory regretted that he had not accepted the invitation of one of his fellow passengers on the voyage across the Mediterranean to visit Madras. He had long dreamed of exploring the land where the nabob had made his fortune and several years before, in 1851, had been promised a welcome both by friends and Lord Dalhousie, the Governor-General. But the cost, which he had then estimated at £1,000, and the length of time he would be away, perhaps a year, and this a period of political instability and hence electoral opportunity, had dissuaded him from going. Now a second opportunity had been lost and who knew whether another would arise. Of more immediate concern, however, was the drain of his funds caused by the unexpectedly long stay in Cairo, first while he waited for Graham and then while he sought another companion. Fortunately, he found an admirable partner in Arthur Kennard, the son of a Scottish ironmaster. Young Kennard proved to be full of fun and good temper and deeply interested in antiquities. [21]

They set out from Cairo on the second day of 1856, having hired a bark which they rechristened *The Flea*, in tribute to the ubiquitous and inseparable associate of all travellers in Egypt, and for which they designed their own flag — a black flea on a blood red streamer. The vessel came with a captain, a steersman and a crew of six, who were all Nubians, and thus 'honest', 'merry', and 'obedient', whereas Egyptian Arabs were 'a set of scheming, grasping rascals always playing tricks and getting well flogged in consequence'. Not that the Nubians honesty prevented them from demanding 'the intolerable buckshish,' which Gregory concluded was 'the sleeping and waking idea of every inhabitant of this country'. Nor did their honesty discourage him from hiring a Dragoman. He spoke French and Italian 'pretty fairly', as did Gregory himself, and this 'one-eyed fanatical Arab' and his well-bred Irish employer found themselves as one in their anti-semitism. Although characteristic of his class, Gregory's prejudice may have been heightened by his increasing dependence upon money lenders. Whatever the reason, his one complaint about the sea passage from Marseilles to Alexandria had been the presence of 'two beastly Jews', one of whom got 'beastly drunk' and the other 'beastly sick'. There were no complaints about the stately progress up the Nile, however. The weather was perfect — cool in the early mornings, hot at midday but even then the dry air made the heat bearable, and pleasantly mild in the evenings. Gregory and Kennard rose at 8.00 am, and breakfasted on eggs and coffee one hour later. If there was no wind they would then go inland to shoot, for pigeons and wild duck were plentiful, visit the square-housed villages and explore the tombs and temples. Gregory soon fancied that he was quite expert in the reading of the hieroglyphs. With the wind they travelled, slowly making their way through the verdant alluvial soil either side of the river, 'green beyond the power of paint with its early products,' and occasionally passing hills that rose craggily and perpendicularly from the river. In addition to observing, Gregory wrote. He decided to keep a full account of the adventure, 'neither historical, nor statistical, nor topographical,' but which would 'beguile a summer evening at Coole'. The country was worthy of a good pen, he informed his mother, and every year new archeological discoveries were being made. Then at dusk, and no matter whether the day had been one of relaxation rather than exertion, he and Kennard sat down to dine. The cook they had employed was soon revealed as a gastronomic impostor but Gregory's servant Hubert came to the rescue, having served time with a noted restauranteur in his native Belgium. Having feasted themselves, the travellers retired at 10.00 pm.[22]

As *The Flea* advanced into Nubia the country became somewhat more stark and the band of cultivation alongside the river narrowed. Outside of that lay the desert, 'with golden sand and great round, baked, terrified hills rising out of the desert plain — sometimes a fringe of palms and mimosas intervene — and beyond that not a vestige of vegetation, but the atmosphere is delightful,' Gregory wrote to his mother, 'and the light on the hill sides varies with the day, and the broad reaches of the Nile closed in by hills at the distance gives one the idea of voyaging on some long lake, mountain girt.' Nor were the temples quite so imposing as those they had seen in Egypt, for not only were they smaller and inferior in conception but being constructed of sandstone they had suffered greater damage at the hand of time.

Gregory and Kennard did dally with the idea of pushing on to the confluence of the White and the Blue Niles, but at the second cataract they decided to turn back. Another thousand miles of intense heat, the fear of fever as the spring advanced, and rumours of revolts among the wild tribes of the interior dissuaded them from going any farther. In Gregory's case there was also the problem of money. Happily when he arrived back in Cairo in April he found a draft for £90 awaiting him, which his mother had forwarded, and with these funds he set out for home via Trieste, Vienna and Paris.[23]

The success of the Egyptian expedition saw Gregory return to North Africa at the end of the year. Reunited with Sandford Graham, and attended again by Hubert, he sailed from Marseilles for Tunis on 30 October 1856. Here was another land of obvious fascination for a student of the classical world, and Gregory retained his deep interest in the classics throughout his life. The British Museum had an employee busy at work in Tunis excavating the site of Carthage, though Gregory was to be disappointed by the ruins and quickly alienated the Museum's man by challenging his classification of some mosaics he had uncovered as Phoenician when they were evidently Roman. It was an elementary mistake Gregory attributed to the weakness of the archaeologist's classical education. Nevertheless, he did establish a lasting friendship with the British consul general, Richard Wood, and his charming Irish wife Christine. Not only did they encourage the travellers to explore the interior of the beylik, which was reportedly full of Roman and ancient remains, but Wood obtained an audience for them with the Bey. A foray inland was certain to be an adventure, perhaps even dangerous, despite the reforms of Muhammad's modernizing predecessor Ahmad Bey, thus some form of official protection was desirable. Of course, one of the attractions of such a journey was the knowledge that the territory had been penetrated by so few Europeans. The Bey provided them with an escort of five soldiers and letters to all the chiefs and heads of tribes they were likely to encounter, calling upon them to supply the intrepid pair with food, forage and lodging, and making them answerable for their security. Also, he granted them permission to visit Kairouan, the oldest Muslim city in North Africa and one of the seven sacred cities of Islam. Although two members of their guard had to be sent packing, for their extortions and brutality antagonised the local Arabs wherever the party camped, the trip passed without serious incident.

Years later Gregory recalled the expedition proudly. It was 'no mean feat,' he wrote, to have 'quartered the whole Regency of Tunis as carefully as a well trained pointer quarters a Norfolk turnip field.' This was no idyllic progress, like that up the Nile, but a hard trek on the back of a horse which was made no easier by a bout of fever which weakened Gregory for a time. Not that North African travel lacked great charm, for 'while you have excitement and entertainment of scenes and of people little known and of a society which totally disassociates you from Europe, yet during every day's march some monument, some inscription recalls your thoughts to the past history of the soil, to famous names and famous times. You have not the gorgeous flowers or the fierce hot chase of South Africa, but the triumphal arch, the ruined temple, the half intelligible inscription all remind us of old names and of fights fought long ago and by the bivouac fire of crackling rosemary amid keen eyed wondering Alis, Kassims and Mohammeds, it is pleasant to talk over past time. . . .' Here were places which possessed 'the special magic' of association with immortal events and men. All of this he sought to capture 'carelessly and playfully' in the two volumes which he wrote recounting his experiences in Egypt and Tunis. They were printed privately in 1859 and he distributed a number of copies to friends, but the remainder were to be destroyed in a fire in 1873. [24]

The long and quiet journey up the Nile and into the past, and the ride through the 'vast and noiseless solitudes' of Tunis, encouraged reflection. Gregory had greeted the new year of 1856 with the fervent hope that it would prove 'more auspicious than the last two or three which have born with them many troubles and anxieties.' Writing to his mother from Cairo, following his return from Nubia, he announced that he had taken a vow to lead a life more in consonance with God's wishes if ever restored to his former position. He did not claim to have undergone any dramatic conversion 'except in the horror of a life of speculation and anxiety and in an ardent desire that I may be permitted to be of use hereafter to those with whom I am brought into contact.' Perhaps his belated commitment to do 'right' would 'be some atonement for high opportunities thrown away, position abandoned, and everything but *honour* forfeited.'

Bess Gregory did all that was within her power to assist her son's rehabilitation. Convinced that a return to public life would indeed be the remaking of him she approached Clancarty in May 1856, seeking a promise of the family's 'influence' should William decide to stand at the next election. Clancarty was pessimistic about the chances of any Protestant landlord in Catholic Galway, hence his delay in launching his son and heir, Dunlo, into political life, and he thought Gregory would be better advised to obtain an English borough through his powerful Peelite friends. However, he did not refuse assistance and when Palmerston went to the country the following spring Clancarty supported Gregory's efforts to wrest a seat form one of the sitting Members, both of whom were seeking re-election. For his part a some-what obsequious Gregory not only committed himself to the system of national education favoured by the Earl but also mounted another Clancarty hobby horse — the establishment of a national board to regulate and inspect all schools whose efficiency would be the sole test for assistance. 'The adherence of the first men in a county, give a candidate not merely a number of votes,' he wrote, 'but a moral position which enables him to dispense with much clap-trap and nonsense and I would willingly consult your wishes and opinions on a subject which you have studied and understood far better than I do.' This was not a stand likely to win much favour with the hierarchy, but in 1857 the political intervention of the Catholic clergy proved to be doubly advantageous to Gregory.[25]

When the Archbishop of Tuam and the Bishop of Clonfert again endorsed Thomas Bellew, though only after some hesitation, for they had not been enamoured of his conduct in Parliament, Gregory rallied fellow landlords with the argument that by electing him they would reassert much of the political influence they had lost to the priests in 1852. As Clancarty emphasised to his fellow Tory magnates, Clonbrock and Dunsandle, to oppose William was to assist MacHale's nominee. But neither that warning nor a personal appeal from Bess Gregory could persuade Dunsandle to forgive Gregory for aiding Clanricarde against his brother in the last election. He stuck to his resolve to offer a tit for tat.[26]

If Bishop Derry's coming out for Bellew suggests that Gregory's efforts to conciliate the hierarchy had failed, the situation was somewhat more complicated than that because in Galway as elsewhere in Ireland the priests were not united politically in 1857. Even as he labelled Bellew the hierarchy's man, in order to unite landlords behind his own candidacy, Gregory was enjoying the support of two of MacHale's other bishops, those of Kilmacduagh and Galway. His long quest for clerical backing had been given an initial fillip in the autumn of 1852 with the appointment of Patrick Fallon as Bishop of the united diocese of Kilmacduagh and Kilfenora. A native of Clonfert and a graduate of Maynooth, Fallon had distinguished himself as a missionary priest in the west and was a man of simple and unostentatious piety. He had been befriended by Robert Gregory, who had thoughtfully forwarded

newspapers to him in his remote parish of Lisdoonvara, and the friendship had been inherited by Robert's son. William had consolidated the
relationship and improved his standing among Catholics generally as a
result of a much publicised clash with the local Anglican Dean over the
Ecclesiastical Titles Bill.

The Patriotic Fund launched in 1854 to aid the widows and orphans
of men who fell in the Crimea threatened to be bedevilled in Ireland by
sectarian suspicions and continuing Catholic sensitivity on the subject
of the Titles Bill. The local organizers of the Fund in Tuam had been
castigated by the *Herald* for their failure to address John MacHale as
Archbishop of Tuam. As chairman of the Gort Committee, Gregory had
secured from the Secretary of War, his old friend Newcastle, an
assurance that the money raised would not be distributed in any dis-
criminative fashion. Catholic and Protestant families were guaranteed
identical treatment Gregory declared at the public meeting he chaired in
Gort on 27 November 1854. But no sooner had he put Catholic doubts
to rest on that score than another ugly problem raised its head. Gregory
asked Bishop Fallon to move the first resolution, only for the Dean of
Kilmacduagh to protest the precedence accorded a Catholic bishop. Not
content with this disruption of the meeting, Dean Bermingham pursued
the issue in a correspondence with Gregory which was soon published
in the *Galway Vindicator*. Bermingham protested 'the very illegal and
unwarrantable indignity to me, and the Protestant clergy of my Chapter
and the diocese', and also Gregory's addressing of Fallon as the Bishop
of Kilmacduagh. In doing so he exposed himself to a crushing retort.
Any other form of proceeding than that which he had adopted would
have subjected the Bishop to an 'unmerited and unwarrantable
indignity,' Gregory responded. He ridiculed the Dean's pretensions,
reminding him that his 'Chapter' was composed of two clerics, and
pointed out that at Fund meetings elsewhere precedence had been given
to members of the Roman Catholic hierarchy. 'This I am sorry to say
must be a catastrophe to you as a believer in the Divine right of Deans,'
he added maliciously. Nor did he overlook the opportunity to deplore
the Ecclesiastical Titles Bill, sarcastically describing it as 'this most wise
and effective concoction of recent legislation.' Finally, he carefully
paraded his liberal religious opinions. 'I do not consider contention to
be the synonym for Christianity nor Protestantism for presumption,' he
observed, and then went on to deplore the Dean's 'act of intolerance'
and his 'Pharisaic craving for uppermost rooms at feasts and chief places
in Synagogues.'[27]

The *Vindicator* recommended Gregory's response to all Irishmen 'who
admire genius, truth, eloquence, and educated Protestant principle, as
contra distinguished from the mean, pettyfogging, partisanship of an
intolerant class.' Fallon certainly appreciated the stand Gregory had
taken, as did McEvilly in the neighbouring diocese of Galway. Bishop
McEvilly was highly regarded as a scholar, having published learned
and lucid commentaries on the Epistles of St. Paul, and was much

admired for his youthful energy. He visited each parish in his diocese at least once every three years and set aside a full day to examine the children in their Christian doctrine. Both men were useful allies and with the calling of the general election Gregory publicly reaffirmed his belief in 'perfect religious equality'.[28]

Assured of the assistance of two members of the local hierarchy, and the 'influence' of the two most powerful Tory landlords, Gregory required the backing of only one other dignitary to complete a coalition of exceptional breadth. He had first approached Clanricarde in mid-March. He promised to support a Palmerston ministry if elected and requested the Marquess's 'neutrality' in the forthcoming campaign. 'By that I mean,' he explained, 'that your influence should be exerted for Tom Burke alone.' Clanricarde, conscious of the debt he had owed Gregory since 1852, replied reassuringly that he would not aid anyone against him, and he immediately honoured that promise by declining to endorse Thomas Redington (another relative) who belatedly and briefly entered the field as a second Whig-Liberal. Moreover, when friends came to him for guidance, asking whether they should 'plump' for Burke or give their second ballots to Gregory, Clanricarde quietly urged them to use both their votes. Yet there was a danger of a revival of that mutual suspicion and acrimony which had undermined the electoral understanding in 1852, and the sense of *déjà vu* was heightened by the decision to put Dunkellin up again in the borough. Some of Bellew's artful friends spoke of Burke as the most vulnerable of the three candidates, hoping thereby to panic his supporters into withholding second ballots from Gregory. Naturally, this led to talk of Gregory's friends retaliating by plumping for their man. To prevent a breach opening between them, Gregory worked feverishly to convince Clanricarde that his supporters would loyally vote for Burke. Indeed, he had Clonbrock forward to the Marquess one of the cards the Tory lord's agent had distributed among the voting tenantry and which made it clear that second votes were to be cast for Clanricarde's cousin. Gregory issued similar instructions to his own tenants and wrote to Clancarty requesting him to do the same. In return, Gregory now expected greater assistance from Clanricarde. 'I have a very hard card to play and am playing it entirely for Tom [Burke],' he informed him, 'I ought to get something in return more than neutrality.' If Clanricarde merely freed his tenants and friends to use their second votes as they wished many of them might succumb to the pressure of Bishop Derry and opt for Bellew, he warned. Surely it was not in Clanricarde's long term political interests to see the Catholic clergy triumph yet again. 'The gentlemen of the county will always feel great deference for your wishes,' he continued, but should 'the priests get the upper hand they will not be satisfied with one member.' He repeated his earlier pledge of support for a Palmerston Government and was able to produce a letter from the Lord Lieutenant, the Earl of Carlisle, in which the former Lord Morpeth, whom Gregory had vanquished in Dublin fifteen years earlier, endorsed his candidacy. Finally, Gregory re-emphasised the breadth of his own support, coming as it did from both landlords and clergy, which if it plumped for him might imperil Burke's chances of re-election. In fact, there was no danger of the understanding collapsing and Clanricarde, without formally coalescing, continued to give Gregory strong backing.[29]

Illness which confined him to his bed for several days prevented Gregory from attending the nomination meeting held in the County Courthouse on 6 April, but his friends were out in such force that even the *Tuam Herald* was impressed by their number and diversity, being 'a mingled array of Liberal and Conservative principles and an amalgamation of interests hitherto unprecedented in this great county.' His nominator described him as liberal in his opinions and hailed him as a friend of the poor, the latter claim being greeted with some dissent. When the High Sheriff called for a show of hands he declared that Burke and Gregory were the choices of the meeting. Bellew's men immediately demanded a poll, which was set for later that week.[30]

In a frantic effort to deny Gregory the victory which at last seemed to be within his grasp Bellew's supporters charged that he was an Orangeman and revived the sensitive issue of the quarter-acre test. His past difficulties with Tresham Gregg, his more recent conflict with Dean Bermingham, and the backing of Bishops Fallon and McEvilly effectively nullified the accusation of Protestant extremism. As for the hated clause which had borne his name, Gregory insisted that it had been introduced to prevent a far more sweeping measure from being adopted, one which would have deprived the poor of everything, even their gardens. More convincing than this excuse, however, in meeting and countering the charge, was Gregory's admirable record as a landlord. One of his Catholic supporters issued a handbill in which he asked: 'Can you possibly believe that model for Irish proprietors, nicknamed "quarter-acre Gregory," "to be a ruthless member of the crow-bar brigade," the rack-renting, house-levelling, exterminating landlords, when his tenantry are some of the best housed, best clad, best fed, well-to-do people in this county; living in comfortable cottages with schools and chapels in all directions about them.' Nor was anyone able to contradict Gregory's claim in his election address that the principle of fair compensation for real and bona fide improvements made by tenants was the guiding one at Coole. Further, he recommended it as an equitable solution for the landlord-tenant question. Equally, his leadership of the agitation for railway extension was paraded as further proof of his concern for the welfare of the poor. 'Who are the fools that would exchange that real Irish diamond [Gregory] for that bit of French paste [Bellew],' one supporter asked, 'that clear headed politician and able statesman, Gregory, for that butterfly of fashion, Bellew, that employs French cooks and foreign servants in preference to natives.'

Although polling took place during Holy Week this coincidence did nothing to sober the carnival atmosphere or discourage unruliness and intimidation. Cars, caravans and every other description of vehicle brought freize-coated freeholders from out-lying districts to the city of Galway. They were welcomed by the hoarse and repeated shouts of the 'botheen boys', who bawled out the name of their candidate. Thirty minutes before the opening of the poll at 9.00 am the constabulary and military assembled, but they were unable to maintain the peace. Some of Gregory's close friends, such as the Eyres of Eyrecourt, not only canvassed on his behalf but escorted their voters to the polls in order to protect them from violence and tampering. The stewards and under agents who were usually entrusted with this task might have been tempted to counsel their charges to vote for Bellew. Yet neither the presence of the police and the military, nor of landlords armed with revolvers or life preservers, prevented outbreaks of violence. At Ballinasloe, a mob of Bellew's sympathizers attacked Gregory's partisans and forced them to seek refuge in the offices of the *Western Star* and Burke's tally rooms. Eventually, they were rescued by the police and escorted to the poll. At Tuam, the mob attacked not only Gregory's supporters but also the cavalry who came to their aid. Here again those intending to vote for Gregory had to be marched under guard to the poll. Nevertheless, the end of the first day found Gregory comfortably ahead of Bellew while Burke was well in the lead. Still fearful that MacHale and Derry might engineer a rally on the second day of voting both Gregory and his agent anxiously urged Clanricarde to send in his Portumna voters to split between him and Burke. They need not have been concerned. Having spent close to £4,000 already, Bellew decided to cut his losses and thus Gregory's expenses by conceding defeat. Gregory later put the cost of victory at £750, but that was probably too low an estimate for Thomas Burke's expenses exceeded £800.[31]

'The Catholic constituency of this county have returned a Protestant gentleman to Parliament in preference to a Catholic,' the *Galway Vindicator* trumpeted. 'The down-right papists of Connaught, in the teeth of the expressed wishes of an influential portion of their clergy, and notwithstanding their supposed bigotted adhesion to Romish influences, have put their trust in Mr. Gregory and confided to his hands their political interests.' The excited victor was quick to thank Clanricarde for his 'kind and valuable support', and to flatter him that no one had reason to be happier at this result. 'It shows that Tuam will no longer dictate to the County,' he averred. 'Had Bellew succeeded, Thom would have been next attacked, and in spite of his great popularity and your influence, he would have a hard fight. . . .' Indeed, Clanricarde had reason to be doubly pleased, for Dunkellin had been returned in another scandal-marred borough contest. But the haste with which Gregory wrote to Clanricarde was not a mark merely of his undoubted gratitude, nor were his immediate and public statements of support for Palmerston simply the honouring of his pledges. Instead, he was also advertising himself for office. 'To great Parliamentary powers and practical qualities of mind Mr. Gregory adds a brilliant and striking capability of discussion and a capacity of reply truly astounding,' the *Galway Mercury* proclaimed. Gregory appears to have thought that he might be offered the post of Chief Secretary for Ireland in the new Palmerston Government. He was to be quickly disappointed and on reflection undoubtedly realized that he would need to prove himself again before he could expect promotion. One consoling thought remained, as his grandfather's old friend Sir Philip Crampton pointed out — his luck had turned at last and if he turned with it 'Fortune will stand to you for the rest of your life'. [32]

6
Champion of the Confederacy

Gregory celebrated his forty-first year in 1857. The slim and elegant youth of a decade and a half earlier had filled out in middle age. One observer judged him to be above average height, perhaps within an inch or two of six feet, with 'a rather robust figure, deep chest, a tolerable head, thick dark hair, and a very unsatisfactory, undecided longish face.' If time had not as yet left many of its marks upon him, the newly elected Member for Galway was all too aware of its passage. He was beginning political life anew at an age which seemed to deny him the luxury of patience in realizing his ambition to secure office. Nevertheless, the exiled Frank Lawley urged him to take as his motto: 'To him that works, and only him, The Past returns again.' Proceed cautiously in the Commons, he counselled, and do not quickly attempt to make too big a splash. Establish the reputation of 'a sensible, thoughtful, practical man, and not that of an orator. There is time enough for oratory hereafter.'[1]

Initially, Gregory quietly bent to the task of consolidating his support within the constituency. The fall of the first Palmerston ministry in 1858 brought the Conservatives led by Lord Derby into office, but theirs was a tenuous grip on power. Seeking to tighten that hold, the government looked to Ireland where memories are long and Whig responsibility for much of the misery of the Famine and Whig authorship of the Ecclesiastical Titles Bill had not been forgotten. 'We believe the chaotic state of the Whigs to be a providential punishment for their misdeeds against God's Church and God's poor,' the hierarchy's organ, the *Tuam Herald*, intoned. Gregory was in the forefront of the county's leading figures who capitalized upon the Tory Government's receptivity to Irish requests to press successfully for the testing of Galway as a transatlantic packet station. It was a scheme which excited visions of commercial and industrial growth, of mills rising on the banks of Lough Corrib and thousands of Irish operatives happily returning home from Manchester and other English cities. The Tories' promise of a postal subsidy to the Galway Packet Line, headed by John Lever, appeared to be a long step in the right direction even though the Treasury had given no indication of responding favourably to a request for the £150,000 which would have to be expended on improvements to Galway harbour in order to raise it to the standard of a transatlantic station. Consequently, when in March 1859 the Tories faced defeat on a Reform Bill, Gregory was reluctant to toe the Opposition line. With Lever lobbying hard among Irish Members, and evidence of the government's popularity in Galway as elsewhere in Ireland, Gregory feared that he might be inviting difficulties if he helped to turn the Tories out before the contract with Lever had at least been signed. But defeated the government was and Lord Derby obtained a dissolution.[2]

Gregory opened the election campaign confidently. He reminded voters of his devotion 'to all measures having for their object the advancement of the prosperity of the Town of Galway', and his honouring of the commitment given before the last poll to promote 'Civil and Religious Equality'. When in 1857 the Palmerston Government introduced an Industrial Schools Bill to provide training for vagrant children it had been Gregory who moved an amendment designed to 'lull the apprehensions now felt that the religious principles of the children would be tampered with by the managers of the proposed schools'. Had the minister 'witnessed the heartburnings and outrages which had arisen in Ireland from the system of proselytism, he would wish to place his scheme above all suspicion in that respect,' Gregory explained, 'and make it a blessing instead of a snare to the lower classes of the community'. By his intervention he won no more in the House than a proviso which would, in certain circumstances, see children placed in schools conducted on the religious principles to which in the opinion of local JPs their parents had adhered, but in Galway he at last won the respect of John Derry, the influential Bishop of Clonfert.[3]

Bishop Derry had found Gregory both helpful in securing copies of proposed legislation and responsive to his concern for the spiritual welfare of Catholics. A particular grievance was the practice of raising children in workhouses as members of the state Church whenever the religion of their parents had not been conclusively established. Catholics outnumbered Protestants 30:1 in Galway, and few of the latter were to be found among the ranks of the destitute, therefore it did seem probable that most if not all foundlings had been born to Catholic parents. So, in March 1859, Gregory had introduced a bill to amend the Poor Relief (Ireland) Act. He sought to restrict the discretionary power of the Poor Law Guardians to those cases where there was no clue to the parents' religion. A child found with a rosary around its neck, for example, would be registered and educated as a Catholic. Not that this advance satisfied Derry, who argued for the acceptance of baptism as proof of a child's religion, knowing full well that those Catholic Irish who found abandoned infants took them to their local priests and that they promptly baptised them. Yet, if he criticised Gregory's proposal as one still open to abuse, the Bishop expressed himself 'thoroughly convinced' of the MP's desire 'to act with the utmost fairness' and handsomely acknowledged that he had misjudged him during the previous election. More to the point, he made known his wish to see him 're-elected as the representative of our County', and when

Clancarty unexpectedly put up his son and heir, Lord Dunlo, against Gregory, Bishop Derry attributed the challenge to 'chagrin at the fair and impartial course you have adopted, as much as unwarrantable personal and family ambition. . . .'[4]

Clancarty's efforts to capitalise on the Tories' popularity to recapture one of the Galway seats for his immediate family and his party did perturb Gregory. Conceding the county's 'wonderfully Conservative state', and admiring the skill with which Dunlo's election address had been composed, for its promise of support for Church schools funded by the government might well 'catch the priests', an uneasy Gregory quickly entered into another informal alliance with Clanricarde. He traded the votes of his supporters in the town to Dunkellin in return for the backing of the Marquess in the county. However, it was soon apparent that Gregory's fears had been groundless. Tory popularity could not be translated into electoral support for Clancarty's son. The government did press its friends in Galway to rally to Dunlo, only to encounter objections from those who declined 'to ask Roman Catholics to vote for a man who calls their religion idolatrous and heaps abuse on them. . . . Voters can't be used precisely as if they had no sense or feeling.' With Archbishop MacHale coming out strongly against Dunlo and three bishops declaring for the sitting Members it was clear that Gregory's Catholic support would hold firm. The *Tuam Herald* denounced Dunlo as an enemy of civil and religious rights, offered tepid support to Tom Burke, but hailed Gregory as 'an active member of Parliament, attentive to the local matters of the county, liberal in his votes', who deserved 'the thanks of the Catholic people of Ireland for introducing into Parliament his bill to have defined the religion of deserted children'. Every honest Catholic and every liberal minded Protestant would vote for Gregory and Burke, the newspaper predicted. Among those Catholics were Thomas Bellew, whom Gregory had defeated in 1857, and John Reynolds, the Repealer who had turned him out of Dublin ten years before that. The owner of a small parcel of property in Galway, Reynolds now made some useful 'agitating speeches' on his former opponent's behalf. As for the liberal minded Protestants, they included Lord Clonbrock. Though a Tory, he promised his considerable political interest to Gregory once again.[5]

The nomination meeting was held on 9 May 1859, and at 10.00 am precisely the doors of the County Courthouse were thrown open to admit 'an eager crowd of the lower orders of the populace — many of them reckless under the excitement of whisky' — who occupied the gallery. Throughout the day they maintained 'a most deafening noise by shouting, blowing a hideous trumpet, and uttering in the most discordant sounds'. When the moment came for the candidates to address the meeting Burke stepped forward and asked: 'Boys, will you now hear me?' Shouts of No from the crowded gallery and blasts from the 'hideous trumpet' saw him retreat to his seat. Dunlo and Gregory, being made of somewhat sterner stuff, in turn 'gesticulated for some time, as if delivering a speech, but with the same result, as it was impossible to hear them.' Eventually, on a show of hands, the sheriff declared that the electors present favoured Gregory and Burke. Dunlo immediately demanded a poll, but the outcome was never in doubt. 'I think he must be blue-molded for want of a beating,' Gregory confidently observed, 'but he won't be so.' Gregory outpolled his cousin in every one of the county's seven electoral districts.[6]

Although the Conservatives made significant gains in the General Election they still did not command a majority when the new Parliament met. The inevitable confidence motion was quickly moved by a member of the Opposition and as the day of the decisive vote approached Gregory found himself in something of a quandary. He was reminded by Clonbrock that his re-election had 'been much assisted by conservative support by men of moderate views who were willing to accept an active useful member pledged to no particular party, ready to support useful measures, no matter by whom proposed, and certainly not ready to support a mere factious vote promising no other result than the substitution of Ld. John Russell for Lord Derby.' On the other side Clanricarde was demanding loyalty to the Whig-Liberal cause and warning darkly that a vote to sustain Derby would 'entirely disconnect' Gregory from the party both in the county and in Parliament. Clonbrock, with whom he discussed this threat, reassured him that it was mere bluster and urged him to make the protection of his broad base of support within the constituency his prime concern. If he explained his vote as one motivated by the desire to guard the Galway Packet subsidy it would get him 'no end of popularity', and if he kept up his popularity Clanricarde would continue to back him in future contests. Sound as this advice was, the decisive influence upon Gregory was probably that of John Derry. The Bishop thanked him for offering 'unrestricted communication to me of your views of public duty at this moment', but expressed a personal inability to distinguish between the political parties in their approach to Ireland's problems. He fancied that only through 'an independent armed neutrality' could concessions be extorted, and his personal list of essential reforms was a lengthening one — measures to protect tenants from capricious evictions and secure them compensation for improvements; good laws to regulate public fairs, markets and municipal affairs; separate workhouses for Catholic indigents; separate religious facilities for Catholic prisoners; denominational schools; the surrender of the Queen's Colleges at Galway and Cork to Catholic control and the creation of a similar Catholic college in Dublin. 'I have no doubt that an honest comprehensive system of aid to Catholic separate Education or a with-drawal of all government aid from *all* Educational projects or systems in Ireland can alone solve the problems in Ireland,' he added. If this ambitious programme was not one either party was likely to implement, hence the Bishop's talk of armed neutrality, he did indicate to Gregory that an abstention on the confidence motion would be readily understood. On reflection, he was even prepared to accept a vote for the Derby Government. There was talk of the Tories introducing Tenant reform and they had been far less sympathetic than the Liberals to the *risorgimento*, or, as Derry described it, the revolutionary and Anti-Catholic policy of Italian nationalists, which threatened what remained of the Pope's territories. Unstated but surely not misunderstood was the Bishop's opposition to a vote for the Whig-Liberals.[7]

The defeat of the Derby Government saw Palmerston rather than Russell emerge as the leader of a coalition ministry which included a number of leading Peelites, among them William Gladstone who had also voted with the Conservatives on the decisive division. Lacking Gladstone's political weight and denied Clanricarde's influence, Gregory must have realized that in bolstering his position in Galway he had sacrificed any immediate hope of promotion even to the bottom rung of the ladder of advancement. Frustrated ambition was one reason why Gregory sailed for America at the end of the summer. He had always intended to go abroad at the close of the session, if for no other reason than to place himself beyond the grasp of those remaining creditors with whom his solicitor was attempting to settle. Now that the major debts had been cleared Gregory hoped to pay off the remainder at the rate of five shillings in the pound. Moreover, the United States had long interested him. He had found Americans the most enjoyable of fellow travellers. As a family friend of the Cramptons he had followed closely in 1856 the troubles of Philip Crampton's son John, who had been expelled from his position as British Minister to the United States, along with three consuls, for a breach of the Republic's neutrality laws. They were all accused of recruiting British subjects resident in the United States for service in the Crimea. But it was the exiled Frank Lawley who finally tempted him to brave the Atlantic with the argument that a North American journey would be not merely enjoyable and instructive but also helpful to his career.

You are giving 'too much attention to North Africa to the exclusion of the great country from which I am now writing,' Lawley chided when he discovered that Gregory had followed his expedition to Egypt with one to Tunis. 'For 2,000 years and more the northern shores of Africa have contributed little or nothing to the political experience of the world, and deeply interesting as the study of hieroglyphics and ancient monuments must be to the refined mind I do not think that it is comparable in utility to being a prominent actor in living and stirring scenes and to an active and intelligent comprehension of the newest forms of political life.' America possessed attractions equal to those of Africa in wild life, he went on, and had a political importance 'transcendantly superior' to that of the teritories bordering the southern shore of the Mediterranean. All men of the modern school of English politics ought to make themselves 'intimately acquainted' with American affairs, for this was another period of Anglo-American tension and the United States was destined 'to be greater than the greatest'.

Given this immediate and prospective significance it was evidently 'more useful to a public man in England to be "au courant" with American politics than to be versed in the intricacies of effete European diplomacy'. The reputation as an expert on American affairs might well strengthen Gregory's claims to office. Thus Lawley recommended that he immerse himself in 'good books', such as Alexis de Tocqueville's *Democracy in America,* and pay a visit to the rising Republic. So, at the end of August 1859, Gregory bid friends farewell as he set out 'to do' North America and he expected 'a good deal of doing in visiting modern cities by steam boat and steam cars'.[8]

The voyage began as it was to continue. Gregory and his fellow passengers had difficulty boarding the *Anglo-Saxon,* which was moored in the Mersey, because of foul weather. Even after they had managed to clamber aboard from the tender their vessel remained in the river for almost a full day, prevented as she was by high winds and heavy seas from crossing the bar. However, the delay did allow Gregory to change cabins. He moved in with an acquaintance, Geoffrey Browne, risking the future Lord Oranmore's reputation for wilfulness in order to escape a Yankee from Mobile. This American seemed to be less than a gentleman, perhaps even capable of using Gregory's toothbrushes. The Atlantic passage was one of perpetual storms, and most of the passengers 'suffered awfully' during this 'terrible bad time'. Although Gregory was 'quite well all through', and marvelled at the 'mountainous, green raging sea', this experience was not one he ever wished to repeat. 'Such sights are quite enough once in a life,' he assured his mother, 'accompanied as they are with the reflection that a screw loose in the machinery, or a faulty bit or iron ..., would have been our condemnation to certain and immediate destruction for no boat could have lived an instant in such a sea.' Happily, the 'hard headed Scotchman' who commanded the *Anglo-Saxon* inspired confidence and many passengers took courage from a Sunday service conducted by an American clergyman. All breathed a sigh of relief when after eight uncomfortable days they passed safely through a field of icebergs and the strait of Belle Isle and found sanctuary in the sheltered waters of the St. Lawrence.[9]

One young passenger with whom Gregory had been thrust into contact and whose company he enjoyed was John Head. The only son of the Governor of Canada, Sir Edmund Head, he had already shown much promise in 'scientific matters' and was returning from two years at Heidelberg before going up to Cambridge. Naturally, Sir Edmund and Lady Head extended a warm welcome to their son's shipboard companion who was also a Member of Parliament. When Gregory pressed on to Montreal from that 'most beautifully situated, but most ill-paved dirty town' of Quebec, he found 'a really fine city, fine streets, admirable shops, Churches built with great regard to taste, and a Roman Catholic Cathedral that would be a noble building in any capital of Europe.' The extensive use of limestone in the construction of private and public buildings added to the pleasing appearance of the city for it gave the impression of solidity associated with granite but was more cheerful than that cold stone. In the company of the Heads and the Canadian premier, George Etienne Cartier, 'a little brisk cock sparrowish French Canadian', he toured the Victoria Bridge which was to span the St. Lawrence. 'This bridge will be about the greatest work in the world,' he admired, 'two miles in length and well-worthy of the noble river it traverses.' From Montreal he travelled to Trois Rivières on 19 September to attend a public dinner and ball held in the Governor's honour, and then joined the Head family for what promised to be an idyllic trip by canoe up the St. Maurice river. They camped beside the magnificent falls at Shawinigan, then moved on to those at Grand' Mère and finally reached Grandes-Piles. The scenery either side of the river had been a breathtaking mass of colour, for like most Europeans who toured at this time of the year Gregory acknowledged that Canadian woods 'are inconceivably beautiful, every tint of purple, yellow and red'. The romantic nature of the experience was heightened when the 'Indians, half-breeds and Voyageurs' who manned the paddles broke into Canadian boat songs. In the evenings there was singing and conversation around roaring camp fires, and the rather stiff and formal Sir Edmund finally relaxed when he and Gregory discovered their common love of the classics.[10]

Suddenly, on 24 September, disaster struck the happy party. Under the good natured ribbing of his father John Head decided to bathe in the river. From a distance he appeared to be diving in the water but was in fact desperately attempting to attract assistance. By the time those on the bank realized that he was in grave difficulty it was too late to save him. After twenty minutes they did manage to pull him from the water and throughout the three hours of frantic efforts to revive him the Head family sat in mute disbelief. There then followed two agonisingly slow days by canoe back to Trois Rivières, and from there the sad group travelled to Quebec for the funeral. John Head was buried in a cemetery overlooking the St. Lawrence. 'One maple in its gorgeous beauty was waving over the grave, and solemn ancient pines added to the impressiveness of the scenery.'[11]

Throughout this ordeal Gregory sought to comfort the bereaved parents, and in the best Victorian manner urged the desolate father to immerse himself in his duties. The Heads much appreciated his support and the warm friendship which was now established long survived. Once the funeral was over Gregory hurried away from Quebec, stopping only briefly in Montreal before setting off for Ottawa — the magnificent site which had been selected for the Canadian capital — and then on to Toronto. Gregory found the vastness tedious. 'There is no great pleasure in travelling here, the distances are so enormous,' he complained. 'Two hundred miles is quite a short trip, and there is a sameness in the towns and the country which affords no great amusement after a few days.' Yet, it was impossible not to be impressed at least with the cleanliness and spaciousness of the streets of even the smaller centres. However, two visits to Toronto, to enjoy the company of one of his favourite maternal uncles, Colonel Walter O'Hara, left him with a very low opinion of it. 'This Toronto is about the most hideous and detestable place I ever was in,' he informed his mother, 'there is not a single pretty walk in the neighbourhood. Dusty high roads, and a most uninteresting lake on one side and flat uninteresting meadows on the other.' Moreover, the climate was 'as detestable as the scenery'.[12]

It was the second week of October before Gregory crossed the border, entering the United States at Niagara Falls. 'They come here,' one distinguished American wrote of British visitors, 'run around the country for three months, and think they understand it.' But Gregory quickly concluded that America was 'unquestionably the place to spoil an Englishman'. 'In spite of the splutter and gasconading of the Press' he discovered that the British traveller was 'as popular as man can be' and to be assured of 'the warmest welcome' he had simply to behave himself and assume 'no airs'. His own grand tour took him to Detroit, Chicago and across Illinois to Quincy, then down the Mississippi to St. Louis. From there he travelled to Louisville where he met a group of his former tenants, and then at Cincinnati he encountered a former maid. Continuing east from that city he passed through Cumberland, on the border of Maryland and Virginia, then Washington, D.C., and Baltimore (where he met Lawley), before pausing for breath in New York. Although he disliked American rail carriages, for often there were as many as 70 people in each car and the seats were uncomfortable, the vast distances had prompted the construction of sleeping cars 'wherein you get a capital bed, and a sound sleep'. The Mississippi river boats had been even more impressive, for they were of immense proportions, had very comfortable cabins, offered excellent living and were 'gorgeously fitted up'. Most impressive of all, however, were American hotels.[13]

Gregory was astounded by the information that his 5th Avenue hotel in New York boasted 1,000 beds and could seat 1,500 people at dinner. The hotels 'are something quite astonishing to a weak mind,' he wrote home, enormous in size, run with clockwork regularity, and with a bar for gentlemen, drawing rooms for ladies, reading rooms, smoking rooms and 'the spittoons in every hole and corner and the floods of tobacco juice spirted into them'. Unlike other British visitors, Gregory was less concerned with the Americans' habit of bolting down their food than he was in awe of the quantities they consumed. The eating and drinking were seemingly perpetual — breakfast, lunch, tea, dinner, supper — and he considered the fare to be excellent. All of this and a bed for the equivalent of eleven shillings a day. Exhibiting remarkable self-discipline, he held fast to his custom of eating but twice a day and drank water instead of the brandy cocktails. Of course, abstinence alone preserved him 'from corpulency and apoplexy'.

When at the end of October Gregory reflected on what he had observed during three weeks of hectic travel he revealed how closely he had read Tocqueville and he was conscious of an ambivalence in his own response to American society and institutions. He had been confirmed in his 'most sincere regard for Americans in particular' and his 'great admiration for much of their character'. He had encountered none of the incivility, obtrusiveness and inquisitiveness of which other visitors had complained, and he wrote admiringly of the general level of public behaviour. 'There seems pervading even the lowest ranks a strong sense of self control I may almost call it dignity,' he noted, 'and you hear very little of that boisterous tipsiness you would witness at home among the same classes of society. They liquor a great deal or rather very often but do not get drunk.' In no country that 'ever yet existed was [there] such an aggregate of happiness,' he conceded. 'In fact no Kingdom in the world ever was better governed or with more universal order and propriety than the New England States — the inhabitants of which are the acute, drawling, nasal-toned wooden-nutmeg selling Yankees for whom we have no particular prepossession.' Nevertheless, he shrank in horror from what he believed to be the results of universal suffrage.[14]

He witnessed elections in Baltimore and New York, where even judges, magistrates and police officers ran for office. In both cities the contests were marred by violence and intimidation. 'Plug Uglies' armed with gimlets, which being fastened to the arm with India rubber flew up the sleeve and out of sight when released, stood guard at the polls and jabbed persons they suspected of having voted the wrong way. Nor did the secret ballot appear to afford any protection, because every man's vote seemed to be known. One far reaching consequence of brawling elections, or so Gregory believed, was the retirement of the 'better sort' from political life leaving the mob to govern. 'There is no such tyranny as mob tyranny,' he remarked darkly, 'no such uncompromising and unrelenting master as the party organization here.' Laying all of these evils at the door of universal suffrage, he concluded that if only every Member of Parliament was forced to travel through the United States 'he would modify many a democratic opinion, and become, if not before, most apprehensive of constitutional changes on an extensive scale.'[15]

In November Gregory moved south, where he had long expected to have an even more pleasant time. This region, despite an external democratic character, was reportedly less a democracy than an aristocracy. He had already found Baltimore, the most Southern of Northern cities, 'one of the most aristocratic towns in the Union and the Society refined and agreeable.' When he revisited Washington, on his way south, he was presented to President Buchanan, attended debates in Congress and he put up for several days in a Southern 'mess'. There he was befriended by three prominent Virginians, including the State's two senators, Robert Hunter and James Murray

Mason, and Representative William Porcher Miles of South Carolina. He immediately felt a social affinity with these men, for they were all 'most agreeable polished highly educated gentlemen in the fullest sense of the word.' Miles, in particular, proved to be scholarly and interested in poetry. Indeed, the South Carolinian became his 'guide, philosopher and friend' in the American capital and convinced the Irishman of the South's right to secede from the Union should the growing controversy over the expansion of slavery not be resolved in a way acceptable to that section. [16]

Gregory was impressed with the complexity of the slavery question. Conversations with his otherwise quiet and refined Southern friends persuaded him that there was 'no proposition too enormous which they are not ready to accept in order to secure the stability of what they call their "peculiar institution," no theory too monstrous by which they do not seek to justify it'. A 'kind, warm hearted old gentleman' like Mason 'defended the propriety of dividing families and selling them apart', and told Gregory 'in so many words that it was his full conviction that no man could be placed in so high a moral position as the slaveowner for that the unlimited control over his fellow men brought out the highest and noblest features of his moral nature, and that it was the nearest approach to the patriarchal virtuous rule of the early Hebrew.' They accepted the theory of those 'scientists' who contended for more than one act of creation, including that of a black Adam, because it simplified the explanation of racial inferiority. That inferiority then rendered the compulsory servitude of blacks justifiable, expedient and necessary, 'for they advance from the justice to the necessity of the case'. Thus in many states the negro was denied education on the grounds that his duty was to labour with hands not head, and knowledge might nurture dissatisfaction with his lowly position, 'while at the same time [slavery's defenders] illogically rest the arguments as to the negro's destiny to servitude upon his notorious intellectual inferiority'.

Obvious as the flaws in the Southern defence of slavery were, and sad the violence the institution did to the minds of otherwise intelligent and sensitive men, Gregory did not debate the issue with his new-found friends. Aware of just how aggressive Southerners were on the subject, courtesy and prudence dictated silence. After all, he had seen the weapons some of these men carried into Congress. But silence was also a reflection of sympathy for the Southerners' plight. Gregory insisted that 'we must make great excuse for Southern feeling on the question of Slavery.' He did not dispute the self-serving American contention that the British had forced slavery upon reluctant settlers during the Colonial Period. Further, he was swayed by those who argued that the issue of emancipation was 'not merely one of absolute and hopeless ruin, and the loss of the enormous capital sunk in sugar, rice, cotton and tobacco plantations,' but involved 'the extirpation of the black or white race in the South'. The British experience in the West Indies had been widely misinterpreted by Gregory's fellow Harrovian Anthony Trollope, among others, as proof that negroes would not work without compulsion, and that if freed, and able to find land on which they could squat and raise enough to support life, they could not be forced to labour through want. Yet, were they not the only labour force providentially supplied to work the land in the subtropical American South? Even more frightening than the prospect of economic ruin was the possibility that freed blacks would demand the rights of citizenship and in those areas of the South where they outnumbered whites would seek to override the other race. Here were the ingredients for a race holocaust, Gregory fancied. Nor was he unmindful of the consequences for Britain of this imagined economic and social turmoil in America. 'As for us we should be ruined,' he concluded, 'every cotton mill in England would be stopped [for Britain imported 80 per cent of her cotton from the United States], and the great manufacturing cities become pauperized — We in Ireland should also be ruined as these cities are our best customers, and Ireland's agricultural prosperity pulsates with Lancashire.'

To regard slaveholders with sympathy and to fear the consequences of emancipation should not be confused, at least in Gregory's case, with support for the peculiar institution. On leaving Washington, he travelled through Virginia, the Carolinas, Georgia and Alabama on his way to New Orleans. In the capital of South Carolina he witnessed the savage employment of the mob in the defence of slavery. A Northern stonemason who had been either brave or foolish enough to profess abolitionist sympathies was seized by the local authorities and handed over by them to a Vigilance Committee. He was lashed with cowhide, the infliction of the punishment being delegated to a negro as an added humiliation to both men, and then tarred and feathered from head to feet. This episode and his personal observations of the institution during his progress through the Slave States satisfied the sardonic Irishman that slavery was not 'calculated in the most eminent degree to develop man's moral nature.' Privately, he ridiculed the assertions that the negro was intended for servitude, and that the purest motives of humanity and religion therefore prompted 'nigger driving'. Although he saw little sign of ill-treatment, he mordantly observed that a man in Britain seldom abused his horse and a negro could not work unless clothed and reasonably well fed. However, he did concede that a few years residence in the South would erode the moral sense of most men on this issue. They also would come to believe that it was no hardship to separate mother from child, and that God looked with favour upon slave breeding farms where women were valued for their fecundity not their chastity. Nor did he fail to note, or be shocked by, the substantial number of mulattoes among the slaves. In short, Gregory was repelled by the institution.[17]

On 27 December 1859, after almost four months of exploration and discovery in North America, Gregory sailed from New Orleans. To have recrossed the North Atlantic by a Line other than that running into Galway would have been politically unwise, but he had been warned that this was not the season to entrust his life to its care. By all accounts the fare was bad, the company worse and the 'sea going merits of the boat worst of all'. Recalling the ordeal of his outward voyage, Gregory had elected to return by the more southerly and reputedly the gentler passage via Cuba and the West Indies to Southampton. This route had the added attraction of providing the opportunity, which he grasped, to stock up on cigars. Offered Cuban cigars at the bargain price of £1 per 100, he was carrying 1,200 of them in his baggage when he embarked at Havana on 10 January 1860, for what proved to be an uneventful crossing. [18]

From Britain Gregory watched without pleasure the growing sectional antagonism in the United States. Much of the excitement would blow over, he believed, if a man of tact and moderation were to be elected president in 1860. By 'tact and moderation' he appears to have meant a Democrat, for he had long recognized that the victory of any man of 'strong Northern views' would precipitate secession and had predicted that this would in turn be followed by civil war. In November Abraham Lincoln, the nominee of the exclusively northern Republican Party, triumphed in the Presidential election and Gregory's dismal prophecies were soon fulfilled. Led by Miles's South Carolina, the Slave States began to secede in December. By February seven of them had withdrawn from the Union and delegates from six of these states (the Texas delegation did not arrive in time to participate) gathered in sleepy, uncomfortable but central Montgomery, Alabama, and founded the Confederate States of America. In April the Confederates attacked Fort Sumter in Charleston harbour. The Federal garrison, after a prolonged bombardment, surrendered and withdrew but President Lincoln immediately called out 75,000 militia to suppress the insurrection. This action drove four more Southern States, among them Virginia, into the Confederacy. Next, the Union, having already taken advantage of the withdrawal of the South to enact a new protectionist tariff which promised to curtail British trade, proclaimed a blockade of the Confederacy which threatened to cut off the supply of cotton to the textile mills of Lancashire and Cheshire.

Britain's response to conflict in the United States was certain to be an ambivalent one. We British would have 'all our commercial sympathies with free trade and the South,' Gregory reasoned, 'and yet our social and moral instincts will be with the North as the antagonistic element to slavery.' He resolved this painful dilemma for himself by giving precedence to racial and material considerations — those long held fears of the economic and social consequences of emancipation — yet his subsequent emergence as the Confederacy's champion in the Commons is not so simply explained. He was bound by ties of friendship to particular Southerners and did feel a sense of social affinity with the residents of the South in general. It was an identity William Porcher

Miles was careful to strengthen. He described the Montgomery Convention, in a letter obligingly forwarded by the British consul at Charleston in the diplomatic bag, as 'a delightful Assembly of gentlemen' and assured his British friend that Confederates were 'sincerely desirous' of having 'Old England' as their 'friend and Ally'. They had broken irrevocably with New England and 'all her *isms* so baleful to Southern gentlemen, whose traditionary tastes, ideas and sympathy are so decidely English.' Gregory was convinced of the right of the Southern States to secede and of the strength of independence sentiment. His reaction was also shaped by a natural aversion to warfare. If Britain promptly recognized the Confederacy would this act not serve to dissuade the Union from launching a senseless struggle to recover the disaffected states by force of arms? Finally, his championship of the Confederacy would provide him with a Commons platform from which he might yet establish his claim to office. From Frank Lawley he received the assurance: 'You have turned the corner, and it rests with yourself now to make your life a triumphal march to a strain of Beethoven's.' 'Many eyes are upon you and you can do more than any living man to show that "best men are moulded out of faults." '[19]

In the House Gregory began by drawing attention to the growing list of irritants in the relationship with the Union, which was a somewhat negative but not ineffectual means of prodding public opinion and the ministry southwards. On 12 April 1861 he enquired whether the government had received a copy of the new American tariff? At the beginning of May his question concerned the sensitive subject of the blockade. Had the Northern government been informed that none but effective blockades were legal? However, it was in reply to yet another of his questions on 6 May that he drew from Lord John Russell, the Foreign Secretary, the remark that the Confederacy 'must be treated as a belligerent'. This observation appeared to advance Britain one long step closer to recognition of the South, as indeed did the formal British Proclamation of Neutrality on 13 May. Under this constant quizzing Russell, usually 'Dry and cold to a degree, and aristocratic to a fault,' complained that it was 'not convenient to the public interest that the state of our foreign relations should be made the subject of weekly discussion in this House.' And it was the argument of public interest that Russell, Palmerston and several other members of the Commons employed to good effect in eventually prevailing upon Gregory to drop his motion 'To call the attention of the House to the expediency of the prompt recognition of the Southern Confederacy of America.' Each party to the American dispute would take offence at what was said against them and pay little heed to what was said for them in any debate, Palmerston feared, and all would say that Parliament had 'no business to meddle with American affairs'. When the objections were phrased in these terms by the Prime Minister personally the ambitious backbencher was ill advised to ignore them. 'I warned him that if he sought to embarrass the Government he wd do harm to nobody but himself as neither the H. of Commons [n]or the public wd permit anyone to make political capital for himself out of the American question,' one influential figure reported to Russell. 'The argumentum ad hominem seemed to have some weight with the Galwegian. . . .' But cooperation had been only grudgingly extended for Gregory was committed to the Confederate cause and had worked long and hard preparing a major address to introduce the motion.[20]

He had seen the speech as an opportunity to make a truly 'big splash' in the Commons. He would be able to demonstrate his knowledge of the United States, his grasp of the many and complex problems which had caused the Civil War and were posed by it, even show his countrymen how they might choose materialism without sacrificing morality and support the independence of 'Slaveownia' with an easy conscience. He had received both advice and information from the Confederate Commissioners, William L. Yancey and Ambrose Dudley Mann, who had come to Britain in search of recognition of their new nation. They had immediately sought out the Irishman, reading to him their official instructions and speaking unreservedly of their plans and strategy. For his part, Gregory had arranged their informal meeting with Lord John Russell in May and obtained passes for them to visit the great ironclad warship, the *Warrior*. 'How can I ever make a suitable recompense for your numerous kindnesses,' Mann asked?[21]

In his speech, Gregory had planned to weave the threads of philanthropy, humanitarianism and self-interest into the whole cloth of recognition. Speaking with the authority of a recent visitor to the Republic, he intended to sketch for his audience the 'irreconcilable differences' which had long divided section from section. Twice before there had been secessionist movements, at the Hartford Convention in 1814 and during the Nullification crisis less than two decades later. In both these instances the heart of the conflict had been the divergent commercial interests of North and South, he would have argued, before advancing the proposition that the dispute over the extension of slavery to the territories of the United States was no more than a reflection of the Southerners' determination to maintain an equilibrium between Slave States and Free. In this balance they saw the only effective protection of those economic interests. By the same token, it was important for him to show the insincerity of the North's position on slavery and this he had expected to do by citing chapter and verse of Northern hostility to blacks. From this point it was but a short step to the conclusion that recognition of the Confederacy would advance not retard the cause of freedom. Recognition would strengthen the hold on power of the 'higher classes' whose opposition to the revival of the slave trade had been given constitutional force by the founding fathers of the Confederacy. And, as Gregory was able to inform the House in a short speech during the debate on the Slave Trade in July, 'It was notorious that the real traffickers in the flesh and blood of their fellow men were citizens of the Northern States. It was in Yankee ships, floated by Yankee capital, commanded by Yankee skippers, sailing forth on their abominable errand, with the connivance of bribed Yankee authorities, that their work of the devil was carried on.' Finally, he had intended to argue that with the separation of the South the Union's Fugitive Slave Law would die and with its expiration the area of freedom would be enlarged. Slaveowners in the Confederate Border States, the argument went, would of necessity have to convert to a system of free labour.

If Gregory's preoccupation with slavery was an acknowledgment of his concern that Britain's traditional opposition to the institution would be an obstacle to recognition of the South, it was the thrust of his argument that this 'feeling should not bear down every other consideration'. Had not Britain an obligation to act if by recognition of the Confederacy she might save a 'kindred' people from a senseless conflict, senseless because the notion was 'perfectly preposterous' that a territory 'as large as Europe occupied by a free population of eight millions, can be overrun, held and subjugated'? Nor could or should the British ignore their own national self-interest. What would be the consequences of a protracted war for the estimated £60 million of British investments in America, for the millions of persons dependent in some way on the cotton trade and the textile industry, or for British commerce, in the event that the American belligerents resorted to privateering? As the South met the tests of recognition — it possessed the will, wealth, numbers and territory, or power, to maintain itself — and as recognition was consistent with philanthropy, humanitarianism and self-interest, then it ought to be extended.

Gregory's understandable disappointment at his inability to deliver his carefully crafted speech, and thus the loss of an opportunity to shine in the Commons, was surely compounded by the news soon afterwards of Palmerston's tinkering with the ministry. When Lord John Russell went to the Lords in June the Prime Minister required another spokesman for the Foreign Office in the Commons. Perhaps a powerful and convincing elaboration of an acceptable national policy towards the Civil War and the South might have put Gregory's name in his mind. What is certain is that, in the absence of such a tour de force, Palmerston elected to strengthen his support among Radicals in the House. He appointed Henry Layard, the discoverer of Nineveh and subsequently a close personal friend of Gregory's, as Under Secretary of Foreign Affairs. The Prime Minister does appear to have approached the Member for Galway, but only with a sorry junior lordship of the Treasury in hand. At Gregory's age this place would be a way station to obscurity not a rung on the ladder of advancement. Such appointments 'were generally bestowed on young members whom it was convenient to rescue, but who were not good at doing anything.' Thus he found an excuse for politely declining the offer.

Throughout the summer Gregory followed the news from America closely, and maintained contact with the Confederate Commissioners.

To them he expressed surprise at the failure of the Southern troops to push on to Washington once they had defeated the Union army at Bull Run in July. He proposed that Mann and Yancey exert more diplomatic pressure on Palmerston and his colleagues by exploiting the anomalous position of the British consuls in the South who were still accredited to the United States. To Henry Layard he forwarded a pair of letters from Mann which hinted at the likelihood of the French extending recognition before Britain and thus garnering the lion's share of the credit and commercial rewards in the Confederacy. He urged the Under Secretary to read them to Russell. He also mentioned that his friend Robert Hunter, who had recently been appointed Confederate Secretary of State, was a 'very prudent sagacious man and a gentleman in every respect' who 'writes full of confidence as to the prospect of the South.' For their part the Southern Commissioners, perhaps sensing that the Irishman's advocacy of the Confederate cause was not entirely disinterested, flatteringly declared that whenever recognition was extended Gregory would be the natural choice to serve as the first British Minister to their nation. His presence would be a great bonus for British interests, Mann wrote, because 'You are known throughout my country as the European friend par excellence.'[22]

Gregory had planned to spend the winter in the warmth of North Africa. The expedition was to have begun at Bengasi, the site of an exciting excavation of the ruins of the Pentopolis. Already a number of 'very fine objects' from it were enriching the British Museum. From Bengasi he had hoped to trek along the coast to Alexandria. However, he journeyed first to Nice to visit his mother and was promptly 'laid up with boils one after another on that part of the person which in equitation would have been sorely affected.' Sensibly, he decided after his recovery to travel no further than Naples and after a short time there, and a few days in Florence admiring the art, returned to Nice.[23]

It was while Gregory was relaxing on the Continent that a sudden crisis blew up in Anglo-American relations. Two more Confederate Commissioners — one of them Gregory's Washington 'mess'-mate, James Murray Mason — had been despatched to Europe. They successfully ran the blockade and embarked at Havana on a British mail steamer, the *Trent*, only for the vessel to be stopped by a Federal warship commanded by Captain Charles Wilkes. Mason and his vulpine colleague John Slidell were removed and taken back to the United States as prisoners. News of the incident created a sensation in Britain where the action of Captain Wilkes was regarded as a violation of 'international law' and an insult to the mistress of the seas. The government demanded the return of the Commissioners and an apology from the United States, demands they backed with ostentatious military preparations which included sending troop reinforcements to Canada and strengthening the naval squadron in the North Atlantic. Throughout December and into the New Year people waited anxiously for the American reply, the Confederates hoping naturally for the refusal which seemed certain to be followed by British intervention in the war. However, President Lincoln and his Cabinet chose to surrender Mason and Slidell and the British Government did not insist upon the apology which had not been forthcoming.

When Gregory arrived in London for the reopening of Parliament in February he found his friend Mason waiting for him and they quickly bent to the task of planning strategy. 'I have had long conferences with Mr. Gregory, who will be an earnest and efficient coadjutor,' Mason reported to Hunter, 'all agree that I could not have a more useful or safe adviser.' It was Gregory who arranged the Confederate's unofficial interview with Russell on 10 February, though Mason emerged from that meeting convinced that if left to themselves the members of the Cabinet would not steer a more interventionist course in America. Hoping to force the government's hand, the Confederacy's friends decided to press the question of the blockade's effectiveness and thus legality. Armed with the proof of massive violations which Mason provided, Gregory agreed to take the lead in the House. There seemed to be evidence enough that the blockade was working hardship in the textile towns. His dismay at the war's prolongation was also accentuated by the pathetic letters he now began to receive from his former gamekeeper, Michael Connolly, who had emigrated to America and joined the Union army with the outbreak of the war. They underscored, written as they often were from hospitals, the suffering and savagery of the conflict. Finally, there were the repeated warnings of his friend Lawley — soon to be appointed a special American correspondent of *The Times* — that in the aftermath of the *Trent* affair 'the deep-seated, bitter, aversion and detestation felt towards England' in the North defied description. The only way to avert a war once the rebellion was settled was to ensure that the Union emerged from the conflict with the South incapable of fighting on, he counselled. 'This being the case, is not England justified in joining the rest of Europe and in lifting the blockade of the Southern ports? It may be selfish policy; but it is a step forward to checkmate the most hostile and dangerous move ever contemplated against England. That we shall be covered with the filthiest abuse, do what we may, is undeniable. Had we not better do something to justify all this venom which is about to be discharged at our heads and put ourselves in a better position for encountering American rancour?'[24]

The chamber was packed when Gregory rose to speak on 7 March. Although one hostile observer noted his 'peculiarly offensive and whining tone', the speech was cleverly constructed and he surely shared the pleasure of his Southern friends 'at the rapt attention and unexpectedly hearty applause with which it was received'. Secession was a right, separation a fact and reconstruction an impossibility, he declaimed. If Britain could not be convicted, therefore, of determining the outcome of the war by any act of intervention, the problems created by the futile blockade were of national significance to her and of importance to the world. On the Continent the charge had already been laid, he warned, that Britain was conniving at an ineffective and thus illegal blockade in order to facilitate her own evasions of international law in any future conflict in which she became embroiled. By recognizing a blockade, which he was able to show had been run by as many as 400 vessels, Britain was making access to the South for her traders 'a mere smuggling and gambling speculation'. Similarly, there was 'the welfare of the working classes of this country' to be considered and protected. Moreover, if the ports of the Confederacy were open Southerners would willingly take all those goods shut out of the Union by the protectionist tariff. Finally, Gregory met head on the sensitive issue of slavery. He skilfully developed the argument that Confederate independence would eventually promote freedom in all areas of the new nation except 'that portion of the South where white labour would find the climate insupportable', and mocked the claim that the cause of the Union was that of freedom. 'Nothing is to me so extraordinary as persons in this country persisting to look on the North as the friend of the negro,' he remarked. 'Why, it is perfectly notorious that these wretched people, when in the North, are treated like vermin and shunned like leprosy.' All of which brought him to the recommendation that Britain in association with France — a pairing which would discourage any thought in the North of retaliation — offer to mediate the conflict. This action would encourage the many thousands in the Union who sought peace to speak up, having long been silenced by 'violence' and 'the intoxication of success'. Should their offer of mediation be refused then the two European nations ought to extend recognition to the Confederacy, for 'when the interposition of Europe is announced, the war bubble in America will burst'.[26]

Government spokesmen astutely deflected the thrust of the debate, persuading Members that this was not the moment to meddle in the American war. All Britain had to do was wait a little longer, Russell announced in the Lords. 'I trust that within three months — perhaps even sooner — we may see the close of this unfortunate civil war in America.' The decision not to divide the House on the American question bitterly disappointed Mason, but his British friends continued to grasp every opportunity to evoke sympathy for the South and excite enmity towards the North. The news that the Union had captured the important city of New Orleans provided a welcome fillip for its beleagured supporters in Britain. However, within a few weeks this propaganda advantage had been lost. Reports reached London early in June of an astonishing order issued by the commander of the occupying Federal troops. 'As the officers and soldiers of the United States have been subject to repeated insults from women (calling themselves ladies) of New Orleans in return for the most scrupulous non-interference and courtesy on our part, it is ordered that hereafter when any female shall, by word, gesture or movement, insult or show contempt for any officer or soldier of the United States, she shall be regarded and held liable to be treated as a woman of the town plying her avocation.' The order could not have been more successfully composed had its intent been to provoke Victorian Britain. Here were men who sought 'to protect themselves from the tongues of a handful of women by official and authoritative threats of rape', the *Saturday Review* savagely observed.

Gregory was quick to seize upon this sensational development, denouncing the order in the Commons as a 'proclamation repugnant to decency, civilization and humanity' and warning that even if the most generous construction was placed upon its wording ladies would find themselves 'locked up in the calaboose with drunken negroes and all the rascality of New Orleans'. And disdaining to address himself to Layard, he demanded to know whether the Prime Minister intended to 'protest against this, the greatest outrage which had been perpetrated against decency in the age in which we lived'. Although he succeeded in drawing from Palmerston an intemperate denunciation of the order — 'Sir, an Englishman must blush to think that such an act has been committed by one belonging to the Anglo-Saxon race' — and the following month was on his feet again to raise yet another delicate topic, that of American seizures of British vessels for violating the blockade, and what amounted to a virtual American blockade of the British port of Nassau, Gregory was beginning to lose faith in the ability of the Confederacy's supporters to force the government's hand.[26]

When in July 1862 the South's parliamentary friends, after some confusion and indecision, resolved to introduce a motion calling for recognition of the Confederacy, they again looked for leadership to the 'early, constant, and ardent advocate' of the Southern cause. But the Irishman declined the honour. The time had come to show the world that there were other staunch adherents of that cause in the Commons, he lamely explained. He also questioned the wisdom of reviving the issue of recognition at this moment. If the motion passed what would it accomplish, he asked, and then answered 'Simply Nothing.' Recognition 'would not add one rifle or one pound of gunpowder to the Southern resources.' If the motion failed, however, the vote would be widely interpreted as a triumph for the Union. Confederate interests aside, Gregory was growing concerned that the Tories intended to take up the American question as a stick with which to beat the government. Mason had been rubbing shoulders with several of the Opposition's luminaries of late, and Gregory, who believed that his support of the Derby Government in 1859 had cost him promotion, had no wish suddenly to find himself at the head of a partisan assault on the Palmerston ministry.

Although he refused to take the leading role Gregory did promise to attend the debate and it was as well for the Southern cause that he was as good as his word. The motion was introduced on 18 July 1862 by the shipping magnate William Schaw Lindsay, but he quickly bored the House and lost much of his audience. It was at this point that Gregory stepped in. He chided Russell for his remarks in March that ninety days would see the war settled and recommended to the Foreign Secretary Palmerston's aphorism 'that for a statesman, if he must prophesy, the best thing is to prophesy after and not before'. He then restated the case for recognition, still founding it on humanity and enlightened national self-interest, and made much of the fact that Britain would be acting in a manner fully consistent with her historic support of peoples asserting their independence. It was a 'strong and well argued' performance which impressed the Prime Minister and prompted at least one influential Tory to bemoan his Party's want of men of the 'Gregory stamp,' men with 'pluck and talent, without the wretched provincialism of our fellows'. But Palmerston deftly turned aside the challenge to his policy and the House left the government 'free to determine what to do, and when, and how to act if any step towards the restoration of peace in America shall appear likely to be attended with success'.[27]

Gregory remained a supporter of the doomed Confederate cause throughout the civil war, if an increasingly silent one. In September he initiated two thoughtful schemes to aid the South. Ever conscious of the moral obstacle to sympathetic British action, he quietly enquired of the Confederate mission whether a means might not be devised 'whereby the intelligent and industrious negro may be able to elevate and educate himself, and, eventually, if he has the good fortune to accumulate money, be able to purchase his freedom'. Unbeknown to Gregory, President Lincoln was at that very moment preparing to issue his preliminary Emancipation Proclamation. However, that document initially proved to be no more popular in Britain than it did in much of the Union and *Punch* reflected a widely held opinion when it depicted a desperate President playing his last card — the Ace of Spades. Had the South embarked even at this stage upon a more conservative course, one which promised to be less disruptive both economically and socially, then the hand of her British allies would have been strengthened. But Gregory's proposal was too radical for the Confederate Commissioners, who were content to list the 'insuperable obstacles in the way of the consummation of such a measure.' An intelligent and industrious slave rarely wants his freedom because he recognizes that his condition is superior to that of the poor white labourer, Mann insisted. 'The tendency of the civilized negro, when thrown upon his own resources, is decidedly in the direction of retrogradation. This seems to be the law of his race.' Beyond these arguments of racial inferiority there lay that of constitutional impediment. The 'Central government can exercise no authority what-ever over the slaves in any of the States,' he went on. 'All regulations relating to the improvement of their condition, or otherwise, must proceed from the State in which the slaves live.' Not until the war was irretrievably lost did the Confederacy resolve to emancipate voluntarily a limited number of slaves if they would fight for its independence.[28]

Mid-September 1862 also saw Gregory lead a group of fellow

Southern sympathizers in a discreet effort to bring 'very strong pressure' to bear upon the government. The latest reports from the United States were of Confederate military victories and there was talk of the imminent fall of Washington and Baltimore. If those cities were lost would the North be able to hold on to Philadelphia and New York? So Gregory wrote to his friend Evelyn Ashley, Palmerston's private secretary, and requested that he forward a letter to the Prime Minister. This partisan of the South attempted to convince Palmerston that Britain's continuing refusal to recognize the Confederacy constituted a 'positive act of favouritism' towards the Union, and that the granting of recognition, together with the recent Federal reverses in the field, would finally embolden those timid Northerners anxious for the war to be concluded on any terms to speak up. Palmerston needed little persuading, for he, Russell and Gladstone, a formidable triumvirate within the Cabinet, had concluded that some form of Anglo-French intervention to halt the conflict was desirable. However, by the time the issue came before the full Cabinet in October there were indications that the tide of battle might have turned against the South. This possibility had already cooled the Prime Minister's enthusiasm for action, even before the stout resistance of several ministers to any meddling in the war settled the matter. The question of intervention was shelved, at least until the spring.[29]

Following his unsuccessful twin efforts on behalf of the Confederacy in September Gregory played little part in the subsequent activities of its British friends. He continued to follow events in America. The autumn of 1863 was to see him greet thankfully news of Confederate military successes. 'It has greatly raised my spirits, for I was really trembling for their fate when we left England,' he admitted to his mother. He did serve on the committee which was struck to raise by public subscription the funds required to finance the building in Britain and erection in Richmond, Virginia, of a statue of the fallen Confederate hero Thomas 'Stonewall' Jackson. He did join the Southern Independence Association, an ambitious project to marshal public opinion and exert popular pressure on the government, but he did not play a prominent role in its affairs. In fact, he had long since abdicated his leadership of the Confederate lobby in Parliament.

The autumn of 1862 had taken Gregory to the Swiss resort town of Baden and its hot sulphur baths, and the winter found him comfortably established in Nice and in filial attendance on his mother, who was unwell. From there he declined to answer a summons to return to London early in the New Year to prepare for a fresh parliamentary campaign by the South's friends. Moreover, when he did at last reach the capital in February 1863, he not only refused to lead but even to participate in another debate on the American war. Evidence of disaffection in the North, and reports of further Union disasters in the field, news which others greeted as an opportunity to revive the issue or recognition he interpreted as reasons to remain silent. Now that the

South was 'perfectly secure', he explained to puzzled friends, it was
foolish to risk reuniting the North beneath a banner of resistance to
British insolence and meddling. Nor was he convinced that a motion
would pass. 'Although 90 out of 100 of our Members of both Houses are
hearty well wishers to the South,' he informed William Porcher Miles,
'there is a universal feeling on both sides, Whig and Tory, not to
interfere.' Then again, recognition without interference would be an
'empty compliment'. Finally, Gregory acknowledged the success that
John Bright and other Radical admirers of the United States had enjoyed
during the winter months organizing popular demonstrations of
support for the Union as the instrument of emancipation. For the
government now to take part with the South 'would expose it to great
risks and loss of support in large towns.'[30]

There was an unspoken motive for Gregory's reticence — ambition.
He still hoped for promotion and it was obvious that additional changes
to the ministry could not be long delayed. From the Prime Minister
down it was one of old men, and Gregory's Peelite friend the Duke of
Newcastle, the Colonial Secretary, was a victim of chronic ill-health.
Ironically, Sir George Cornewall Lewis, one of the Cabinet's youngest
figures was the first to pass away. Confident that Henry Layard would
be promoted in one of the enforced ministerial shuffles, perhaps still
hopeful of replacing him at the Foreign Office, Gregory had good cause
to separate himself from the American question. So far it had served him
well. The American Minister to the Court of St. James's, Charles Francis
Adams, privately conceded that the Confederate cause 'had its best
advocate at first, in Mr. Gregory', and that it lost ground 'in each
successive transfer'.[31] However, with the Tories showing signs of
making American policy a partisan issue it was time for Gregory to sever
his intimate association with that cause. He did intervene briefly during
the debate of another recognition motion in July 1863, but merely to urge
that the discussion be terminated. Moreover, he had sensed rather more
quickly than other Southern sympathizers the declining political interest
in the American war. After two years of fighting, one disconsolate
Confederate agent reported to his government from Britain, the conflict
had 'worn off its startling effects'. Instead, British attention was drawn
to Europe by a succession of crises — the revolution in Greece; the
mounting tension between Denmark and the German States over
Schleswig and Holstein; and the Polish rebellion.

For a philhelline the attractions of the Greek problem were natural
but in Gregory's case they were also political. Here was an opportunity
to demonstrate the breadth of his interest in foreign affairs. 'It is not
merely the sentimental feeling, which of course must more or less
influence a man to whom Homer and Aeschylus, Thucydides and
Aristophanes are the daily friends and companions, that makes me so
deeply interested in the fortunes of Greece,' he informed one Greek,
'but it is the conviction that by the progress and strength of Greece
there will be progress and enlightenment and encouragement spread

throughout the Christian dependencies of Turkey, and thereby will eventually come the real and right and just solution of what is called the Eastern Question, that terrible question that stares us daily in the face and threatens Europe with conflagration.'[32]

Gregory shed no tears for the unpopular monarch the Greeks deposed in October 1862. His first thought had been to run down to Athens from Nice in order to make himself 'thoroughly acquainted' with Greek politics, but on reflection he decided against the journey. However, he showed no timidity on the Eastern Question in the House. The search by the Great Powers for a successor to the Greek throne proved to be appropriately byzantine. To hold the Greeks steady in their support of a monarchical state, as the quest dragged on, the British Government was willing to put up the Ionian Islands. They were of little strategic significance and their occupation had been less of an asset than a liability. For their part the islanders had profited from the association to the extent that they enjoyed good roads, cricket and a form of ginger beer. The cause of *Enosis* was one Gregory passionately espoused in the Commons — he subsequently supported the union of Crete with Greece — as part of a larger strategy of creating a Greater Greece in the Balkans. Here was a more sensible and proper policy for Britain, he argued, more sensible and proper than her traditional one of sustaining the decrepit and brutal Turkish Empire as a bulwark against Russian expansionism. Similarly, he called for British assistance to Serbia rather than to Turkey, and 'wished to see the Turkish Government warned that every massacre of Christians which it was too weak to prevent or too fanatical not to connive at, would be punished by the loss of territory'. 'This gentleman spoke ably it seems to me on his brief', the British Ambassador to the Porte conceded, though he resented not only Gregory's attacks upon the policy with which he was identified but also the failure of any minister other than Gladstone to speak up on his behalf. And the Chancellor's remarks scarcely constituted a stout defence. Ironically, had Gregory's recommendation been adopted it would have saved a later Tory government from serious embarrassment at the hands of Gladstone. The massacre of Bulgarian Christians in 1876 was to provide him with a powerful and emotional weapon against a Disraeli ministry which, still wedded to the Turkish bulwark policy, sought to minimize the horrors.[33]

Much praised in Greece for his 'devoted and enlightened zeal in behalf of this classic land', (and later to be decorated by the Serbians) Gregory did not flatter himself that much had been changed as a result of his activities. By selecting a monarch acceptable to Britain the Greeks did indeed secure the Ionian Islands, but the Irishman lamented that the arrangement had not been accomplished with the 'kindly feelings' he had forseen. Nor had he been any more successful in his efforts to persuade the government to adopt a new Eastern policy, one which would no longer see Britain sacrifice the hopes, progress and civilization of Greeks and Slavs 'merely to prop up the worn out dynasty of an incorrigible race of barbarians'.[34] Finally, for all of the prominence he had won with his advocacy of the Confederate cause and of the interests of the Greeks and Slavs, he continued to be overlooked when appointments were made to the government. 1865, which saw the Confederacy surrender, found Gregory approaching the age of fifty and still languishing on the back benches. His ambition to win office remained unfulfilled.

7
Constructive Unionist

Impatient for advancement, the restless Gregory had been constantly reassured by well-meaning friends that he was destined to be a leading figure in the Whig-Liberal party. The old stagers could not go on for ever and in the Commons he had won a measure of recognition already. He served as an Irish representative on the Committee of Selection, which arranged the groups of Private Members' bills and selected Members to serve on private committees. He sat on the Committee of Standing Orders, 'a most confidential and important committee', which disposed of all cases of petition for the relaxation of those orders. He was appointed to the Chairman's Panel, whose members investigated petitions for the overturning of election results. However, what Gregory continued to thirst for was the recognition of office and a place on the Treasury Bench and he was reduced to pressing his mother into service as he sought to slake it. Bess Gregory called upon an old friendship with the Earl of Clarendon, a former Irish Viceroy and Foreign Secretary who continued to move on the periphery of the Cabinet, to protest her son's long exclusion from office.[1]

Clarendon admitted that 'there are few men of his age so clever and rarely as well informed or whose society (to me at least) is so agreeable', but pointed to 'the manner and extent' of Gregory's 'foolish pursuit' of the Turf as one reason for his being shut out 'at first from the offical careeer that his talents would naturally have opened to him'. More recently, his behaviour had given rise to the suspicion that he was an unreliable friend of the government. Then again, the excuse Gregory had given Palmerston in 1861 for declining an office he considered unworthy of his talents and experience now proved double-edged. The difficulty of his securing re-election in Galway had discouraged thoughts of advancing her son, Clarendon replied to Bess Gregory in the spring of 1865. The cruel irony of this explanation was underscored by William Gregory's unopposed return for the county in the general election later that year.[2]

Palmerston's electoral triumph in July, for he was assured of a handsome majority in the new Parliament, was followed within three months by his death. The new ministry, with Russell at its head and Gladstone leading the Commons, soon gave every sign of responding to the pressure for the franchise reform Palmerston had effectively resisted. But sitting behind the front bench were several opponents of

159

long standing to any movement towards democracy, among them William Gregory. Thus the Prime Minister, seeking to minimise dissent within his own ranks, took advantage of a rearrangement of minor officeholders in December to invite the Irishman to join the Government. 'I should be very glad to have the benefit of your talents and power of speaking in the office,' Russell wrote flatteringly, 'and I have no doubt the public service would gain by such an arrangement.' The fact that the office was an insignificant one, being that held by a civilian in the Board of Admiralty, and that he did not much care for the 'soldiering and sailing department', does not entirely explain Gregory's decision to refuse it with the novel excuse that his mother's poor health would prevent him giving due attention to his duties. The Prime Minister's Ecclesiastical Titles Bill had neither been forgotten nor forgiven by Irish Catholics. Furthermore, news of the offer had excited the unflattering speculation that Russell either had 'great faith in the power of place to alter men's convictions' or that the coming reform bill would be 'one of a very moderate kind'. Besides, the subordinate nature of the proffered position suggested that the Prime Minister would not enter into discussions with Gregory on such important questions as that of reform. Anyway, 'Johnny's antecedents' did not encourage confidence in any assurances of moderation he might have been willing to provide. Gregory surely agreed with the friend who remarked that 'He could not have accepted with credit to himself. After all that has passed he would have lost himself had he accepted office from L[or]d Russell.' How could he now vote for a measure he had already so 'strongly condemned?' So he took his place among those traditional supporters of the government who broke with it on this issue and were to be ridiculed by John Bright as dwellers in the Cave of Adullam, the haunt of 'everyone that was in distress and everyone that was discontented'.[3]

Gregory spoke for many of his fellow Adullamites when he declared: 'I am looking for something which partakes of the quality of permanence, something large and liberal and yet thoroughly safe, something that will touch a stronger and higher chord throughout the country ... than this unseemly apologetic *ad misericordiam* plea of — "We must do something —." ' Of course, his definition of safe excluded even an inching towards universal suffrage. This aversion to democracy dated from his first election campaign in 1842, when he had contemptuously dismissed the demands of the Chartists. However, the journey to the United States and his experience of Irish politics had converted distaste to dread. The nature of his opposition to parliamentary reform had been clearly developed in 1860, when he attacked the Representation of the People Bill which Lord John Russell (as he then was) had introduced with the undisguisedly lukewarm endorsement of Palmerston. The stance Gregory then adopted he held for the length of his political life, and years later he fondly recalled the 'immense applause' his remarks drew from both sides of the House.

In 1860 he had found himself in the happy position of capturing the mood of the great majority of his listeners.

He criticised the proposal to extend the franchise through the establishment of a £6 householder qualification as a dangerous interim measure. Once it had been lowered to that level there would be no firm ground on which to prevent its reduction to universal suffrage. Both this immediate proposal and its likely result he deplored as enfranchising 'the lowest class of voters', those 'most deficient in education, and the most exposed to corruption and pernicious influences'. And he was horrified by the social and political implications of this prospect, which to his mind threatened to be little short of revolutionary. The effect would be, he warned, to 'transfer the direction of public affairs from the employer to the operative, from the master to the workman, from wealth, intelligence and education to mere numbers. . . .' For the conclusive proof of democracy's dreadful consequences he had only to turn to the United States, and to a lesser extent the Australian colonies — the best men fleeing or driven from public life; unbridled corruption and pervasive venality in every department of the country, the fountain of public justice polluted at its source; the tyranny of the majority. Yet he was careful to deny that he was opposed to all representation of working men in Parliament, and conceded that 'it would be infinitely better for them and for us that they should have their own advocates, and that their own questions should be argued by themselves in this House instead of out of doors'. But he foresaw token representation at best, certainly not the enfranchisement of working men as a class which would place them in a position to disturb 'the equipoise of intelligence and property'.

Nor did Gregory see extension of the franchise as a solution to the electoral troubles of Ireland, where intimidation and corruption were notoriously prevalent. To enlarge the electorate would merely compound the problems, he insisted. His posture may well have reflected an underlying conviction, which for obvious reasons it would have been imprudent to avow, that the ordinary Irish 'were a fine race when under control, but unfit to be their own masters'. It would have been surprising had Gregory remained entirely immune to the doctrines of Ango-Saxonism and Celtic inferiority, although disparaging Irish references to the 'Saxon' indicated that racialism was not the exclusive possession of the English or the Anglo-Irish. He consistently fought that remedial measure — the secret ballot. Once again he dwelt upon the experience of the United States, where the secret ballot had not eradicated corruption. And standing the corruption argument on its head, he purported to believe that instances of intimidation and venality would be exposed and punished only so long as votes were cast publicly. If the ballot was secret then the 'money bag, without detection, would be a new power before which every thing would go down, landlord, priest and public opinion'. Finally, and with more ingenuity than consistency, William Gregory predicted that this particular political reform would precipitate a social disaster. Admitting and deploring the conduct of those landlords who drove their tenants to the polls, he questioned whether they would keep so many tenants on their lands if they had no means of controlling their votes. 'We know that many a tenant is now retained upon estates to swell the landlords' parliamentary influence,' he observed, 'but if the landlord sees that the very men he is keeping up, encouraging and assisting in time of need, if he sees that they are antagonistic to his views, that they are the very persons instrumental in returning to Parliament men diametrically opposed to his opinions, rely upon it that there will be a clearing of estates of which the famine of 1848 will be the parallel.' Men would be replaced by cattle, for it was only the concern to maintain his political interest which had dissuaded many a landlord from transforming his estate into a profitable graziery.[4]

The withdrawal of Russell's bill, in June 1860, had been followed within a year by another cheering development for the opponents of reform. Radicals, such as John Bright, had long lauded the United States as an inspiring example of what might be achieved through a policy of 'peace, retrenchment and reform'. Consequently, their domestic opponents gleefully grasped the American Civil War as a stick with which to beat such 'unthinking and unprincipled demagogues'. The Union's collapse afforded further proof, conservatives charged, that the 'widest enjoyment of the electoral franchise' was more akin to 'tyranny than true liberty'. However, by the end of 1864, that stick was in the other hand. Now, the inexorable advance of the Union armies and the re-election of President Lincoln were acclaimed by sympathizers of the North and reformers — often one and the same — as the victory of democracy over aristocracy. Abraham Lincoln was held up to the British working men as one of their own class. Here was a man who had raised himself, 'by his force of character and unaided efforts, from the position of day labourer to the chief magistrate of the great American Republic'. This triumph was a tribute not merely to his native abilities but to a political system founded upon the 'legitimate and uncontrolled suffrage of the people' which made such careers possible. But this was only one of the American lessons as taught by the National Reform League created to agitate for a broader franchise and redistribution of seats. Another was that recited by William Gladstone, who stunned the House and his colleagues on the Treasury bench with the declaration, uttered during debate of a bill to lower the borough franchise, that every man who was not 'incapacitated by personal unfitness, or whose admission would not be attended by political danger', was 'morally entitled to come within the pale of the constitution'. The working men had shown in Lancashire throughout the long cotton famine that they could safely be entrusted with the vote. They had demonstrated 'self-command, self-control, respect for order, patience under suffering, confidence in the law, regard for superiors'.[5]

The fillip given to the reform cause by the approaching vindication of the Union was a development doubly repugnant to William Gregory, the Confederacy's first parliamentary champion. Speaking in the borough franchise debate, Gregory had repeated all of his earlier objections to a sharp increase in the size of the electorate. He identified himself with those 'Palmerstonian Conservatives' who were 'quite prepared to move on with the times, but not prepared without rhyme or reason to run violently down steep places and be choked in the sea of democracy and universal suffrage'. He struggled to define liberalism in such a way as to exclude reform at this time. All liberals were agreed on certain matters and objects, such as 'Liberty [to write and to speak], peace, enlightened views with regard to commerce and the distribution of taxation, and the purity of elections'. And the outcome of the American Civil War notwithstanding, he pointed to the violation of these liberal principles in the democratic Republic — free opinion stifled, four years of internecine warfare, a prohibitive tariff, and electoral corruption.

Early in 1866 James Clay, a Radical, introduced a bill which provided for an extension of the borough franchise to those men who were able to pass an education test — 'writing from dictation . . ., simple addition, subtraction, multiplication and division of money'. The fact that the Adullamites rallied to this proposal almost to a man has generally been attributed to little more than a desire to embarrass the government and obstruct the measure which it intended to bring forward. But William Gregory's act in putting his name on the back of Clay's bill was not one of simple mischievousness or insincerity. The two men were close friends — Clay being one of those fortunate regular recipients of Coole woodcocks which were as 'large as turkeys' — and Gregory was eventually to marry into the same family. Further, his co-sponsoring of this proposed reform was fully consistent with his oft expressed support of the principle of limited working class representation. The existing franchise provided for the property qualification, he observed, 'and the bill of my hon. Friend provides for the question of education and intelligence.' Equally, it raised no immediate prospect of universal suffrage and if that was the ultimate result the inherent dangers would have long passed, or so Gregory reasoned. The 'educated and reflecting body' who won the right to vote under these provisions would have been 'long in training in a course of political education'. 'If we are to be smothered or to be swamped,' he added, 'I had much rather be drowned in a butt of malmsey than in a barrel of swipes.'[7]

Small beer was an accurate enough description of the bill Gladstone introduced on behalf of the government in March. It sought to lower the householder qualification to £14 in the counties and £7 in the boroughs, thereby enlarging the electorate by some 400,000 voters of whom approximately half were likely to be working men. In all, less than one quarter of the adult male population of England and Wales would have been enfranchised. Although the measure was a far cry from universal suffrage the Adullamites reacted furiously to its introduction. Here was proof, they fumed, that the government had fallen under the influence of Bright and the Radicals and that Gladstone was their 'willing, impulsive, and unreasoning instrument', for once electoral power had been conceded to mere numbers there could be no halting of the flight to democracy. In the Cave's darker recesses Gladstone was accused of having taken as his motto: 'the more the merrier', while Bright was viewed as striding purposefully towards his 'long sought object' of radicalizing the Liberal party. Alarmists predicted that the working class would constitute a majority of the electorate in forty per cent of the boroughs, involving 133 parliamentary seats. Nor did the release of the statistics compiled by the Poor Law Board, from which it was possible to argue that one quarter of borough voters were already working men, weaken either the Adullamites' arguments or opposition. They poured scorn on the bill as another interim measure devoid of principle, one which would lower the franchise down to the mass of the adult male population instead of requiring the lower classes of men to bring themselves up to it. [8]

Gregory had attended the strategy sessions of the Cave since the beginning of the year. The Adullamites met or dined together, most frequently at Lord Elcho's house in St. James's Place, and persistently lobbied fellow Members. Gregory had a prominent role in these activities. He supported with voice and vote Lord Grosvenor's proposed amendment to the Reform Bill, calling on the government to bring forward the companion piece of such a significant broadening of the franchise — a redistribution bill. The Adullamites, no less than the government, realized that any redistribution scheme was likely to cost the ministry the votes of those suppoters who discovered that their seats were in jeopardy. Yet Gregory was never an Adullamite pure and simple, root and branch. He drifted in and out of the Cave during this hectic spring, and his meandering course was a response less to indecision than to the dictates of principle, personality and political calculation. He scorned association with the shabbier parliamentary tactics of the anti-reformers and their Tory allies. Thus he voted with the government and against the ploy to attach to the bill clauses which were designed to prevent bribery and corruption, for notice had already been given of a private Member's bill on this sensitive subject. Of course, by successfully adding these provisions to the bill the Adullamite-Tory coalition made it anathema to some indignant and uneasy Members. Gregory also sided with the government in resisting the move to substitute a ratal for the rental qualification in the counties. Nevertheless, when Dunkellin moved that the ratal test be extended to the boroughs he supported the amendment and thereby helped to bring down the government. [9]

Gregory had been subjected to strong countervailing pressures throughout the extended crisis over the Reform Bill. Frank Lawley had returned to Britain and was now a member of the staff of that 'growing power' the *Daily Telegraph*. He cautioned his Irish friend that the

Adullamites would receive rough handling in the Liberal press as disappointed office seekers; as puppets of Robert Lowe, that most acerbic and powerful spokesman of the anti-reformers, who was suspected of being motivated by a desire to strengthen his position within the Liberal party at the expense of Gladstone; and as dupes of the Tories. It was well known in the Clubs, Lawley reported, that Grosvenor's amendment had been written out in Disraeli's hand. Yet those who looked to the future saw that England would remain Liberal so long as Gladstone lived, thus if Gregory remained within the Cave he would blight his career. The same cautionary notes were sounded by Henry Brand, the Chief Whip. He privately warned Gregory of Disraeli's cunning, encouraged him to accept the offer of another minor office, and protested that it would be possible to effect moderate reform 'without putting in peril the integrity of the Government and of the Liberal Party'. Also, Gregory was left in no doubt as to the attitude of his clerical supporters in County Galway. Bishop McEvilly wrote to report that the county had been swept by a rumour, put about by Tories and bigots, that he intended to vote 'with the rabid Tory faction against the present Government'. Although Russell as the author of the Ecclesiastical Titles Bill remained anathema to Roman Catholics, the Bishop had detected in Gladstone and other leading members of the Cabinet an anxiety to bring about a settlement of 'the great questions.' Consequently, 'the Catholic County of Galway would strongly deprecate such a misfortune [as the fall of the government] at the present time.'[10]

Yet Gregory's ties to the Adullamite were strong. His aversion to democracy had not weakened nor his fears of the bill's consequences eased, and they prompted his foolish remark, which went the rounds of London society, that the Radical *Morning Star* was now the organ of the ministry. He was bound by friendship to Lord Elcho, who worked tirelessly to hold the anti-reformers together, and by friendship and interest to Dunkellin, who had joined him as a county Member in 1865. Clanricarde, whose political influence in Galway could never be forgotten, made no secret of sharing his son's views. But in moving the adoption of the rating principle in the boroughs Dunkellin was not merely serving as the agent of the anti-reformers. He acted from conviction, as Gregory well knew. Out of Britain for much of the damp winter, he had maintained a correspondence with his friend while seeking relief in Cannes from gout in both feet, both hands and elbows and one knee. Eventually, he stoically bore the painful remedy of blistering practised by his former regimental surgeon. In his letters to Gregory, Dunkellin had long endorsed the rating test. 'A £6 rating in towns would surely let in all the superior class of mechanics *who chose to pay it,* and whose exclusion we are told is such a blot and anomaly in the present system,' he argued. 'If they chose to live in a house under 3/6 a week, or to compound for their rates, that would be their look out.' In short, here was a 'principle' which provided a barrier to universal suffrage for it would exclude all those 'compounders' who paid their rates with their rents to their landlords. Indeed, this test would have reduced by half the number of working men the government's bill promised to enfranchise. Moreover, as the decisive vote on this appealing amendment approached, Gregory was reassured by Elcho that the Tories were not seeking to exploit the reform issue for partisan advantage. They had abandoned all idea of office and were ready to assist in forming or supporting a moderate Liberal government, he reported. [11]

The prospect of a realignment of politics and the organization of a 'moderate Liberal' ministry embracing 'Palmerston Conservatives' and liberal Tories, and led by some compromise figure, whether Clarendon, Granville or Derby's son Stanley, had long been aired. Gregory, in common with several other leading Adullamites, certainly expected in the aftermath of Russell's resignation to be invited to join a fusion ministry. The Cave proposed to the Tories that Clarendon — who had entered the Russell Cabinet as Foreign Secretary — head the government and Stanley lead in the Commons. Stories were soon circulating that Gregory (he had in April 1865 volunteered to serve under Clarendon and had in December offered him a detailed explanation of his 'temporary' reasons for declining the Admiralty post proffered by Russell) was so confident of being appointed Chief Secretary for Ireland that he had discussed with friends the measures he intended to adopt. But the hopes of the Adullamites were quickly dashed by the Tories, who were far more ambitious and calculating than Elcho and his colleagues had preferred to believe. When the Cave rejected a counter-proposal that several of its dwellers serve as junior partners in a Derby-led coalition, the Conservative leader went ahead with the formation of a Tory government. He did make one further attempt to attract Adullamites, among them Gregory. However, the secretaryship of the Admiralty was no more enticing now than it had been six months earlier when offered by Russell. Had Derby, or even Russell, extended the Chief Secretaryship Gregory might have found the temptation to grasp it too strong to resist. He had dreamed of holding this office ever since his re-election to Parliament in 1857. It was, after all, 'the highest Parliamentary appointment which an Irish commoner holds in his native country', and for William Gregory it held particular meaning. At last he would have lived up to and even exceeded the great expectations his grandfather had vested in him so long ago. This appointment would restore the name of Gregory to its former eminence in the government of Ireland and provide an historical sequel to the career of the Under Secretary. Moreover, as London gossip intimated, William Gregory did have a policy for Ireland. He believed his measures would pacify the island, preserve the Union, and finally emancipate the family name from its earlier association with the most conservative Ascendancy elements. Indeed, suspicion of his liberal sentiments with respect to Ireland went far to explain Derby's resistance to the suggestion that Gregory be made Chief Secretary. [12]

Gregory was a precursor of the constructive unionists who, somewhat later in the century, worked with a missionary zeal 'for the betterment of their country and the welfare of their fellow-Irishmen.' As a Galway Member he was naturally to be found in the vanguard of those who struggled to keep the Packet subsidy afloat. It was not an easy task, for the Company had fallen victim to poor management and was victimized by ill-luck. Yet here was an enterprise, Gregory contended, which gave the lie to the all too familiar accusation that Irish Members were forever engaging in projects of agitation instead of devoting themselves to the practical improvement of their native land. Furthermore, the Galway Packet Company enjoyed widespread popular support in Ireland, as investors and shareholders to the number of 1,750 attested. Thus with the granting of a postal subsidy by the Derby Government 'All Irishmen felt that at last they had got something more than words'. The Company had negotiated two contracts. The first, signed with the colony of Newfoundland in October 1858, provided for service between Galway, St. John's and the United States and an annual subsidy of £13,000. The second, with the Imperial Government, obligated the Company to maintain a fortnightly service between Galway and Boston/New York and in return for transporting mails and telegraphic messages it was to receive £3,000 for each round trip. The government also required that the vessels employed be of a certain minimum standard, at least in their displacement and power, and the Company promptly contracted for four at a total cost of £400,000. Over the course of the following two years ships of the Galway Line carried more than 13,000 passengers out to North America and returned with some 4,000. These travellers had all escaped the inconvenience of a transfer at Liverpool, Gregory reminded the House, and thus avoided the robbery and spoilation to which the unwary were exposed in the English port city. 'I am also able to declare,' he continued in fine Victorian style, 'that Irish girls going to America by these steamers escaped the debauchery and contamination to which they would have been exposed in emigrant ships, which I regret to say have been instrumental in stocking the streets of New York with unfortunate girls seduced, degraded and then abandoned.' But the Line's contributions to social hygiene could not mask its financial troubles. [13]

Given the arduous task confronting it, the Company had sought and obtained a delay of fourteen months in the operation of a full service. Nevertheless, the annual report for 1860 disclosed a loss of £100,000 during the first year of business. More than one quarter of this sum had been paid to John Lever for his interest in the Line, and his shady dealings had been another of its embarrassments. Nor was the Company's public image improved by the revelation that the vessels it had ordered did not meet the government's specifications. 'The Company is doing very badly and the directors who we fought so hard for have verified the opinion I always entertained and frequently expressed to you,' a choleric Dunkellin later observed to Gregory, 'of their being a pack of scuts.' Of course, there were extenuating circumstances. One of the Line's new vessels, the *Connaught*, proved to be ill-fated. Her maiden crossing of the Atlantic in June 1860 had been delayed by a mechanical failure — the bottom of her port cylinder blew out. Then, in October, during her second outward voyage, she sprang a leak while still some 150 miles east of Boston and rising water in the engine room eventually immobilized her. It was while the hapless vessel was wallowing in the swell that fire broke out. Fortunately, a distress signal was seen by an American brig and by the time she completed the transfer of passengers and crew the starboard side of the doomed *Connaught* was red hot. Indeed, the American captain was very much the hero of the hour for he courageously took his own ship alongside the sinking packet when several boat crews from the *Connaught*, having rowed to safety, refused to return to bring off more passengers.[14]

An even more crippling blow to the Company's reputation and prospects was the prolonged uncertainty over the future of the postal subsidy. The fall of the Derby Goverment in 1859 and the formation of the second Palmerston administration had brough renewed criticism of the subsidy. A committee appointed in July 1859 to examine postal contracts, did not report until the following year and the issue of the Galway contract was not settled until August 1860. Thus the Company had effectively been held in suspense for a full sixteen months, and neither its confidence nor its profitability had been strengthened by the Imperial Government's insistence that it surrender the Newfoundland subsidy but continue carrying mails to St. John's. Not surprisingly, full implementation of the contracted service had again been postponed, this time until June 1861. But in March of that year the government announced the cancellation of the postal subsidy. Infuriated by this action, which was legal but harsh, Gregory led a delegation of fellow Irish Members to protest to the Prime Minister and he may have been party to the negotiations which were held with Disraeli and looked to the unseating of the Whig-Liberal Ministry. The government survived, thanks largely to a number of Tories who absented themselves when the vote was called, either because they shunned involvement in a 'conspiracy' over the Galway contract or had no wish at this time to drive the conservative Palmerston from office. However, the Prime Minister had taken the added precaution of promising not to oppose a select committee inquiry into the cancellation of the contract, thus mollifying some of his Irish supporters. A few days later Gregory successfully moved for the appointment of such a committee, and he was named to the chair.[15]

Gregory's skilful conduct of the inquiry won him high praise, at least at home. Instead of seeking to pack the committee he 'manfully encountered the foes of our Irish Packet Station — defeated their malignant attempts to damage it; and by his sagacity and intelligence invariably elicited the testimony that told powerfully in its favour with the majority of the committee'. The leaking to the press, on the very eve of the report, of Palmerston's offer of a minor office to the Galway

Member smacked of an attempt to discredit Gregory and his findings. For as Irishmen had confidently expected, the committee urged the government to treat the Company with leniency and indulgence and recommended that the contract be renewed if it was able to provide satisfactory evidence of its ability to maintain an efficient service. The publication of the report was followed by a long struggle to convince the government to implement its recommendations. Gregory again took the lead, badgering Palmerston with questions in the Commons, drafting the memorial urging renewal of the subsidy which 86 Irish Members signed, and escorting the delegation which delivered this and a number of other petitions to the Prime Minister. At last, in February 1863, the indefatigable Gregory drew from Palmerston an assurance that if in the opinion of the Admiralty the Company's vessels were capable of fulfilling the terms of the contract the government would sanction its renewal. But the eventual renewal of the subsidy came too late to rescue the Company. The failure of its vessels to complete passages within the contract time brought heavy financial penalties, and when in February 1864, two of the packets were involved in accidents the Directors had no choice other than to ask the Post Office for a suspension of the mail contract. This request amounted to 'an ignominious finish to the Atlantic Company, and to a deplorable end to the project of the Galway Packet Station'. Shares which had once been valued at £10 were now being quoted at 11/- and in June the Directors decided to wind up the Company and the contract was finally annulled in August.[16]

The long, frustrating and ultimately unsuccessful struggle to save the Company and maintain Galway as a transatlantic station saw William Gregory increasingly give voice to a moderate if negative form of Irish nationalism — that of national resentment. Within the Commons and on public platforms in Ireland he complained of discriminatory policies which sanctioned such miserly expenditures on one side of the Irish Sea while generosity prevailed on the other. Mail contracts to the value of £900,000 had been approved for English ports, he pointed out. Huge sums 'were spent in England for various public undertakings — for arms, ships, clothing, dockyards, etc. — and that the Irish people, who were taxed for all those purposes, were entitled to some share in the benefits of the national expenditure.' The real question at issue was not the 'miserable dole' of the £72,000 annual subsidy, he informed the House, but 'whether, while English enterprise is met with favour, Irish enterprise is met with disfavour?' And accusations of discrimination were not silenced by the refusal of the Public Works Loan Commissioners to grant the £50,000 (for which Gregory had lobbied hard at the Treasury and the Board of Works) required to finance improvements to the port of Galway. It was 'scarcely proper', Gregory informed a meeting of the Royal Galway Society, that £180,000 had been spent on the harbours of England and Wales but less than one tenth that sum on those in Ireland. This sense of national indignation, even bitterness, which characterized Gregory's response and that of other

Irishmen to the rejection of the loan application and the collapse of the Packet Company, and the end of the quest to make Galway a point of departure for North America, was not unconnected to the persistent poverty of the residents of the island's west coast. Now one more hope for prosperity had been dashed and one more instrument of relief cast aside.[17]

Famine had returned to Galway in 1861. The report of the relieving officer for the region had made dismal reading that autumn — wheat: deficient in quantity and quality, the yield being only one half that of the previous year which had itself been no better than average; barley: scanty and what there was in poor condition; oats: a good crop but much of it still in the fields uncut because of the miserable weather; potatoes: a poor crop and much of it diseased; turf: still lying in heaps in the bogs, wet and unfit for use as fuel. By the spring of 1862 the situation had naturally deteriorated and relief committees were at their wits' ends, because to the suffering labourers there were now added small farmers who had no means of seeding their plots of land. In some areas, such as the islands of Boffin and Shark off the Connemara coast, the absence of regular medical inspection and adequate care compounded the tragedy. As one appeal for help revealed, the islands' residents were 'left, when sick, lying very often on a little straw, with a poor covering over them, without doctor, without medicine, to the mercy of God, to live or die'. Moreover, many among the destitute preferred to risk death rather than enter the workhouse.[18]

The obvious and pressing need was for employment which would enable the poor to see themselves and their families through this latest disaster. Thus there were angry protests against a government which on a point of honour (the *Trent* affair) had been ready to rush into war with the United States yet did not stir in a crisis where national honour was truly involved. 'Surely no civilized government will refuse to cope with a calamity which threatens to depopulate whole districts,' the normally moderate *Galway Vindicator* remarked. The Irish people remained the 'worst housed, worst fed, and worst clothed people in Europe', the *Tuam Herald* charged, and it concluded that the infamy and the disgrace 'of this state of things mainly rest with England, whose partial and one-sided legislation has ever sacrificed Irish to purely British interests'. Not that the hierarchy's organ exculpated the Irish. They shared the responsibility for Ireland's misery because they had failed to send to Parliament 'really sincere, earnest and zealous and competent representatives'. One representative excepted from this indictment was William Gregory.[19]

Gregory made modest private donations to relief funds, and by his personal interest in the plight of the residents of Boffin and Shark prompted the Clifden Poor Law Union, within whose jurisdiction the islands fell, to send the medical and relieving officers there. Nearer to home, he set a 'noble example' to fellow landlords. He cut timber on the Coole desmesne and distributed it for fuel 'amongst the poor of the locality', where there was general acknowledgment that Gregory's 'private benevolence and philanthropy are only limited by his means.' One year later thankful tenants and their families marched to Coole to offer tangible proof of their appreciation — they dug up and stored the entire crop of potatoes. 'May such reciprocity of good feeling between the peasantry and the proprietary of this country become more common,' the *Vindicator* rhapsodised. [20]

Nor was Gregory loath, at least in one celebrated instance, to condemn a fellow landlord who failed his tenantry. It was during this period of acute distress in western Ireland that he launched his long campaign against the Law Life Assurance Company. Law Life was one of those new capitalist landowners of the post-Famine era, having foreclosed on the vast and heavily encumbered Martin estate in Connemara. Its more businesslike approach towards landownership was all too soon in evidence. The traditional rights of small farmers, such as those of pasture on mountain lands and free turbary, were either withdrawn or a charge imposed. Even the seaweed collected from the seashore and sold as manure now had to be paid for. As a result, the Company was able to sell off one third of its property yet earn from the remainder more income than the Martins had derived from the entire estate. With the return of severe distress in 1862 Gregory privately approached Law Life's land agent seeking action, for it continued to be the largest landowner in the hard hit Clifden Union. Money spent on road works that opened up this remote area would be well invested, he wrote to Henry Robinson. Although he recognized the 'military' significance of better communications, Robinson was not an enthusiast of public works but he assured the anxious Member of Parliament that he was willing to sell both fuel and seed potatoes to the Company's tenants at reduced prices. Of course, such magnanimity was wasted on those who did not have the cash to make purchases. He did provide some work, building fences and embankments, but the task work was so demanding that the daily wage averaged out at less than fourpence, and this at a time when other landlords were paying tenpence a day. Manifestly, the Company had failed in its duty 'to set an example of judicious liberality and enlightened philanthropy to the other property owners of the district'. Wearying of discretion, Gregory decided in the spring of 1864 to embarrass Law Life into the fulfilment of its responsibilities. After all, one of its directors was the Home Secretary in the Palmerston Government. At Gregory's request the Commons ordered that a Poor Law Inspector's report which detailed the niggardly conduct of the agent and his masters in London be produced and printed. Then he moved for and obtained a report on the ejectment cases Law Life had prosecuted since coming into possession of the estate in 1852. The total exceeded 3,000. Consequently, when another Irish Member launched an assault on the Company in May 1864, Gregory was ready with the evidence of its 'unpleasant behaviour'. [21]

Yet it was to the government rather than to individual landlords that

Gregory's correspondents, many of them local priests, principally looked for assistance. When Chief Secretary Peel, citing workhouse statistics, insisted that conditions in western Ireland were far from serious, Gregory explained to the House that such figures were misleading because many of those in dire need held land and were therefore ineligible for this form of relief. Contradicting Peel, he assured the House that there was a 'very great amount of destitution and distress' in Galway. And what were the sufferers requesting? Nothing more than a 'fair day's wages for a fair day's work till the next harvest came in'. Assistance in this form would be far more productive and far less dangerous than the extension to Ireland of traditional outdoor relief, he added, for that 'would result in the paralysis of every honest exertion, and reduce the peasantry of the country to the level of a shameless habitual mendicancy'. The government's ignoring of these pleas but its introduction of a bill to relieve the distress of the textile operatives in Lancashire, victims of the cotton famine popularly attributed to the American Civil War, nourished Irish bitterness. Here was one more example of English discrimination against Ireland. 'When will our representatives realize to themselves the fact that, cruel justice, heartless indifference, cold blooded apathy, are the distinguishing features of British policy towards Ireland,' the Galway press asked? In fact, several Irish Members gave voice to their anger at the exclusive attention focused on Lancashire's distress, and Gregory was again in their van. In June 1863 he reminded the House of the sad conditions in western Ireland and warned his listeners that people were being driven to emigrate and that they carried abroad with them an enmity for Britain 'which not only rankles in their own breasts, but which they bequeathed to their children'. Nor did he fail to contrast the treatment of Ireland with that of Lancashire. 'What was given to Ireland was, in the first place, given grudgingly,' he observed reproachfully, 'and, in the second place, it was given, as far as possible, in a manner to prove nugatory.'[22]

Gregory's alarm at the number of embittered Irishmen departing their native land, and the great majority of those who quit the British Isles still made for the American republic, was well-founded. The formation of the Fenian Brotherhood in the United States in 1856, and of an Irish counterpart, the Irish Revolutionary Brotherhood, two years later, had inaugurated a republican conspiracy against British rule which for all its elements of burlesque eventually managed to embarrass governments on both sides of the Atlantic and throw much of the island and areas of England into panic. Not that the Fenians ever ought to have taken the British authorities by surprise, for there was never any shortage of informants. But during the tense Anglo-American relationship immediately following the Civil War, as Irish-American veterans of that conflict disembarked in Ireland, the British Government responded nervously to reports that insurrection was in the offing. In September 1865 the Dublin police raided the offices of the nationalist newspaper, the *Irish People*. By a rigorous enforcement of the police powers, and the suppression of the Fenian organ, the Irish administration had hoped to induce Irish-Americans, easily identified by their square-toed boots, and generally accepted as the trunk if not the root of the conspiracy, to return home. Instead, they merely became more cautious. Another setback for the Castle was the escape from prison of James Stephens, the leader of the Irish Revolutionary Brotherhood, less than two weeks after his capture. Under pressure exerted by worried members of the Ascendancy, and determined to lay hands on the arriving American Fenians, the government rushed the suspension of habeas corpus through Parliament in mid-February.[23]

Although North America appeared to be the focus of Fenian activities in 1866, the end of the year found the British Government anxiously preparing for insurrection in Ireland. There were reports that Stephens was on his way back to Ireland from the United States, where he had gone in an effort to make peace among warring Fenian factions and in order to secure more assistance for action in Ireland. Informants reported that he had 20,000 men available for service around Dublin, that the Fenians had already examined the forts and magazines located near the city and were equipped with the scaling gear needed for attacks upon them. There was talk of an elaborate strategy which involved the use of Greek fire to distract the authorities, the cutting of the telegraph wires and then a call for the people to rise. The semblance of a 'civil war' would permit the American Congress, where indignation over Britain's conduct during the war to save the Union was still high, to recognize the Fenians as belligerents. Far-fetched as much of the information was, there were signs of mounting concern in both Dublin and London. More troops were ordered to Ireland, bringing the total to 22,500, exclusive of police, and men-of-war and gunboats were despatched to watch the coasts and all ports. Even the collapse in February 1867, of a scheme to raid Chester Castle and seize its store of arms, and the failure of several sadly mismanaged uprisings in Ireland, only relieved the tension temporarily. Soon, there was disconcerting evidence of sympathy for the imprisoned Fenians 'among a comparatively respectable class of the south Irish population'. 'Provisions and little luxuries are being constantly supplied to prisoners by tradesmen and persons in that rank of life,' the Irish administration noted. No less disturbing, the 'feeling among the Irish peasantry' seemed to be 'growing worse and worse'. In the words of one Cabinet member, 'the language now openly held is, that neither the church nor the land grievances are what they complain of, they want independence, and nothing else'. Moreover, with the continuing suspension of habeas corpus in Ireland, there was prompt recognition within the government of the danger that the Fenians would carry their struggle to the mainland.

Steps were taken at Liverpool and London to guard the docks from possible incendiary attacks. There were also reports and rumours of plots to blow up the Houses of Parliament, to kidnap the Prince of Wales, to set fire to houses and theatres in London, to assassinate the leading figures in the goverment, and to murder the Queen. Nor was the task of protecting the monarch facilitated by her refusal to allow any-one to accompany her during her drives around Windsor in the company of her ubiquitous gillie, John Brown. Two armed members of her suite were obliged to travel a discreet distance behind the couple. The successful liberation of a leading American Fenian while he was being transported across Manchester in a police van in September, and the tragically bungled and bloody effort to free another from Clerken-well prison in London in mid-December, gave credence to the wildest rumours and reports of hair-raising plots. The Queen was sufficiently alarmed to propose that habeas corpus be suspended in England, and while the Cabinet was not prepared to go that far, and some of Disraeli's colleagues suspected that he saw the Fenian schemes less as a serious problem than as a means of diverting attention in the House during the coming session, there was a 'prevailing anxiety to do something that should look energetic'. With this thought in mind, the government announced that the Metropolitan Police would be strengthened and the numbers of detectives increased. However, no less obvious and pressing was the need for remedial measure in Ireland. [24]

From the security of Italy Dunkellin advocated summary punishment of Fenians. 'It would have a good effect if the Police were to shoot a few of the blackguards that are illegally assembled and armed,' he wrote to his close friend and fellow Member for Galway. [25] No doubt Clanricarde's heir was representative of much Ascendancy opinion, but William Gregory elaborated a far more thoughtful response to this new manifestation of Irish disaffection. Indeed, his reaction reflected his own growing sense of national resentment of English discrimination against Ireland; his awareness of what Fenianism signified; and his complex relationship with the Roman Catholic clergy in his locality.

Initially, Gregory's dealings with the hierarchy and local parish priests had been governed almost exclusively by the realities of constituency politics in Catholic Galway. His consultation of the Bishops, and his liberal stance on those questions in which the Roman clerics took a particular interest, were one side of an exchange which saw them continue in return to offer him electoral support. When the Lord Lieutenant expressed a desire in 1861 to nominate Gregory a Visitor of Queen's College, Galway, the county Member promptly sought the advice of Bishop McEvilly. Reminding Gregory that these institutions were condemned 'by the Highest authority' of the Catholic Church, the Bishop warned that connection with the College 'would be made a great election cry against any candidate however great his merits and might put the supporters of such a candidate in a very unenviable light before the country'. The nomination was politely declined. Nor was the

Bishop any more enamoured of national and model schools, insisting that they were Queen's Colleges in infancy. 'Rest assured as regards the Question of Education,' he informed Gregory, 'we will never be content till each religious denomination of this country are (*sic*) placed on a perfect equality and education rendered denominational.' And Gregory responded to such pressure. He called in the Commons for the extension to Ireland of those benefits of denominational education which England enjoyed. He pointed both to the discrimination implicit in the existing policy and its puzzling contradiction. 'Those impressions of reverence, faith, obedience, and religious duty, which are deemed necessary for a comparatively sober, calm, matter-of-fact race, are deemed unnecessary for a race quick, susceptible, ardent, imaginative, ready for good, but also ready for evil purpose.' Thus one result of the experiment in Ireland with mixed schools and the 'absolute indifference to all doctrinal teaching and distinctions', had been 'a gradual, insensible, but certain drifting into practical infidelity' and 'the fruit of all this was Fenianism'.[26]

Another traditional subject of episcopal concern was proselytism in the workhouses. Responding to Bishop Derry's requests for action, Gregory had in 1859 introduced a bill which sought to prevent the automatic raising of foundlings as members of the Established Church. Then, in August of that same year, the Poor Law Board had issued an order directing masters of workhouses to ascertain, if possible, the religious creed which had been professed by the parents of orphans and to ensure that no other creed was taught to them before the age of 12. But this instruction had often been ignored, and it was at Derry's prompting that Gregory intervened in the debate of the Poor Relief Bill (1862) in an effort to tighten the regulations concerning the religious registration of children and to broaden the authority of the hierarchy over the institutions' Roman Catholic chaplains. Also, as the Member for a Catholic constituency Gregory attacked the oaths still demanded of Roman Catholics who held office, or which excluded them from office. Such oaths 'irritated and wounded' without giving the State strength, he observed. He ridiculed the notion that Catholics be compelled to renounce the doctrine that princes excommunicated by the Pope might be dethroned and murdered by their subjects. The Protestants of England had executed Mary, Queen of Scots, sent Charles I to the scaffold, and his son James II into exile. 'Why not, then, impose the oath taken by Roman Catholics on the Protestants and Dissenters of this country as well,' he inquired facetiously? What could be more ridiculous than the present spectacle of 'the strong imposing oaths on the weak pledging the weak not to infringe on the privileges and emoluments of the strong?' Moreover, if they believed that their Church was founded 'on this miserable quicksand of oaths instead of the affection and esteem of the people, then of all men Protestants were the most weak and miserable'. This comment soon illustrated just how fine the line was that a Protestant Member had to walk in a Catholic constituency, for the *Tuam Herald* was quick to chide Gregory for leaving any impression that the Established Church rested in Ireland upon 'the affections of the people'.[27]

The *Herald* attributed Gregory's performance in the debate on the Obnoxious Oaths' Bill in May 1865 to the dictates of Galway politics. In order 'to curry favour with all sides and to disarm hostility, either from Catholicity or Protestantism, on the critical eve of a general election', he had voted for the former and had flattered the latter. If his 'zeal in reference to the rights of Catholics' can never be entirely separated from an elemental preoccupation with personal political survival, more elevated considerations and greater interests steadily loomed larger in Gregory's mind. 'What has been the main cause why Ireland has remained so long alienated and disaffected,' he had begun to ask, and his own reply to this question was 'Religious Injustice — It is that which has poisoned all the springs of Irish society hitherto, from that have poured forth the waters of bitterness over the land.' This was the very same metaphor, significantly, the hierarchy had employed to describe the root of Ireland's woes. Gregory's recognition of this source of social and political instability was paralleled by his growing awareness of the conservative and restraining role the Catholic Church might play, if only it was treated with respect and generosity.

Gregory's admiration for the great mass of priests was less than unbounded. Privately, he bemoaned their provincialism. After a visit to the Irish College at Salamanca in 1863 he commented: 'I wish with all my heart that Maynooth was transported bodily to Salamanca, the foreign Education, and the society in which these young men are received would introduce into Ireland a class of priests that would be very different from many that we have at present.' Yet he had long co-operated successfully with several of them and on many important issues they had revealed a congenially conservative cast of mind. Patrick Duggan, the parish priest at Athenry who appears to have influenced the editorial policy of the *Tuam Herald*, and was ultimately to succeed John Derry as Bishop of Clonfert, assured the Adullamite that 'In this country we do not now care much about an extension of the suffrage. Its total abolition would be the greatest boon to the poor — tenant at will people.' Bishop McEvilly averred that there was nothing he deplored more than the prospect of any serious permanent disagreement between landlords and clergy. Finally, the hierarchy's general response to Fenianism had been most helpful to the authorities. Throughout 1864 and 1865 its organ in Connaught had campaigned against extra-parliamentary solutions for Ireland's woes and had applauded the vigour of the Executive in suppressing the conspiracy. 'Popular representation can achieve almost everything that Ireland requires,' the *Herald* consistently argued. The National Association was founded in an effort to channel Irish energies into constitutional agitation for the redress of grievances. Specifically, it sought compensation for the improvements effected by the occupiers of land; disendowment of the

Established Church; and freedom and equality of education for the several denominations and classes of Ireland. Two other demands were those for the encouragement of native manufactures and the recognition of the 'religion and race' of the Irish people. 'The Government must act so that we shall have no grievance to complain of,' the *Galway Vindicator* insisted. 'That once done Ireland will be pacified, and there will be an end for ever to all secret societies and conspiracies.'[28]

Listening to and learning from the demands of the Catholic clergy, Gregory had come to regard the Roman Church as the 'one body which could have bridged over the chasm between England and Ireland'. Unfortunately, 'that bridge had been wilfully broken down' by such absurdities as the Ecclesiastical Titles Act, 'and each successive administration had shut its door in the face of the persons with the greatest influence in Ireland, and whose religion would primâ facie have induced them to ally themselves, if they could have conscientiously have done so, with the constituted authorities of the realm.' With the influence of Ascendancy landlords clearly on the wane across the island here was their natural replacement, one 'favourable to law and order' and able to 'control the passions of the masses'.

What Gregory envisaged was a wide range of remedial measures which would pacify the tenantry and conciliate their Church, thus ensuring the security and stability so long sought by Ascendancy and successive governments alike. For 'everyone who had resided much in Ireland must feel in his heart that the day of separation from England would be the prelude of anarchy and bloodshed as terrible as any of the catastrophes of the past.' Hence it was essential to diagnose Fenianism as the secondary infection of a more deep-seated disease. 'Irrespective of the base motives of vanity, love of notoriety, hopes of plunder,' Gregory informed the Commons, Fenianism 'was a mixture of the recollection of past wrongs, of the sense of present grievances and neglect, and of the hope of a future nationality; but as past wrongs and future schemes were sentimental, and as present grievances were real, let them deal with what they acknowledged to be wrong.' And the Fenians carrying of the national struggle to England in 1867 supplied a Parliament dominated by Englishmen with an added and unprecedented incentive to resolve the Irish problem.

Addressing the House on the eve of St. Patrick's Day 1868, Gregory enumerated the measures that men both wise and prudent would adopt in Ireland. The first item on his as on other lists was reform of the landlord-tenant relationship. On this subject he spoke with the authority of an Irish landlord who freely admitted that everything he had was derived from his estate, and one who had loyally defended his class against unreasonable criticism. The landowners of Ireland were no longer the stereotypes familiar to readers of Jonah Barrington's memoirs or Charles Lever's novels, he protested. They were now more interested in saving than wasting their inheritances. Nor did he overlook any opportunity to remind the Commons that those new men who had obtained their lands through the Encumbered Estates Court pressed their tenants harder than did the traditional landed families. He thanked God that the Law Life Company was an *English* landlord in Ireland, and noted that among its managers were Members of Parliament who called themselves Liberals. He expected his colleagues to recognize that there was a landlord as well as a tenant side to the question. Little had been said, he had observed during the debate one year earlier of the Tory Government's land bill, of 'the reckless and ruinous destruction of the land by tenants' and the fact that far more of it was returned to the landlord 'deteriorated and worn out than had come back to him with improvements'. The true policy was not to exterminate the landlord class but to root out those 'bad agencies' which bred discontent. Thus Gregory rejected the 'wild and preposterous views' espoused by some who claimed to be the tenants' friends and which appeared to be inspired by 'wild and communistic principles'.

Although he did voice a willingness to see a proposal which John Bright sponsored, to effect a peasant proprietary voluntarily, given a reasonable trial, Gregory never wavered in his belief that no land settlement would endure which failed to guarantee security of tenure. He had in 1866 put his name on a bill drawn up and introduced by Colman O'Loghlen, which sought to spur landlords to abandon tenancies at will — a term which he applied to all yearly arrangements entered into without benefit of lease. In the absence of a written contract there would be a presumption of an agreement to lease for twenty-one years. To discourage landowners from resorting to annual written leases, a yearly tenant would be permitted to deduct from his rent one half of the county cess and the landlord would be denied the right to distrain for rent. Finally, to check the abuse whereby an evicted tenant lost all the improvements for which he had paid, ejectment for any other cause than non-payment of rent would entitle a tenant to compensation. In support of this measure Gregory had marshalled the arguments of landlord self-interest. The existing insecurity of tenure, and he estimated that of every one hundred tenants fully ninety-five held the land at will, discouraged the investment of labour and capital. Insecurity also spawned disaffection. For the Irish tenant eviction was 'tantamount to ruin, expatriation, and the breaking up of every family tie; and the fear of this, the chance of this, made men rebels in thought if not in acts.' In the words of one of Gregory's clerical correspondents, 'when more than 95, probably 98 per cent of the people live upon the breath of the nostrils or caprice of the few what interest can they take in the *British* Constitution!!!' Thus did insecurity of tenure injure landlords by lowering the value of their land, by sparking agrarian outrages, and by encouraging demands for fixity of tenure. Also, those tenants whose families had held undisturbed possession of land for generations on tenancies at will were confirmed in the dangerous belief that they had an inherent right to the soil of which the law had unjustly deprived them.

It was in the name of social and political peace that Gregory urged the House to concede the merits of denominational education, as a second step towards a lasting pacification of Ireland. Religious education was more essential for the Irish people, he affirmed, than for the less excitable and more 'law-loving' races of the other parts of the British Dominion. He cited the experience of English towns as evidence that the influence of the Roman Catholic clergy was more potent on their co-religionists than that of the law, for wherever that influence was weakened some Irish immigrants resorted to crime and brutality. And once he had established the significant role the Catholic Church had played in England and might play in Ireland, Gregory moved on to a discussion of a triad of measures which he believed would conciliate the latter island's hierarchy. He accorded pride of place to a reform of the Church Establishment. Catholics, clerical and lay, had every reason to complain of a religious endowment which was applied exclusively to a mere fraction of the population, and thus deprived the masses who were also the poorest section of society of these emoluments. If only at union in 1800 the Protestant, Presbyterian and Roman Catholic Churches had been treated with equality, he observed with all the advantages of hindsight, Ireland would have been spared the upheavals of Catholic Emancipation, the Tithe War, the Ecclesiastical Titles Bill and the present campaign against the Establishment. So, rather than sweep away the Establishment and the Presbyterians' Regium Donum, which might add to the ranks of the disaffected the middle and upper classes who were members of those Churches, he 'would wish to see every religion in Ireland placed on precisely the same footing as regards the State, and all impartially assisted'. Evidently, he favoured a form of concurrent endowment though he described the state grant as a 'round sum' and stipulated that it be given once and for all and without strings, for they would cause the Roman Catholic clergy to reject it. With this money the Presbyterians might go on much as before, the Church of England put itself in order, and the Catholics educate their priests, establish their university, support their diocesan schools, and provide a glebe and a few acres of land for every rural parish priest.

But a programme of religious conciliation, if it was to succeed, would have to include the eradication from the statute book of the Ecclesiastical Titles Bill. Gregory decried it as 'one of the most wantonly insulting, needless, and inoperative Acts' of the century. Further, he urged the establishment of official and cordial diplomatic relations with the Holy See in order both to terminate the existing 'hole and corner' dealings with the Papacy and to facilitate understanding of the religious questions affecting a large body of British subjects.

Beyond the problems of land and religion, but by no means unrelated to them, lay the need to emancipate Ireland from chronic poverty. The commercial jealousy of England in earlier centuries, the absence of mineral wealth, the years of insecurity, the religious animosities, had all contributed to the crippling of the Irish economy, Gregory charged.

Ireland required, and deserved, policies which would promote material development, for prosperity was another indispensable instrument of pacification. With such political and economic ends in mind, the island's resources demanded development. Year after year the Shannon and its tributaries overflowed their banks and inflicted heavy damage on the surrounding area, thus money invested in a system of drainage would be usefully and reproductively spent. No less urgent was the improvement of Irish railways which combined 'the minimum convenience' with 'the maximum extortion'. Although the poorest of the sister Kingdoms, Ireland's rail fares were the highest and the rates for the carriage of agricultural goods were prohibitive. How could the economy improve when it was cheaper to send goods by sea from Dublin to Sligo via Liverpool than to ship them directly by rail? His solution to these problems, and one which he predicted would stimulate the Irish economy, was for the state to purchase the existing railroads, and complete those under construction, thereby providing the island with an efficient and less expensive transportation system.

Lastly, Gregory appealed for a greater measure of English liberality in the treatment of his native land's scientific and artistic institutions. 'It was wise and politic to attract to the metropolis of Ireland the literary, artistic and scientific talent of the country,' he reasoned. 'It was wise and politic that from this national centre should emanate institutions to awaken artistic taste and evoke the scientific aptitude of the Irish people.'[29]

Gregory did not expect his far reaching programme of reforms to be adopted by the Tory Government which was still clinging to office in the spring of 1868. And while his ambitious and generous proposals were advanced with an eye to ending the traditional English policy towards Ireland — ' 'Too late! too late!' had been the reply from Ireland' — they were also intended to advance his career. Gregory had not abandoned hope of being appointed Chief Secretary, and his speech on 16 March 1868 served to remind his listeners of his qualifications for that office. Indeed, he had given some thought to the problems of the Irish Executive and had concluded that the office of Lord Lieutenant ought to be abolished. Lady Clanricarde had once observed that 'The chief business of the Lord Lieutenant is to flatter the Irish people by making promises which he is not allowed to keep.' To this Gregory would have added that the Viceroy 'though potent to do mischief is really impotent to do good'.[30] It fell to the Chief Secretary to explain and defend Irish policy in the Commons, and if weak he did this half-heartedly and even if active and strong he could always throw the blame for failure upon his nominal superior. Moreover, the nobleman appointed to that august post went to Ireland as the representative of a party and naturally sought to strengthen it there, but whenever that party was unpopular the unpopularity extended to the Viceregal office. In short, it was Gregory's belief that instead of promoting loyalty the Lord Lieutenant often had the very opposite effect. The answer was to do away with the

A photograph of Mr. W. H. Gregory, M.P. for Galway, probably in the late 1860s, or the time that he accepted the offer of the governorship of Ceylon.

Viceroyalty and assign the Chief Secretary a seat in Cabinet. There, he could initiate the policy he considered requisite for Ireland. In the spring of 1868, with the tradition of a Chief Secretary of Cabinet rank well on the way to establishment, for Palmerston, Russell, Derby and Disraeli had all recognized the office's importance, and having described in some detail the measures he would introduce, Gregory waited for the general election which if it returned the Liberals to power might be followed by an invitation at last to accept the office he craved.[31]

He had prudently kept his distance from the Conservative governments of Derby and Disraeli. Although he privately used what little influence he did possess with the Tories to secure the appointment of moderate men to the minor posts in Irish administration and prevent that of a rabid Protestant who had the misfortune to be deaf as Lord Justice of Appeals — the irony of this physical ailment would not have been lost on Catholic appellants — Gregory had every reason publicly to steer well clear of the Adullamites' former allies. Predictably, the Conservatives' response to the Irish problem fell far short of the measures he believed necessary if the island was to be pacified. When Lord Naas introduced a Land Bill, and thus set out along the path which *The Times* likened to the route to Salt Lake City — 'Covered with the skeletons of those who have trodden the way before him' — he found himself criticised both for going too far and not far enough. Provisions which looked to encourage tenants to make improvements to their holdings, by making loans available to them and permitting the removal of their fixtures if on eviction they were unable to obtain satisfactory compensation from the landlord or the incoming tenant, incensed the landed interest. 'Once admit that a tenant holding at six months' notice may mortgage the land without the consent of the lessor,' *The Times* thundered, 'and there is nothing that may not be asked and conceded by a legislature liberal of the rights of property and careless of those principles upon which property rests.' Gregory was among those who deplored a measure which so 'needlessly violated the laws of property', but his objections were no less firmly rooted in the conviction that unless it incorporated security of tenure the bill was doomed as an instrument of Ireland's pacification. His attempt to amend it along those lines failed, for Naas was not alone in querying how he would compel landlords to grant leases without infringing the rights of property. Indeed, the issue of Tenant Rights was beginning to drive a wedge between Gregory and even his liberal Conservative supporters in County Galway. Increasingly, Lord Clonbrock stigmatised the Member's views as those of an 'advanced Radical'. However, the obverse side of this coin bore the image of the hierarchy. Bishops Derry and McEvilly still identified 'Insecurity of Tenure as the crying injustice of the existing code and practice', and the latter continued to insist that if only the measure Gregory advocated became law 'every peasant in Ireland would be a special constable as attached to the throne and the Institutions of the country as Mr. D'Israeli and Mr. Gladstone'.[32]

Another thorny Irish issue confronting the Tories was that of denominational education, together with the associated question of a Catholic university. The Cabinet sought to evade the former by the time-honoured device of appointing a commission, this one to enquire into the national schools' system, but they did announce in March 1868 their intention to charter a Roman Catholic University. The proposal was quickly attacked in the Commons, not least as a concession to the hierarchy rather than to the population. Gregory immediately came to the defence of the Bishops, pointing out that there was no evidence of the Irish laity desiring protection from their doctrinal teachings. And while John Derry, who had been despatched to London by the hierarchy to negotiate with the government, expressed to Gregory his disappointment at the unhelpful behaviour of Gladstone and other Liberals on the education question, there were some grounds for optimism. The Bishop granted that the right of Roman Catholics to receive education at all other levels on terms of equality with Protestants was steadily being recognized in England. Moreover, in dismissing the Tories' concession on the university as one of little account in the struggle against Fenianism, Gladstone had declared for a more thorough-going measure — disestablishment. And the defeat of the Disraeli Government on the Liberal leader's motion on the Established Church brought an end to the negotiations for a University Charter.[33]

Even as he made plain that he was not an 'independent' supporter of the Conservatives he had helped put into office in 1866 Gregory was re-emerging from the Cave. The fact that the Tories had soon introduced a Reform Bill more radical than that of Russell had long since given him ample cause to reflect on the wisdom of his earlier conduct. 'No political act of turpitude ever exceeded his Reform Bill of 1867,' he wrote many years later of Disraeli. At the time he took little part in the debate, except to observe with understandable sarcasm: 'The theory of the hon. Gentlemen opposite now seemed to be that the Constitution of the country could be best maintained by making its foundations to rest not on wealth, character and education, but on poverty, venality, and ignorance.' He declined to serve as an Irish Boundary Commissioner, whose task it was to redraw the constituency boundaries under the terms of the Irish Reform Bill, explaining to Disraeli that he strongly objected to many of its details and that acceptance of the position 'would not be understood in Ireland'.[34]

Differences over Ireland had served to loosen Gregory's ties to the Adullamites. He found himself at odds with them over their inflexible defence of property rights against those of tenants, while they criticised his calls for security of tenure as 'real tenant right' speeches and ridiculed the claim that long leases would convert tenants-at-will into special constables. And when in a letter to the Editor of *The Times* Lord Grosvenor appeared to signal an effort by the Cave to form a third party Gregory hastened to inform Gladstone that he rejected any such strategy and remained a 'moderate Liberal'. Undoubtedly, this reaffirmation of political allegiance reflected the calculation that the moment had long since passed to effect successfully a political realignment and the belief that the Liberals were destined soon to regain power. Yet at the height of the crisis over the Liberal Reform Bill, in April 1866, he had shown himself reluctant to sever his ties to that party. Within the Cave he had counselled moderation, urging that Lowe avoid in his speeches a 'personally hostile and acrimonious tone'. In the House he had called upon the occupants of the Treasury Bench to give him and others 'credit for submitting to what he trusted would be the temporary severance of party ties and political friendships, and under an overwhelming conviction that there was something far above friendship and party; he meant, their duty to their country'. Further, he had denied all knowledge of any scheme to topple the government or weaken the position of Gladstone within the party. 'He, for one, looked forward to the great financial abilities of the Chancellor of the Exchequer being employed for many years in settling questions of the greatest magnitude as affecting the prospects of this country, which, he believed, no one can handle but himself.' By March 1867 Gregory was declaring allegiance to Gladstone as the only man who could 'settle the great questions uppermost in the Irish mind, and which must be settled ere we can have Ireland peaceful and contented'.[35]

By describing in some detail the measures he considered necessary in Ireland — disestablishment, security of tenure and an alliance with the Catholic priesthood — Gregory was clearly seeking to stake a claim to the Irish office in a future Liberal government. 'I know your anxiety about Ireland,' he wrote to Gladstone, 'and therefore I think any contribution from one who understands it, and who has the confidence of the Roman Catholic Clergy and peasantry about him, cannot come amiss to you.' 'You and you alone can pacify Ireland,' he flattered, 'or at least lay the foundation of a thorough and hearty reconciliation, and I am as confident, as that I now write, if God spares your life, you will do it.' Was it mere coincidence that he chose to remind Gladstone of his eligibility for the post of Chief Secretary, by elaborating in the Commons his earlier private suggestions on how to pacify his native land, on the very day in March 1868 of the Liberal leader's declaration of support for disestablishment? What part if any Gregory's urging of Gladstone to take this question into his hands, and to do so while in opposition in order to give the fashioning and shape to Liberal policy, played in the decision now to commit himself is difficult if not impossible to determine. Did Gregory's letter in 1867 prompt him to take the opportunity presented two months later by a discussion in the Commons of the position of the Irish Church to express his sympathy with the cause of disestablishment? His more emphatic statement the following year has been attributed by some historians to the Fenian outrages. Whatever the stimulus, Gladstone's choice of this issue proved to be an inspired one. He reunited a party which had been split by Reform two years earlier, and in Ireland his supporters were assured of the hierarchy's support at the polls in November. 'It could not be called with truth a political issue,' Bishop McEvilly observed, 'it was essentially religious.'[36]

'I do not hear the faintest rumours of a contest which is a blessing,' Gregory confided to a friend in September, 'as I cannot afford the expense without great inconvenience and pinching afterwards.' At the nominating meeting on 26 November he found himself unopposed, having been handsomely endorsed by the *Tuam Herald* as a representative worthy of the 'unanimous gratitude of this great Catholic county', and by the *Galway Vindicator* as a figure of 'unlimited influence in the Liberal section of the House'. If the accompanying calls in the local press for Gregory's appointment as Chief Secretary in any Gladstone Government were unlikely to be heard in England, Henry Layard, himself a strong candidate for a portfolio, had written encouragingly: 'You must now take office. There cannot be any difficulties in the way and you ought to take the position to which you are entitled and in which you could be of use to the country.' But Chichester Fortescue, who had served in the Russell Government as Chief Secretary and had an influential and ambitious wife, soon seemed earmarked to return to that post in a Gladstone Cabinet. So, Gregory turned with more than a hint of desperation to the Earl of Clarendon, whose claim to the Foreign Office the new Prime Minister could ill afford to ignore. 'At present if any office for which I have a taste were offered to me I would gladly accept it, for certain reasons which did not exist when I preferred my liberty to work,' Gregory wrote beseechingly. 'It is possible that Gladstone may consult you about appointments, and if so pray do not forget an old friend — especially if there be a chance of serving under you.' Although this note was duly forwarded to Gladstone, not even the comparatively minor office of Under Secretary of Foreign Affairs, for which he had so carefully prepared himself several years earlier, was offered to Gregory. The Prime Minister in overlooking him may have been actuated by dislike or distrust, but personal reservations and political suspicion proved no obstacle in the case of Robert Lowe whom he appointed Chancellor of the Exchequer. Of course, Lowe had been a junior member of the Palmerston Government and if a disagreeable man was certainly one of unquestioned cleverness and iron resolution. Perhaps, Gladstone was somewhat less impressed by William Gregory. Moreover, at a time when he was anxious to conciliate not only Ireland but also the United States Gladstone would have been ill-advised to appoint to the Foreign Office the man most closely identified in American minds with British sympathy for the Confederacy. Finally, Gregory could be more easily ignored than others seeking promotion for he lacked a highly placed and energetic sponsor. In forwarding the Irishman's plea for advancement to the Prime Minister Clarendon had refrained from adding a strong recommendation that it be granted.[37]

8

Political Dilettante

The Irish Church had found few defenders during the Commons debate in the spring of 1868. In the words of one surprised Conservative minister, 'it seemed as if the Fenian trouble had turned a languid sentiment of disapproval into an active determination to get rid of the thing altogether.' Benjamin Disraeli did strive to make defence of the Protestant Establishment an issue in the ensuing general election but even his intimates acknowledged publicly that there were 'good reasons why the position of the Irish Church, confessedly the Church of a small minority, should be reconsidered, and why a portion of its wealth should be devoted to more useful public purposes — such portions of its wealth, that is, as may reasonably and fairly be considered public property'. Those who would justify it as a missionary Church had to face up to the fact that its membership had contracted rather than expanded over the past thirty years. Indeed, in 199 parishes there was not a single congregant and in 575 others there were less than twenty. Yet, however indefensible the status of the Church, Ascendancy friends of William Gregory in Catholic County Galway warned darkly that to tamper with it would 'disgust' those who formed the bond of union between the two countries. Protestant proprietors would draw their own conclusions should the Church discover that treaty rights and 300 years of occupation afforded it no real defence or security. Would there then be an estate in Ireland which could not be appropriated and dealt with in the same fashion, they asked? Further, the 'banishment' of the Protestant clergy would seal the doom of 'this most unhappy country' and an 'ignorant Peasant proprietary and Peasant clergy' would 'render it the most detestable residence on earth'. The Anglo-Irish would either emigrate or be converted to Catholicism, and allegiance to England thereby eroded. [1]

If these were the convictions and fears on which William Gregory had been weaned by his grandfather, the religious scepticism to which he had surrendered in adulthood now smoothed the path of accommodation with Catholic Ireland. Divine Service gave him neither pleasure nor comfort. 'I have no patience with that class of people who think they honour God by absurd dresses and absurd gestures, which have recondite meanings of so deep a nature that if God were not vested with omniscience he would never comprehend their aim,' he informed his devout mother. He disliked most hymns, dismissing them as

186

'generally a mere jingle of uninteresting and silly rhymes' fit only for schoolboys. He offered the familiar and conventional criticism of most sermons, growling that it would be far better for the clergy to read out 'some good printed sermons instead of preaching nonsense which sends everyone to sleep or to think of something else'. He did wrestle with the difficult problems posed for all men of reason by the miraculous and the supernatural, but his conclusions, while in this instance somewhat more original, were less than profound. Pondering the accounts of the resurrection and the ascension following the crucifixion, Gregory found his own explanation in the lack of education of the writers of the scriptures and their belonging to a nation 'proverbially credulous'. As a result, their stories had been accepted as certain without the slightest proof and with the passage of time had assumed fresh consistency and a defined form. [2]

But no account of Gregory's advocacy of disestablishment would be complete which disregarded the extent to which the verities of youth had been disputed by experience. He grew to oppose a state paid Church Establishment on principle, and his visit to North America in 1859 had pointed him in this direction. Travelling through one small Canadian town after another he was both struck and impressed by the number and architectural taste of the churches. He wrote to his mother: 'I can assure you the manner in which the churches are kept up in Canada by a poor people solely on voluntary contributions would put to shame the condition of too many of our Irish churches supported as they are by such immense wealth, and by the richest portion of the community.' Nor had he ever witnessed services either better attended or more decorously conducted. There was a lesson in all of this for Irish Protestants, he concluded. The voluntary principle not only worked well but 'by it religious animosity loses its point'. While the brief Canadian journey helped to convince Gregory that the Church of Ireland ought to be able to survive disestablishment, long residence amidst Catholics had led him to question another article of Anglo-Irish faith — that the Protestant proprietors were the only bond holding the union together. There was a larger proportion of Roman Catholic land-owners in Galway than in any other county and they were 'respected, true and just in all their dealings, and eminently loyal'. [3]

Unfettered by spiritual anguish or soul-searching, Gregory took a decidely pragmatic view of the Church question. Religion was a bulwark of law and order and in Ireland the Roman Catholic Church was the 'great central fortress'. Popery, he explained to one anxiety-ridden friend, was the 'only teaching for our own people that will keep them moral and well behaved'. When Bishop Derry wrote to him shortly after the election to express his concern that the triumphant Liberals would now back away from an immediate disestablishment and disendowment of the Church, and to warn of the political and social consequences, Gregory responded immediately. He sent off a long letter to Chichester Fortescue which the Bishop had seen in draft and believed would be of 'the greatest service to the Cabinet', providing as it did 'correct and authentic information of the feelings and opinions of their supporters in this country'. The strictest adherence to the principle of equality must be its guide, Gregory instructed the government. No one objected to the Irish Church retaining life interests and property derived from sources other than state endowment but to go beyond that would be misguided generosity which, without lessening Protestant irritation, would inflame Catholic opinion by confirming inequality. In that event, the whole measure would 'lose its savour'. Those Roman Catholics who had worked to return supporters of Gladstone would have reason to feel betrayed and whatever hope still flickered 'in the minds of the Irish masses as to English honest dealing' would be extinguished. The result 'would be utter despair of English treatment, utter scorn for English statesmen, and an almost universal persuasion that nothing but revolution could bring things right.' The present opportunity 'to make a discontented, and justly discontented people, loyal and concordant with the rest of the Empire' must not be lost, he argued, for 'we shall never live to see such another.' In summary, it was preferable that a measure of strict equality failed than one of inequality succeeded. 'In the one case confidence in the honour of the Liberal party would be preserved, in the other case every denomination in Ireland would be left dissatisfied, distrusting and resentful.'[4]

Fortescue forwarded Gregory's letter to Gladstone and the Prime Minister returned it with the comment: 'I agree very much with his opinions but I think he has no cause to be uneasy. To let us know however of any uneasiness which prevails is a friendly act.' As keen as Gregory had shown himself to be in this and other instances to conciliate and reassure the Catholic hierarchy he had detected a subtle but significant difference of opinion within the ranks of the Roman Catholic clergy on disestablishment and disendowment. Although the Bishops rejected out of hand all suggestions that their Church share in the funds involved, the local priests showed signs of wanting to have at least some of the proceeds forced upon them. Thus Gregory privately pressed the government to provide in the Church Bill for a glebe house and a few acres of land for parish priests. If this was done every one of them would then feel a different man and bless the hand that carried this gift, he prophesied, and in every parish the most influential figure would be a proselytizer for the country's institutions. 'Surely such a stake as this is worth a risk.'[5]

In fact the risk was too high as Gregory soon publicly acknowledged. Speaking immediately after Benjamin Disraeli on the first night of debate of the Church Bill, on 8 March 1869, and he gave the Tory leader's 'laboured triviality' short shrift, the Irishman conceded that the government had acted prudently in omitting from the legislation any provision concerning glebes. The probable opposition of non-conformist members and others to any scheme which smacked of re-endowment, and the likelihood of the Conservatives exploiting any crack in Liberal unity, dictated caution. Moreover, when an amendment was attached to the Bill in the Lords, giving free glebes to the clergy of the three denominations, it was denounced by Cardinal Cullen as 'a device to get an argument to defend the renewed endowment of the Protestant Church, and to silence us by throwing us some crumbs'. Gladstone was able to secure removal of this promise of concurrent endowment, but the following year the government did pilot through Parliament a bill which permitted Irish priests to obtain generous loans from the Commissioners of Public Works in order to purchase glebes.[6]

Disestablishment and disendowment as enacted in July 1869 clearly fell somewhat short of Gregory's expectations. Nor was he heeded when he called for the application of the surplus revenues — the funds that remained once the property of the former Established Church had been capitalized and provision made for the life annuities of the clergy and officials who had lost their income — to such great national objects as railroads. Instead of being invested in the material and industrial development of Ireland the surplus was to be used largely for charitable and educational purposes, as well as to encourage agriculture and fisheries. Nevertheless, Gregory continued to regard the measure, its limitations notwithstanding, as the vital first step towards the conciliation of his native land. 'If Catholic Emancipation was the foundation of religious equality in Ireland,' he declared in the Commons, 'this was the coping stone of the edifice.' Even Patrick Duggan, whom he regarded as a representative parish priest, and who in their correspondence had initially condemned the Church Bill for allowing 'the robber of three centuries' to walk away with one half of the capitalized property and for failing to provide glebes, had eventually accepted it as the nearest approach to justice that was possible in the complex circumstances. The money was a trifling affair compared with the equality involved in disestablishment, Duggan allowed. However, the establishment of religious equality and the lessening of religious animosity were, as Gregory had long realized, insufficient in themselves to quieten Ireland. There were other important questions that demanded attention, he reminded his fellow members, including the landlord/tenant relationship and education. Nor was he ignorant of the problems they posed. 'Do not delude yourself with a hope that any half-measure on the land question will have any effect in tranquillizing the people,' Duggan had written as the Church Bill was still making its way through Parliament. 'Until the greater or at any rate a great portion of them is put in a position where it will become their interest to side with the law, bid adieu to tranquillity.'[7]

A solution of the land question was complicated by the indelible myths of absentee ownership, rack-renting, confiscation of improvements and massive evictions. If some landlords were absentees, most of them chose to reside for part of the year in Ireland; they did not charge their tenants unreasonable rents or throw them off the land in large number, while many tenants elected to invest whatever capital they accumulated in livestock rather than make improvements to their holdings. Yet there was a tendency even for observers as acute and knowledgeable as William Gregory to reduce the problem of land to one or more of these issues, and this simplification had the advantage of making it more comprehensible to English listeners. In particular, the despised Law Life Assurance Company served a purpose as an intelligible and ironic (being English) example of the many landlord/tenant ills of Ireland. 'All the Society wants is to get as much as they can, and the people may starve or emigrate,' one of his correspondents wrote. 'The houses on the property are a disgrace to any civilized country.' Moreover, like the classic absentee, it was accused of carrying the entire income from the land out of the country. Beyond this, its behaviour illustrated 'the real grievance' of which Irish tenants complained — 'uncertainty of tenure'. 'Now what must they think of this great Company whose practice it has been to serve annual notices to quit upon their tenantry,' Gregory planned to ask the Commons, 'by means of which either on the 1st of November or the 1st of May the wretched peasant might find himself cast out from the house he had built and without one farthing of compensation left friendless and homeless on a bleak hill side in Connemara.' However, he always intended to add the important qualification that he 'did not say these things were done, but they might be done and the poor people knew that the agent was a man of good nerves who would have done it without scruple and eaten his dinner afterwards without a pang.'[8]

How to remove the sense of 'uncertainty of tenure', that remained the nub of the matter. Long an advocate of twenty-one year leases, Gregory learnt that they no longer answered the tenants' demands for security. 'We are in for a period of great change and restlessness,' Duggan predicted in May 1869, 'and spurn *now* what a few years ago we would accept with gratitude.' The call in the *Tuam Herald* was for *absolute* security of tenure and protection against 'capricious' increases of rent. What tenants sought, it seemed, was legal recognition of their claim to a proprietary right in the land. Certainly, this was the tenant right which the extension of Ulster custom to the other provinces would confirm. A landlord never evicted a rent paying tenant under this arrangement, while a tenant leaving a holding sold the right of occupancy to his successor. Such notions of security had a familiar ring to those landlords who could recall the three Fs (Fair Rents, Fixity of Tenure and Free Sale) specified by a Tenant Right conference in 1850, and they exceeded anything Gregory had ever contemplated or was yet willing to entertain. He deplored the remarks of Sir John Gray, the proprietor of the *Freeman's Journal*, the Member for Kilkenny and an intimate of Archibishop Cullen, who declared that compensation for improvements and the granting of leases, even those for periods of thirty-one years, would be regarded as confiscation. When Gray went on to demand the extension of Ulster custom, Gregory urged Chichester Fortescue to impress upon 'the worthy Knight' that by his encouragement of 'wild schemes' he was impeding a land settlement.

Conservative by nature and education, Gregory instinctively resisted 'grave innovations' which were tantamount to granting tenants a share of what he had always regarded as his property. A progressive landlord, he had continued to improve his tenants' condition in such traditional ways as the enlargement of grazing farms. 'Many [landlords] begin to see they will get better rents from their *own* and become beloved by their neighbours by following your idea,' Patrick Duggan wrote approvingly. 'That is one of the methods to put it out of the power of "Monkeys" to make the "mischief" you deprecate.' But mischief was abroad. Lord Clonbrock, an old friend, assailed him for doing 'evil work' and noted with asperity that the Liberals' 'message of peace to Ireland seems only to be productive of increase of trouble and crime'. He, together with his gardener and his steward, had received threatening letters. Infuriated rather than afraid, Clonbrock summoned his entire staff to inform them that if any injury befell the two servants he would shut up his home and retire from Ireland, thus throwing them all out of employment. Gregory became even more familiar with the violence when he returned to Coole for the summer. He was appointed foreman of the County Grand Jury which sat with two justices as a special commission to hear cases of agrarian outrage. Although these were only four in number they included the attempted murder of a local landowner. Elsewhere, a High Sheriff had been murdered and in November a by-election in Tipperary saw a convicted Fenian returned though as a felon he was disqualifed from taking the seat. This event 'will open the eyes of people here to the real wishes of the middle and lower classes in Ireland', one prominent English politician observed.[9]

The 'state of feeling' in Ireland — 'terribly bitter and dangerous' — may have briefly unnerved Gregory. He was afraid that the island was being drawn into a vicious circle of disorder as 'impunity gives encouragement to fresh outrages until crime becomes an ordinary transaction'. In his alarm he left undelivered the stinging attack on the Law Life Company which had been prepared with characteristic thoroughness. He worried that the 'good fruit of the Church Act' was being squandered by those who made 'wild speeches and impossible proposals'. In a letter to a conference on the land question which met in Dublin in October he warned that extremists on both sides, landlord and tenant, were complicating the issue but called upon his fellow landowners to be 'wise in time'. A meeting of the Gort Board of Guardians, at which he presided, passed unanimously a resolution which endorsed the concession of 'secure occupancy'. This carefully ambiguous term evidently fell short of fixity of tenure. Privately, he reaffirmed his support 'for a broad measure involving security of tenure' but complained that 'when the people get it fixed in their heads that they are to have permanent possession of the land at a government valuation, no measure however liberal and wide will satisfy them, and that which a few months ago they would have accepted with joy and gratitude, they will next year receive with sullenness, certainly without gratitude or increased loyalty.' And when he wrote to the editor of *The Times* he signed the letter 'Moderator'. [10]

Speaking with greater freedom from behind his mask, though it was penetrated with disconcerting ease by at least one friend, Gregory drew a stark portrait of a land inhabited by a lawless people of 'thriftless, squalid habits, resulting in overpopulation and destitution'. He chastised those guilty of fostering the peasantry's 'wild dreams', for 'Saxon moderation' not 'Celtic rhapsodies' would determine the land settlement. As remedies for those problems beyond the reach of legislation he proposed the residence of proprietors (still believing absenteeism to be another of the island's curses); the emigration of the surplus population or, through the promotion of manufacturing, its employment off the land; and the cultivation of moral, social and mental education. This last cure might yet be effected if the role of the priest was enhanced, he argued. 'What more dangerous element in a semi-barbarous people can you have than a low priesthood,' he mordantly inquired from the refuge of a pseudonym, 'half educated, but wholly organized, whose interest it is to keep the people in squalid darkness, to set them against their landlords, that they may themselves become their crooked counsellors, to promote early marriages and passionate ignorance, — for by these means they gain their pitiful subsistence.' Having abdicated his place and deputed his functions the landlord would be wise to elevate the status of the priest above that of 'the absolute cottier'. The way to do this was to provide him with a decent home and glebe and endow him, 'if not as a priest, at least as a teacher so that he may cease to subsist entirely on the passions of the people'.

The importance Gregory continued to attach to state supported denominational education as an instrument of alliance with the clergy as well as of pacification of the peasantry was matched by his insistence that more effective police action was essential to counter the inevitable disorders when the tenantry discovered that 'wild aspirations' would not be fulfilled. The present detective establishment must be strengthened, he declared. For the evil of absenteeism he, like others, urged a royal residence in Ireland. Were the Prince of Wales to reside there for a period each year he would be followed by the society which had left since the Union. 'When we have kept from them their natural leaders,' he wrote of the peasantry, 'what wonder if they look elsewhere for help or indulge in visionary abstractions.'

What of those aspects of land question which might be dealt with by legislation? He would provide tenants both with compensation for improvements and the greater security of tenure offered by leases. And as Ulster custom had worked so well in that province he saw no objection to *some* of its provisions being extended to the whole country. A Gregory land bill would define improvements and confirm landlords in their right of pre-emption. Further, the landlord would compensate an outgoing tenant for improvements but charge the cost to the incoming one in the relatively painless form of a small but long term rent increase. 'This would relieve the new tenant of payment of goodwill [occupancy] and so return the economical division of labour,' he explained. Nor, on reflection, was he quite so tolerant as he had once been of John Bright's scheme to transform peasants into proprietors by advancing them government loans. The government would become a landlord on a massive scale, he now protested, and if the peasant was able to draw on the government why not the trader, shipowner or landlord? How will subletting and subdividing be effectively prevented, he asked? The task of the legislature was 'to remove every obstacle in the purchase and sale of land', he insisted. Thus the Encumbered Estates Court might be extended and in land transfers all but nominal fees and stamps abolished. The actual financing of purchases should be left, however, to companies and banks who would extend loans on the traditional security of a mortgage. Clearly, Gregory had not conceded free sale or virtual fixity of tenure.[11]

Gregory's restraining influence reached within the Cabinet. The Home Secretary, H. A. Bruce, consulted him as a representative of the landlord class who had sympathy for the tenants and was a 'master of the whole subject.' Chichester Fortescue's instinctive conservatism on this issue was buttressed by Gregory's warnings that agitation in Ireland was becoming dangerously unreasonable. 'What a country ours is,' the Chief Secretary wrote to his fellow Irishman early in November. 'All the isms — Fenianism, Ribbonism, Orangeism are in a state of inflammation.' Fortescue's proposals in Cabinet — that the legislation guarantee to tenants compensation for improvements, facilitate the emigration of the surplus population and encourage the consolidation of holdings — had a Gregory ring to them. But measures which had been too radical for Gladstone when introduced by Gregory and O'Loghlen in 1866, because they would interfere with 'the management of a man's property', no longer sufficed. The Prime Minister now advocated nothing less than the full extension of Ulster custom. He met stern resistance from his colleagues. They were angered by the increase in violent incidents in Ireland and the evidence that land agitators were cooperating with Fenians, and were fearful that rights established throughout the island would promptly be claimed by tenants in the rest of the United Kingdom. Faced by a Cabinet in no mood to meet the Irish tenantry's demands, the Prime Minister slowly retreated from his advanced position. However, the contents of the land bill were as yet unknown when Gregory returned to Britain in mid-January.[12]

He had been out to the Eastern Mediterranean to attend the festive opening of that great feat of nineteenth century engineering — the Suez Canal. Nor had he undertaken the journey as one of Thomas Cook's excursionists, but as a guest aboard the steamer of John Pender. A textile merchant, Pender also found employment for his considerable entrepreneurial skills in the promotion of submarine telegraphic communications. Presumably his initial preoccupation with the laying of the Atlantic cable had seen him strike up a friendship with the most persistent advocate of the Galway Packet station. Now, as a supporter and intimate of Ferdinand de Lesseps, Pender could assure his guests of a prominent place in the armada of vessels which entered the canal on 18 November 1869 for the ceremonial first journey through to the Red Sea. From Egypt Gregory moved on to Palestine and the Holy Land, taking the opportunity to visit the real Cave of Adullam — 'a marvellous place' — and carry back a piece of rock as a gift for Elcho. 'I have had a most delightful two months in the East which I ever spent,' he wrote to Henry Layard. 'All a bed of rose leaves and not a crumpled one.'

The situation which greeted him in Ireland was far less comfortable. Gregory quickly discovered on his arrival home that there had been no moderation of the tenants' demands. The edition of the *Tuam Herald* which welcomed him back to Galway repeated the calls for fixity of tenure except in cases of non-payment of rent; protection against capricious rent increases which would endanger this right; and recognition of the tenants' claim to 'the value of their occupancy title' even in those cases where they had been unwilling or unable to pay their rents. All of which amounted to a continuing insistence that the rights enjoyed in Ulster be extended to the other provinces. From Rome, where he and his colleagues were attending a Vatican Council, Bishop McEvilly wrote to express the hope that the Land Bill would go far enough to put 'a quietus on Fenianism' and make every tenant as anxious as the Prime Minister for peace and order in Ireland. If the legislation failed to root the people in the soil or protect them from capricious evictions then the consequences would be 'very bad', the cleric warned. [13]

Inevitably, there was dissatisfaction in Ireland when the Bill was at last introduced in February. 'It utterly ignores the "tenant's right of property in occupancy" outside Ulster,' the *Tuam Herald* complained. In fact, the custom was recognized wherever it was already established but this fell far short of universal application. Moreover, financial devices to provide tenants with greater security, through a limited compensation for disturbance as well as for improvements, were less than reassuring. Such protections stood in obvious danger of being vitiated by the landlords' rights to raise rents and then evict for non-payment. At a well attended 'indignation meeting' held in Tuam on 2 March a statement was adopted 'requiring' the county Members to inform Prime Minister Gladstone that continued Irish support of his government depended upon its willingness to withdraw the present Bill or to amend it in a way acceptable to popular opinion. In his correspondence with Gregory, Patrick Duggan speculated that the Catholic clergy would be obliged to withdraw from politics 'because the people say they have been long enough following their lead to no avail'. England 'has lost her last chance of tranquillizing Ireland by pacific means,' he added gloomily. Nor did Bishops McEvilly and Derry hide their disappointment, though the latter still strove to be constructive and was willing to applaud the 'generous spirit' with which the Bill had evidently been introduced by the Prime Minister. Indeed, fearful that an opportunity to effect reform might be lost, Bishop Derry urged Gregory to amend the Bill rather than to oppose it. [14]

Violence, popular agitation and clerical pressure were a persuasive combination in bringing Gregory to the realization that the land settlement he had envisaged would no longer suffice. No doubt his long standing sympathy for tenants played its part. 'He knew instances in which, under a threat of a notice to quit, tenants were obliged to make their purchases in the shops of their landlord, to cut his corn, to dig his turf and potatoes.' He may also have been influenced by the pamphlet of the Indian civil servant, George Campbell, whose arguments for ratification of the tenants' right of property so impressed Gladstone. Certainly, the beginning of March found him sounding out the Prime Minister, informally and indirectly, on the possibility of extending Ulster custom throughout the island. The response, as relayed by the intermediary, Frank Lawley, was discouraging. Making no reference to his own earlier espousal of this solution, and its defeat in Cabinet, Gladstone pointed to the impossibility of creating or conjuring up a custom; to the difficulty of defining one in precise language so as to adapt it to provinces where it had failed to grow spontaneously; and to the fact that Ulster tenants had purchased their exceptional rights with higher rents. 'I am sure Gladstone will battle to the death ag[ain]st perpetuity of tenure,' Lawley concluded, 'and ag[ain]st the universal diffusion of Ulster Tenant Right.' Consequently, it was surely a privately pessimistic Gregory who accompanied the deputation, composed of representatives of the National Association and of the Tenants' delegates gathered in London, which met with the Prime Minister just two days later, on 5 March, to plead for those concessions. In rejecting their plea Gladstone offered an explanation and issued a warning to the Irishmen. Any measure of justice for Ireland had to be acceptable to opinion in England and Scotland, he emphasised, and popular sympathy for that country might weaken if a 'fair' settlement framed in accordance with this reality was rejected by the Irish people. [15]

In the House Gregory struggled to overcome this and a number of other objections to appeasement of the tenants. Rights granted in Ireland need not be automatically extended to England and Scotland, he argued, for in the past there had often been different provisions for that kingdom and the rest of the nation. With an eye to Gladstone's threat and Derry's advice, he attempted to discourage fellow Irish Members from opposing the government, lest it throw up its hands in frustration. They would do far better to seek to amend the legislation instead. Leading by example, he introduced a series of proposals that had already been endorsed by the Tenants' delegates. He would solve the contentious and difficult problem of rents through a two-step procedure. First, the present rents would be accepted as the general basis of settlement but a Land Court created to hear landlord requests for an increase and tenant appeals for a reduction. Second, he recommended the establishment of a relatively simple mechanism to provide for periodic rent revisions at fixed periods. A regular review, perhaps every fourteen years, tied to a local standard of measure, such as the average price of a group of agricultural products over a specified number of years, would go far to reduce the friction between landlords and tenants, he believed. The assurance that capricious rent increases would no longer be possible was accompanied in the Gregory plan by a second guarantee. A tenant would have the right to sell his goodwill even in cases of eviction, subject only to a landlord veto 'on reasonable grounds' of the tenant offered by the outgoer. All arrears of rent were to be paid from the goodwill and tenants were only to be evicted for specific statutory causes — non-payment of rent, subletting, ill-treatment of the land, and the commission of any serious crime 'not political'.

William Gregory did not attempt to disguise the fact that expediency had dictated his conversion to full Tenant Right. However, in the context of the debate, that promised to be a larger consideration and hold greater sway than appeals for justice. 'The whole of the bonds of society' seemed to be breaking up in Ireland, he reminded the House, but a land bill which met with the general approval of the Irish people 'would be the best Coercion Bill they ever could enact, and no repressive measures at all would be required.' Those Members who took the trouble to read the reports of the Poor Law Inspectors would discover that wherever Ulster right existed 'there was perfect content [sic] on the part of the tenant, great improvement was going on, and the landlord felt secure as to his rent'. Under the provisions of the government's unpopular Bill every landlord became more or less an annuitant, Gregory claimed, 'but under the system which he proposed he would at least be an annintant with an annuity, while under the Bill he might be an annuitant without one'.

Concern to effect a lasting settlement in Ireland also led him to endorse Bright's land purchase scheme, which had been included in the Bill. Here was one way to increase the gradations and thus the stability of Irish society by multiplying the landowners. And with this object in mind Gregory wisely strove to lengthen the period of repayment and secure a reduction in the rate of interest on the loans in order to reduce the annual charge, thereby enabling greater numbers of tenants to take advantage of the scheme. He failed. [16]

This performance in the Commons saw the *Tuam Herald* shower Gregory with praise. 'The whole speech evidences deep thought, and a searchingly comprehensive knowledge of the principles, which, if put into legislative operation, would set the question at rest for ever, without interfering with the rights of property,' this local organ of

Tenant Right affirmed. However, there was precious little chance of the government incorporating any of the Galway Member's proposals in the Land Bill. His conversion to thorough-going reform, like that of his friend Lord Dufferin, who earlier had been an even more forthright defender of landlord interests, came too late in the day to be of service to Gladstone. The battle within the Cabinet had been fought and lost, thanks in part to the moderate conservatism of people like Gregory and Dufferin. But there was an alternative course of action, as Gregory had hinted in his speech on 11 March. If compulsory Tenant Right was unacceptable why not provide for its voluntary adoption? The Tenants' delegates had welcomed this solution when Gregory put it to them, as had a meeting of Irish Members. With the assistance of Sir John Gray he had secured the signatures of the bulk of their colleagues on a document which had then been forwarded to the government. However, the cold reception given this proposal by Chichester Fortescue convinced Gregory that the situation was hopeless and despite Gray's pleas he refused to go on with the matter. Nevertheless, when the Kilkenny M.P. introduced their permissive Tenant Right proposal in the House on 19 May Gregory considered himself honour bound to give him every support. He made an effective speech, emphasising the benefits to landlord and tenant alike. The landlord who consented to create a tenant property in his estate — and he promised to be among the first himself — would receive compensation in the form of 'secure rents, perfect peace about his home, and a relief from all the litigation involved in the Bill'. From the other standpoint, 'He knew if he was a tenant on any property on which this principle should be adopted that he was perfectly secure, except for certain causes [non – payment of rent, wilful neglect and dilapidation of the holding, subletting]. He knew if he fell into arrears he was sure to be able to sell his goodwill. He knew that every improvement he made increased the value of that goodwill.'[17]

Although Gladstone paid Gregory a handsome compliment; describing him as a 'worthy representative of an admirable class of landlords,' that was merely the sugar coating on the pill of the permissive scheme's rejection. This the latest defeat for Tenant Right brought ominous word from Ireland. Patrick Duggan, soon to be promoted from the parish of Athenry to the see of Clonfert, informed Gregory that the government's measure was widely regarded by the people as a curse. Evictions would only cease when Irishmen passed in their own parliament another land bill, the priest concluded. This endorsement of the reawakening repeal sentiment, the demand for Home Government or Home Rule, was accompanied by renewed protestations of the clergy's inability to check popular frustration and anger. 'Now, we priests, are utterly helpless to arrest the current of dangerous feelings,' he wrote. 'Gladstone has made us as mute as dumb dogs.' While some landlords, such as Lord Longford, did express confidence that 'our virtues will protect us from spoilers', and that 'I and my fellows will keep our estates, and die in our beds', there was, in truth, scant cause to be sanguine.[18]

Manifestly, Ireland had not been pacified. The Land Bill went in tandem through Parliament with the Peace Preservation Act, which bolstered the detective establishment — something Gregory had proposed in his letter to the editor of *The Times* — and sought to control more effectively the possession of firearms and facilitate police operations in proclaimed districts. Nevertheless, the following year saw the suspension of habeas corpus in certain areas. There was no alternative, Gregory conceded. The 'reign of terror' in Westmeath was a 'scandal and disgrace to civilization'.[19] Nor did the land settlement revive the island's stagnant economy. Landlords had lost in the Land Bill their absolute property in land and were unable to create farms of an efficient size worked by improved techniques so they declined to invest capital.[20] But the tenants were few who could take advantage of the land purchase scheme in the Bill. Yet the economy continued to be almost exclusively agricultural. This situation might have been less pregnant with disaster had Gregory's proposals in 1868, to promote economic diversification through substantial investment in transport-ation and manufacturing, been adopted. Part of the population would have been drawn off the land and the chances for social peace improved. But the large sums released as a result of disestablishment and dis-endowment were to be invested in agriculture and fisheries.

Another integral and vital part of Gregory's comprehensive programme of appeasement was an alliance with the Catholic clergy. Several of the conciliatory steps for which he had called were also taken by the Gladstone Government. Not only had the Irish Church been dis-established but in 1871 the Ecclesiastical Titles Bill was finally repealed. Unfortunately, the latter concession to Catholic opinion made little impact. Three or four years earlier it would have been viewed as an act of greater significance. However, the report of a select committee appointed in 1867, on which Gregory sat, and which by the barest majority recommended removal of this obnoxious law from the statute book, had been rejected at that time by the House. Equally, if Duggan's attitude was as representative as Gregory often believed, those parish priests alienated by the terms of the land settlement were unlikely to be won back as allies of the civil authorities even by the welcome provision of loans with which to puchase glebes and a few acres.

The hinge of the relationship with the hierarchy, as Gregory had long understood and warned, was the government's willingness to sanction and support denominational education. 'The land is a very difficult question to deal with,' John Derry had written to him in 1869, 'but there is really no excuse for not disposing of the Irish Education question in a way just to all religious Denominations in Ireland — in accordance with their views, their rights, or even their reasonable preferences.' Bishop McEvilly, who had always insisted that without its satisfactory settlement 'peace and contentment' could never be expected in Ireland, wrote from Rome after the passage of the disappointing Land Bill to remind Gregory that education was 'the sorest question'. Not surprisingly, the Galway M.P. in turn exhorted Chichester Fortescue to follow the Church and Land Bills with an Education Act. 'You can hardly form an idea how much more easily the mechanism of government would work here,' he informed the Chief Secretary's ambitious if not domineering wife, 'if the Bishops were disposed to apply the oil.' Moreover, the royal commission established by the Tories finally reported in 1870, and it was highly critical of both the national and model schools. But Gladstone shied away from the political danger to which a bill founded on the commission's recommendations would have exposed his government — that of being perceived in England as 'truckling' once again to the Roman Catholic clergy. Disappointed by his inaction on the schools, the hierarchy finally broke with the Prime Minister in 1873 over an unsatisfactory University Bill. [21]

The failure of Gladstone's first mission to pacify Ireland also suggests the weakness of the Gregory master plan, even had he obtained the office he sought and with it a measure of control of Irish policy. He possessed greater knowledge of Ireland than either Fortescue or Gladstone, and was more sensitive to its needs, but neither of these virtues would have enabled him to overcome English resistance to much of the necessary remedial legislation. He would have been just as confined by a crabbed popular opinion in the other kingdoms and in Parliament. English and Scottish Members had delayed the repeal of the Ecclesiastical Titles Bill; English and Scottish members of the Cabinet had prevented the extension of Tenant Right; the Queen frustrated a proposal to establish a royal residence in Ireland; and the revival of anti-Catholic prejudice in England dissuaded Gladstone from making concessions on education. *Ireland's English Question* remained.

While the dogged and unsuccessful pursuit both of high office and the conciliation of his native land undoubtedly dominated Gregory's parliamentary career after 1857, thriftless ambition did not ravin up his political life. He made time and found the energy for an impressive variety of interests and causes. 'He is prepared to discuss with you the history of every land, and of every race from Indus to the Pole,' an ironic *Tuam Herald* commented in 1865; 'and at a moment's notice, to rush into the discussion of every subject from the highest aesthetics of the fine arts down ... to the latest patented improvement in the mechanism of a rat-trap.' [22] Catholic in his secular tastes, he chaired in 1864 a select committee on the Scientific Institutions of Dublin which frustrated the attempt of the Department of Science and Art at South Kensington to acquire control of the Irish Museum of Industry and recommended that greater liberality be shown to the Royal Irish Academy. Chartered in 1786 'for the promotion of the higher branches of Science, Polite Literature and Antiquities in Ireland', it was too impoverished to employ the custodial and clerical staff necessary if the public was to be admitted to the collections and to the library. However, another three years were to pass before the government was prevailed upon to be more generous.

William Gregory also took a prominent part in the squabbles surrounding the British Museum, rejecting the notion that as a mere Irish Member 'he ought to employ himself in wrangling over some grand jury bill, or some pleasant religious squabble'. Moreover, he spoke with authority on this topic. 'From taste and inclination ... he was frequently at the Museum, and well acquainted with the affairs of the place.' Conditions there were a scandal. Want of space prevented many collections, ever increasing in number and size, from being made available to men of science or for the amusement of the public. Priceless objects were condemned to the basement and 'concealed in impenetrable darkness', or in the case of Assyrian antiquities exposed in a 'miserable and unseemly cistern'. One solution was to remove the natural history collections from Bloomsbury to Kensington, but Gregory fought a long and doughty rearguard action against this particular dispersal. In 1859 his motion for the appointment of a select committee was defeated by the dissolution, but the following year he chaired the Committee on the British Museum which reported in favour of the enlargement of the Bloomsbury site. When the government responded in 1862, and again in 1863, with schemes to remove part of the Museum's holdings to South Kensington, Gregory helped engineer its embarrassing defeat in the House of both occasions.[23]

The intensity of his involvement in what may seem a somewhat mundane, if not arcane question requires explanation. Certainly, he was responding to a larger ambition to ensure that London had public institutions worthy of its position as the world's greatest and most important capital. Visits to museums and galleries in continental cities filled Gregory and some of his friends with shame at the 'discreditable conditions of our own Museum'. 'I had the grand idea of turning the present British Museum into what would have been the finest and most scientifically arranged Museum in the world,' he recalled twenty years later. The patchwork nature of the government's proposals would, he feared, bring 'discredit' on the nation. But the conflict over the Museum's future was also part of a bureaucratic struggle for power, one which the energetic and skilful director at South Kensington, Henry 'King' Cole, appeared to be winning. 'He did not wish to see all the institutions of the country fall into the grasp of that craving, meddling, flattering, toadying, self-seeking clique that had established itself at Kensington,' Gregory informed the House. However, at the heart of his concern to keep the natural history collections at Bloomsbury there lay a nobler consideration.

Gregory looked upon the Museum as an educational and recreational institution for all classes of society. He repeatedly called for the establishment of lectures there, arguing that by 'this means those who were unable to purchase the catalogues would be enabled to appreciate the value of the collections there assembled'. He had never forgotten his introduction years earlier to a group of remarkable Coventry weavers who passed their weekends making collections illustrative of the entomology of the neighbourhood. Yet it was obvious that 'without proper books or oral instruction many a working man who might otherwise under more favourable circumstances achieve distinction, must forever forego pursuits on which he might have shed much honour'. In some small way the Museum might aid similar groups of London working men to overcome these obstacles. Nor was it fair that working people who had contributed in taxation to the £2,000,000 which had been spent on the Museum between 1823 and 1850 were unable to participate 'in the advantages of the expenditure'. Finally, the evidence taken before his committee in 1860 had established that the natural history collections were by far and away the most popular. Thus this was for William Gregory a 'working man's question'. To transfer those collections from central Bloomsbury to the 'distant suburb' of Kensington 'would be taking them from the poor and giving them to the rich'. The well-to-do could drive out there in carriages but the working man would not be able to afford the cost of the journey.[24]

Proof of the sincerity of Gregory's interest in the enrichment of the lives of working people was afforded by his recurrent and at times quixotic jousts with the champions of sabbatarianism. Proposals to throw open to the public on Sundays places which offered 'recreation of a pure, elevating and intellectual kind' raised the hackles of many of those who considered themselves God-fearing. They denounced sabbath-breaking and railed against the raising of competition with places of worship. They warned working people of the frightening consequences of breaching the custom of one day's rest in seven, for someone would have to work at the places of recreation and employers would exploit this precedent. 'Think, ye sons of toil, how large a portion of your life is made up of Sundays,' the Working Men's Lord's Day Rest Association implored. The labourer who had toiled 49 years had enjoyed 7 years of sabbath rest, it calculated. Had he been compelled to work seven days a week during that period 'what a weary life his work would have been. His frame would be worn out long before its time, and his existence would be shortened by some years'.

When working people showed themselves willing to brave the dangers of an earlier grave and a harsher day of judgment, Gregory proved to be a sympathetic ally. In 1861 he secured the opening on Sundays of the Glasnevin Gardens, Dublin. But the broad local and parliamentary support which made this Irish victory so effortless could not be reconstituted when he turned his attention to Scotland. Petitions from thousands of working men, seeking the opening on Sunday afternoons of the Botanical Gardens, Edinburgh, had been quietly ignored by a government and private Members united in a healthy respect for the power of the Scottish Church. And when Gregory bravely took up the cause in 1863 he was promptly excoriated by one clergyman who declared that 'It was a painful thing to have the Scotch sabbath interfered with by the representative of an Irish Papist constituency, one of the most degraded communities in the world.' Defeated in this instance, though the vote was surprisingly close (123–107), he took up the cudgels again and this time on behalf of 47,000 people who petitioned for the Sunday opening of museums and galleries. 'If they really wished the [British Museum] ... to be accessible to the working classes,' he informed the Commons in 1867, 'they would get rid of some of their Pharisaical notions and open it on Sunday.' In March 1869 he escorted the deputation from the National Sunday League which called upon Gladstone to press the case, and in June made what he always regarded as 'one of the best and most exhausting speeches' of his entire career in support of the request.[25]

There were a variety of reasons why Gregory took up the issue of Sunday opening with such zeal. His own scepticism in spiritual matters surely heightened his awareness of the confusion which evidently existed in the minds of the members of the Society for Promoting the Due Observance of the Lord's Day over the 'Christian Sunday' and the 'Mosaic Sabbath'. From his reading of the New Testament he understood that the tendency of the former had ever been towards a relaxation of the latter, and the League insisted that it was merely seeking to ensure that Sunday was devoted to its original purpose — 'a day of devotion, of rest, and of innocent enjoyment'. No less important, and by no means unrelated to his personal scepticism, William Gregory 'repudiated in the strongest terms this assumed right of one man to subject others to burdens and annoyances and restrictions on account of his conscience and religious scruples'. He agreed that every effort ought to be made to induce the 'mass of the population' to attend religious worship in the morning but believed that in the afternoon they should be able to enjoy 'innocent or profitable recreation'. In short, he was calling as a liberal for recognition of liberty of conscience and for conduct tempered by respect and honour for the devotional observances of others. He challenged on principle the right of sabbatarians, even when a clear local majority, to impose 'pains and penalties upon a minority'. Nor was he unmindful of the strong odour of class as opposed to religious prejudice enveloping this discussion. The working people who wrote to him, many of their letters laboriously if not painfully composed, were informed that they were to be kept out of parks and museums on Sundays in order not to offend God and to protect the sanctity of the day of rest. But it was common knowledge that the Prince of Wales had visited the Zoological Gardens on the Sabbath and on many a Sunday the roads around Regent's Park were blocked by the carriages of the wealthy who were promenading there.[26]

Yet it was William Gregory's social and political conservatism that went far to determine his stand. The National Sunday League was at pains to emphasise that neither it nor its supporters were 'innovators'. They quoted approvingly the observations of one London magistrate who had declared: 'Encourage the people to take innocent recreation on Sunday and you will confer a great benefit on society [for] in proportion as you give people better taste they will relinquish low sensualities.' To those who warned that sabbath breaking would encourage drunkenness Gregory replied that the deplorable scenes he had seen on the streets of Edinburgh were only to be equalled by those he had witnessed in Glasgow. 'It was very certain that Scotch asceticism in the observance of the Sabbath produced no effect in diminishing the prevalence of drunkenness,' he remarked with asperity. On the other hand, wherever places of pure, elevated or intellectual recreation had been thrown open on the one day of the week when the working class was able to visit them they had proven immensely popular and there had been a significant decline in drinking. All of which gave weight to the argument that the 'National stores of the wonders of nature' and the museums and galleries holding the 'beauties of Art' would 'teach wisdom and decorous behaviour to the "rough" whom curiosity might attract within the building'. In brief, Gregory considered Sunday opening essential 'for the moral and physical improvement of the masses of the great towns'. Those unfortunates who lived in ugly and crowded cities, their homes all too often squalid rooms and dwellings where young and old were herded together, where the wife cooked, washed, weaned, and the husband carried on a trade, required and deserved a refuge other than the gin shop on dull, or wet, or dismal Sundays. 'You cannot give the pure air, and the green fields and the clear sky,' Gregory preached in the Commons, 'but the little alleviation you can give you refuse, and in doing so you invoke the name of God whose most glorious attributes in the hearts of Christian man are mercy and beneficence.' But he was responding not simply to the prick of his social conscience. Having lost the battle to prevent a significant enlargement of the working class electorate he saw hope through uplifting recreation of minimizing the social consequences of that defeat. And it was with a touch of irony that in 1869 he revived the discussion of Sunday opening in the 'Reformed Paliament', only to have the debate come to a sad and inconclusive end when notice was taken that fewer than forty members were present.[27]

Among the institutions whose doors William Gregory had wished to see flung open at a time convenient for working class visitors was the National Gallery. Founded in 1824 with the Liverpool Government's purchase for the nation of the collection of John Angerstein of Lloyd's, it no less than the British Museum became an annual subject of controversy. The belated establishment of a public gallery, for most European states had long since recognized the importance of such collections 'to art and to the cultivation of public taste', fueled arguments over its purpose and policy. Some pessimistic patriots concluded that the slow start had completely hobbled Britain in the race for Old Masters. Treasures held in private collections had already been largely bought up, they gloomily counselled, while Italy no longer offered a rich harvest. In earlier years regulations forbidding the removal of masterpieces had been all too easily circumvented. Paintings had been purchased from churches and other religious institutions with the connivance of 'greedy priests and ignorant monks' and copies substituted. However, by mid – Century the laws were being enforced with greater vigour. 'After allowing works of the highest interest and beauty to perish from absolute want of common care, after permitting those in churches and public galleries to be tampered with and ruined by the cleaner and restorer, after exposing them to every injury which ignorance, indifference, and neglect could inflict,' one Englishman complained in 1859, 'the Italian Governments bethink themselves of making a merit of keeping their remains in the country, and have recourse to measures equally illiberal and unjust to retain them.' Indeed, in 1859, the Gallery's Old Masters numbered no more than 259 out of a total collection of almost 600 pictures. Moreover, such important schools as the Dutch and the Flemish were poorly represented. Certainly, works 'by the early Flemish painters — so important and interesting for the influence they exercised on the development of the art of painting — were almost entirely absent.'

These circumstances and deficiencies were grist for the mills of those who advocated a Gallery devoted predominantly to 'national productions'. Instead of attempting the impossible by endeavouring to collect 'a tolerably adequate representation of the various schools of painting' the National Gallery, they reasoned, ought to consist of the works of British artists, whose genius was 'of the true British stamp — natural, vigorous, manly and truthful' — such as Hogarth, Reynolds, Gainsborough and Turner. Others, while admitting the importance of the best works of British painters, continued to insist that the National Gallery include 'well selected specimens' of the Continental schools.

Gallery policy was the responsibility of an administration which had been reorganized in 1855. An unwieldy body of Trustees charged with 'general superintendence' was slimmed down to a board of six; a salaried Director was appointed to recommend purchases and a Travelling Agent 'to ascertain and describe the contents of private and other collections abroad, and to obtain the earliest information of any sale'. Purchases were to be made from a grant of £10,000 annually voted by Parliament, but the Treasury wisely agreed that the sum 'need not be annually expended, but might accumulate, and thus enable the Trustees and Director to purchase a fine collection at once, if such an opportunity should offer'. Finally, a Keeper was named to act as custodian of the collections and to serve as secretary to the Trustees.

The choice of Sir Charles Eastlake, the President of the Royal Academy and a former Keeper, to be the first Director proved to be a happy one. Rejecting provincialism, he adopted the plan common to most of the great European galleries. The National Gallery would provide a selection of the works of the different schools of painting 'arranged historically and chronologically for general instruction', and in his first four years of office more pictures were purchased than in the preceding three decades. An admirer of the Italian schools of the 14th and 15th Centuries Eastlake concentrated on acquisitions representative of their work. Although the years between 1824 and 1862 did not see the purchase of a single work by a British artist, the Gallery received a number of handsome and significant gifts. Among the most important of these was J.M.W. Turner's bequest of hundreds of his own finished and unfinished pictures and thousands of water colours and drawings, though the terms required that room be found to put them on show. ·

Sir Charles Eastlake's aggressive purchasing policy, which saw 145 pictures added to the collection, together with the gifts and bequests, merely exacerbated the problem of space. Originally located 'in the dull and dingy rooms of a private dwelling in Pall Mall', the Gallery had removed in 1838 to a new building on Trafalgar Square which it shared with the Royal Academy. This arrangement simply ensured that much of the collection was consigned to the cellars. Another concern was the damage done by the soot and smoke of industrial London and the 'impure mass of animal and ammoniacal vapour' given off by the hordes of visitors. The 'effluvia of so many human bodies' produced a greasy substance which softened varnish and caused dust to adhere to the paintings. Yet proposals to despatch the Gallery to Kensington or some other suburb were fiercely resisted. 'Its very existence would be speedily forgotton by the millions or they would look upon it as inaccessible as Pompeii or Pekin,' the *Gentleman's Magazine* protested. In short, there was widespread agreement that the advantages of a central location outweighed the dangers of industrial grime. Nevertheless, Eastlake hoped to see the Gallery relocated in Piccadilly. Believing that the 'vast area' around Burlington House would ensure sufficient space for a half-century to come, he prompted William Gregory to recommend this solution in 1864. 'I will only beg, if you refer to it either publicity or privately,' the Director wrote, 'that you will not mention my name in connection with it.' In supporting the removal of the Gallery to the Burlington House site Gregory stressed the unworthiness of its present home. 'The whole of Europe must be ransacked without finding a building so unfitted in every respect for the reception of a national collection of pictures,' he observed. Such disdain also extended to many of the visitors to the Trafalgar Square building, for soldiers from the adjacent barracks made use of it as a convenient place of rendezvous with 'housemaids'. The proposed move was unlikely to inconvenience the general public, Piccadilly being no less central. Parliament decided, however, that the National Gallery should remain where it was.[28]

Gregory's interest in art was life – long but grew with age. There was, of course, a strong aesthetic tradition in the family. Uncle Richard had been a dedicated and determined collector, both of paintings and sculpture, and during their European wanderings before taking possession of Coole William's parents had picked up additional 'booty'. These influences may have been strengthened during his undergraduate years. Christ Church Library housed the Guise Collection, which boasted fine examples of the Italian schools and included works by Holbein and Vandyke. The political acolyte of Sir Robert Peel was surely also inspired by his hero's love of art. One of the earliest Trustees of the National Gallery, Peel was the proud owner of a large collection of masterpieces. Finally, it was fashionable in the 1850s and 1860s to take an interest in and be knowledgeable of the fine arts. The Prince Consort gave his backing to Eastlake and his policies and such close Gregory friends, personal and political, as Layard and Elcho, were dilettantes.

As he advanced into middle age William Gregory increasingly combined European excursions and tours of continental galleries. His visit to the Low Countries in 1861 was undertaken primarily to study Dutch and Flemish masters. Writing to an American friend the following year, he reported: 'I have for some time been wandering through North Italy giving myself up to my chief hobby when away from the House of Commons; namely, the study of early Italian architecture and early Italian painters.' In the autumn of 1863 he took himself off to Spain, although the physical discomforts of this experience appear to have blighted his opinion of Spanish art. Transportation proved to be a disagreeable challenge, for there were few railroads and the excellent high roads did not compensate for carriages without adequate springs. The inns were cheerless and extremely uncomfortable, and he was forever encountering fleas, grease and garlic. Predictably, he fell victim to diarrhoea and this prolonged misery, together with a persistent low grade fever, did nothing to improve his disposition. 'Neither it nor its inhabitants will inspire me with the slightest feeling of regard,' he remarked of Spain at the height of his misery. 'It is the most hideous country in the world, and all classes except the peasants who are good people, are proud, jealous, superstitious, dull, ignorant, and rogues.'

Debilitated and depressed, he admitted to being disillusioned with Murillo. However, nothing could lessen his 'inordinate admiration' for Velasquez whose 'portraits, even matched against those of the greatest of the great, can hold their own in strength and vigour with those of Titian'. Moreover, when he travelled further south and his health improved he was ready to concede, as he stood looking down from the Alhambra across a marvellously fertile plain surrounded by rugged mountains, and saw in the east the huge range of the Sierra Nevada covered with eternal snows, that Granada was one of the loveliest places in the world. Moorish architecture and decoration also struck him as beautiful. Nor did he scorn the opportunity to revisit Spain and tour Portugal in 1865 in the company of an art expert, and it was during this expedition that he purchased cheaply in Léon an 'Assumption of the Virgin' which was long to hang at Coole.[29]

The death of Sir Charles Eastlake in December 1865, just a few months after his reappointment as Director, brought a legion of would-be successors into the field. A measure of Gregory's growing reputation as a politician of some influence in these matters was the decision of at least one of the candidates to seek his support. The difficulty of finding a replacement for Eastlake saw a weary Lord Russell offer the post to Henry Layard on the understanding that he would serve without pay and continue as Under Secretary of Foreign Affairs. He declined. William Boxall was eventually appointed. He had been backed by Lady Eastlake, amongst others, and was described as a man of 'exquisite taste, literary achievements, a wide knowledge of art, and engaging manners'. Unfortunately, he lacked the drive and self-confidence of his predecessor. A portrait painter of 'great refinement', he was, as one essayist later delicately observed, 'of so scrupulous and sensitive a nature, that he was rarely satisfied with his own work, and left much that he undertook unfinished. He consequently did not attain that reputation to which his undoubted abilities entitled him.' Such indecision suggested that Boxall would require the support and the pressure of active Trustees, and when in 1867 a vacancy opened on the Board William Gregory successfully solicited the appointment from Disraeli. [30]

The following year the new Trustee was named to the Council of the Arundel Society for Promoting the Knowledge of Arts, where he joined such old friends as Layard (another Trustee) and Elcho. Founded by Charles Eastlake and a group of 'distinguished amateurs' in 1848 the Society's membership eventually grew to some 500. These dilettantes paid an annual fee of one guinea and thus provided the fund from which the Council financed diverse activities and publications. If the chief purpose was 'to obtain and reproduce in a popular form correct drawings' of those Italians frescoes in danger of ruin, the Society also issued reproductions of paintings in oils, scale facsimiles of sculpture, classical and medieval, even illustrations of sepulchral monuments.

From his position on the Council William Gregory was soon urging the Arundel Society to extend its operations from the reproduction of threatened frescoes to the publication of the many fine pictures hanging in out of the way churches and thus little known and rarely seen. However, it was to the affairs of the National Gallery that he continued to devote most of his time out of the House. William Boxall's purchasing policy had excited criticism. He was accused of nibbling at things and of talking too much about possible acquisitions, which merely served to drive up the price. Nor did he silence his critics with his bold purchase for £7,000 of *Christ blessing Little Children*, for it was not the Rembrandt he believed it to be but merely a schoolpiece. There was further criticism when in 1868 he acquired a Michelangelo, *The Entombment of our Lord*. Purchased inexpensively by Robert Macpherson, an Edinburgh surgeon who had taken up photography in 1851 and with his residence in Rome elevated it to an art with his photographs of the city's antiquities, cleaning revealed the painting's true quality (though some experts still challenge the attribution). There was a sensation in Italy but an attempt to reclaim it failed in the courts and Macpherson was permitted to ship the picture to England. Nevertheless, many observers considered the price Boxall paid Macpherson (£2,000) too high 'for such a mutilated and unfinished work'. Although Gregory sympathised with this opinion he defended the purchase.[31]

Stung by the attacks, Boxall required a gentle but firm push from Trustees organized by Gregory for that express purpose before he would purchase a second Michelangelo in 1870. Moreover, the Director showed himself reluctant to travel abroad in search of additions to the national collection. In 1869 he complained that his official expenses were insufficient to cover his costs and that he had returned from an expedition the previous year to Spain and Italy £180 out of pocket. In 1870 the outbreak of the Franco-Prussian War provided him with an excellent excuse to remain at home. 'I wish you could tell me where to find some *first rate* works in England,' he wrote to Gregory in September of that year. As a result of this inactivity, and indecision, the Gallery failed to spend its annual grant and revisions to the Treasury regulations now required the return of any unspent balance. In 1871 that sum promised to be £8,800. The anguish Gregory suffered as a result of this turn of events, for there were fine pictures on the market in London and Paris, was not lessened by the evidence that Chancellor of the Exchequer Lowe had concluded that this was the time to dispense with the annual grant. 'He says we have pictures enough,' the incredulous Trustee reported to Layard. Yet it was against this unpromising background that William Gregory played an important role in the successful negotiations which led to the acquisition of the Peel Collection. 'We have made a glorious purchase,' he wrote ecstatically. 'They fill up every gap.' More accurately, the National Gallery was now very strong in the Dutch School. Significantly, it fell to Gregory to explain and justify in the House the special grant of £75,000 needed to make the purchase, and he gave short shrift to one member who protested that the nation could no longer afford such expenditures. There was, then, no immodesty in his private boast that he and Layard (for he was writing to his friend) were the two Trustees of vigour. It was well and good that the majority of the Board be 'men of contemplation,' he observed, but it was essential that at least a couple of them be men of action and energy.[32]

The primacy Gregory gave to the welfare of the National Gallery was underscored by his acquiescence in the decision finally taken in 1868 to remove the natural history collections from Bloomsbury to South Kensington, for he understood that a number of drawings by Old Masters would eventually be transferred from the Museum to Trafalgar Square. However, the chronic problem of overcrowding had become acute there. The response of the Tory Government had been to announce in 1868 the removal of the Royal Academy to Burlington House and E.M. Barry was commissioned to redesign the National Gallery. Although Disraeli and his followers subsequently went down to defeat in the general election, a select committee of the new

Parliament did recommend the erection of a museum of Natural History and the enlargement of the Gallery. Gregory sought to exert additional pressure on the Gladstone Government to implement these proposals by organizing a memorial signed by prominent figures in the worlds of science and art. The response of the Treasury was far from sympathetic. It sent an 'ill-written, absurd, aggressive letter' to the Trustees which, in the name of economy and utility, demanded a definition of 'the principles and the extent to which British Pictures ought to be represented in the collection at Trafalgar Square which represents the pictorial art of all ages and peoples'. What was more, the Treasury suggested that the overcrowding might be relieved by the despatch of 'superfluous pictures' to other galleries on loan. Most Trustees saw the hand of 'King' Cole in all of this and suspected him of scheming to establish an English Gallery at Kensington by grabbing the National's English School.

Alone among the Trustees Gregory opposed a blunt rejection of the Treasury request. While he, no less than other members of the Board, feared that to specify principles would establish limitations on acquisitions which might in turn discourage gifts and bequests, Gregory was willing to surrender some of the works of British artists. At his suggestion the Trustees sent a 'modified reply' to the Treasury. The National Gallery would not part with any of its 'first rate' English pictures but would be content with a single example of the work of 'moderate' native painters. This somewhat more accommodating stance may have strengthened the position of the Gallery's advocates within the government, and that summer saw the Gladstone ministry commit itself to a Natural History Museum and a large addition to the National Gallery. Not that this decision solved all problems. The land purchased by the government, and on which the extension was to be built, had once been a burial ground for victims of the plague. Reports that the Church would insist on a costly and time-consuming re-internment of all remains in consecrated ground provoked Boxall to complain that 'surely nothing so absurd can be suffered to delay the commencement of this long promised Gallery. A firm and compact bed of concrete would thoroughly protect the poor plague-struck bones till Doomsday'. Meanwhile, architect Barry viewed the extension as merely an interim settlement. The fact that the new galleries could even then be filled, and that fresh acquisitions would certainly be made during the two years of construction, prompted him to label this a 'make shift scheme' in his correspondence with Gregory.[33]

In addition to the struggles over the British Museum and the National Gallery, William Gregory was in the thick of the fight over the location of the new Law Courts. These public institutions were part of the whole cloth of his desire to ensure that London had buildings worthy of her international position. Perhaps he and other British visitors to the French capital during the Second Empire had at least a sneaking admiration for the great schemes of Napoleon III's Prefect of the Seine, even though *The Architect* deplored 'the destruction of ancient buildings and thoroughfares'. What is more certain is that the bitter disappointment of his own omission from the Gladstone Government is 1868 had been tempered by pleasure at the inclusion of Henry Layard as First Commissioner of Public Works.[34]

A short man with a large head and a 'restless irritable look', Layard's bulldog appearance and temper did not endear him to many of his parliamentary colleagues. This 'mighty self-sufficient gent' had too high an opinion of himself and was too discourteous in debate to be popular. Dubbed 'Mr. Lie-hard' by one antagonist he was more accurately described by *Punch* as 'the Bull in the Chinaware shop for he smashes everything about'. Despite occasional and sharp clashes in the Commons, he and William Gregory established an intimacy which saw the Irishman stand as best man at his wedding in March 1869. Exact contemporaries, the two men were drawn together by the wide range of their shared interests. Both were dilettantes, reading widely, enjoying music, loving beauty and fascinated by art. And Layard entered office in 1868 determined, with Gregory's help, to give Britain the public buildings she deserved.[35]

Having written to the editor of *The Times* in August 1868 to endorse the campaign for the decoration of the capital with imposing structures, Gregory was chosen by the friends of that cause to take the lead in the House. He gave notice of motion in the spring of 1869, calling attention to the construction of the Law Courts and urging that they be built on the Thames Embankment. This would be the first step towards the erection of a series of buildings which would 'make it the glory of the world', and in February he was named as a member of the Thames Embankment Committee formed by the Society of Arts. But Layard's subsequent announcement in the Commons that the government intended to build the new Law Courts on the Embankment let loose a storm of opposition. It was led by indignant law associations who prefered the original choice of site, one bordered by the Strand on the south and Carey Street on the north, which was somewhat closer to the chambers in Lincoln's Inn and Chancery Lane. Their argument rested not merely on convenience but also on economy, humanity and philistinism. What of the huge sum of money already invested in the Carey Street site, they asked? They expressed concern for the health of lawyers and solicitors plodding daily up and down the 120 steps between the embankment level and that of the Strand. Finally, they insisted that the 'misfortune of our public architecture is the interference of irresponsible dilettanti'. The 'notion of ornamentation of the metropolis' ought to be excluded from the discussion, they declared, for what was required was a building in which business might be carried on 'with the greatest amount of expedition, economy and efficiency in a locality as central as possible for those who have to conduct their business'. Before this onslaught, which *The Architect* described as 'Lincoln's Inn against All England', the Gladstone

Cabinet gave ground. It agreed to the appointment of a select committee to re-examine the question. Both Layard and Gregory sat on that committee but they were unable to hold the line against the powerful legal forces marshalled by the former Attorney-General and future Lord Chancellor Roundell Palmer, and it recommended a return to the Carey Street site.[36]

Defeated on the location of the Law Courts, and with his plans to beautify the British Museum and import Italian mosaics to decorate the Houses of Parliament the objects of parsimonious scorn, Henry Layard threw up office and went into political exile as Minister to Spain. Although Gregory chided him for abandoning their great mission, the Irishman fleetingly harboured the hope that he might succeed Layard. Instead the Board of Works went to A.S. Ayrton, who as Parliamentary Secretary to the Treasury had in the name of economy done so much to frustrate Layard. He was opposed, Ayrton informed his constituents in the London borough of Tower Hamlets, to public expenditures on 'painters, sculpturers (sic), architects and market gardeners'. With public affairs and public taste under the control of the likes of this man, a disdainful Layard observed, 'it is time that men of feeling and those who feel any pride in their country should move off'.[37]

Disappointed that his claims to promotion had been ignored yet again, scornful of the new First Commissioner, Gregory also gave thought to moving off. He had at last found an influential and assiduous sponsor in the person of Lady Waldegrave. A colourful figure and a remarkable woman, she had survived three husbands before marrying Chichester Fortescue. She, along with Lady Palmerston and Lady Molesworth, had been one of the great hostesses during the hey–dey of the political salon. And while the day of the salon had long since passed invitations to Strawberry Hill, her gothic castle overlooking the Thames and Richmond Park, were still prized and accepted by the powerful and the aspiring. Without either education or refinement, and haughtily dismissed by some contemporaries, such as Lord Stanley, who remarked that she had the bad taste to flatter him even though they had never met before, Frances Waldegrave possessed an extraordinary power of 'attaching' people. 'None of her visitors, however eminent,' it was said, 'ever deserted her.' She had been a devoted admirer of Sir Robert Peel, had promoted the Duke of Newcastle as a possible Prime Minister, and was a confidante of the Clarendons. This strong Peelite tradition may have been the basis of her friendship with William Gregory, who had as a much younger man attended her masked balls but did not become an intimate until the late 1860s.[38]

At Gregory's request, Lady Waldegrave sounded out Earl Granville in October 1869 about the possibility of the Irishman securing a colonial appointment. The governorship of Ceylon was the post he had his eye on. The Colonial Secretary's initial response was not encouraging. He noted that the Ceylon post would not fall vacant before 1871, and then expressed disappointment that he had not known of Gregory's interest

'An Art Critic'. The cartoon of Mr. Gregory, as a Trustee of the National Gallery, that appeared in *Vanity Fair*'s issue of 30 December 1871.

sooner because he had recently been seeking a Governor for Mauritius. This remark, and a flattering acknowledgment that there was 'no more competent and Cosmopolitan man' than Gregory, smacked of a polite refusal. However, Lady Waldegrave did not give up the cause and she continued personally, and through her husband, to seek a private assurance of an appointment for Gregory. Pessimistic about the outcome, he also secured her aid in an effort to stake a claim to an Under Secretaryship of Foreign Affairs. Here his prospects appeared somewhat brighter, for Clarendon headed the Foreign Office. There was no 'general shuffling of the cards' in the offing, the Foreign Secretary replied, but he declared himself happy to propose Gregory's name should a vacancy occur. Within a few months Clarendon was dead and a government shuffle could not be avoided. Chichester Fortescue wanted to move from the Irish to the Colonial Office and succeed Granville who after some hesitation agreed to take the Foreign Office. Lady Waldegrave worked strenuously to advance her husband and among her agents was William Gregory. He was deputed to see John Delane, the editor of *The Times*, and he lobbied among fellow Liberals. Of course, Gregory would have been less than human had he not again hoped that his own moment had come. There was talk of the unpopular Ayrton being eased out of the Board of Works and of Gregory taking his place there. Then again, Fortescue's promotion would open the Chief Secretaryship. But neither of these changes were made. The Earl of Kimberley not Fortescue went to the Colonial Office and Ayrton continued as First Commissioner. Gregory knew that his last chance for high office had gone. Even the redoubtable Frances Waldegrave had been unable to rescue his political career from the obscurity of the back-benches. 'I can only say that knowing what has occurred I am satisfied you have as usual been my truest friend,' he wrote to her. For her part she sought to prevent him from sinking into despondency at this final setback, sending the message: 'Tell Gregory that when the right moment comes we shall take very good care of him.'[39]

The promise of eventual recognition was not enough to console the Irishman, not least because the private assurance of a colonial appointment which Lady Waldegrave had eventually extracted from Lord Granville might prove worthless with his change of portfolios. Wounded, resentful, depressed, he quit London for Coole long before the end of the parliamentary session. Then, in October, he set out on another tour of Italian galleries, but the foul weather he first encountered on the Channel crossing to Antwerp dogged him across the Continent. Driven from Venice by the elements he arrived in Rome to find the city deserted and the Vatican museums shuttered. The arrival of snow saw him hasten further south, only to fall victim to the worst conditions on the Mediterranean in living memory. The passage from Naples to Palermo took 26 hours, which was double the normal time, and he was almost drowned entering the Sicilian port when his boat sprang a leak. Nor was his return up the Italian peninsula any happier.

Trapped for five days by more snow and intense cold in Florence he occupied himself examining a private collection whose contents were 'filth'. The young lady showing them 'was very pretty and frisky', he informed Henry Layard, 'so I paid them a longer attention than they deserved, which she seemed quite aware of and highly amused at.' But neither relaxation nor reflection brought contentment. His once promising political career lay in ruins, at least to the extent that a place at the Despatch Box was the true mark of success. For reasons he did not understand the offices which others considered him eminently well qualified to fill had all eluded his grasp. He was too old at 54 'to climb the ladder by beginning at the lowest rung'. He was tired of Parliament, and for all his protests to the contrary was worried that passage of the Ballot Act would make more difficult the task of winning re-election. How could landlord and clerical control be maintained when the electorate voted in secret? And he did not relish the prospect of 'being dragged through the dirt' as a result of his opposition to such measures. Nor was his growing and discouraging sense of failure diminished by the fate of the causes he had so energetically and passionately championed — the appeasement of Ireland, the Sunday opening of places of 'pure' recreation, and the adornment of London. He began to fear that even the National Gallery extension would reflect the new and triumphant spirit of 'Ayrtonism' and be 'as bald and bare as a Quaker's Meeting House'. In short, he saw no hope of plucking the country out of the 'bog of vulgarity and bad taste in which she is immersed'. One other woe was his persistent financial troubles. The hint of desperation in his quest for a colonial appointment had been both monetary and political. Hence he greeted with a mixture of joy and relief the confidential news early in 1871 that Kimberley had confirmed that the Governorship of Ceylon was soon to be his. The salary was generous and would enable him to save. No less important, he had finally been given the long-craved opportunity to make a 'name' for himself. If he occasionally succumbed to self-pity — 'sic finis Gregorii,' he wrote to Henry Layard — he could truthfully add: 'I have no regrets by my departure.'[40]

News of William Gregory's colonial appointment and retirement from Parliament brought tributes both traditional and unusual. Across the Atlantic, the *New York Tribune* was moved to observe that his loss to 'art and social progress' in Britain would be Ceylon's gain. From the nobility, gentry and clergy of County Galway he received an address and from 'a few Catholic prelates priests and laymen' an inscribed silver claret jug. The parish priest of Woodford, near Loughrea, wrote to request a photograph 'of your own good self' which he intended to place alongside that of the Holy Father 'so that I may be constantly remined to pray for your good health, long life and safe return to your country and your friends'. Praise of the departing M.P. was mixed with apprehension that the struggle to succeed him would destroy the political peace in the county. There had been a hint of future difficulty during a by-election in February 1871, which had seen Mitchell Henry nominated to join Gregory as a representative of the county. The son of Irish parents who had emigrated to England and made a fortune there, Henry had once sat for the constituency of South Lancashire. However, the previous decade had seen him spend more of his time in western Ireland than in Britain. He built a gothic castle at Kylemore, Connemara, invested heavily in a Galway factory, and was recognized as a 'resident proprietor'. With the discreet assistance of Gregory, who solicited the support of Bishops McEvilly and Derry, Mitchell Henry had been returned. His calls for denominational education, for British championship of 'the dignity and independence of the Pope', and for home government, had taken the wind out of the sails of some 'ultras' on the Home Rule question. And he celebrated his victory in great popular style, staging a magnificent display of fireworks at Kylemore, followed by a ball to which tenantry and tradesmen were also invited, and throughout the night an Irish harp and shamrock formed by gas illuminations decorated the castle.[41]

The hierarchy's backing of Henry had been at the expense of Captain John Nolan, a Catholic landlord, and they were loath to deny him twice. Nolan had been embarrassed during the 1871 by-election by the charge, made by a parish priest, that he had evicted tenants in 1864 and 1865. He immediately withdrew from the contest and took the unprecedented step of submitting the tenants' claims for compensation to arbitration. When the arbitrators recommended that the dispossessed be restored to their holdings the contrite landlord lost no time in launching legal actions to recover the tenancies from those 'middlemen' now in occupation. His popularity restored and his conduct paraded by tenant spokesmen as a model of how an injustice ought to be corrected, Nolan was a formidable if not unbeatable candidate in the contest to succeed Gregory. 'I think we'll put in Nolan,' the Gort parish priest wrote to the retiring Member of the approaching by-election. 'If there be a contest it will be Landlord v Tenant. The gentlemen of the former class are I understand as a rule enraged at the precedent set by the gallant Captain. Well let them be — the people are proud of it.' When landlords, Catholic as well as Protestant, Whig/Liberal and Tory, did unite behind a candidate — Lord Clancarty's son, Captain William Le Poer Trench — they found themselves in a bitter battle with not only the tenantry but also a united clergy.[42]

Trench approached old Archbishop MacHale, looking for clerical endorsement, but received a stinging rebuff. He was advised 'not to disturb the peace of the county by a contest with Captain Nolan, a contest which he could not hope to win but by the unconstitutional coercion of the Catholic constituents, who form the great mass of the Galway electors.' Throughout the campaign the *Tuam Herald* exhorted the faithful to give their votes to Captain Nolan, 'the chosen of the Priests and the People,' while poor Trench was regularly traduced. Evidently, the broad based coalition constructed by William Gregory, embracing prelates and liberal landlords, had fallen apart and he was powerless to halt the unequal trial of strength. Privately, he deplored Trench's nomination and rued the early death of his friend Dunkellin. Had he lived, Gregory later argued, Clanricarde's elder son would never have countenanced this foolish effort to reassert landlord political control and would have dissuaded his father from joining hands with Clancarty.[43]

Nolan's landslide victory at the polls was widely regarded as a triumph of 'priestly influence'. Not content simply to win, a choleric Clonbrock wrote to the former Member, the clergy had invoked heaven and moved earth in order to 'trample' the landlords. Tom Burke, one of Trench's most important Catholic supporters, had fled the country under a deluge of 'petty, venomous slander'. Another embittered landlord, Denis Kirwan, amended his will to ensure that he was not buried in Catholic Galway and that not one of his tenants touched his coffin. These proved to be timely provisions, for he died three weeks after the election. And Bishop McEvilly, while he criticised the landlords for their refusal to put up a 'presentable' candidate, thereby contributing to their own humiliation, did admit to Gregory that 'some four or five priests went to lengths that I would be the last to palliate, the more so as the extreme measures resorted to were utterly unnecessary'. The evidence of 'spiritual intimidation,' which well-dressed Trench supporters had thoughtfully taken the precaution to gather at Nolan meetings and in chapels, was the foundation of the petition to unseat the victor. The trial of that petition, which opened in April 1872, and lasted for six weeks, saw more than 300 witnesses called. Then, on 27 May, the mercurial Judge Keogh delivered his opinion in an extraordinary pyrotechnic performance. Unstinting praise of Oliver Cromwell was mixed with furious denunciations of prelates and priests, but throughout this extended exercise in mass provocation he comported himself in a way which did nothing to lend solemnity to the occasion. 'At one time treading in furious form the narrow arena of the bench; at another, smiting the ambient air in the vehemence of his exuberant elocutionary efforts' and beating the judicial bench; he occasionally descended 'to the softest cadences of the most approved stage whisper, to ascend presently to the highest pitch of oratorical intonation'. Keogh upheld the petition and Trench was subsequently seated in Nolan's stead.[44]

Some of William Gregory's correspondents applauded the Judge's resort to his vast storehouse of epithets and praised his 'truths', but even from his safe colonial port in this storm the former Member of Parliament deplored the harangue. Indeed, he supported those friends who disassociated themselves from it or, like Mitchell Henry, contributed to the National Insult Fund launched to assist Nolan pay his costs which were estimated at £15,000. From a member of his family Gregory learnt that cousin Trench had spent £9,000, and there was never any doubt of the pyrrhic nature of the victory. His membership of the Commons was certain to be shortlived, and when a general election was called in 1874 he prudently retired from political life. A group of liberal landlords did attempt to deny Nolan and the clergy the satisfaction of sweet revenge that year, by putting up a candidate of their own on 'national' principles, but this ploy failed. Captain Nolan topped the poll, followed closely by Mitchell Henry who had already announced his full conversion to Home Rule. The Liberal finished a distant third. In short, the Galway results mirrored those elsewhere. Home Rulers and nationalists had profited from this miserable affair and the Liberals had been ruined by it. In the words of one ironic Gregory friend, William's parliamentary career had 'a striking tableau for the end'.[45]

9

Governor of Ceylon

Coming from a family of intelligent and strong willed women the mature William Gregory was at his ease in the company of females and flourished in their society. The leading London hostesses invariably added his name to their lists of guests, and during the parliamentary session his life was a never-ending round of dinners and receptions. Always engaging and frequently witty, with a fund of stories and anecdotes, cultured, attentive, a faithful correspondent whose letters were pleasantly gossipy and invariably cheerful, he established and sustained many close friendships with members of the opposite sex. He was such an attractive bachelor that friends urged him to capitalize upon his evident charm. 'Why do you flirt with every woman,' James Clay good naturedly inquired. 'Marry one instead.' Another well-wisher picked out a 'handsome and well jointured' American widow, and invited her to his estate so that Gregory might look her over. In 1863 reports of his engagement to a Trench relative were promptly contradicted but four years later he was informing intimates: 'I believe I am going to be married — that is to say my marriage is declared but there are some difficulties in the way which retard it.' The difficulties were probably financial and his intended wife Elizabeth Temple Bowdoin.[1]

Elizabeth, or Lizzie as she preferred to be called, was the widow of James Bowdoin, a soldier. She was also one of the six daughters of Sir William Clay, the head of an important merchant house and a politician of some distinction. He had represented the constituency of Tower Hamlets for twenty-five years at the time of his retirement in 1857, and had held a minor office in the Melbourne administration. Along with her husband, Elizabeth belonged to that society of refugees from the British winter (which included the Gregorys, mother and son) annually gathered on the Riviera. There she and William Gregory may have first discovered their mutuality of interests, for Lizzie 'was a woman of many accomplishments, a good linguist, extremely fond of art, and remarkably well read'. In London, Gregory lived on Grosvenor Street West which was just off fashionable Eaton Square where the Bowdoin home stood. The summer of 1867 found him increasingly in the company of the handsome widow, dining at her home and escorting her to the opera. But hopes of an alliance must surely have foundered on the rock of Gregory's inadequate income. He was living on an allowance which varied between £65 and £75 a month during the session and before the year was out had been obliged to remortgage, with his mother's consent and co-operation, a part of the Coole estate in order to raise £5,500. Under these circumstances a union may well have been unacceptable to Lizzie's family. [2]

No sooner had his appointment as Governor of Ceylon been confidentially confirmed by Lord Kimberley than William Gregory advised Henry Layard of his impending marriage. The post carried an annual salary of £7,000. In their marriage settlement Elizabeth Bowdoin, on whom her father had settled £5,200 a year at his death in 1869, helped loosen the snare of debts in which William had entrapped himself. The 1867 mortgage had been secured by a series of life insurance policies but the premiums were certain to rise dramatically when Gregory went off to the tropics. Thus in return for an annual rent charge of £1,000 on the Coole estate in the event of William's death, Lizzie put up £4,000 as security for the outstanding debt. On 11 January 1872, the day following this act of emancipation, they were married at fashionable St. George's, Hanover Square. Now in his fifty-sixth year, the arched eyebrows and sharply chiselled nose gave the groom a faintly sardonic air. Equally, the thin and untidy whiskers that framed the lower half of his face, for they grew beneath but not on the chin, accentuated his age. His bride was considerably younger, only just entering middle age and seemingly still capable of bearing children. Yet her 'saxon type', for she possessed both a fair skin and a fair complexion, did not extend to her physique. She had a 'frail form' and ill health may well have been the cause of the wedding's postponement from the summer until the very eve of their winter departure for Ceylon. Moreover, the Gregorys quit England in the full knowledge that she might not be able to remain long in the colony. In the event that Lizzie's health broke down William intended to give up his office and return with her to Britain. [3]

Thoughts of Ceylon filled William Gregory's mind and study of the colony filled his days in the months before he and Lizzie set out for the East. Some friends were aware of the fascination and 'mysterious charm' that region of the world had long held for him. There his great-grandfather had made the fortune which raised the family from obscurity. However, those intimates who sought to dissuade him from going into this distant exile received only the most superficial explanation of his determination to take up the appointment. 'To save money is a great object to me, I like a warm climate, and there is much to interest one in the island.' At other times he quipped that he would busy himself 'amassing snails, or improving the breed of Cingalese caterpillars or making a collection of White Elephants'. Yet all of the while he was preparing with great care for his new responsibilities. An obvious starting point was Sir James Emerson Tennent's *Ceylon An Account of the Island Physical, Historical, and Topographical with notices of its Natural History, Antiquities and Productions*. A fellow Irishman, and one

whose home in County Fermanagh was reputedly the *Castle Rackrent* of
Maria Edgeworth's famous novel, Tennent had served in the colony as
Colonial Secretary and Lieutenant Governor. His portrait of an ancient,
beautiful and exotic land was calculated to entrance readers and to
titillate them with just the hint of danger. Moreover, he wrote
reassuringly of the climate. The heat was not in itself unhealthy, he
reminded propective visitors, and the malarial regions were well known
and therefore easily avoided. He insisted that 'a lengthened residence
in the island may be contemplated, without the slightest apprehensoin
of prejudicial result', and that ladies, 'from their more regular and
moderate habits, and their avoidance of exposure [to the sun],' were
likely to withstand the climate even better than men.[4]

The quest for more information about this small part of the Empire
took William Gregory to see Lord Torrington, Tennent's superior during
his service in Ceylon. Torrington's term had dramatically illustrated
some of the pitalls of colonial government. A supercilious manner and
clumsily executed policies had first alienated the Governor from the
European community and then contributed to the outbreak of a native
revolt in 1848. Thus the discussion must surely have served both to
strengthen the Governor-designate's resolve to enter upon his duties
with a sound understanding of the colony's problems and to remind
him of the need to treat with sensitivity the various ethnic groups that
made up its population. He continued his education at the Colonial
Office. The official correspondence and the Blue Books offered a detailed
insight into the current situation and officials briefed him on the
Downing Street view of some of the major questions which would confront him on arrival. Gregory corresponded privately and unofficially
with the man he was succeeding at Queen's House, Colombo, who
happened to be a fellow Galway landowner. In addition to profiting
from Hercules Robinson's intelligent advice he took full advantage of
the presence in Britain of A.M. Ferguson, the editor-publisher of the
Ceylon Observer, to add to his knowledge of the island's European
community and establish cordial relations with the press. After more
than six months of careful and thoughtful preparation Gregory had
every reason to look forward eagerly and confidently to his government
of Ceylon. Success there would help erase memories of the many
disappointments of his political career.[5]

The Right Hon. William H. Gregory (he had been appointed to the
Irish Privy Council in July) and Mrs. Gregory left England immediately
after their marriage. They travelled at a leisurely pace across France and
into Italy, embarking at Brindisi for Egypt on 22 January 1872. At
Alexandria they had their first taste of the trappings of office. The
Khedive's barge came out to take them ashore, their baggage passed
through customs unopened, and as they strolled to the special train
which had been laid on to carry them to Cairo they were preceded by
an imposing official carrying a large silver rod. No less pleasing was
Gregory's ability to befriend a group of Americans who had been fellow

passengers from Italy, thereby saving them from the horrors of the Customs House and Alexandria. He and Lizzie remained in Egypt for three weeks but were unable to see as much as they had planned. The short voyage from Brindisi had prostrated her and she was still suffering more than a fortnight after their arrival. Nevertheless, there was time for a short trip up river to see the huge sarcophagi and they attended a performance of Giuseppe Verdi's *Aida* at the Khedival Theatre. Commissioned by the Viceroy and intended to be one of the great artistic celebrations of the Suez Canal's opening in 1869, the first performance of the work had been delayed for a variety of reasons until the month before the Gregorys' arrival. And it was the judgment of William Gregory that the Khedive's total investment of £50,000 had not been a wise one. 'Verdi was paid £5,000 and a drearier article was never yet purchased,' he remarked critically. Although the staging was 'wonderful' the music was the 'dreariest' he had ever heard. On this strange note, for the adjective he employed to dismiss the score could scarcely have been more inappropriate, Gregory and his wife left Egypt.[6]

They set sail from Suez on 16 February aboard the P & O steamship *Australia*. She was a large vessel, indeed one of the largest in service, and her size, the fair weather, and entertaining company, were the essential ingredients of a 'wonderful' passage which even Lizzie survived in 'fine style'. The long journey from England had given the Gregorys ample time to adjust to their new intimacy. Lizzie's 'clinging dependence' upon those she loved might have been expected soon to irritate a bachelor of William's age but her unfailing good humour and unselfishness even during the miserable trial of the Mediterranean crossing left a deeper impression. Nor could any husband have failed to respond to 'her excessive pride and delight' in his importance as well as his company. 'She is one of the pleasantest of companions,' he informed his mother, 'so clever and agreeable to everyone and at the same time so nice and sweet tempered that I consider myself a very lucky fellow to have such a helpmate in my exile.'[7]

Most voyagers approaching Ceylon from the southwest were struck by its beauty, the low coastline even creating the illusion that the coconut palms were growing out of the sea. William Gregory proved to be no exception. Entering the harbour at Galle, and passing the fortifications built by the Dutch, he marvelled at the richness of vegetation and the brilliance of the colours. After a weekend of rest at a government residence the Gregorys steamed up the coast on Monday, 4 March, for a ceremonial entry into Colombo complete with flags, bands, escorts and salutes. They remained in the hot and sticky capital for three additional days only, just long enough to tour the city by carriage and explore their imposing official residence, and then sought refuge in the mountains from the heat and humidity.[8]

The distance from Colombo to Kandy is a mere 70 miles but the latter's elevation offers assurance of a less oppressive atmosphere. An earlier governor had built an attractive Italianate residence there, the Pavilion, which was set in beautiful grounds. Moreover, the city was one of historic and religious importance. The collapse of the unitary Sinhalese realm in the Fifteenth Century had seen the rise in Kandy of an independent kingdom which through military skill and diplomatic finesse had resisted successive native, Portuguese and Dutch efforts to subdue it before the British finally triumphed in the Nineteenth Century. Fifty-five years after that conquest William Gregory found the 'Old Palace' of the Kandyan kings occupied by the Government Agents for the province, and since a revolt in 1818 the colonial authorities had tended to view the native chiefs with suspicion and had generally sought to curtail their power and influence. Yet this policy had contributed to the lawlessness which culminated in the 1848 revolt, and if that episode served to reinforce the ambivalent official attitude towards the Kandyan aristocracy the new Governor responded positively and sympathetically to these proud and noble men. He employed the influential chiefs as native officials in the Kandyan districts. Nor was he unmindful of the former capital's religious significance. It boasted the Temple of the Tooth, which housed that sacred relic of Buddha. The Kandyans believed that whoever possessed the Sacred Tooth was the province's rightful ruler and the rebels of 1818 had seized it. Gregory quickly established a friendly and relaxed relationship with Dunawilla, the Sacred Tooth's guardian, and it paid a handsome dividend. The Governor tended to believe the rumours that the guardian like a number of priests was 'a bit of a rogue', and in 1872 and again in 1876 he made proposals to increase supervision of the Buddhists' scandal-plagued affairs, but he later admitted that Dunawilla always gave him 'excellent counsel on matters concerning the customs and feelings of his countrymen'. [9]

    After several enchanting days in Kandy, during which they toured the famous botanical garden at nearby Peradeniya, rising temperatures drove the Gregorys higher into the mountains. Their destination was the hill station and sanatorium of Nuwara Eliya, some thirty-six miles to the south-east but almost 5,000 feet above Kandy. The steep climb by carriage on narrow roads that often ran along the edge of precipices imbued Governor Gregory with a zeal for road widening and protective embankments. Happily, journey's end was worth the tortuous approach. The climate at the mountain retreat was ideal for British expatriates, at least during the first four months of the year. Clear sky and clean air, a soothing wind so unlike the 'rusty sawlike gusts' of home, these could be enjoyed in temperatures that rarely rose much above a very comfortable 65°. In the refreshing chill of the evening there was the additional pleasure of a crackling wood fire. Not surprisingly, the Governor, who had been loaned a small cottage there, decided that the acquisition of an official residence was a matter of some urgency. After four months in the damp and hot city of Colombo, from September until December of each year, retirement to a cooler and invigorating climate would be 'indispensable for the maintenance of health and vigour', he wrote to the Colonial Office. Lord Kimberley readily conceded that it was 'very desirable in order to secure the efficiency of government that the heads of it should have the means of passing some of their time in a salubrious climate', and he endorsed the proposal. Gregory artfully forestalled possible resistance by selling the residence in Galle, which he dismissed as virtually useless, and thus had £1,500 in hand to apply against the purchase price of £2,600 for the 'commodious house' and 26 acres of land he had quickly picked out in Nuwara Eliya. Subsequently, the colony spent a further £1,400 on decorations and improvements to Queen's Cottage and its grounds. [10]

The Gregorys designed an English garden for their new home, filling it with strawberries and roses, and then supervised the construction of a 'fine fowl yard' which would guarantee them regular supplies of fresh eggs and fat poultry. To this they soon added pens for sheep and pigs, for William had savoury recollections of the small legs of pork with the least dash of salt on which he had frequently feasted at the Garrick Club in London. Before long, this passion for improvements had transformed the surrounding area. More drives, walks and rides were cleared and an 'ungainly swamp' converted into an attractive lake, to which the Governor gave his name. Idyllic as it seemed, life at Nuwara Eliya was not to the taste of everyone in the Gregorys' entourage. Late April brought the rain which signalled the approach of the south-west monsoon. The cool, damp weather, together with the cramped quarters of the small cottage the Governor and his staff initially inhabited, proved too much for the French chef. Declaring the climate a threat to his delicate health, he resigned. His loss was a serious one to Gregory who had travelled to Paris in the autumn of 1871 for the express purpose of finding someone 'to cook into something eatable the bad and fresh provender of Ceylon'. Moreover, the man had proven to be pleasant, courteous and economical as well as an excellent chef. While they waited for a replacement to arrive from France, William and Lizzie were obliged to employ a native cook who almost poisoned them yet fancied himself 'a perfect cordon bleu'. [11]

Despite these culinary problems, when Governor and Mrs. Gregory moved down to Kandy for several months at the beginning of May they gave weekly dinner parties at the Pavilion and the Queen's Birthday was celebrated in fine style. There was the traditional ball and while a great deal of champagne was consumed no one drank to excess. But they saved the most lavish entertainments for the four months of residence in Colombo beginning in September. By this time a replacement chef had arrived and there was a dinner party at Queen's House each Saturday for some 30 guests and more intimate gatherings during the week. Gregory had thoughtfully ordered 50 dozen bottles of champagne and reports of his 'satraphical magnificence' quickly reached and delighted friends in Britain. Years later he wrote: 'I may in justice to myself and without boasting attest that neither before nor since my Government have such excellent dinners and wines appeared on the tables of Queen's House.' He repeated in Colombo the Monday croquet parties that had proven so popular in Kandy, and there was a ball every other week. Disliking late nights, the Governor arranged for the band to bring all dances to an end at 12:30 a.m. by striking up God Save the Queen.[12]

If by no means scintillating, this sprightly social life provided diversion and served the useful political purpose of sustaining Gregory's initial popularity. Yet he earned acclaim as well as courted it. He was greeted as a welcome and refreshing change after his dull and dour predecessor. Lizzie proudly informed William's mother that he fully deserved the high praise he received, 'for he is so active and energetic, so anxious to see and judge everything for himself, so courteous to high and low, and has such unfailing good spirits and temper'. William Gregory had taken to heart the advice of the earnest Hercules Robinson to take advantage of the long and otherwise inactive period between his landing at Colombo and the opening of the legislative session there in September to see something of the island and study its inhabitants. Indeed, the new Governor undertook the investigation of his colony with such thoroughness that his admiring and long suffering wife was moved to protest the small amount of time they were spending together.

'I am determined to visit every station, go over every road, and know and talk with every public servant in the island,' the enthusiastic new Governor wrote to one friend. 'It is the only way to act when Government is personal.'[13] Once Lizzie was safely and comfortably settled in the cottage loaned to them at Nuwara Eliya, he undertook a four day inspection of the coffee planting district south of Kandy and then set out on a month long tour of his dominion. He boarded the Colonial steamer at Colombo and sailed up the west coast to the northern port city of Jaffna. It was the centre of the colony's Tamil population, the descendants of immigrants and of the waves of invaders from Southern India who had been the bane of ancient Ceylon. The Tenth Century had brought the destruction of the Sinhalese capital of Anuradhapura by conquerors who founded another further to the south at Polonnaruwa. When the resurgent Sinhalese finally expelled these invaders the following century they retained the more secure city as their capital, but in the face of renewed invasions they eventually retreated to the south-west. By the Thirteenth Century a Tamil kingdom centred on the Jaffna peninsula had arisen. The Portuguese ended its independence three hundred years later. However, a visit to Jaffna served to remind the Governor of the ethnic and religious cleavages (the Tamils were Hindus) within the native population. The next port of call was Trincomalee, and then it was on to Batticaloa situated about half way down the island's east coast. At this point the comforts of the steamer were abandoned and Gregory continued his journey on horseback. He rode some thirty-five miles south along the coast road to

Karunkoddittivu before swinging inland and describing an arc which brought him back close to Batticaloa only then to turn south and west for Badulla. As he approached that town he was at least able to transfer to a carriage, thanks to the road building of Hercules Robinson, and in this more stately fashion make his way back to Nuwara Eliya.

After a brief period of relaxation Gregory was off again, first examining more coffee plantations in the mountains and then riding eighty miles north in July to inspect the unfinished arterial road to Jaffna and see for himself what was required in order to speed construction. This trek also gave him an opportunity to examine the rest houses, wells and medical facilities provided for the thousands of transient labourers, or coolies, who came to the colony each year from India to work the coffee plantations. The fact that a substantial number of these 'poor people' perished was a source of concern and Gregory had crossd the narrow strait separating the island from India during his trip to Jaffna in April to learn more of the 'coolie system'. Finally, the July expedition saw him visit Anuradhapura — the first Governor to do so in fifteen years. The region had an evil reputation, Tennent describing it as 'pestilential', but Gregory discovered that the dangers to health were less serious than he had believed. He attributed the improvement to Robinson's very modest expenditure of £160 to clear back the jungle from the ancient city, though it now boasted only a handful of huts. The former capital's attractions for Gregory were its antiquities. The ruins of palaces, temples and private dwellings, and the inscriptions, were all magnificent relics of an erstwhile grandeur. 'There is much that is grotesque and bad in taste,' he observed, 'but much that is very beautiful.'

Despite his exhausting itinerary Governor Gregory showed no sign of flagging enthusiasm or failing energy. Quite the reverse, he had been rejuvenated by his first few months in the colony. He faithfully followed Lizzie's instructions not to spend too much time in the sun and to eat only in moderation the sour fruits he liked so much. Equally, he was careful not to sample too generously the fine fare he served to guests. Having given up all spirits and beer, and usually taking cold tea with both breakfast and dinner, he sensed a recovery of youthful strength and vigour. Soon, he was boasting to his mother that he was never knocked up or drowsy and was able to stand the heat and fatigue rather better than the younger members of his staff who had guzzled the champagne, claret, or brandy and soda water. Practising moderation, even abstemiousness, but brimming with good health, confident that he had loosened the grip of time's devouring hand, the Governor returned exhilarated from his journeys of exploration and investigation. 'I am perfectly charmed with this island,' he informed Henry Layard, 'the beauty is beyond anything that even you with your imagination can conceive.' He liked the natives. 'The people are very good,' he reported, 'no amount of serious crime, and I suppose in the enjoyment of greater comfort and ease than any population in the wide wide world.'

No less intoxicating was the knowledge that he at last possessed the power to do 'much good' and 'both by legislation and public works to leave a good name'. In short, he had 'the feeling of being free and able to work with his hands unfettered.'[14]

A Governor's domination of this Crown Colony was no longer as absolute as it had once been, yet he remained supreme. Reforms adopted in 1833 required him to consult an Executive Council composed of a handful of senior officials and officers, such as the Colonial Secretary and the officer commanding the colony's forces, but he was under no obligation to accept their advice. The five members of the Executive Council also constituted the larger part of the official majority of the Legislative Council, where there was a minority of six unofficial members. All appointed, they were intended to be representative of colonial society and opinion. Thus there were three Europeans and three natives — a Sinhalese, a Tamil and a Burgher (the last being the descendants of unions between the earlier European colonists, Portuguese or Dutch, and native women). But the Governor's power of veto, his control of financial measures, and the official majority, all ensured that a Legislative Council he chaired and where he possessed an original and a casting vote was responsive to his wishes. Of course, he could never forget that all ordinances had to be forwarded to London for confirmation, amendment or rejection by the Crown. Inevitably, there had been calls in the colony for a liberalization of this form of government. Some reformers had demanded that the official members be permitted to speak their minds and vote on the Legislative Council as their consciences dictated. Then, in 1864, a dispute over the military expenditures brought to the boil the long simmering struggle to establish a measure of popular control over the Council. The Ceylon League was formed in 1865 for the purpose of forcing recognition of the right of the unofficial members to command the budget. That was not a concession the Colonial Office was willing to contemplate let alone grant. 'The Europeans, who are temporary settlers have, as a rule,' the then Colonial Secretary, the Earl of Carnarvon, replied in 1866, 'no real sympathy with the natives and will only advance the interests of the latter, so far as they do not conflict with their own interests; the natives are not sufficiently advanced to be entrusted with power. Once withdraw the control which the Home Government have now over the Revenues and Legislation of the Country and that day will prove the beginning of the end of Ceylon. Do what the natives will, the dominant race has means of asserting and maintaining its interests which the natives will not enjoy for a long time.'

Hercules Robinson had advised his successor not to seek any change in the constitution or powers of the Legislative Council before he had gained some experience of the working of the system. But Gregory lost little time seeking a limitation upon the tenure of the Council's unofficial members, which was effectively for life. To his mind renewable terms of seven years would help ensure that these men remained responsive to and representative of the colony's changing conditions. Further, he sought to reconcile the surviving Ceylon Leaguers to his government by inviting one of their leading figures to join the Legislative Council. 'My old Parliamentary habits have made me well aware that vigorous, searching, independent criticisms of government measures are the very salt of good legislation,' he declared. 'I do not deprecate but welcome such criticism if applied in a fair and manly spirit and I am confident it will ever be by you.' Although he failed to get his man in 1872 Governor Gregory soon succeeded in his larger purpose of conciliating Leaguers. He revived the practise first introduced in 1855 of appointing nominees of the Colombo Chamber of Commerce and the [Coffee] Planters Association to fill vacancies in the unofficial membership, and this arrangement satisfied a number of the former dissidents that their interests were now fairly represented. Nor was he unsympathetic when in 1875 the Chamber of Commerce revived the old proposal that official members be allowed to vote according to their private opinions. Not that Gregory intended to surrender any of his power. 'So long as a Colony remains a Crown Colony the Governor is really the only person responsible,' he continued to believe. Thus he would never have conceded all that the Chamber sought, and certainly not the freeing of the five members who also constituted the Executive Council. As the Government's ordinances were first submitted to them and their objections were noted in the minutes they 'could not be allowed to stultify themselves by opposing measures they had prepared'. Yet he did recommend the conditional emancipation of the other four official members. They ought to be free to vote their opinions unless expressly required to support the government. Greater liberty would encourage the four to give closer attention to the proposals submitted to the Legislative Council, he argued unavailingly in a despatch to the Colonial Office. It opposed any meddling with a Council which was working so well. [15]

William Gregory had also given thought to the composition of the Executive Council, for he was less than impressed with the advice he received from that quarter. The heart of the problem, he rapidly concluded, was the fact that the majority of the members were men without long experience of Ceylon. Consequently, they had little knowledge of administrative details, of the various races, customs or systems of land tenure, and not one of them spoke either Sinhalese or Tamil. Therefore, he suggested that the officer commanding the troops be removed from the Council and that at least one Government Agent, and possibly two, be appointed to it. The Colonial Office scotched the first proposal but endorsed the second. However, Governor Gregory had long since created an alternative institution which gave him the informed advice he sought — the 'durbar'. He summoned all of the Government Agents to a meeting at Kandy in the summer of 1872 to discuss the forthcoming legislative session in Colombo, and the gathering proved so helpful and successful that he made it an annual event. [16]

It was a well schooled Governor who returned to Colombo that first September to preside over the Legislative Council. The preliminary course of study in England had been capped by personal tours of the colony and consultation with the Agents who administered its several provinces. Consequently, his address to the Council revealed an impressive understanding of the island's needs and a remarkable knowledge of its conditions, while the programme of action he envisaged won the admiration even of old Colonial Office hands. 'Mr. Gregory does not mean to let the grass grow under his feet,' one permanent official minuted. The new Governor sought to reassure the powerful coffee planters that he recognized their importance to the economy and intended to assist them. The Dutch had grown a small amount of coffee near the coast in the Eighteenth Century but the British defeat of the Kandyans and the building of roads made possible the exploitation of the far more suitable highlands. Encouraged by a rising demand for coffee in Europe, especially in those areas where the consumption of wine was falling, and aided first by the collapse of that market's traditional West Indian suppliers (whose labour system had been dislocated as a result of the emancipation of slaves) and then by colonial preferences in the British market, Ceylon planters invested heavily in this crop. Although excessive optimisim had been punished during an extended crisis at mid-century, bust turned to boom as the 1850s wore on. The construction of the Colombo-Kandy railroad, financed by the colony and opened in 1867, was obviously of immense benefit to the planters but their appetite for public works was insatiable. Indeed, the agitation for popular control of the Legislative Council had originated in the planters' discontent with government expenditures on such works. Mindful of this, and keen to effect a reconciliation with the remaining members of the Ceylon League, the new Governor declared it to be the government's 'bounden duty' to facilitate the cultivation of coffee by pressing ahead with new and improved roads, the extension of the railway, and 'outlets' for the crop — a reference to the development of Colombo as a harbour. However, he was careful to insist that works undertaken essentially to promote the coffee industry not be financed with long term loans.

Without being alarmist, Gregory expressed his unease at the colony's dependence upon this single cash crop. He had noted the many deserted estates during his tours of the Kandyan districts. Wasteful methods of cultivation by planters who did not work the land with any thought of handing it down to their children had resulted in soil exhaustion and a rapidly shrinking area suitable for planting. 'I cannot therefore but fear that all this prosperity of coffee planting is but transitory,' he wrote privately to Lord Kimberley within three weeks of stepping ashore at Galle, 'and that unless science supplies new and cheap applications to renew the exhausted properties of the soil, the end of this Century will witness the extinction of by far the largest proportion of the coffee plantations of Ceylon.' The Governor's pessimism deepened as his friendship grew with Dr. D.G. Thwaites, the Superintendent of the Botanic Gardens at Peradeniya. They had been introduced by Joseph Hooker, the Director of the Royal Gardens, Kew, who described Thwaites in a letter to Gregory in July 1871 as an 'accomplished naturalist and a skilful horticulturalist'. A scientist with a European reputation, Thwaites successfully communicated to the new Governor his alarm that the 'coffee bug,' a fungus which had recently appeared and was slowly spreading throughout the district attacking the leaves of the coffee trees, would eventually destroy the entire industry. 'The precarious nature of the crop, its liability to disease and ravages of insects, do not distinguish it from any other agriculture,' the Governor warned the Colonial Office in August 1872.

Fearful for the future of a coffee-based economy, Gregory's response was twofold. First, he argued 'that if any debt be incurred for the promotion of Coffee enterprise, it should be on condition of its being paid off as rapidly as possible out of the surplus revenue which is dependent on the prosperity of that industry.' Second, he advocated economic diversification. Thwaites had long been experimenting with tea and recommended the planting of cinchona (the bark much valued for its medicinal properties was used as a tonic and as a remedy for ague, and quinine proved to be its most important derivative). The ever energetic William Gregory promoted both these alternative crops. He personally urged planters to cultivate cinchona and saw to it that the excellent price the bark from Ceylon commanded in London was well publicised in the colony. As for tea, he ordered the planting of some thirty acres next to the Botanical Garden at Hakgala and sent to India for experienced hands to work the experiment. 'The planters will then be able to obtain every information as to proper manipulation and they will be able to see the annual balance sheet and count the cost,' he explained in a private note to Lord Kimberely who quickly applauded this initiative. By 1874 4,700 acres were cultivated with tea. One other possibility was to start a silk industry. Encouraged by the information that mulberry trees grew quickly and that the worms were hardy he sent to Japan for a small quantity of eggs.[17]

A second question demanding the attention of the Legislative Council, and one which the Colonial Office considered far more urgent than the colony's long term prosperity, was the treatment and care of the 50,000 coolies who came each year to work the plantations. Gregory's visits to the coffee districts had convinced him that few labouring populations anywhere in the world could be so well off, for the coolies had a shrewd appreciation of the importance of their labour and would quit if aggrieved. The planters, for their part, dreaded disputes with these indispensable labourers. But if self-interest and humanity combined to ensure that the coolies were rarely ill-treated on the estates, Gregory readily admitted that more might be done to care for those who fell ill. The central hospitals that had been set up in the provinces were usually too distant from the plantations to be of aid in emergencies, so he planned to establish medical districts of a more manageable size where the coolies could obtain advice and medicines. Also, he adopted Lord Kimberley's suggestion that a small cottage or hut be required on each plantation, or group of neighbouring plantations, to which the sick might be removed and assured of cleanliness, ventilation and elementary hospital appliances. Planters opposed these reforms, though less on grounds of ideology or expense than dislike of constant prying and interference by officals. Instead, they proposed that medical relief be organized and administered on a voluntary basis by themselves.

Concern for the coolies' welfare extended to the operation of the gangs in which they entered the colony at Jaffna and were marched south to the plantations. The Colonial Office proposed that these labourers be provided with rations for the journey, that the gangleaders, or Kankanis, be licensed, and that the number of immigrants be restricted. Two of these suggestions won precious little backing in the colony. The first excited visions of hordes of Indians descending upon Ceylon to claim the rations, thus making it 'A Pauper Asylum for Southern India'. The last raised in planters' minds the spectre of a rise in their labour costs. As for the licensing of Kankanis, Gregory stressed the difficulty of effectively enforcing this form of regulation when some 2,000 gangleaders were involved. How would immigration officials verify that the possessor of a license was the person to whom it had been issued? He favoured a resort to passes. Every Kankani would be required to carry a form on which the number in his gang at journey's beginning was recorded and he would have to account for any discrepancies in this figure at its end. And Gregory's conviction that this modest measure would suffice had been strengthened by his own trek up the northern road in July. He described as adequate the accommodation provided for the coolies, and found the settlements convenient to pure water. In those places where the wells had run dry he ordered others to be sunk. Moreover, these clusters of huts invariably attracted bazaars where the migrating labourers could purchase all the rations they required. Indeed, those he encountered appeared to be in good condition and excellent spirits. Although officials at the Colonial Office greeted the Governor's reports with some scepticism, unable as they were to square 'the capital condition of the coolies from first to last' with earlier explanations that the worrying mortality rate in some hospitals was due to the exhausted state in which these labourers reached the plantations, they decided to rely on his good judgment.

William Gregory's cautious and intelligent response to the coolie problem avoided the friction which might so easily have developed with the planters. Passes promised to compel Kankanis to pay closer attention to their gangs' welfare during the hike south. When the coolies reached the plantations responsibility for their medical care still devolved upon the planters. Bowing to that powerful lobby's demand for a voluntary system, the Governor accepted an ordinance which gave to the planters the power to appoint a committee which would make the medical regulations for their district. But as a long time chairman of a Poor Law Board, Gregory knew the value of state supervision of medical relief. Thus all rules and arrangements established by the planters were subject to the approval of the Governor and Executive Council. If in the opinion of the government a district had failed to proved adequate health facilities it was empowered to intervene and take over their management, financing the necessary measures with a tax on cultivated land. Further, the government required the prompt removal of all sick coolies to hospital, and it appointed each district's medical supervisor.[18]

The suspicion that Governor Gregory was overly solicitous of the interests of the European planters and insufficiently mindful of the welfare of the native population was quickly allayed. William Gregory had not thought deeply about the responsibilities of empire before his colonial appointment. In the Commons he had taken more notice of foreign rather than imperial affairs. Yet his Irish background and experience moulded his general approach to his duties as Governor, just as it influenced particular policies on medical relief and a number of other issues. 'It is for the glory of our nation, in the vulgar sense of the word glory,' he observed, 'that we should wield the sceptre of the Indies; but it is for our glory, in the true sense of the word, that we should promote, as of late years they have been, and now are promoted in Ceylon, and on the mainland of India, the happiness, and the social, moral, intellectual well-being of the peoples.' Nor in his case was this profession mere cant. He bridled when planters and 'merchants clerks', themselves 'the sons of pastry cooks and ladies' maids', assumed offensive airs in their dealings with natives some of whom had been educated and accepted in England. For his own part, he took as his guide the dictum that 'a native gentleman should be made to feel that you regard him as your equal, in short as an Englishman.' He favoured the introduction of 'natives into situations of responsibility', and not only in the Kandyan districts, though he revealed a common prejudice in supporting their exclusion from revenue departments. On the other hand he insisted on the dismissal of an Assistant Government Agent and District Judge, whose services he sorely wished to retain, because the man had used his offices to extort money from his native charges. The traditional course was to allow such transgressors to resign, but William Gregory was determined to impress upon native and European alike his intolerance of official misconduct. Not surprisingly, a prominent Sinhalese paid tribute to his 'impartial and liberal administration' by endowing a Gregory Scholarship at St. Thomas's College, Colombo.[19]

To the extent that William Gregory's conduct was governed by a single, overriding concern it was his determination as a genuinely benevolent paternalist to improve the well-being of the island's indigenous population. He made thorough, repeated and surprise inspections of every hospital, prison and asylum at the various stations he visited and in his first address to the Legislative Council gave notice that his government would spend substantial sums on these and other facilities, such as schools. He immediately launched an investigation of the 'mysterious and grievious disorder' called 'Parange disease', appointing an especially able medical officer to the Northern Province where the problem was most serious. In much the same spirit he declared war on the curse of drinking, considering it to be the cause of most of the crime and much of the misery on the island. The fact that liquor had been introduced by the British as a source of revenue, or so he believed, was in his mind 'a horrible reproach to the name of Christianity'. The ordinance which he introduced and the Council enacted established licensing regulations modelled on those in Britain; it prohibited the importation (except for medical and scientific purposes) of white spirits, an ingredient of a particularly poisonous home-brew; and forbade the adulteration of any drug with alcohol (other than those specified under English law) and the sale of liquor to children. Gregory's term saw more than 400 arrack taverns suppressed but 1,000 were still flourishing at its end.[20]

More successful and significant were the new Governor's endeavours to repair the island's once elaborate irrigation system. It had been developed by the Sinhalese in the First Century A.D., and involved the construction of canals and enormous reservoirs, or tanks, complete with a sophisticated method for regulating the discharge of water. An irrigation network of such complexity required constant maintenance, but the successive invasions from southern India prevented this. Abandoned, the waterways fell into disrepair and provided an ideal breeding ground for malaria-bearing mosquitoes. By the Fifteenth Century the entire system had collapsed. Four centuries later the British began the work of reconstruction. Governor Sir Henry Ward had spent some £80,000 on repairs in the 1850s, concentrating on the two giant tanks of Irakkaman and Amparai in the Eastern Province. When Gregory visited the province in April 1872 he did so primarily to examine these works, which had already increased the total area of rice paddy from 5,000 to 23,000 acres. Wherever cultivation was introduced 'the people became strong, vigorous and independent,' he learnt. Could there be any better way of spreading contentment, health and wealth? 'I am going to take up the subject with the greatest vigour,' he immediately confided to his mother, 'and form a separate department for the sole purpose of carrying it on without the loss of a day so far as our resources will permit.' The visit in July to the Nuwarakalawiya district around Anuradhapura did nothing to weaken his resolve. In this the former granary of ancient Ceylon he found 1,600 tanks, not one of them in a state of repair. The consequences were plain to the eye — waste, bare land or jungle infested with wild beasts, and an impoverished, emaciated population of 60,000 souls. Contrasting these conditions with those in the Eastern Province, he asked the Legislative Council to sanction measures which he hoped would expand and expedite the work of repair. In January 1873 it passed an ordinance which established a more flexible scheme for the repayment of the costs of these works. Gregory's personal investigation had satisfied him that an earlier provision, requiring villagers whose tank had been restored at state expense to pay back the advance in ten instalments, was too harsh for an impoverished people. Now the villagers would not have to begin repayment until they had begun to reap the benefits of their newly irrigated lands.[21]

The irrigation schemes had a direct bearing on the Governor's campaign to improve the health of the population. Abundant and wholesome food promised to curtail the ravages of disease, including the dreaded 'Parange'. Similarly, those schemes were essential for the success of his conservation policies. Gregorys had been planting trees at Coole for generations, thus William was dismayed to find in Ceylon vast tracts of jungle denuded of timber and left as wretched, unhealthy scrub. There were several reasons for this sad state of affairs, among them the absence of rational cutting operations and the want of proper forest reserves. However, the chief cause was the practice known as *chena*. This primitive and wasteful form of agriculture saw natives clear a patch of ground, throw seed on it and then surround the clearing with a fence. Within fifteen years the soil had been exhausted and abandoned. The cycle was then repeated on another virgin tract. 'It is for this miserable cultivation that the finest and most valuable timber has been exterminated,' the Governor reported to the Colonial Office. 'It is a wretched system in every respect as bad for the cultivator as for the Government. It confirms his natural laziness and indifference,' because less labour was involved than in working the paddy fields. 'It discourages any attempt at permanent improvement by draining, clearing and manuring — a close unhealthy jungle takes the place of open forest. It interferes with Paddy cultivation.' Yet inadequate supplies of water in areas such as Nuwarakalawiya prevented the prohibition of *chena*. Hence the link between irrigation and conservation. What Gregory did do was warn headmen of severe punishment if their villagers cleared good timber land unnecessarily; he created forest reserves; appointed a forester for each province; fixed rational cutting procedures; required some reforestation; and called for the establishment of nurseries to provide seedlings.[22]

William Gregory was as anxious to protect the island's game as he was its trees. He had seen only two deer and heard but a single pea-fowl while travelling through the Northern and Eastern Provinces. 'I wish it distinctly to be understood,' he declared to a responsive Legislative Council, 'that this is not an Ordinance to preserve game for the amusement of sportsmen, but to prevent the complete extermination of those animals which, a few years ago, supplied food to a large portion of the native population.'

The Governor's progressive and expensive measures — and he promptly announced his support for the long debated scheme to build at a cost of £600,000 a breakwater which would make Colombo a 'magnificent harbour' — were contingent upon healthy Government revenues. He acknowledged in his address to the Legislative Council that his predecessor had bequeathed to him an enviably prosperous colony, and his successful completion of the negotiations Hercules Robinson had opened with London for a reduction of the military budget resulted in an annual saving to the government of £50,000. 'The enormous price of coffee, and the fine crop has done wonders,' he wrote to Henry Layard early in 1873. With everyone full of money and the government assured of another fine surplus 'every man in the island is taxing his invention to spend it in the most reckless and unprofitable manner'. Not that he intended to permit waste. The surplus was earmarked for his ambitious programme, and no single aspect of it was more important to him than the cultural. Freed at last from the penny-pinching restraints of 'Ayrtonism', he intended to erect a 'museum of the Natural History and Antiquities of Ceylon' and 'redeem the island from the perfect indifference hitherto manifested for its history and products.' As befitted a leading member of the Arundel Society, he ordered a survey of the two ancient capitals, Anuradhapura and Polannaruwa, and the reproduction of every inscription, whether by photograph, casting, hand copying or rubbing. 'They are very remarkable, not merely religious, but moral precepts, historical narratives, ordinances on social questions and from every date indeed,' he explained to a fellow dilettante. It was his intention to remove all inscriptions of interest and no great size to the museum, so long as their removal would not give offence to the native population.

In less affluent times this project might well be regarded as an inexpedient luxury, Gregory admitted to the Legislative Council. The money being available, however, the opportunity must be seized to establish an institution 'which shall not be a mere random collection of miscellaneous objects, but a scientific, teaching exhibition, — which, while ministering to the amusements of many, may convey instruction to all who seek it.' In modern society men engaged in business for a portion of the day deserved and required opportunities 'for intellectual employment in the study of the works of nature and of man' which a properly organized museum affords them. Nevertheless, only too aware that this enlightened conviction was not held by all men and that many were moved by more bourgeois considerations, he spoke soothingly to the Council on the sensitive topic of cost. The museum would not become a constant financial drain on the colony, he promised. Attributing the expensiveness of such institutions in Europe to their insatiable appetite for objects from every part of the world, he emphasized that the acquisitions' policy in Ceylon would be insular. Although the Legislative Council sanctioned construction, progress on the museum quickly stalled. Lord Kimberley regarded 'literary and anti-quarian gentlemen' with jaundiced eye, believing them to be notoriously spendthrift. Thus when Gregory slipped into his estimates in March 1873 an appropriation for a museum the Colonial Office promptly took exception to it. Advised that he had not yet made his case for a building 'which appears to be designed on a large scale', he was instructed to go no further until he had secured Crown approval. 'How difficult it is to have one's own way in this world,' Henry Layard sympathised when informed of this development. 'But I have no doubt that with your energy and perseverance you will overcome all difficulties — especially not having a House of Commons to deal with.'[23]

Despite the temporary setback to his museum, William Gregory had every reason to be well pleased with his first legislative session and to greet the second year of his governorship in a continuing state of euphoria. At last his life had purpose and his career seemed destined to be crowned with achievements. 'I hope and feel that I am making amends for a wild past life by working heart and soul for my fellowmen,' he wrote to a mother who had devotedly supported and sustained him throughout his indiscretions and the years of political disappointment. He continued to enjoy the rudest health and the island appeared to have worked its magic on his frail wife. 'She is so fat and strong you would hardly know her again,' he happily reported home. 'This warm climate has had a most extraordinary effect on her, a complete revival — every ailment seems to have entirely disappeared.' Their marriage was also thriving, William's happiness and success in office infusing their relationship with gaiety and laughter. They were still separated too often for Lizzie's liking but she had found pleasure and enjoyment sketching the island's rich varieties of flowers and butterflies and in the companionship of Constance Gordon Cummings, an artist. He soon detected the benefit of this association in her work and predicted that she would take back to Britain, whenever they returned home, 'some excellent sketches of various points of interest in the island'. Lizzie never made that journey.[24]

Anxious to escape from the petty and tedious administrative duties of his office, such as deliberating in Executive Council on the constant stream of requests for leaves of absence, or making recommendations for pensions, the Governor decided to go off on another tour. A second visit to Anuradhapura would enable him to re-examine its antiquities, and from there he could travel south and west into the North Western Province. He agreed to allow Lizzie and her companion to accompany him as far as the ancient capital, having first checked to ensure that the weather would be tolerable. Setting out from Kandy on 7 June they reached Anuradhapura three days later. Lizzie arrived in good spirits and seemed well even though she had complained before their departure of a mild case of diarrhoea and had wakened William one night en route with abdominal pains. They had been relieved by a warm bath and the Government Agent who met them at Anuradhapura, and had some experience of tropical diseases, saw no reason for concern. Lizzie declined the service of a native doctor and bravely made light of her discomfort, determined not to be the cause of an abrupt end to William's expedition. Reassured, he left the ladies at Anuradhapura.

Within a day Lizzie's condition had deteriorated, and she decided to return to Kandy. Ever considerate of others she stopped for two days on the way to permit Miss Cummings to sketch, but pain and apprehension (she became somewhat morbidly preoccupied with the lines of one of John Keble's religious poems written on Pascal's motto 'Je mourrai seul') drove her to complete the last forty-seven miles to Kandy in a single day. There she collapsed, exhausted. When William reached Kuranegala in the North Western Province on 22 June 1873 he found a telegram awaiting him. Informed that Lizzie was seriously ill he telegraphed the principal doctor in Colombo to come up to Kandy immediately and hastened there himself. Fortunately, at Kuranegala he was no more than twenty-five miles away. The diagnosis was alarming — dysentery — but the doctors by no means pessimistic. Lizzie's condition while serious was not critical, they concluded. She had a good night on 24 June, even showed interest in nutriment the following morning, and the attending physician spoke optimistically of her being well enough in a few days to travel down to Colombo where the medical facilities were somewhat superior. Later that same day a fever set in. Again she rallied, only to suffer a relapse and die peacefully early in the afternoon of 28 June. Throughout this ordeal she remained composed, 'well aware of her position' but 'perfectly calm and resigned to God's will'. To the very end William remained at her bedside, holding her hand while she recited a favourite hymn and voiced less fear of death than sorrow at leaving him alone.[25]

'She was the light of my eyes the very joy of my heart and now that light is quenched and my life is darkened forever,' a grief-stricken son wrote to his mother. 'No one but myself can know the intense love I felt for her.'He performed the melancholy task of ordering a tomb, which was shipped from England, and the polished red granite bore the simple inscription 'Elizabeth Gregory Died at Kandy 28 June 1873'. Thwaites, who kept the bereaved husband company during the first few weeks, later designed and planted the surrounding bed of flowers she loved and had copied so diligently. Next, there was her estate to be settled. The Gregorys had had no difficulty saving £2,000 from his first year's salary, while Lizzie had touched little of her large annual income. As a result, William Gregory had expected to be finally clear of all debts within three years. Lizzie's death altered radically his financial circumstances. Apart from a few small bequests she left everything to him. He would receive the sum of £9,000, an annual life income of £1,200, and revenues from a substantial trust fund which had recently been swollen by £10,500 from the sale of her house in Eaton Square. Inevitably, the management of this fund subsequently created tension between Gregory and one of his wife's brothers, Arthur Clay, a trustee. However, they always overcame their disagreements and mended their strained relations.[26]

The combination of desolation and affluence caused William Gregory to waver briefly in his resolve to make his name in Ceylon. For weeks after his wife's death he would not permit her room to be touched, except to have a fresh nosegay placed in it each day. 'I have no thought or theory of what death is,' he acknowledged, 'but I know that my present life is a living death.' Why remain in lonely colonial exile now that he was was 'so extremely well off'? Yet simply to throw up the appointment was unthinkable, for 'I should put the whole Colony out of gear as no one but myself can carry out the large measures for its advancement which I mean to propose.' Moreover, what would he do if he resigned? A return to public life in Britain held no attraction for him, and he was not ready to resign himself 'to sitting down with nothing to do' at Coole. The thought of a peerage was an inviting one and he discreetly enquired as to his prospects, only to hear that Gladstone would not consent to recommend him to the Queen. Another possibility was travel, and he was keen to see the Orient and the Antipodes. But this was all in 'the misty future'. He was content for the time being to look forward to three months' leave in Britain in 1874. Meanwhile, he would resort to that traditional therapy of the bereaved — work and more work.[27]

William Gregory called the Legislative Council into session a full month earlier than the traditional date. The evidence that revenues in 1873 would exceed expenditures by 800,000 rupees (£80,000), a jump of 10% in the very healthy figure for the previous year, justified his boast that the 'financial position of the Colony is one of unqualified prosperity'. He had not forgotton the fundamental weakness of this thriving economy — its narrow base — as he made clear in his address on 30 July. Once again he reverted to the need to lessen the dependence upon the coffee crop. He advertised the profitability of cinchona, adverted to the possibility of developing cocoa, and advocated an expansion of tea planting. He reminded the Council and beyond them the planters that in two decades the quantity of Indian tea shipped from Calcutta had risen from not a single pound to more than 17,000,000. What India had done Ceylon might repeat, particularly as the tea grown experimentally and cured on the island had been well received in Britain. 'I am deeply interested in the cultivation of this plant which I am sanguine will yet become one of our prominent exports,' he added, 'and shall do all in my power to establish and promote this industry.'

If the swelling Treasury surplus ensured that the Governor's calls for economic diversification went unheeded it did enable him to press on with the other far-sighted measures introduced the year before. He recommended to the Council an impressive list of public works — bridge construction, road and railway extension, the advance of the Colombo breakwater. All of these were music to the ears of the planters, but William Gregory's zeal to promote the welfare of the Sinhalese showed no sign of waning. The liberal provision made by previous administrations for medical institutions which served European stations, while the mass of the population in outlying stations was left 'at the mercy of ignorant quacks and devil dancers', reflected discredit on the government. Thus he made the establishment of a proper system of medical relief for the entire population a priority. Calling on his long experience as Chairman of the Gort Poor Law Union he sought to recreate in Ceylon the dispensaries provided for in the Medical Charities Act. Each medical district would have a dispensary staffed by trained natives and attended by a medical officer once or twice a week. All serious cases would be removed to the central hospital. Rudimentary though it was, this system did represent a significant advance in the care of the native population. But the Governor's dedication to the islanders' well-being continued to be most evident in his untiring efforts to restore the irrigation system, for irrigation 'implies health, progress, in some cases even existence.'[28]

William Gregory's determination to rescue the residents of Nuwarakalawiya from destitution and the terrible wasting disease called 'Parange' had been fired anew by his fateful visit to the region in June. No longer would the government tolerate as almost normal the poverty to be seen there. First, he secured approval from the Colonial Office for the creation of a new province. The fact that Anuradhapura and the surrounding countryside had been administered from distant Jaffna, as part of the Northern Province, explained why even the most active of Government Agents had been unable to give to it the close attention in which it desperately stood in need. Moreover, this arrangement had bound uneasily together populations — Tamil and Sinhalese — ethnically separate. The small size of the new North Central Province, both in area and population, made it more manageable. Then, Gregory carefully selected as Agent a 'man in the complete strength and vigour of life, full of spirit and love for his work.' Once these preliminary steps had been taken he was able to develop a comprehensive plan for the province. He decided to employ the local population on the work of repairing the tanks and building roads, paying for the labour either in money or seed paddy for the newly irrigated fields. However, a third visit to the area, in February 1874, convinced him that more had to be done. An initial reluctance to involve the government in the management and distribution of food, tasks which as a liberal he believed properly belonged to and were more efficiently completed by private enterprise, was quickly overcome. Perhaps recalling the Whigs' mistakes during the Irish Famine, he had no intention of tolerating misery and premature deaths in the name of economic orthodoxy. He shipped 50,000 bushels of rice to Anuradhapura, the new provincial capital. To put more money into the hands of natives he expanded the public works programme, sanctioning the building of a series of minor roads to link the villages and ordering a quickening of the pace of construction on the arterial route to Jaffna. He transferred a large portion of the experienced irrigation staff from the Eastern Province to the new one, to begin immediately the reconstruction of a very large tank near Anuradhapura. In the case of small village tanks the villagers concerned were to provide the labour and the government a skilled officer to supervise them and the installation of a free masonry sluice to regulate the flow of water. Earlier repairs had often come to naught because villagers had been obliged to break the banks of the tanks in order to release the water. Although they then re-dammed them the weakened section invariably gave way during a rain storm and all the water was lost. The masonry sluice would not only solve this problem but Gregory believed that their work on the tank would provide the villagers with the skill needed to maintain the irrigation system and eventually encourage them to undertake repairs on their own initiative.[29]

The vast expansion of public works prompted the Governor's re-organization of a Department which now controlled an annual budget of £350,000. Unfortunately, his proposal to open it to natives proved too liberal for the Colonial Office. What Gregory had in mind was the introduction of Sinhalese through a somewhat simpler examination than that taken by European candidates, and consequently at lower pay. Promotion for both groups would be dependent upon their passing a common higher examination. Kimberley accepted the entrance of some natives under this 'probationary scheme' while rejecting the Governor's suggestion that they and Europeans fill vacancies in alternation. That procedure, the Colonial Secretary feared, might in time result in the Department of Works being overweighted 'by officers of inferior calibre and training'.

As the time of his departure for Britain neared, William Gregory could reflect with understandable pride and satisfaction on the achievements of his two years as Governor. The Legislative Council had given him practically everything for which he had asked, and this record of support was a tribute to the skill and tact with which he had handled that body. Of the twenty-one ordinances enacted during the first legislative session the Crown had disallowed only one, and while Kimberley had on occasion checked Gregory's progressive instincts he applauded 'the energy and care devoted by Mr. G[regory] to all branches of his duties. . . .' More heartening than official praise was the dismayed response of the Sinhalese to the rumour that he intended to resign. This popularity was attributable, at least in part, to his visibility. More islanders had seen this governor than any of his predecessors. Ten days of travel in the 'beautiful' Southern Province in August 1873 had been followed in February 1874 by the trek of 300 miles through the impoverished Northern districts. It was the information so arduously gleaned which shaped the Governor's policies. He could legitimately boast that 'no previous Governor ever obtained a greater amount of native confidence, because they know how deeply interested I am in promoting their interests and in apportioning the annual expenditures to benefit all classes impartially.'[30]

All thought of resignation had probably been banished from William Gregory's mind before he sailed for home on 17 April 1874. He had regained the fourteen pounds in weight that he had lost after Lizzie's death, and one of her brothers —'the ugliest little fellow I have ever seen'— had come out to keep him company and serve as an aide. Nevertheless, he found the lack of female companionship a hardship, complaining that the 'long dreary evenings without a woman to speak to are terrible'. Moreover, the beguiling knowledge that he was finally free of financial worries must still have tempted him from time to time to end his exile. Yet there was little self-deception in his private protest that 'Wealth and ease are matters of little care to me now.' That strong sense of responsibility and public service which had long characterized his family had reasserted itself. Resignation might place in jeopardy much of what he had already achieved and only if he returned to Ceylon and carried through the policies he had initiated could he be sure of establishing securely a reputation for enlightened and progressive colonial administration.

10
Resignation and Remarriage

William Gregory reached London on 13 May 1874, and there he remained for three weeks seeing friends and catching up on gossip. He was more sombre than they remembered, much of his gaiety having died with Lizzie. No doubt he found the cosmopolitan life a refreshing change from the provincial atmosphere of Ceylon, but neither the civilized ease of the Athenaeum nor meetings of the National Gallery Trustees and of the council of the Arundel Society caused him to doubt the wisdom of his decision to continue as governor. Further, he found the Liberal Party in disarray following its defeat in a general election earlier in the year. Criticism of Gladstone's somewhat quirkish decision to seek a dissolution and uncertainty about his future saw potential successors jockeying for position. 'No cohesion, plenty of jealousy, and few to follow' were the more obvious difficulties confronting Lord Hartington as a stand-in leader of the Opposition. This unpleasant state of affairs surely hardened William Gregory's resolve to keep his distance from political life. Nor had the change of government created problems in Governor Gregory's relations with the Colonial Office. Before leaving Ceylon he had established the same informal arrangement with the Conservative Colonial Secretary, the Earl of Carnarvon, that had worked so well under Lord Kimberley—he discussed awkward and delicate matters in private notes. His predecessor's misfortune to see a 'confidential' despatch published in London had taught Gregory an important lesson—official correspondence, however it was marked, should only contain material that could be read 'at the Market Cross'.[1]

He had shipped to Britain in his baggage samples of Ceylon tea, which he distributed to family and friends. Though some of them disliked the 'new and perfumed flavour' he forwarded a pound to Carnarvon and repeated his belief that tea would soon become a 'very large' export of the colony. During Gregory's meeting with the Colonial Secretary at Downing Street they discussed the island's food supplies, the irrigation works, and a number of personnel problems. Significantly, the Governor's main concern was to make the colonial administration more responsive to the sentiments and ambitions of the native population. 'To be respected by an Oriental people particularly tenacious of outward decorum, a public servant should be possessed of gentlemanly feeling and deportment,' he explained to Carnarvon in winning his support for a more careful selection of Englishmen sent out to the colony. There

241

were to be no more 'rough fellows' who drank, swore and abused their subordinates appointed to the Department of Public Works, no matter their qualifications as engineers. In the same spirit, he won the Colonial Secretary's endorsement of a scheme which required a form of apprenticeship for young men arriving in Ceylon to begin life as magistrates. Inexperienced, stationed in isolated communities, they often succumbed to natural temptations, and their conduct did little to increase respect for the law they administered. Gregory intended to employ them on the island for several years before allowing them to preside over a court, hoping that through this probationary service and their contact with 'the better class of natives', as opposed to the miscreants who appeared before the bench, they would also be cured of racial contempt. Moreover, whenever they received a judicial appointment, senior magistrates would supervise and report on their work for some considerable time. Finally, William Gregory urged that natives be appointed to minor magistracies and he pointed to the success of those whom he had already named to such positions on a temporary basis as proof of this proposal's practicality. His aim was not simply to improve the system of justice by ensuring that it was staffed by men familiar with the island and its inhabitants, important as that was. He was looking to achieve more. 'Exclusion [of natives] from high places is not a wise policy for the British Government to pursue in view either of its own prestige or of what is due to the natives,' he reasoned, 'and each year the expediency of holding out prizes for their laudable ambition becomes more and more apparent.' Here was one way of continually reconciling 'the better class' to colonial rule. [2]

His discussions at the Colonial Office satisfactorily completed William Gregory travelled to Galway early in June to see his mother and check his estates, the latter now cleared of all debts. At Coole he made a melancholy discovery. The butler had, with the assistance of a kitchen maid, drunk his way through the entire wine cellar. That misfortune did not prevent the newly prosperous landlord from giving a dinner and a dance to his tenants, all of whom were 'contented and peaceable.' However, at the end of his leave in mid-July, Gregory was quite ready to return to Ceylon. He embarked at Southampton on 16 July 1874, a little swollen with good food, excellent wines, and pride. Friends wrote that Carnarvon was full of his praise and had named him as one of the three governors in whom the government placed full confidence. No doubt this knowledge helped to sustain him throughout an otherwise tedious voyage. Although his old horse trainer Trean was aboard and proved to be 'very good company', there were few other diverting passengers. He devoted his mornings to Homer, which seemed appropriate on the classically named *Hydaspes*, gave his afternoons to French novels, a store of which he had thoughtfully laid in, but early dinners and the lack of partners even for a rubber of whist meant that the evenings became 'intolerably long'. It was with relief that he stepped ashore at Galle on 14 August. [3]

William Gregory's life in the colony resumed its earlier pattern. He again divided the year equally between his three residences and the periods at Nuwara Eliya and Kandy were interspersed with tours of the provinces. Throughout the legislative session in Colombo he entertained on a scale reminiscent of that before his wife's death. Each week he hosted two dinners — one large, one small — a whist evening, and a garden party. Nor was there much change in the colony's affairs. The island continued to prosper on the strength of coffee. Success in utilizing higher ground (up to 5,500 feet) for planting had let loose the speculative spirit and the government began to profit handsomely from the increased value of public lands. As his old fears of the exhaustion of the area suitable for coffee cultivation were dispelled, and the 'coffee bug' showed little sign of spreading rapidly, Gregory committed a cardinal error. He still spoke encouragingly of tea, cocoa and cinchona as alternative crops to coffee and began planting teak trees, but there was less urgency in his words and actions. Swept up by the renewed optimism he relaxed his efforts to diversify the economy and invested some of his own funds in new coffee plantations, only to pay dearly for the mistake when the 'bug' subsequently devastated them.

Prosperity facilitated progress. The Governor applied an unexpected windfall of 70,000 rupees from the pearl fishing industry to a number of 'fancy' reforms — construction of a Seamen's Home; the erection of fountains in a number of towns where water was desperately needed; further improvements to Nuwara Eliya; and the restoration of ancient monuments at Kandy. He pointed to the colony's bursting Treasury to justify the acceleration of the museum, which would also contain an Oriental library. It was to be an imposing building in size, and represented an attempt to embellish Nineteenth Century municipal architecture with a touch of Eastern influence. Proud as he was of its appearance William Gregory took even greater pleasure from its success. 'Judging from what I see every Sunday,' one colonial resident wrote to him a decade later, 'its influences for developing intelligence, enlightenment, and other most healthy results among the masses are both already assured and invaluable.' The preservation of Ceylon's 'national monuments and literature', Gregory had every reason to believe, was an important legacy of his rule. 'If the same had been done from the beginning in all our Colonies,' one friend observed, 'what precious things might have been preserved.'[4]

There were other monuments to Governor Gregory — the Colombo breakwater; a Customs House; new schools for the island's young; new roads. And to dramatize the advance of the northern arterial route he promised to drive a carriage and four the 275 miles from Colombo to Jaffna before the end of his term. Yet of all these important public works there was never any doubt which held primacy in his mind. 'My great object is to restore the prosperity of the Northern part of the island and rescue it from utter extinction,' he reaffirmed in November 1874. 'Nothing can be more gratifying than the perfect success of my measures hitherto.' He kept up his tours of inspection, visiting the Western Province in August 1875, but he had already been back to the north earlier that year and he went there again in March 1876. He spent £6,500 restoring the huge Kantalai tank, about forty miles due east of Anuradhapura. Covering 6,400 acres, with banks that were $1\frac{1}{2}$ miles in length and 60 feet high, it promised to irrigate thousands of acres. Meanwhile, natives were responding with enthusiasm to the scheme he had devised to speed the repair of village tanks. By 1876 twenty-six of these, complete with free masonry sluices, had been restored and work was continuing on another ninety. Happily, the Governor ordered a further 100 sluices from England. For their part villagers discovered that they had more than enough water to irrigate the land they possessed, and were soon in the market for adjacent crown lands. Anxious that these 'timid' people not be discouraged, Gregory relaxed the rules of sale. They were able to buy directly from the government without the necessity of bidding in the competitive atmosphere of a public auction. Finally, he ordered an extensive survey of the North Central Province as a first step towards the completion of a ten-year irrigation scheme which would see the restoration of all the tanks and their connection, as of old, by a network of canals. It was a mark both of their respect and apreciation that one group of villagers invited the Governor to remain among them for a month to sire a new generation. He politely declined.[5]

As before, the work of irrigation went hand in hand with that of health and conservation. A painful riding accident, which left him lame for weeks and kept him out of the saddle for a month, together with an unpleasant ear infection (prompting one acquaintance to remark that it was no bad thing for a Governor to be deaf in one ear), probably account for his uncharacteristically slow reaction in March and April 1875 to an outbreak of cholera first in Colombo and then, more seriously, in Negombo forty miles up the coast from the capital. Nevertheless, it was to his credit that Ceylon escaped the famine then threatening parts of India. Moreover, he had continued to wage an energetic and successful struggle to protect the island's resources. In particular, he acted with laudable vigour to halt the Europeans' extermination of that 'noble, useful, and at present harmless animal', the elephant. Having seen tame animals at work, and astonished by their 'fine temper, patience and marvellous sense', he recognized their importance to the colony and was appalled by the evidence that wild elephants were being hunted indiscriminately. 'It is a miserable cruel sport at the best,' he observed, 'just the same as stalking a herd of cows and dropping a couple right and left.' Equally, he deplored the cruel trapping methods employed by those hunting beasts for sale in India. Rather than drive them into a 'kraal' these hunters resorted to crude practices which resulted in the death of as many as five animals for each one captured. Those they had secured were then starved into submission. But tied to trees the elephants frequently injured themselves so badly that they had to be put down. With the consent of the Colonial Office, Gregory decided to declare a five-year moratorium on killing, except of rogues and beasts that trespassed on cultivated lands, and he more than doubled the royalty on those exported, thereby raising their price and cutting the demand for them in India. Of course, the moratorium did not apply to the Prince of Wales, who visited the colony in December 1875, and was determined to go on an elephant hunt. [6]

Privately, William Gregory had greeted the news of a royal visit without enthusiasm. The governors of honoured colonies were expected to dig deeply into their own pockets to ensure a social success, and he was soon purchasing carriage horses from Australia and importing wines and cognac in quantities sufficient 'to float an ironclad'. 'I am not to be reimbursed one penny for my expenditure,' he complained to his mother, having put that figure at £1,000. Meanwhile, the colony had been ordered not to spend more than £5,000 from the public purse. However, as the preparations went ahead — redecorating Queen's House, Colombo, and the Pavilion at Kandy; the elaborate illumination of the temples and ruins of the capital of the Kandyan Kings with 10,000 lamps; the preparation of a suitable site for the elephant hunt — the costs quickly exceeded the budget and eventually reached £11,000. Inevitably, there were disputes over the adequacy, nature and progress of the preparations, and as the delays lengthened so tempers shortened. Adding to the Governor's worries were the instructions he received from the Colonial Office. On him fell the responsibility for the Prince's safety, from fever and wild animals, a reminder which prompted his forlorn effort to discourage the royal party from going on a hunt. He was expected so to arrange the itinerary that the sabbath and the anniversary of Prince Albert's death, should the Prince still be in Ceylon on 14 December, were both respected. From the most distinguished correspondent accompanying the heir to the throne, W.H. Russell, an acquaintance of Gregory and a fellow Irishman, he heard that he would be expected to 'cut' another member of the Fourth Estate who was suspected of being the source of an embarrassing report that the Prince and his entourage had a woman aboard their vessel. Fortunately, the reporter in question contradicted the story and was thus deemed to have purged himself of the lese-majesty.

In the midst of these hectic arrangements — the problems were not eased by the royal party's insistence that the hunt be in the neighbourhood of Colombo rather than of Trincomalee, where a camp was being prepared — William Gregory was confidentially informed that he was to be knighted by the Prince. The fact that he was to be invested merely with the order of St. Michael and St. George, the second class of Knights Commanders, angered the Governor. 'Being a Privy Councillor and of superior rank,' he later remarked, 'This distinction was by no means a grateful one and I would probably have refused it, but as it was to be conferred by the Prince himself, I was obliged to profess myself highly gratified.'

The Prince of Wales landed at Colombo on 1 December 1875,

Ceylon: above left, a cartoon of Mr. Gregory as King Nusanka Mala, one of the most famous kings of the island, seated on a stone lion. This lion was included as the Governor had brought down just such a lion from the interior for the Museum in Colombo. Above right: the clay model of the bust of Sir William Gregory by Sir J. E. Boehm, which still stands in the Museum in Colombo. Below: the recently knighted Governor with the Prince of Wales in Calcutta on 6 January 1876. Between them sits Lady E. Baring, the daughter of the Viceroy of India Lord Northbrook, who sits on the Prince's right.

appropriately attired in the tropical kit of a Field Marshal. Everywhere there were flags, flowers, fruit, palm-leaves and triumphal arches. The next morning the party moved on to Kandy, where the Pavilion's grounds were 'literally ablaze with brilliant flowers, and the air was heavy with the perfume of yellow champac and of the white roses of the iron-wood trees'. They visited the Botanical Garden at Peradeniya, driving through the avenue of magnificent india rubber trees to Thwaites's Swiss-style chalet where the Superintendent had organized an exotic exhibit of plant and insect life. That same evening, and at the Prince's suggestion, the old Audience Hall of the Kandyan Kings provided the setting for the dignified little ceremony which saw William Gregory kneel before the royal heir, receive the accolade and rise Sir William. [7]

When the Prince embarked at Colombo after his week-long visit to the colony, having enjoyed a somewhat more exciting elephant hunt than that planned, a relieved Governor had every reason to be satisfied. The only disappointment had been the disruption of the spectacular reception at Kandy when driving rain extinguished the illuminations and the bonfires set on the surrounding hills. The popular warmth of the Prince's reception convinced the Irishman that such tours did much to stimulate and sustain loyalty to the Crown, and he had taken this opportunity to raise with his royal guest the oft-discussed establishment of a regular royal residence in Ireland. The Prince indicated that his mother was the obstacle. Indeed, almost in spite of himself, Sir William Gregory formed a high opinion of the Heir Apparent's abilities. Instead of the shallow if not empty-headed and frivolous figurehead he had expected, the Governor encountered a high spirited and astute man who showed good sense and clear judgment in speaking of home and foreign affairs. He concluded that Great Britain was fortunate to have such a future King, and he gladly accepted the Prince's invitation to follow his party to Calcutta. Sir William welcomed the chance to see something of the magnificent sub-continent which his great-grandfather, the nabob, had left little more than a century earlier weighed down with riches. But he combined business with pleasure, inspecting jails, hospitals, factories and sewerage systems as well as participating in the festivities. And the pomp of the royal investiture of eight Indian princes with the Grand Cross of the Star of India moved him to meditate on Britain's role there. 'What bloodshed and desolation would ensue, for a period at all events, if we went,' he mused, 'and on the other hand how these princes and every man who feels the elements of greatness in him must groan and travail in spirit under the iron or rather leaden hand of England.' Nor was this sombre mood lightened by the news of his mother's death. He was not unprepared for these mournful tidings. She was 76 years old and had long been in poor health, her eyesight impaired by cataracts and her breathing by bronchitis. Her physician had warned him that the strain on her heart might prove fatal at any time. Yet the predictability did not lessen the grief or the inevitable sense of guilt. He knew that his triumphs in Ceylon had not fully repaid her long life of love and devotion. 'I cannot say how lonely and desolate this last bereavement has left me,' he declared simply and sadly to Henry Layard. [8]

'The loneliness of my life is unbearable,' Gregory had confessed to friends even before his mother's death. He determined to resign his office but had difficulty in settling on the appropriate moment. Disappointed with the honour conferred upon him he had somewhat peevishly fixed the Prince's departure from the colony as the time to inform the Colonial Office of his decision. On reflection he thought better of this plan fearing that resignation might be widely interpreted as an act of disrespect. Yet the desire to give up his office did not weaken. He was finding less pleasure in his role and grew increasingly bored by his duties. Despatching the daily business that came before him in a couple of hours, and cursed by a prolonged period of less than robust health which necessarily dampened his enthusiasm for exhausting tours of inspection, he occupied himself rereading Homer and Tacitus. Equally, it was evident that his popularity was waning among the members of the European community. 'I do not think the deep interest I take in the fine country and very fine people in the north contributes much to my popularity here,' he admitted to Carnarvon. 'The planters and Europeans grumble much that our surplus balances are not applied in schemes for making roads to every estate, and in relieving the richest town in the island [Colombo] from taxation.' Proud of his public works, not least the roads, he resented accusations of parsimony when he insisted that projects for the extension of the railway be carefully examined and the proposed routes professionally surveyed. He was righteously indignant at the ill-disguised European hostility towards those programmes which benefited natives almost exclusively. His feelings were summarised by a friend who wrote encouragingly to the besieged Governor: 'I have but little sympathy for the Europeans in their relations with the natives. They can take good care of themselves, and it is for a just government to take care of the weaker portion of the community.' Inevitably the antagonism extended to the Legislative Council, where Gregory met resistance from the unofficial members to his policies. By 1876 he was compelled to turn to the Colonial Office for assistance in overcoming the opposition to his proposals for heavy expenditures on hospitals, prisons and asylums, though as he was quick to point out the total cost of these vital social works was no more than that for $1\frac{1}{2}$ miles of railroad. But this resort to London was an additional discouragement, for Gregory's relations with the Colonial Office had also deteriorated as he grew to suspect it of being keen to criticise him. [9]

His dealings with Lord Carnarvon had begun to sour early in 1875 when the Bishop of Colombo resigned and the Governor's attention was directed to the all too familiar problem of an Established Church which served a mere fraction of the population. Non-conformists, such as

Gregory's press ally, A.M. Ferguson of the *Ceylon Observer*, resented the contribution they were obliged to make to the support of Anglican clergy. Nor were they interested in talk of concurrent endowments, fearing that the principle of equity would result in state aid to 'atheistic Buddhists' and the 'foul idolatry' of Catholicism. However, it was the existing injustice to the Roman Catholic community that most concerned the Anglo-Irishman. In a population of 2½ millions the Anglicans and Presbyterians did not exceed 13,000. The annual charge on the colony for the support of this miniscule number was more than £10,500, and that figure did not allow for the pensions paid to retired clergy. Meanwhile, the 184,000 strong Roman Catholic Church, its size a tribute to the earlier missionary zeal of the Portuguese, received a paltry annual sum of £100. In short, the arguments employed to justify disendowment in Ireland applied with equal if not greater force to Ceylon. What Gregory proposed was not an abrupt and complete termination of the establishment but its steady and painless contraction. He urged the Colonial Secretary to leave the see of Colombo vacant and simply strike off the salaries of clergy as other vacancies occurred. Carnarvon had in fact already named a successor to Bishop Jermyn before Gregory's letter reached London but he made clear that he would have gone ahead with the appointment anyway. He believed it important to preserve the Established Church in Ceylon and tartly reminded the Governor that the wisdom of disestablishment and disendowment in Ireland had not been universally acknowledged and accepted. Subsequently, Sir William took a certain malicious pleasure in the turmoil Carnarvon's Bishop created within the Anglican community. A High Churchman whose diocese was decidely Low, Bishop Coplestone's 'Roman pretensions' in matters of doctrine, ceremony and authority, and those of the flock of young curates he brought with him to the colony, provoked a series of controversies. 'I cannot tell you how sorry I am to write an adverse opinion as to the Bishop's writings and doings,' the Governor reported with more than a hint of insincerity. 'He is an excellent man — his whole soul is in his work — his simplicity, geniality and unselfishness attract every one, but they are repelled by those lofty pretensions and by the follies and nonsense of his curates.'[10]

The rejection of his scheme of disendowment and disestablishment did not deter the Governor from making other concessions to the Roman Catholic Church. He had to tread warily, however, in order to avoid provoking the resignation of those members of the Legislative Council opposed on grounds of conscience to anything that smacked of 'special privileges' for Catholics. When he learned from the Roman Catholic Bishop that the admirable work of education was being impeded by the narrow minded and 'sectarian bent' of a civil servant — inappropriately named Helps — who denied Catholic schools grants to which they appeared to be entitled, the Governor quietly reorganized the Education Department and placed a more sympathetic officer in charge. Not surprisingly, Bishop Bonjean did not expect to find in

Governor Gregory's successor, whoever he might prove to be, an equal appreciation of Catholic feelings and the same sympathy with their wants. Indeed, the Bishop was so appreciative of the Irishman's beneficent rule that he wrote to the Bishop of Galway in order to inform 'the people at home' that 'one can be kind to Catholics and yet be a great Governor'. [11]

Sir William Gregory informed the Colonial Office in July 1876 that he intended to retire in February of the following year. It was a costly decision, for in resigning a full year before the expiration of his term he forfeited £700 in passage money. Similarly, the fact that his salary, like that of subordinate officers, was converted into rupees at the fixed rate of ten to the pound, and the rupee had suffered a significant devaluation, had worked to the Governor's disadvantage. An income of £7,000 at his appointment had fallen to the equivalent of £5,600 by the time of the Prince of Wales's visit. Nor was the loss of purchasing power made any less of a hardship by the need to send to Britain and Europe for some victuals (Gregory estimated his own annual wine bill at the princely sum of £1,000), and before leaving the colony he did secure a 20% increase in civil service salaries which compensated for the 18.5% fall in the value of the rupee.

The conviction that it would be impossible to maintain the dignity of his office on £5,600 a year, though in his first year he had saved £2,000 from his salary, influenced Gregory's decision to quit his post. Having escaped so recently and tragically from a lifetime of financial anxiety he was acutely even hysterically sensitive to any threat to this new-found security. Why remain longer in lonely colonial exile, performing duties that had lost much of their interest for him, struggling for policies that were meeting resistance in the colony and winning less than complete support at the Colonial Office, when to do so forced him to dip into his own funds. 'Nostalgia is too strong for me,' he confided to Henry Layard. Moreover, he had achieved much of what he had set out to do. His rule had seen great internal improvements, especially in irrigation and communications; the beginning of the breakwater; and the erection of several fine public buildings. He had reorganized the various departments of the colonial administration and had opened a much greater number of places in it to natives. Yet with admirable frankness he admitted that the time had come for a fresh man with new ideas. Progressive and important his 'brave programme' certainly had been, but it lacked in his final two years as governor the earlier energy and originality. Entering his sixty-first year, tired, lonely, homesick, frustrated and occasionally depressed, sure that he would be unable to achieve a great deal more for the colony and its inhabitants, his decision to resign was both sensible and understandable. 'I am not surprised that you should have resolved to give up your work next year and to return to England and your friends,' Layard wrote supportively. 'After all absence from one's own country, even under the most favourable circumstances, is an exile, which one feels the more as one grows older.' [12]

Although the permanent Under Secretary at the Colonial Office, the urbane and gracious Robert Herbert, did write to express the wish that Gregory remain in Ceylon for an additional year, Lord Carnarvon made no effort to persuade the Governor to change his mind. He did applaud Sir William's achievements and acknowledge their agreeable relationship but the Colonial Secretary soon had reason enough to rue even that traditional response to the resignation. Gregory decided to depart in a blaze of controversy. He ordered the beginning of construction on a lunatic asylum which he described as such an earthly architectural paradise that it would almost be worthwhile to go mad to secure admission. He planned to commit £4,000 he had in hand and thus leave the Legislative Council with little alternative except to find the balance required to complete the building. Where 'the fore wheel goes the hind must follow', he observed. If the adoption of this timeless bureaucratic strategy infuriated the planting interests, greedy for more railways and roads, some of Sir William's other actions excited howls of rage at the Colonial Office. Carnarvon's failure to support the Governor's request for the dismissal of a civil servant who had proven a disgrace to the service — he had been permitted to resign and claim a pension — provoked Gregory to sarcasm in a despatch suggesting similar treatment for another miscreant. 'A more unjustifiable attack upon a Secretary of State by a Governor I have never read,' minuted one permanent official, while Carnarvon described it as an 'outrageous document'. The indiscretion was attributed to Gregory's inability — having entered the service late in life — 'to appreciate the necessity of absolute loyalty and deference to Her Majesty's Government'. That residual tolerance did not survive the news two weeks later that the Governor had spoken and voted with the minority on the Legislative Council against a continuation of the subsidies to the Ecclesiastical Establishment. The infuriated officials at the Colonial Office fumed at this 'swan like proceeding' and complained that 'Sir W. Gregory, with all his ability, has been unable to learn his constitutional position as a Governor'. One of them acidly concluded: 'As regards Sir W. Gregory individually he is the type of man who I consider usually well qualified for a post such as he now occupies and it is unfortunate that he should somewhat ostentatiously air his independence as he has been recently doing. My chief wonder however is that he managed to restrain himself from delivering a grand oration upon the occasion in question. It is so unlike him that I can only assume that the gallery was inadequately filled, a circumstance which has several times deprived the House of Commons of an intellectual treat at the hands of the ex-Member for Galway.' Despite the advice of his officials, who counselled against entering any controversy with Gregory, Carnarvon insisted on a response which would let the service know that he took a poor view of the Governor's conduct. [13]

In the midst of this flurry of excitement Sir William set off for a visit to Australia. He sailed from Galle on 15 January 1877, and spent a month on that continent. His host was Hercules Robinson, now the Governor of New South Wales. For the first time in twenty years Gregory was able to examine closely the workings of democracy 'in its most extreme form', and this inveterate anti-democrat was surprised by his findings. Notwithstanding the reports and evidence of jobbing and bribery, he discovered that the colonists had managed their affairs well and concluded that 'no other form of government would have been equally successful'. He was particularly impressed by the liberality of the democracies in all matters of health, improvement and education of the people. Education was universal, the hospitals, museums and public libraries princely, and everyone in this 'manly honest country' addressed you with 'extreme civility'.

If his Australian journey forced Sir William Gregory to reconsider some of his long-held views on the nature of democracy it also revived his health and spirits. Friends noted that he had recovered his 'erect and cocky gait', and on his return to Ceylon he briefly regretted his decision to resign. He would miss the native people, for they were 'quick witted and intellectual and the highest classes singularly well bred'. What higher compliment could he pay them than admit: 'I have known some whom I trust as implicitly as I would an Englishman.' Suddenly, he began to doubt whether he would be so happy or enjoy such health at home. Those regrets and doubts were laid to rest, as so nearly was he, by a 'nasty attack' of dysentery in May. After this 'narrow squeak' he left the colony once he was fit enough to travel, though in parting he knew that 'the happiest and most important' period of his life had come to an end.[14]

It was mid-summer when Sir William Gregory landed in England, where he was wined and dined by friends before gratefully retreating to Ireland for a period of peace, quiet and reflection. Throughout his residence in Ceylon he had thought of Coole, sending instructions either to his mother or to his cousin Charles Gregory who was administering the estate in his absence. 'I long to hear your report about Coole — I gave strict orders to re-roof the laundry,' he wrote on one occasion. At other times he insisted that fires be set during the winter, arguing that losses likely to be incurred as a result of damp would exceed the cost of the coal; sanctioned the setting aside of part of the desmesne where the poor could gather firewood; inquired about the progress of the garden wall and trellis work, the planting of roses, and the placing of 'spouts' around the barn to get the ivy up. He planned a number of additions, including two servants' rooms, a dairy, another laundry and a poultry yard. He supported his mother's scheme to build a school on the estate, providing a set of plans which had been drawn up by an architect in the colony. Once he was home he found Coole decidedly 'fusty' after the bright and fresh houses of Ceylon and quickly set to work supervising its redecoration and embellishment whenever the weather permitted. He also rearranged his library of almost 4,000 volumes which he proudly described as 'large for an Irish country gentleman'.[15]

Gregory had no intention of passing his remaining days in bucolic isolation, nor did he wish to reside at Coole during the wet and dreary winter months. By September he had purchased a tall and pleasant London home in fashionable St. George's Place, a little enclosure off Hyde Park. For two months he busied himself hunting furniture in London and Paris (his preference was for Louis XVI) and stocking this second home, all of which ensured that his life in the capital was comfortable and enviable. 'A pretty house, prettily decorated, with artistic surroundings — a good cook and cellar, pleasant friends, and ample income and good health,' one jealous friend remarked from his own colonial exile. But what of employment? Physically sound and intellectually vigorous, Gregory had led too active a life to contemplate complete retirement. While at Coole, he encouraged the formation of a Galway Archaeological Society and agreed to finance the restoration of the remarkable round tower at the nearby monastic ruins of Kilmacduagh. He also gave much of his time during the autumn of 1877 to the flattering task of making arrangements to sit for the statue which a group of residents of Ceylon, European and Sinhalese, had commissioned. He selected the fashionable and successful Joseph Boehm as the sculptor. The monumental Gregory was an imposing figure, standing 8' 6" high. The British India Company agreed to ship the finished work to the colony free of charge, content with the publicity for their faltering line. The statue was finally erected outside the museum in Colombo in November 1879, and unveiled by Gregory's successor as governor.[16]

He found another outlet for his energy at the National Gallery. Friends had dissuaded him from resigning as a Trustee when he was appointed Governor of Ceylon. However, it was not long before he was complaining from his distant island of Boxall's failure to keep him properly informed of Gallery affairs and quietly calling for the Director's replacement. 'Poor old fellow he must soon go,' Gregory declared to Layard in April 1873, 'and if any tolerably good man could be found to take his place the sooner the better.' Indeed, he suggested the name of a fellow Irishman, Frederic William Burton, as a suitable successor. If a trifle eccentric, thus rejection by the most famous Irish actress of his day saw him devote himself first to his mother and then to bachelorhood, Burton was an artist of distinction though he had shunned oils in favour of water colours and chalk drawings. Whatever his shortcomings Burton possessed those attributes Gregory considered essential — 'he has refined taste, technical knowledge and is a gentleman'. Moreover, as a fellow member of the Arundel Society Burton shared Gregory's opinion 'that all reasonable and safe effort should be made to place beautiful things within the reach of all eyes'. Hence his pleasure when Burton succeeded Boxall early in 1874.

The new Director avoided those mistakes of his predecessor which had so chafed William Gregory. He aggressively entered the market for pictures purchasing fourteen important works within a few months of his appointment, among them a Botticelli. He saw to it that Gregory received the annual report and wrote one of his own to the absent Trustee. He agreed with Gregory that the Gallery ought to have works from the French School of the previous century, especially those of Watteau, but explained that his work was rarely up for sale. He wrote flatteringly of the need for Gregory's presence in London. 'We shall be very glad when you return and add strength to the Board. We are crippled by your and Mr. Layard's absence [Layard was still serving as Minister to Spain but was soon to be knighted and sent off to represent the Queen at the Porte]. Also by the want of a representative in the Lower House. Had we had one lately we might have defeated Mr. Barry's encroachments, and at the same time saved the nation some expense.' Barry's sin was his 'execrable' taste. His influence over the First Commissioner of Public Works had resulted in space being wasted for architectural effect. Further, the decoration of the new rooms he had designed impressed only with its vulgarity, especially the 'hideous strawberry cream coloured paper'. Yet, the collection still had a 'splendid appearance'. On his return to London from Madrid, before setting out for Constantinople, Henry Layard reported to his friend in Ceylon: 'With all these drawbacks and mistakes we may be well proud of our Gallery — for quality not for quantity — and for the illustration of the history of Art in all its schools we are before all the European collections.'[17]

One of the first calls Sir William Gregory made on his arrival in London from Ceylon in 1877 was at the National Gallery. He admired Burton's purchases but not some of the English pictures. He urged the Director stealthily to banish the 'vile rubbish' downstairs, insisting that it was a disgrace to the Gallery and the English School, only to discover that 'Burton funks weeding the English pictures. He dreads the gabble of the Academicians.' Gregory also threw himself into the fray to recover the Gallery's annual grant of £10,000, which had been suspended by the Liberals to help compensate the Treasury for a number of expensive special purchases. He met with Disraeli, who had led his Tories to office in 1874, and 'put a pistol to his head,' reminding the Prime Minister of his private admission that as Chancellor of the Exchequer Robert Lowe had behaved 'shabbily' towards the National Gallery. And when in 1878 the Tory Chancellor, Sir Stafford Northcote, proposed that the grant be re-established at half the former figure it was Gregory who pushed the Director and his fellow Trustees to seek an interview with the Prime Minister to make their case for its full restoration. Although the annual grant was set at £5,000 that year it was doubled in 1879. 'In Burton's hands it will be put to good account,' Gregory observed with satisfaction. He applauded the Director's purchase of a number of fine English pictures — an enormous, splendid landscape by James Ward and several small pictures by John Constable, George Morland, George Romney and Richard Wilson (the last had almost starved to death because no one would buy his landscapes) —

which would enhance both the reputation of the Gallery and the English School.

Pleasing as such small bureaucratic victories and large acquisitions were, membership of the National Gallery Trust did not fill Sir William Gregory's days or exhaust his energy. Moreover, he sensed a disturbing deterioration of that body's prestige. No longer was it consulted by the government on all matters concerning the Gallery, including the 'structural requirements'. Instead, it was 'absolutely ignored'. Anxious to reverse this decline, he fastened on a pair of recent 'complimentary appointments' as the cause of the Trust's weakness. The two men in question had proven 'far worse than useless', he advised Layard. The task at hand was to convince Disraeli, both directly and through his private secretary and confidante, Montague Corry, that the idea of a small Trust while excellent in theory had in practice been marred by bad appointments. 'I am sure you could do a vast amount of good if you will make it a point of impressing your views on Lord B(eaconsfield),' he wrote encouragingly to Henry Layard, 'and you can add that I fully concur in them and Burton is also of our opinion.' Meanwhile, Gregory was invited to broaden his interests from the world of Art to that of Business. Frank Lawley approached him on behalf of a group seeking to wrest control of the Erie Railroad from Sir Edward Watkin. Lawley dangled before his old companion on the Turf a handsome prize — the chairmanship of the Company and a salary of £3,000 p.a. — if he would join this sporting endeavour. But a belated entry to the world of high finance held no appeal for Sir William Gregory. However, he did show signs of responding to the pull of politics.[18]

Despite occasional disavowals while in Ceylon of any inclination or ambition to return to public life, correspondents had kept him abreast of developments in Ireland. Also, Gregory conceded that experience of government in a Crown Colony, because of the personal nature of the rule, would prove invaluable to a politician. More specifically, he admitted to a continuing interest in the position of First Commissioner of Public Works. 'It is the kind of work I should like, and I think I should do it pretty well, because I know enough to be profoundly impressed with my want of real knowledge and I should therefore rely on advice of persons competent to assist me,' he avowed. On closer inspection the political waters seemed less inviting. The *Tuam Herald* welcomed him home warmly as the 'bhoy for Galway'. The county 'naturally takes, as every one knows, a peculiar interest in the splendidly successful diplomatic career of their once trusted, tried and popular member,' this organ of the hierarchy proclaimed, 'and we would not be surprised if he will again occupy the position he once so worthily filled.' The banquet held in his honour proved 'a marked and gratifying success'. Nevertheless, there were other less promising omens. The 'bubble' of Home Rule, which from his colonial vantage point he had predicted would soon burst, continued to swell menacingly. Old friends warned: 'There is an ineradicable distrust and dislike of England among the voting classes of these parts, which one cannot sympathize with nor overcome.' Most landlords appeared to be 'afraid' of the people and to have lost most of their political influence over them. Weighing all of this Gregory let it be known that he was not looking to take the political plunge. 'You must not be scared from the House by [the obstructive and unpleasant tactics of the Joseph] Biggars and [the Charles Stewart] Parnells,' Henry Layard goaded. 'They must go down to the bottom at last, like the muddy sediment of a pond. You are too useful a man to be out of public affairs, and you have now special knowledge which will give you even a higher position than you formerly held.' But Gregory held fast some distance from water's edge. 'Five years of despotic government have removed all interest in our wretched Irish squabbles, into which, however, I could not fail to be drawn,' he replied. [19]

Inevitably and inexorably he was drawn into those squabbles. At the request of one of his old clerical allies, Patrick Duggan, he wrote in November 1878 to the Lord-Lieutenant suggesting that he see the Bishop of Clonfert. Although Duggan had recently been 'the intimate friend of men of extreme politics', Gregory still clung to the belief that the hierarchy might yet be won by prudent concessions as allies in the struggle against radical nationalists. It was a hope Bishop Duggan nurtured with his appeal to Sir William to lobby for passage of a Catholic University Bill. One result of its enactment would be 'the closer union if not fusion of Catholic and Conservative elements in the Empire,' the Bishop predicted. 'The Conservative principle is the natural ally of Catholicity.' Conveying all of this to the Duke of Marlborough at the Viceregal Lodge Gregory urged the Tories to mend their relations with the Irish clergy. And beyond 'the higher motives of effecting a great good in itself and of doing an act of justice' he pointed to the probable electoral benefits to the Tories in such an alliance. The opportunity was lost. The clever measure brought forward by the Government in 1879 did not meet the Catholics' demand for a state supported denominational institution. 'The entire grievance of "inequality" will be palpable' in this eventuality, Duggan had warned, and will be 'brought home to every parish in the country in tangible form'. [20]

As the Conservative Government neared the end of its term and a general election loomed Gregory inched closer to a decision on his return to political life. He categorically refused as an Irishman to allow his name to be added to the subscription for an Earl Russell Memorial, identifying the former Prime Minister 'with the most inexcusable and ruinous measure of this Century' — the Ecclesiastical Titles Bill — and denouncing his mismanagement of relief during the Famine. He sent a recent picture of His Holiness the Pope to Bishop Duggan, and was assured by a committee bearing the offer of the Liberal nomination in Galway borough that his conduct in Ceylon had made him the favourite of 'the priests' party'. The local parish priest in Gort cited the testimonial of the Roman Catholic Bishop of Ceylon and Sir William's provision of glebes to priests who resided on his property as proof that he was 'a liberal-minded man always a patron to the Catholic Church'. Thus reassured, Father Hogan of Ennis promised Gregory the backing of the priests if he agreed to contest Clare on Home Rule principles. Of course, that was not a proposal he would ever have entertained but his criticism of Mitchell Henry for refusing to attend political meetings on the sabbath excited speculation that he intended to challenge this former ally and present conservative Home Ruler for one of County Galway's seats. Henry's response was to remind a gathering at Athenry of Gregory's authorship of the notorious quarter-acre test for relief during the Famine. It was a savage blow designed 'to render me odious in the minds of your audience', Sir William protested in a letter to his former colleague, but served to discourage any further thought of attempting to unseat Henry.[21]

This flight from the broil of politics suggests a lack of mettle. Physically brave and at times intellectually courageous, Gregory was too easily discomfited by criticism and over-sensitive to abuse. He expected his many virtues to be acknowledged and was somewhat tortoise-like in his haste to shelter from possible attack in a shell. The popularity he had worked so hard to earn he was unwilling to put at risk. Yet, just as other factors bore heavily upon his decision to retire from Ceylon in the face of opposition that was gathering strength among the Europeans, his final retreat from active political life in Ireland was undertaken against a background of political pessimism and personal depression. The divisions within the Liberal Party, between the 'moderates' with whom he identified and 'rampant Radicals' such as Joseph Chamberlain, had not even been papered over. It simply would not do, he observed, for a man in Hartington's position to be dubbed 'the Vice Chamberlain'. Nor did he take comfort from Gladstone's dramatic re-emergence with his startling Midlothian campaign in late November 1879, concluding that he 'seems to have driven the sober Scotch wild with his eloquence but though he may carry a few seats in Scotland he seems to have added to the difficulties of the Liberal party'. Moreover, amid all the scorn Gladstone heaped upon Disraeli's imperial and foreign policies there had been a declaration of support for a measure of Home Rule. 'He has destroyed every particle of cohesion among us — and is more dreaded and disliked by a large number of good Liberals than even Lord Beaconsfield,' Gregory charged.[22]

Sir William Gregory's gloomy assessment of his party's prospects, and at his age he had no desire to sit on the Opposition benches (and must have doubted whether a triumphant Gladstone would find a place for him in a government), had been much influenced by the death of Frances Waldegrave. He believed that she would have been a tower of moderation and common sense in the search for Liberal unity. But his sense of loss was more personal than political, for he described her as 'my very dear and truest friend'. Adding to his misery was vile weather, a persistent cough, and a growing unease about the wisdom and safety of the substantial sums he had invested in Ceylon coffee plantations. Grim news had arrived from the colony of planters crippled by the spread of the leaf disease and a tight money market. Equally unnerving for holders of first mortgages like Gregory were reports of a judicial decision striking down the preference they had always enjoyed in the recovery of their money when estates failed. Worried and unhappy he withdrew to Coole, quitting a glittering social life in the capital which had lost some of its sheen for him, only to find evidence of mounting unrest in Ireland.[23]

The summer of 1879 had been cruel to Irish farmers. Excessive rainfall and cool temperatures meant poor crops, and this was a formula for disaster in those regions such as the west still heavily dependent upon the potato. To make matters worse agricultural prices remained depressed despite the scarcity, and a sharp drop in the demand for seasonal labourers in other areas of Britain reduced income from this important and traditional source. Suffering hardships, if in many cases far from starving, tenants demanded assistance and relations with their landlords quickly deteriorated. In Galway, the behaviour of the Marquess of Clanricarde heightened the tension. When he succeeded his father in 1874 the dead Dunkellin's younger brother inherited 52,000 acres worked by 1,900 tenants. From these vast landholdings he derived an annual income of £25,000. An absentee, miser and misanthrope, Clanricarde seemed bent on alienating the Catholic clergy and antagonising his tenantry. He created difficulties when the hierarchy sought to purchase a small plot of his land in order to build a cathedral and responded to their protests by reopening the wound of the Galway election of 1872. He refused to release land at a reasonable price and thus facilitate a railroad development which would have provided work. He declined to borrow money to finance improvements, such as drainage, sub-soiling and reclamation, on which the poor would also have found employment. His tenants were unable to borrow. 'Is it any wonder that discontent and deep indignation should prevail at seeing the "dog in the manger" policy acted on at such a time,' Bishop Duggan asked Sir William Gregory. 'And I tell you very plainly,' he added ominously, 'I do not feel called on to interpose.'[24]

Two men who had worked long and harmoniously together were drifting far apart on the land question. Tragically, there seemed to be no middle ground on which they could meet. Duggan, whose father had been evicted from his holding three decades earlier instinctively sympathised with the agitation and established a long-lasting friendship with its organizing genius, Michael Davitt. For his part Gregory, despite his deserved reputation as a just and humane landlord, allied himself in this crisis with the landed interest and thus with some members of that class who were unworthy associates. It was a conditioned reflex of a man alarmed by the growing anti-rent agitation organized by the newly formed Land League and fearful for his financial security. With the upkeep of his London home absorbing most of the annual income Lizzie had bequeathed to him, and his investments in Ceylon unlikely to be profitable, he was dependent on his rents. The agitation also violated his belief as a natural conservative in the sanctity of contracts. If they were not upheld 'the foundations of society would be shaken'. Yet, as Duggan sharply reminded him, he had himself earlier described some landlords as 'rapacious' and Lord Clarendon, when Viceroy, had termed them 'felonious'.

'Are the contracts of "rapacious" ones and felons *Just* ones,' the Bishop sarcastically enquired, before conceding that in Gregory's case a 'sense of honour and humanity' had provided the standard for a just rent. Of course, from Gregory's standpoint the anti-rent campaign threatened to be no more selective than his defence of contracts. 'There is much distress in certain districts and the Government and landlords are called on to alleviate the distress,' he reported to Henry Layard, 'the former by lending the money and the latter by borrowing it to improve the land of the tenants who start by repudiating all existing obligations — Of course landlords will not embarrass themselves for the sake of persons who have been taught to look on them as vermin which should be exterminated.' And the certainty that this social polarization would be reflected in the forthcoming election was reason enough for him to abandon all thought of a return to political life in 1880. Anyway, by the time of the general election his private life had taken a somewhat unexpected turn.[25]

The happiness he had found in marriage, the pleasure he derived from the company of women, the dread of spending his declining years alone, were the separate strands of a single thought — remarriage. Within a few months of Lizzie's death William had resolved to remarry eventually. 'Of course I never can feel as I felt for my late dear wife,' he had then hastened to add. 'Still I could have a warm regard and respect for a woman who suited me and that would be enough.' While in Australia he appears to have had a brief liaison with an actress, Ada Ward, and she had spoken to friends of pursuing him to Britain in search of respectability. But she was waylaid by a Russian swindler and never completed the journey, much to Gregory's relief. However, in 1879, when he returned to Coole so depressed in spirit and in quest of solitude and health, he renewed his friendship with Augusta Persse.[26]

Sir William's neighbour Dudley Persse was twice married and Augusta was the twelfth of sixteen children and the youngest and smallest of seven daughters. The unhappiness of childhood, even the sense of being set apart within her own family, pervades the opening chapter of her autobiography with its impersonal style. Her mother had set her heart on giving birth to another son and made no effort to conceal her continuing disappointment, even though she bore four after Augusta. She supervised an education which was devout but neither inspiring nor imaginative. In a household dominated by boisterous young men who were local Hotspurs, as befitted their descent from the Percys, there was much physical activity but precious little intellectual inquiry. Quiet, conscious that she was constantly being compared unfavourably with sisters who were tall, musically talented or more attractive, Augusta sought and found sanctuary in reading. At the family home, Roxborough, which did not boast a library, necessity and preference directed her at first to religious literature but slowly she expanded her horizons and her taste began to run to poetry, literary essays, Shakespeare and novels. It was this studiousness and depth which interested Sir William in the earnest young woman. They had met soon after his return from Ceylon and before long he had opened his large library to her and amended his will to grant her the choice at his death of any six of the near four thousand volumes. Precisely when he settled on Augusta as the companion and friend for whom he had been searching is not clear, perhaps because the thirty-five years separating them discouraged any immediate thought of a union. But they continued to see one another, and not only in Galway. When Augusta escorted her ailing brother Richard Dudley to the Riviera during the winter of 1878-1879 she again encountered Sir William, and although very early in the spring he travelled on to Rome this season of renewed life may well mark the planting and nurturing in his mind of the idea of marriage. He went to the Italian capital to meet a fellow Irishman, Robert Tighe — whom he described as his 'archaeological Gamaliel' — ostensibly to learn more of the Eternal City's ancient and medieval past. He found Tighe preparing to leave for home in order to get married. Further advanced in years than Gregory, he had found a bride who was approximately the same age as Augusta. 'He told me that their tastes were quite in conformity, that she hated parties and was not going to have an evening dress in her trousseau,' Sir William confided to 'Miss Persse'.[27]

Several months were to pass before Augusta responded to this somewhat elliptical approach. In the meantime the brother she had been nursing died and her eldest half-brother, who had succeeded to the family estate and taken possession of Roxborough on her father's death, fell ill and turned to her for care. 'I was tied as before,' she later observed cryptically. For an intellectually alert woman of twenty-eight, small, plain, one of several children as yet inadequately provided for, a dependent who seemed to be viewed as a convenient nurse, marriage even with a far older man must have appeared an ever more inviting prospect. Moreover, if Sir William lacked youth and was no longer handsome, indeed had the faintly forbidding air of a Victorian father, he had proved on closer acquaintance to be a man of considerable charm, much refinement and without being a great wit was a fascinating conversationalist. To be mistress of Coole with its rich heritage and magnificent library, and to have a London house, was to be assured of a cultural quality of life and to enjoy a security otherwise unattainable. Gregory had twice written to her since Rome, once to offer his condolences on the death of her brother and then in December to invite her to Coole while 'chaperones' were staying there. 'I have but little

Isabella Augusta Presse, a photograph probably taken just before Sir William Gregory's proposal of marriage.

amusement to offer,' he admitted, 'but I do not think that drawback will influence you if your engagements permitted you to come.' He protested to her mother the self-sacrifice the family expected of Augusta. Then, in January 1880, she returned William's copy of *Roderick Hudson* with a note which was something more than a simple critique of the book.

Despite this encouragement Gregory continued to advance cautiously, sensitive as he naturally was to the danger of exposing himself to ridicule as an aged Lothario. Thus he first asked Augusta whether he might 'write freely' on the 'most momentous question affecting man and woman's life', and provided her with a graceful means of closing the discussion by promising to remain her 'true and most sincere friend' even should he learn that he had misinterpreted her note. He did request that she 'refrain from communicating the purport of this letter to any one'. Augusta evidently replied by return for only four days later Gregory, again writing from St. George's Place, proposed to her. 'Long long have I earnestly wished to speak but I refrained from doing so, not knowing how you would have answered me and feeling that I had not the slightest ground to go upon,' he declared. 'Will you be my wife?' 'Will you marry me at once?' 'Will you come abroad after the marriage to Italy and perhaps Constantinople and then home here for the Summer?' He did not ignore the great disparity in their ages, reminding her of the obvious fact that he was old enough to be her father and warning that while in good health even the strongest break down unexpectedly. Further, she would still be young when he was a very old man and as her life had as yet not been a bright one she ought to consider the consequences should he become another invalid for her to nurse. On the credit side of this ledger, however, 'there is this that we have great similarities of tastes, we both love art and books and travelling, we know something of the character of each other, though I know far more of you than you of me. We can both live quietly, if we think fit, without yearning for balls and dissipation. It is great happiness no doubt to see this beautiful world in the companionship that is the most congenial one can select.'[28]

Friends were quick to congratulate Gregory, not least for his good sense in 'choosing with your head as well as your heart, which latter sometimes makes mistakes'. 'She has an original mind, well cultivated and with a sense of humour inherited from her mother.' Yet, he continued to be more than a little embarrassed by Augusta's youth. 'I dare say you will think it a foolish thing at my time of life to marry a young lady, only 27 [29],' he wrote defensively to his closest friend who was himself married to a younger woman, 'but she is far more mature in thoughts and habits than her years. She has been admirably brought up, is clever and well informed, fond of art and literature — so I trust we may get on happily — I found myself of late so lonely especially when in the country and by myself that my spirits and health were giving way and I could no longer live without a companion. It is all very well when you are young, but solitude is bad for the old, and last winter tired me terribly.' This sensitivity was heightened by his bride's small size and appearance, which led most people to underestimate her age. 'I thought you looked quite in your early teens when you appeared in your sealskin and hat the other day,' he wrote shortly before the wedding on 4 March 1880, in Dublin. Naturally, he attempted to make light of the matter, suggesting that the 'Society for the Suppression of Vice' would seize and prosecute him 'for abducting a girl below the proper age', but he was insistent that theirs be a simple and quiet ceremony, one free of feasts, toasts, and 'gossip', and he promptly took his young wife off on a European tour. Nevertheless, there was no escaping the fact that many years separated them or that this gulf made all too likely another long separation. Thus shortly after their marriage he brought home some verse for Augusta which he had found and had copied out at the Athenaeum:

> Till death us part
> So speaks the heart
> When each to each repeats the words of doom
> Thro' blessings and through curse
> For better and for worse
> We will be one, till that dread hour come

There was, however, the assurance of eventual reunion:

> Death with his healing hand
> Shall once more knit the band
> Which needs but that one link which none may sever
> Till, thro' the only good
> Heard, felt and understood
> Our life in God shall make us one for ever.[29]

Having selected a young woman of intellectual pursuits for his wife, one whom he admiringly described as 'quite a student', and whose smooth hair and subdued apparel reminded him of a 'Jenny Wren' when he saw her among more fashionable 'birds of plumage', Gregory was nonplussed by this blue stocking's unexpected and expensive preoccupation with 'chiffons and modistes'. His disapproval did not survive the disarming explanation that her purchases were motivated solely by a desire to please him. Their honeymoon took them first to Paris and then on to Italy. At Naples they embarked for Greece, and from there they journeyed to Constantinople. They were handsomely entertained by the Layards, even though Sir Henry had just received word that the victorious Gladstone had recalled him as Ambassador to the Turkish Empire. Lady Layard judged Lady Gregory to be no more than 21 and considered her 'plain but intelligent looking'. Together they visited mosques and bazaars, were carried by the ambassadorial launch to the entrance of the Black Sea and to Scutari, and walked up to the Crimean War cemetary which was beautifully decorated by Judas trees. After twelve days of sightseeing and exploration the Gregorys set out for home, taking a French mail steamer to Marseilles. They arrived in a cold and wet London on 31 May.

Gregory introduced his wife to the capital's 'delightful society'. They spent the months of June and July in a heady whirl of activity — lunches, garden parties, including a royal one at Marlborough House, receptions, dinners, visits to the Royal Academy, the National Gallery, the British Museum, South Kensington, Christie's for an auction, Covent Garden for a performance of *La Sonnambula*. They entertained at St. George's Place. Slowly, the shy, young, provincial Lady Gregory gained confidence in her prowess as a conversationalist and hostess. She had an excellent instructor in her husband, of whom Gladstone once remarked: 'Sir William Gregory is a very agreeable man. I think the most agreeable I have ever known.' They would gather a select company of a dozen around the small dining table to enjoy good food and fine wines. Gregory scorned 'that odious adultered stuff Moselle' which Layard served, the 'most unsavoury beverage in the civilized world', preferring champagnes. 'We are having small and pleasant dinners, not for mashed-potato headed swells but "convivers" who put something into the part,' the host boasted after one success. The guests included both men of letters and men of politics — statesmen sat down with artists, sculptors, writers and poets. All of this was a far cry from the rural and unsophisticated Galway to which the Gregorys returned at the end of July, and life at Coole naturally seemed both 'trivial' and 'common' in comparison. However, Augusta soon made the exciting discovery that she was with child.[30]

Sir William responded with a surprising lack of grace and enthusiasm to the impending birth. 'People congratulate me on the prospect of being a father which I dread and detest,' he sourly confided to Layard, 'my wife is so poorly that she cannot do anything at present and so as I am likely to be detained at Coole much longer than I intended I have left her there with her sister and come' to London. Indeed, Gregory behaved inconsiderately throughout his wife's difficult pregnancy, complaining that it was 'a horrible business and each day adds to my discomfiture'. Set in his ways at the age of sixty-four, worried about his health if forced to remain at Coole for the entire winter, perhaps fearful of gossip and ridicule, he resolved not to abandon long-laid plans to travel. Even when it became clear that Augusta was too unwell to undertake a foreign journey, he planned to leave her in the care of her family in Dublin and flee to Southern Italy. He did return to Ireland from London to be with her for the New Year celebrations and take her on to Coole but was back in the capital when she fell ill again in March. Conscious of how unpleasant and distasteful William was finding the experience, she forbade anyone to inform him of her condition and it was only after her recovery that he discovered how serious this crisis had been. Shamefaced, he gave up all thought of travelling abroad and hurried to see his wife. Spring found them in London and after 'quite a banquet' at St. George's Place on 20 May 1881, Augusta casually confessed to Enid Layard that her confinement had already begun but that her doctor had given her permission to sit through the lunch. Layard's startled wife immediately rose to leave and urged the other guests to follow her example. At 9:00 p.m. a son and heir was born to the Gregorys, whom they named William Robert, but the father's joy knew its bounds. 'I wish to heavens he could be shut up ... till he reaches the age of 7 *at least*,' he wrote to his son's godfather. [31]

11

The Final Decade

On 25 July 1881, having deposited their infant son with a member of the family, the Gregorys left London for a characteristic visit to the Continent. It was an extended tour of art galleries and churches in the Low Countries and Germany. Sir William studied with particular interest the work of J. Van der Meer of Delft, for he considered him 'the greatest of the Dutchmen barring Rembrandt'. 'We saw ten of his pictures and I got photographs of several,' he reported to Henry Layard. Augusta derived less pleasure from these foreign excursions, which separated her from her child and where the artistic rounds were infrequently interrupted by the social. 'Museum again' was a recurrent and weary entry in her diary during that summer. She masked her boredom and dutifully recorded the names of many of the pictures they saw. Oblivious to the deception, Gregory happily convinced himself that Augusta's interest in art and architecture equalled his own. And no sooner had they returned home at the end of August and were reunited with the baby than William was arranging to winter in Egypt, having been obliged to cancel his plans the previous year. Among Cairo's attractions was its inexpensiveness, but he also insisted that it was a place of 'amusement' for ladies. Little did he realize how decisive this interlude would prove to be in his young wife's life. [1]

Again entrusting their son to one of Augusta's sisters, they set out in October. Travelling at a leisurely pace they made their way to Venice, via Frankfurt, Munich and Verona, where they remained as guests of the Layards for a fortnight before embarking for Egypt. Their arrival in the land of the Pharaohs could scarcely have been less auspicious. William caught a cold 'at that beastly Alexandria' and then fell victim to an attack of eczema. He viewed with dismay the changes 'progress' had wrought in Cairo. Old houses had been levelled to make way for huge, wide streets, and with them had gone beautiful lattice and stonework. The city had been ruined, he grumbled, and converted into a tenth rate French provincial town. Finally, even the seeming unchangeable had changed — the weather. It rained for several days, leaving mud inches deep and a noxious smell. But the Gregorys soon forgot these disappointments. They had 'tumbled into a revolution' and were rapidly caught up in the excitement of Egyptian politics. [2]

Disraeli's purchase of Suez Canal shares had inevitably drawn Britain deeper into the affairs of Egypt, long merely a nominal part of the

Turkish Empire. In 1879 the British and French Governments had deposed the Viceroy, or Khedive, Ismail Pasha, who was heavily in debt and unacceptably independent, replacing him with his more pliable son Tewfik. The Anglo-French Control of Egyptian finances, the rivalry of the English and French Controllers for ascendancy, the great increase in the number of European officials, all served to undermine the Khedive's authority and create a volatile situation. A growing national and religious resistance to Europeanization, to increased taxation to pay European bondholders and the salaries of European officials, found expression and leadership in the army. A military revolt in February 1881 had seen the charismatic figure of Colonel Arabi Bey emerge as the most powerful officer, and a second military demonstration in September had made him the effective ruler of the land.

A natural conservative and an enemy of radical Irish nationalism, Sir William Gregory instinctively regarded Arabi as a 'mutinous rascal' who ought to be exiled to the Sudan. Initially, he saw in the national movement an Egyptian equivalent of the Land League at home. However, on closer inspection he discovered Arabi to be honest, patriotic, industrious and intelligent, if lacking a high level of education and devoid of experience in public affairs. As for the national party, that appeared to be a inchoate political force at best. It was less a party of national unity than a reflection of an almost universal desire for change. He sympathized with the plight and yearnings of the Egyptian peasantry, the unfortunate 'blue shirted fellah', who paid through the nose 'while the Greek, Jew, Levantine usurer and extortioner dwell in magnificent palaces and drive over flagged streets for but one shilling of the expense which he contributes'. Ordinary Egyptians sought the redress of many grievances, including an end to their exploitation by Christians. They wished to see the number and the salaries of Europeans reduced and an end to such privileges as immunity to taxation. They longed to free their government from the grasp of Britain and France and to govern themselves according to their own traditions and ideas. In short, they craved an Egypt which was Egyptian. And this was an ambition Gregory came to support, concluding that Britain's interests in the region would be served by the triumph of a national government.[3]

Convinced that Arabi Bey was being misrepresented by English correspondents, who depicted him as the mere mouthpiece of a turbulent soldiery, Sir William wrote a number of letters to *The Times* in an effort to correct this distortion. He informed British readers of the existence of a national party to which practically every educated Egyptian gave allegiance; advised them that it was a civil movement but one supported by the army; that it was directed by a man of great power, singleness of purpose and noble-minded honesty. Officers and men of the army had behaved well, he insisted, and had guaranteed tranquillity unless there was foreign intervention to crush the national movement. He made light of the incidents so shamelessly exploited by the promoters of intervention, men he contemptuously described as either officials who feared for their sinecures or merchants frightened that the success of the national movement would result in the suppression of 'flagrant jobs'. Thus a 'row' had erupted at a waxworks when an Egyptian soldier had, somewhat indecently, placed his hand on the figure of a half-naked woman, only to be hit on the head with a hammer wielded by the German exhibitor. Do not 'our soldiers sometimes use their belts in the street of London without the imputation of the army being in a state of insubordination,' he asked Henry Layard, having just read another incendiary article in *The Times*. And one of the newspaper's leader-writers acknowledged that 'It is not everday that a successful revolution finds so practised an advocate. ...' The policy Britain ought to have followed was clear, at least to Gregory. Had the British Government recognized the importance of the revolution, abstained from foolish menaces, and extended the hand of friendship, it might have got 'hold of Arabi'. He would have responded by willingly accepting British guidance on a number of major matters concerning the canal if in return he secured freedom of action in dealing with problems that were more minor from the British viewpoint. Equally, Britain would have been well advised to co-operate with him in remedying such injustices as the inequality in taxation and the inordinate salaries and sinecures of foreign employees. [4]

Once it was clear that this policy had not been adopted in London, and that the danger of European intervention was growing, Sir William Gregory struggled manfully to win for Arabi and his followers the additional time needed to acquire experience of administration and to reassure the British that their legitimate economic and strategic interests were not in jeopardy. He proposed that the friends of the national movement exploit British distrust of France, a distrust he genuinely shared. 'Their only object is the gratification of greediness and vanity,' he wrote of the French. 'We are certain to suffer in our material interests if we ally ourselves with them and to be tarred with the same brush in the estimation of Europe and of Egypt for their misdeeds.' Another tack was to dwell upon the risk of anarchy, disorder and insolvency if the Powers meddled, and thus tap the concern of the bondholders. Less attractive was the spasm of anti-semitism to which he succumbed when, despite these efforts, the demands for intervention grew more shrill. 'The main movers of all the attacks against the Egyptian Government and the fomentors of aggression are the Rothchilds and other Jews with their ramifications in every country,' he privately charged. 'To them national aspirations are as mere dust in the balance compared with having the power of keeping their debtors under their heel and taking the pound of flesh, blood and all — Rely on it this is the true clew to the attacks.' [5]

In all of his endeavours on behalf of the Egyptian nationalists William had been supported enthusiastically by Augusta and they had been allied with Wilfrid Scawen Blunt. Sussex squire, poet, writer, hedonist, philanderer, Blunt was ever in search of political crusades to lead. Genuine enthusiasm for a 'good' cause was heightened by a Thespian desire for self-dramatisation. He was a romantic admirer of things Arabian. And it was the single-minded nature of his commitment which always distinguished him from Sir William Gregory. 'I view all these matters differently from Blunt who pushes things to first principles,' he had early recognized, 'but I think that Blunt deserves great credit for the bold and indefatigable manner in which he has fought this battle almost single handed. He has fought for Egypt alone, I have fought for England first and Egypt also.' At first, these differences had been less important than Gregory's recognition in the much younger man (Blunt was 42) of his own impetuous and full-hearted espousal of foreign causes two decades earlier. It was not until the spring of 1882 that they began to drift apart, when Arabi ignored Gregory's advice neither to accept wholesale promotions in the army nor threaten wholesale dismissals of Europeans. Irritated by the Egyptian's 'unyielding stubborness', Gregory proved less immune than Blunt to the hostility their sympathetic attitude had generated in London. The brutal murders in Phoenix Park, Dublin, on 6 May 1882, of the Chief Secretary for Ireland and his Under Secretary, led many Englishmen to equate Egyptian with Irish nationalism and within the Gladstone Cabinet the Marquis of Hartington, brother of one of the slain men, successfully argued that Arabi must be deposed. Removed from office on 20 May 1882, following the arrival at Alexandria of two British warships, he was reinstated the very next day at the demand of the Egyptian populace. From this point, however, relations between the Europeans and Egyptians, the nationalists and the British, steadily deteriorated and the distrust culminated in the British bomardment of Alexandria and military defeat of Arabi.[6]

Sir William Gregory was scornful of the British Government's policy. 'Our exploits in Egypt are very gratifying,' he subsequently observed sarcastically. 'We have been the means of destroying Alexandria and have saddled the Egyptians with 5 millions [pounds] to build it up again, we have slaughtered from first to last some thousand harmless Egyptians, we have squeezed the last penny out of the cultivation so that the canals are neglected. ...' Moreover, he retained a large measure of sympathy for Arabi and his followers. But the dominant consideration in Gregory's mind following the unsuccessful effort to oust the nationalist leader in May, which coincided with the Gregorys' arrival home, was the knowledge that Arabi was 'now so alienated from England by the foolish and petulant manner in which he had been treated that there is no hope of his being guided by us'. It was this conviction which explained his defection from the ranks of Arabi's defenders and not, as Blunt churlishly charged later, a pathetic hunger for popularity among his fellow clubmen. Indeed, it was less his change of position than the evidence of the government's hamfisted policy, which careful readers found in the parliamentary papers published later in the year, that restored his reputation. 'After having been the cockshy of London society during the summer and been heartily abused by all sides,' he informed Layard in October, 'I find myself greeted as a prophet.' When Arabi was placed on trial he quietly urged leniency. On the other hand Blunt arranged for the Egyptian's defence and nobly paid for it out of his own pocket, even though he could ill-afford the large sum involved. 'We have not got the money but we can borrow it,' Lady Anne Blunt remarked, 'and if our income is straightened we have the comfort of knowing it is owing to our having done what is right.'[7]

Throughout the campaign to defend Arabi and save his life Augusta worked closely with Blunt. Her aging, temporising husband, who suffered with his teeth and from an unsightly eczema, and against whom she may have harboured a long smouldering resentment both for his selfish behaviour during her pregnancy and apparent lack of interest in their son, cut a sorry figure beside the handsome, romantic, quixotic, eccentric, even exotic Blunt. In her diary of the Egyptian adventure she reserved for Blunt the intimacy of a first name and her favourite adjective to describe him had been 'radiant'. Then, in the summer of 1883, Augusta found herself standing with Blunt against her husband. Together with Randolph Churchill and others they disparaged the Khedive, a course Gregory deplored as contrary to British interests. 'Blunt is a fanatic and apparently thinks anarchy will create a pure and simple Arab rule, with all European influences eliminated,' he concluded. 'R. Churchill's only object is to discredit and embarrass the British Government and Lady G. thinks if the Khedive becomes impossible her dear Arabi may be recalled to govern the country.' Whether or not he was alarmed by his wife's intimacy or aware of her infatuation with Blunt, Gregory never gave any indication of having suspected that friendship had been briefly transformed into a more passionate and adulterous relationship. Surviving letters to Augusta for this period are affectionate in tone and he continued to employ tender diminutives when he addressed her. Nor did he sever relations with Blunt, at least until 1886 and then the cause of the break was the Englishman's provocative support of Irish nationalism. As for Arabi and his principal associates, all of whom had been sentenced to exile in Ceylon, Gregory fought valiantly for the remainder of his life to lessen their misery and improve their lot. He approached Gladstone and Lord Salisbury, the Tory Prime Minister, he wrote to the Foreign Office, the Colonial Office, the Governor of Ceylon, and a number of other influential figures in Britain, including the editor of *The Times*, seeking an increase in the exiles' allowances and to protest their treatment. By 1890 he was appealing for them to be permitted to return to Egypt or at least to the nearby island of Cyprus, but to no avail.[8]

The Gregorys had sailed from Alexandria for Catarnia on 1 April 1882, but a comfortable boat could not compensate for overcast skies and heavy seas. They spent a month in Sicily, discovering on the island's east coast a society more prosperous than they had expected. Once again they toured museums and admired the architecture, putting up in hotels that combined cleanliness with inexpensiveness. Not that they escaped the darker side of Sicilian life. They took a train to Palermo and at every stop on the way it was met by large crowds and a sound reminiscent of the popping of soda water bottles. They discovered that the multitudes had assembled to cheer and to smack kisses on the cheeks of a fellow passenger, and local banker, who had just been ransomed from brigands for 50,000 francs. It was a story Gregory naturally embellished and added to that fund of anecdotes which made him such a welcome dinner guest in London. After another rough sea passage, this one from Sicily to Marseilles, and several days in Paris, they finally reached London on 18 May 1882. It was another four days before an excited Augusta was able to record in her diary: 'To Redruth & Baba.'

Three months later they were off again, William seeking relief from his eczema in the waters of Ems. Then it was on to Vienna and another fortnight with the Layards in Venice before returning to Britain in October. The spring of 1883 found them junketing through Portugal with an American friend and 'living sumptuously on chicken broth and Quince cheese'. William enjoyed the trip, for he saw a small number of pictures of high merit and some fine examples of architecture. 'There was just too that little amount of roughing which makes a journey pleasant and gives a zest to it — the anticipation of bad accommodations, bad food, and bad smells, generally falsified by scrupulously clean rooms, very good "nourriture," and unodorous lodging, is a very pleasant ingredient in travelling.'

To the delight he took in travel itself William Gregory no doubt counted himself doubly fortunate that his wanderings took him abroad during the period of acute tension in Britain following the Phoenix Park murders in Dublin and the Dynamite campaign in London. And if foreign excursions had long since begun to pall for his young wife they did have a profound impact upon her life. In this sense the briefly passionate relationship with Blunt was less important than the breaking of the ground for her later illustrious literary career. Her short essay on *Arabi and His Household* had appeared in 1882, and before long William was urging her to write 'a corrected vindication of Arabi and the National Party'. She had the 'power of writing well and piquantly', he praised. Her account of their journey 'Through Portugal', which revealed a descriptive ability and paraded literary and artistic knowledge lightened by a fillip of humour, was published in the *Fortnightly Review*. Proudly, he reported that in London she was known as 'the bright and clever Lady Gregory' and that the *Pall Mall* had applauded the piece as 'lively and clever'. He exhorted as well as lauded, demanding that she make full use of her talent. Thus a subsequent and lifeless article in the *Fortnightly* on the Sudan, which was little more than an abstract of a plodding book by a German academic, he extolled as good of its kind before dismissing this genre as unworthy of her. She was too original, he flattered, to convert herself into a kind of 'lemon strainer'.[9]

Generous in his encouragement and constructive in his criticism of Augusta's literary activities, Sir William found employment for his own pen. He began to compose a memoir of his life, dictating to his wife and then correcting the manuscript. More immediately profitable was a long article on the Arundel Society published in the *Nineteenth Century*, and for which the review paid him the princely fee of £14. It was fitting that the first 'literary penny' he had ever earned should be a reward for his long and continuing interest in art. In foul weather as well as fair he journeyed from Coole to the capital to attend meetings of the Society's council and of the Trustees of the National Gallery. The latter were strengthened in the 1880s by sound appointments but Gregory and Layard remained the dominant figures. Relations between Sir William and his fellow Irishman Frederic Burton, the Director, had cooled by 1880. Gregory's frequently voiced concern that the heating and ventilation system was causing irreparable damage to a number of pictures (nightwatchmen reported that they heard some of them go 'pop' in the night), his protests that the annual cleaning of the Gallery was so mismanaged that filth, soot and dust went flying everywhere, and his undisguised irritation at Burton's sudden reluctance to enter the market for pictures ('Sales are dangerous,' the Director wrote to him. 'One is very apt to be led into imprudence at them, either by rashness or timidity.'), created friction. 'I give up all communications with him except at the Board where he has resisted every reform, fruitlessly nevertheless,' in informed Layard.[10] It was the energetic Gregory who led the fight to recover the balance of the annual grant left unspent as a result of Burton's caution and returned therefore to the Treasury. Of the £10,300 surrendered between 1879 and 1881, £9,000 was recouped, only for the purchases made with this windfall to become a subject of controversy. Lady Eastlake announced that Sir Charles would never have wasted public money on these pictures, a statement calculated to confirm members of the government in the opinion that the Trustees were spendthrifts.

That was a charge which the Prime Minister made bluntly to Gregory when both men were guests of Lord Roseberry at Dalmeny Park in September 1884. The Trustees, with a special parliamentary appropriation, had recently completed the purchase of 12 Blenheim pictures including the famous Raphael. The price paid for this masterpiece — £70,000 — was then 'the largest sum ever paid for a single picture.' As a Trustee Gregory had questioned the wisdom of spending more than £30-40,000 on the picture. To the argument of his colleagues, that it might otherwise go to Germany, he had replied: the Germans will then be unable to compete for other great works. Moreover, he had warned that to advocate the expenditure of such an enormous sum (his fellow Trustees had been prepared to go up to £100,000) would seriously weaken their authority with the goverment. Finding himself standing alone he had given way. At Dalmeny he discovered just how soundly based his misgivings had been. Learning of the government's decision to apply the Gallery's annual grant for at least seven years to the repayment of the special appropriation, Gregory protested personally to the Prime Minister. Gladstone did not mince his words in reply. The Trustees appeared to have lost their heads, he complained, and expected the government to find money for pictures that were put up for sale no matter how extravagant or preposterous the price. It was the duty of the Trustees, he insisted, not only to promote the National Gallery but also to protect the public interest.[11]

Before this onslaught of indignation Gregory beat a hasty retreat, but he did cooperate with Henry Layard in the preparation of an article on the 'National Gallery' which was critical of the government's course. Published in the *Quarterly Review* (1886), it scored a number of telling hits on the Prime Minister. Layard pointed to Gladstone's decision when Chancellor of the Exchequer, and 'in the exercise of his own judgment', to purchase for the nation the works of a number of obscure German artists. '£2,800 was paid for these sixty-four worthless pictures,' he noted, 'only four of which have been considered as fit to remain in the National Gallery.' He attacked the decision of the Gladstone Government to suspend the annual grant as 'unfair, unwise, and parsimonious,' having incorporated Gregory's suggestion that he emphasise its failure to present the Trustees with a choice between making the Blenheim purchases and retaining the annual grant. Again following Gregory's advice, he inveighed against the 'short sighted' nature of the action; dwelt upon the Gallery's utter dependence now on bequests; pointed to the gaps which remained in the various collections; and stressed the extraordinary popularity of the Gallery.

'In former days such an article would have excited general attention, but both the Quarterly and Edinburgh have lost that influence which used to be widespread and powerful,' Gregory commented. 'Still it will have many readers and cannot fail to help our objects materially.' The return of the Tories to power in 1886 raised the Trustees' hopes of receiving a more sympathetic hearing and Sir William Gregory again took the lead in a dogged campaign to win restitution of the annual grant. After three years of partial successes they triumphed in 1889. The victory was a timely one, for the competition for pictures had increased with the arrival of American millionaires 'determined to buy the best things that come into the market'. Thus Gregory had every reason to look back with pride on his long service as a Trustee. He could claim a full share of the credit for the National Gallery's dramatic rise 'to the very first rank' of public galleries, 'both as regards the number of its pictures and its importance as illustrating the history of painting.' Ever in the vanguard of those demanding and supporting an aggressive purchasing policy (with the single exception of the Blenheim pictures), and untiring in his struggle to recover funds from the government, whether they were unspent balances or the suspended annual grant, his energy and zest had gone far to make possible the boast: 'No other European gallery has shown so rapid an increase within so short a period.'[12]

The patriotic desire to establish the National Gallery as one of the world's finest collections of art did not entirely explain Gregory's dedicated attendance at the meetings of the Trustees. Restlessness, a need for some change in his life of retirement, often provided an additional incentive during the early years of the decade to undertake the long journey from Coole. In much the same mood he began to give serious thought to a return to political life, particularly when he was invited to stand for a number of English constituencies — Devonport (1884), New Forest Division of South Hants (1885) and the Epsom and Surrey Division (1885). After much debate, with himself and friends, and taking into consideration his age (he was approaching 70) and the November date of the general election in 1885, he concluded 'that a wintry Parliamentary campaign would soon bring my head to the family vault.' Writing to Augusta, he added: 'I have therefore finally decided on never entering Parliament — and I have no misgiving as to the correctness of the conclusion.' However, he had not excluded the possibility of another overseas appointment. His name was floated as a candidate for the Governorship of Bombay and to head the Madras Presidency, the latter being a post his great-grandfather had been urged by supporters in the East India Company to accept a century earlier.

Gregory had remained active in colonial affairs and Ceylon was the natural focus of his attention. He corresponded with old friends and associates in the colony's society and administration, he assisted some of them to find places for their sons in English Public Schools, and in a few instances attempted to advance careers.[13] Occasionally, he intervened at the Colonial Office in an effort to promote the island's interests, though the interference was not always welcomed or appreciated by his successors at Queen's House, Colombo. Sir Arthur Gordon was understandably piqued when A.M. Ferguson, following an argument with him, dedicated a book on the colony to Sir William Gregory 'the best living Governor of Ceylon'. Yet when the former Governor returned to the island early in 1884, hoping to shake off his persistent eczema and to check on the plantations in which he had invested, he received a friendly enough welcome from Gordon despite the triumphal character of his progress. Gregory had begun to swell with pride as he entered Colombo and first glimpsed fourteen steamers riding safely at anchor within the breakwater that stretched for three quarters of a mile. 'My head is absolutely turned by my reception here,' he wrote to friends, 'a public holiday was given on my arrival, the harbour was crowded with boats all decorated with flags and flowers, the guests equally decorated. Lovely ladies strewing roses before me, addresses from all corporations.' He was overwhelmed by the affection of the native population, some of whom travelled from as far afield as Jaffna merely to see him. A visit to Anuradhapura proved equally satisfying. He found the North Central Province prosperous and healthy, the hospitals cleared of victims of 'Parange', and the area around the ancient capital, where a large town had sprung up, 'like a vast gentleman's park with noble trees and green sward. . . .' Here was a monument to his enlightened rule of the colony. There were some disappointments. Nuwara Eliya 'has gone to the bad from sheer neglect since I went away,' he observed. 'In every place I see signs of torpor, want of discipline and neglect.' Nor had the Museum developed as he had hoped and planned, largely because of the unimaginative administration of its directors.[14]

Sir William set out for home at the end of March, bearing gifts for Augusta who had chosen to remain in Ireland with young Robert. They included a gold bracelet studded with rubies, although he hastened to warn her that the gems were very small, and a silver box. He spent much of the voyage from Colombo to Suez trying to avoid 46 'noisy and wilful' children and annotating Homer's *Odyssey* with two new editions. When he finally landed in Europe he went first to Venice and then to Milan, to begin his rail journey to Calais. He had to change trains in Basle and for thirteen hours cooled his heels in this Swiss town. 'I have walked over every street in Basle and rubbed my nose on every shop window and read through Zola's dull and improper "Page d'amour" and am absolutely stiffened with the black cold,' he reported miserably to one friend.[15] On 1 June 1884 he reached Gort.

The exhilarating memories of his reception in Ceylon, and the island's magical powers of rejuvenation, perhaps an understandable wish that Augusta see for herself his many achievements there, all drew Gregory back to his former dominion. No sooner had he decided not to seek election to Parliament in November 1885 than he persuaded his wife to accompany him on an expedition to India and Ceylon. Disembarking at Bombay on 5 December they set off on an exhausting but exciting trek across the sub-continent visiting temples and tombs. Augusta was disappointed with the Taj Mahal, insisting that she could not 'feel' it. William considered it the 'finest single structure' he had ever seen. They also visited the jail in Agra to examine the magnificent carpets woven by prisoners, and learned that the finest and most expensive of these products were bought by Parisian houses. But they were able to obtain several for Coole. From Agra they moved on to Delhi, and then to Allahabad, the Holy City of Benares, and Calcutta, before crossing to Madras to stay with a friend who was Governor of the Presidency. At the end of February 1886 they sought refuge in Ceylon from the detestably hot climate and the swarming, aggressive mosquitoes of the Coromandel coast.

Throughout the Indian journey Gregory had pondered the political setting of this jewel in the Imperial crown. His views mirrored the conservatism which was hardening as he aged. He was not opposed to natives being conceded a greater share of responsibility for the government of their country so long as they earned it 'by degrees'. To every unprejudiced person it was clear, he asserted, that power should only

Above left: William Robert Gregory, Sir William's only child, aged about four. Above right: Sir William Gregory. Lady Gregory's prefered portrait of her husband, used as the frontispiece to the first edition of his *Autobiography* (1894). Below: A family group outside the front door of Coole Park. Sir William and Lady Gregory with their son, and two of the senior servants on the estate in 1887, photographed by Mrs. Ernest Hart.

gradually be entrusted to native administrators. This was not the time to encourage or to precipitate general aspirations, and he dismissed those guilty of this 'folly', such as Blunt, as 'sentimental unreflecting enthusiasts'. The true policy was 'wisely and tentatively' to promote 'individuals of known competency.' To hold in check the ambition of the educated 'Bengal Baboos' and designing 'Poonah Brahmins', controllers of a native press 'which reeks with the most odious abuse of England and Englishmen', he recommended to public men the systematic advance of the Moslems of India. If less clever, less adroit, less accommodating than Hindus, they were more safe and staunch. Obviously, Gregory was quite prepared to seek security for the Indian Empire in a deliberate exploitation of the ethnic and religious divisions within the population. He allowed that this might seem a strange recommendation by a man who 'was looked on as the most philonative Governor who ever ruled' Ceylon, and insisted that he did not want 'to oppose progress, but to go with it very cautiously and to guide it — to do in short what Gladstone has not done and we see the result everywhere of encouraging and accepting every proposal which is backed up by a cry and therefore hailed as the voice of the nation.' This allusion to Ireland in a discusson of the best policy for India suggests the extent to which the tortured affairs of his native land dominated Sir William Gregory's final years. He peered at life through that dark glass. His enthusiastic and prominent participation in the founding of the Imperial Federation League in 1884, which had as its aim the reversal of the drift to separatism and the drawing together of the several parts of the Empire in an Imperial Parliament, was surely the result as much of a hope that this structure might provide a solution to the Irish question as it was a mark of his distinction as a former colonial governor. [16]

For many a landlord, Sir William Gregory included, the Land War had been a traumatic and embittering experience. 'Whatever naughty deeds I may have done I always felt the strongest sense of duty to my tenants, and I have a great affection for them,' he declared to Augusta shortly before their marriage. 'They have never in a single instance caused me displeasure, and I know you can and will do everything in your power to make them love and value us.' A 'generous gift' to aid the poor of Loughrea brought an appreciative note from the local parish priest. 'The cases of helpless want which are around us are not among those who are fortunate enough to be your tenants,' Father Jerome Fahy acknowledged. 'All interested in our district must regard it as a source of pleasure to see the kindly relations which you cultivate with your tenantry,' he wrote a few months later, 'and especially at the present time when in many other districts similar relations are either over strained or rudely broken.' [17]

Those tenants of Sir William Gregory who had shared in the general agricultural prosperity which had been a feature of the third quarter of the century had good reason to be well disposed towards their landlord. On the Coole lands rents remained unchanged as incomes rose. In 1856 the 4,950 acres William Gregory ultimately retained of the more than 15,000 he had inherited yielded an income of £2,670. Twenty-four years later the rents from those same lands totalled £2,820. Moreover, rent stability had been accompanied by security of tenure. There was a truly remarkable continuity among his tenantry. Many of those in occupation of the land in 1880 were either the same persons or evidently members of the same family as those listed a generation earlier. Gregory's generosity during the good times was matched by his kindness during the bad. He had not raised his rents to capture a share of the prosperity despite his desperate need for money during the 1850s and 1860s, thus they were 'notoriously low compared with those exacted by other land-lords,' but he had quickly called his tenants together when he realized how poor the crop prospects were in 1879 to announce a 10% abate-ment. He had acted long before any of his neighbours stirred 'and much to the indignation of other landlords' who knew they would soon be under pressure to follow his lead. As the season advanced and the extent of the disaster became clear Gregory ordered, again on his own initiative, without receiving an appeal, that the rent reduction be increased to 20% for that year. In 1880 the harvest was good but he granted a 10% abatement on the half-year rents paid in November to help his tenants to get back on their feet. And when, during the winter of 1880–1881, there were heavy losses of sheep on his lands he granted another abatement of 20% on the rents paid in May 1881. Finally, he made permanent reductions in those few cases where in the opinion of his agent and cousin Charles Gregory rents were too high.[18]

What Gregory expected from his tenants in return was loyalty and gratitude, and these he briefly received. He and his young bride had been given a rousing welcome to Coole in July 1880, and he had happily perfomed his duties as a country gentleman — attending the petty sessions and presiding at the weekly meetings of the Poor Law Board. He gave a dinner for his tenants, at which 100 sat down, and made a little speech reprobating the activities of 'agitators and communists'. 'Nothing can be better than the spirit apparently of the people about here,' he reported to a friend at the end of August, 'but I dread that all may be changed in a day by some of these violent agitators who lash the tenants into fury against the best landlords.' His premonition proved to be all too accurate. Personally safe, he watched first in disbelief and then with mounting anger and fear the enthronement of terror in a part of the Queen's dominions that was only sixteen hours from the capital. 'Besides assassinations successful and assassinations incomplete, there is cutting off ears and desperate assaults and mutilations of cattle, and orders which dare not be resisted to servants to leave their masters' houses and shepherds and herds(men) to leave their flocks.' Even the priests seemed incapable of halting the violence, and when they did intervene were themselves threatened. Indeed, threatening notices were 'flying like snow flakes'. Inexorably and insidiously the intimidation spread across his estate. On the November rent day the tenants 'behaved splendidly' and the arrears amounted to no more than £100. All of them denied membership of the Land League and declared that they would never join it. But after a week of abuse and persecution they capitulated almost to a man. 'The combination is creeping on like lava filling every cranny,' he fumed, '_____d Gladstone is in the highest spirits while anarchy prevails within a few hours of London.'[19]

The new Liberal Government had hoped to calm Ireland with an interim measure of conciliation. In the summer of 1880 it had introduced a bill which required landlords to compensate for disturbance those tenants evicted for non-payment of rent, thus closing the large loop-hole in the 1870 Land Act. The rejection of this mild reform by the Lords, following its passage through the Commons, had natually given fresh impetus to the violent campaign of the Land League. Consequently, the angry and frightened Gregory was less than just when he indicted the government for 'the dreadful state of things' in his native land. Nor was his faith in the effectiveness of a policy of 'vigour' well founded. When the government prosecuted some of the leading lights of the agitation it was unable to find a jury which would bring in a verdict of guilty. His demand that the Liberals respond immediately to this setback with a suspension of habeas corpus took little account of the government's dependence upon a powerful Radical minority which insisted on conciliation before coercion. Further, indecision reached into the ranks of the threatened landlords. In Galway they could not agree to hold a meeting of magistrates, some fearing that much would be said that was better left unspoken, nor even unite on the composition of a delegation to visit the Chief Secretary to demand protection of life and property. Gregory raised with a number of friends the possibility of founding a Landlords League to combine 'in support of each other against the tyranny of the Socialist aggressors, and to assist poor landlords financially in fighting the Land Leaguers'. For example, 'recoup them to a moderate extent' for farms left unoccupied when tenants were ejected and others 'persuaded' not to take their place. The initial enthusiam for such an association quickly evaporated. Those landlords already unable to collect their rents could ill afford to contribute to the war chest and those whose tenants were still paying were reluctant to invite retaliation by the Land League. And when Lord Leitrim attempted to launch a similar organization, naming it the Secret Vigilance Committee, he and his associates were sadly disappointed with the £600 subscribed to their fund.[20]

Angered by his tenants' defection to the ranks of the League, increasingly pessimistic about the survival of his class, fearful that in England there was a growing weariness and with it a strengthening sentiment in favour of appeasing the nationalists, a dispirited Sir William Gregory declined an invitation to join a group of fellow land-owners who intended to seek a settlement of the land question 'on a liberal and comprehensive basis.' Even when they formed themselves into a committee chaired by his old friend Lord Monck, the former Governor General of Canada, and recommended that the Government legislate the 3 Fs, Gregory shunned identification with them. Why struggle for a measure which had already been rejected on every public platform in Ireland, he inquired? 'I consider also that any proposals which have for their object largely to curtail the present rights of property ought to be accompanied with compensation to the land owners.' He gave form to his fears and vent to his bile in a pamphlet which he published privately in January 1881, even as the Gladstone Government deliberated and debated Irish policy.[21]

It was an essay heavy with foreboding. He warned that 'the complete disruption of the tie which binds the two countries together' was near, and voiced the Unionist's conviction 'that the separation of the two countries would be the absolute and immediate ruin of Ireland and a fatal blow to the power and majesty, and perhaps ultimately to the very security, of England.' Nor was he in any doubt how affairs had reached this gloomy pass. The well intentioned legislation of the past twelve years had 'undermined the structure of the British connection,' for passage of the Land and Ballot Acts had seen power pass 'from the hands of the Crown's devoted adherents into the hands of its bitterest foes.' Indeed, the Ballot Act had not only eradicated landlord influence but had also undermined that of the priests. 'The power is now in the hands of the masses,' he noted, and the emergence of a body of 'Irish Girondins' led by Charles Stewart Parnell, who fused the land and constitutional questions, had given effect to 'the feelings predominant in the hearts of Irishmen — hatred of England and a passionate clinging to their holdings.' Implicit in the present agitation, he warned, were promises that Irish peasants would secure full possession of their farms and that all supporters of the British connection would be expelled from Ireland. Moreover, Gregory despaired of the drift to separation being corrected. Were an election to be called in Galway 'Mr. Parnell might send his umbrella and his walking stick as candidates, and they would be instantly elected, in spite of bishops, priests, and landlords, *vice* the present members,' he opined. A lowering of the county franchise and reform of the antiquated and unrepresentative grand jury system of local government would merely place more power in the hands of the masses, while any land reform acceptable to Parliament, such as the 3 Fs, would fail to satisfy 'the overwrought expectations' of the tenants. In short, little would have been gained and much lost. The Irish country gentlemen would find himself shorn of all influence within the county and reduced to sharing control of his property with his tenants, that is until they seized it all. In these circumstances the gentry would inevitably flee their native land and the English eventually tire of seeking to hold Ireland by force. Forseeing a day when Parnell would hold the balance of power in Parliament, and his capacity for obstructing necessary legislation for England as well as Ireland thereby increased, he predicted that frustrated and weary Englishmen would concede

Home Rule. And to those who argued that such a concession would make of Ireland 'a loyal appendage of the British Crown' he replied that the nationalist leaders and their devoted followers wanted nothing less than an independent Republican Ireland.

Gregory's bleak prediction of what the future held for landlords and the union caused a stir in London. 'It has made a very serious sensation far more than I wished or expected,' he reported to Augusta from the capital, 'and applications for it are pouring in so fast that all my copies are gone and I have been obliged to get 50 more struck off.' John Morley, 'the extreme Radical' editor of both the *Pall Mall Gazette* and the *Fortnightly*, described the pamphlet as one of the most remarkable documents he had read in a long time and admitted that he was not 'over-gratified' by its success. Pleased by this response, the demoralized Irish landlord was further comforted by the behaviour of Gladstone. Resisting the popular pressure of English working class Radicals, who had gathered to oppose coercion in Ireland, his government announced early in January that it would seek legislation suspending habeas corpus. Well placed informants passed on to Gregory encouraging news of the Prime Minister's opposition to the demands of his Radical supporters in the House. Naïvely, they equated Irish disorder with landlord oppression and sought enactment of the 3 Fs. Reassured, the Irishman concluded that the best hope of landowners was to stick with Gladstone now that he was trying to stand by them. 'You and other graceless creatures ought to pray to God every night of your lives and every morning too that his health and his strength may be long preserved,' he banteringly informed his wife. 'So long as he is safe we are safe as he is the only man who can control the democratic elements and I can assure you he is quite as Conservative about Ireland as I am.' But this confidence was cruelly shortlived.[22]

A number of Gregory's friends and correspondents, more optimistic than he, had continued to cling to the hope that removal of 'the real grievance' by 'a just land bill' would gradually bring 'the people' to their senses. Mr. Justice Michael Morris, who planned to visit London shortly before the long awaited bill was introduced, resolved to advise his fellow Conservatives 'to fall in with it as being the only course in my opinion for the peace of the country and as the best course from a party view'. However, much of this support evaporated in the over heated response to the measure the Prime Minister finally presented to Parliament. The reports of two royal commissions, one appointed by Disraeli and the other named by Gladstone himself, had lent support to the Radicals' call for enactment of the 3 Fs and the Prime Minister eventually gave way. The work of 1870 was to be completed and the permanent interest of the tenants in their holdings to be recognized. Yet in conceding the 3 Fs the Act did not define a 'fair rent'. Instead, it established a land commission to which a tenant could appeal in order to have his rent set for a period of fifteen years. Few doubted that in the interests of peace the commission would reduce rents. After all, the judicial fixing of rents while occupancy rights were sold freely meant that a tenant's income would rise by the amount of the rent reduction he obtained. Michael Davitt, the Socialist mastermind of the war on landlords, succinctly observed that the Act was 'a legislative sentence of death by slow processes against Irish landlordism'. All too conscious of this themselves, landlords reacted with natural bitterness. 'It is so like the English,' Lord Dufferin wrote to Gregory, 'they pride themselves upon their "generous" policy toward Ireland, their generosity consisting in trying to bribe the Irish population into loyalty with our money, and while they pretend to sit in sackcloth and ashes for their past tyrannies they are simply repeating them.'[23]

Eleven years earlier William Gregory had urged that the 1870 Land Act be amended in the way Gladstone was now supplementing it, but circumstances had changed and 1881 saw him explode with indignation. He no longer believed that these measures would assure landlords of peace, security and payment of their rents. On the contrary, landowners would be converted into 'precarious annuitants', robbed of all authority on their estates. They would be left powerless in their dealings with tenants who refused to pay their rents or to sell their occupancy rights but threatened anyone disposed to buy, and refused to leave their holdings. 'In the whole bill I fail to see a single provision to compensate the landowner for all he is deprived of,' Gregory raged. 'The least that should have been done is to relieve him of all the odium of ejectments and to have placed it in the Land Court.' In his mind simple justice demanded that the landlord receive something in exchange for all that he had lost. Did he not at least deserve assistance in future collisions with anti-rent combinations through the passage of measures both to ease the recovery of land and to guarantee that when recovered it would not be seized again by the dispossesed holder? To this end, and taking a leaf out of his grandfather's and Robert Peel's books earlier in the century, Gregory proposed that local districts be made liable for the compensation of the owners of farms kept vacant and unproductive by intimidation. But there seemed little chance of the government adopting any of these suggestions. The only glimmer of hope Gregory found in the bill were the provisions to promote the tenants' purchase of their holdings. Here was an opportunity to transform 'down-trodden serfs' into 'full fledged squires', he commented sarcastically. 'I have now only one desire and that is to get rid of all relations with agricultural tenants.' Yet he feared difficulties in coming to terms and gloomily predicted the collapse of land values. There was, in short, a continuing 'strain of despondency and disappointed feeling' permeating Gregory's thoughts and all that he wrote during the summer of 1881.[24]

In one important and unwelcome respect his January jeremiad had proven prophetic. The Land Bill did not still the agitation or halt the violence. The Land League expired only to be replaced by the National League which gave primacy to Home Rule. In Gort, there had been a call for a boycott of a resident who had given lodging to the head of the police detachment. Also, persecution of bailiffs had continued apace. Before an excited mob serenaded by a band in the market square several of these wretched men had apologised for those writs they had executed, had promised not to execute any more, and had agreed to inform the senior police officer that they no longer required protection. This act of abasement had not ended their misery and isolation, as they had been assured it would. They continued to be treated like lepers and were unable even to obtain a meal in the town. Then, in June, the arrest of the organizer of their humiliation had sparked a riot. If there was any consolation for Sir William Gregory in all of this, apart from an unpleasant sense of vindication, it was the information that not one of his tenants had participated in the disturbances or been involved in the intimidation. [25]

He had returned to Coole on 30 August 1881, following the mid-summer visit to Europe. His initial uneasiness about his reception faded in the face of his tenants' good humour, the promise of a 'grand harvest', and the local priest's assurance that he would 'not have any trouble under the Land Act'. There was also encouraging word from his cousin and former agent, Charles Gregory, who had been appointed one of the four sub-commissioners for County Mayo. He outlined the careful investigation the land commission conducted before establishing a fair rent and offered the reassuring information 'that on almost all large estates, which have been in the same families for a great many years, the rents are very little higher than they should be — in many cases we have reduced the rents but little — and in many cases not at all.' Nevertheless, it was not long before Gregory heard from friends whose rents had been reduced by a quarter. The ill-feelings engendered between landlord and tenant by this 'accursed legislation' has 'fairly broke me down', the Countess Dartrey wrote from her husband's 30,000 acres. Prudently, the Galway landowners met on 14 November and set up a fund to pay a competent counsel to attend all meetings of the commissioners, and act on behalf of landlords. Gregory was not present at the gathering (he and Augusta were on their way to Egypt) but he did subsequently contribute 10 guineas to the 'Counsel Fund'. His Egyptian expedition also coincided with the meetings of a somewhat less than resolute Property Defence Association. 'How lucky you are to be out of this confounded country — where everything is going wrong,' one of his neighbours wrote enviously.

Before departing Coole in October Sir William Gregory had sensed unpleasantness in the air. He suspected that his tenants would not appear on rent day and he grimly resolved to fight to the bitter end, even at the cost of quitting Coole. This would be a 'sad blow' for him, he admitted, but a 'far worse blow to the neighbourhood, the poor of which have literally had their lives preserved by my cutting wood annually to give away to all comers for firing — besides timber to tenants and flannel . . . and blankets to the aged, sick and chilly.' Believing that he had earned their respect and appreciation, Gregory expected his tenants to show more loyalty to him than fear of the anti-rent campaigners. They had given assurances that the old rents would be willingly paid when times improved. Now, although crops had been good and prices were excellent, an offer of a 10% abatement as a matter of goodwill was rejected as insufficient.[26]

Infuriated and saddened by his tenants' behaviour Gregory instructed his agent to summon them to a meeting on 20 January 1882, and inform them that non-payment would be met by the process of eviction. In reply, they implored the agent not to go ahead and offered to pay 80% on account if he would wait for Sir William's return to settle the balance after a re-evaluation of the estate. Unfortunately, this proposal was garbled in transmission by telegraph to Egypt and the angry Gregory tersely responded: 'No Proceed'. In the meantime, word of the tenants' action had spread and notices were posted on the estate warning them to withhold rents or face punishment by 'Captain Rentstopper'. The police and a strengthened military detachment in Gort were powerless to prevent this form of intimidation and were themselves subjected to demoralizing attacks — unwary soldiers were assaulted when off-duty; patrols were greeted with catcalls and hooting and occasionally had buckets of water thrown into their faces at night. Reporting all of this to the absent Gregory, a local magistrate declared that there was no evidence of internal dissension among the tenants of Coole. They had simply crumbled under 'a fearful external pressure'. Perhaps it was this knowledge which prompted him to grant them an extension until St. Patrick's Day, but as 17 March approached no more than twenty had secretly paid in full. And when his agent explained to those still in arrears that Sir William simply could not go on without income they had suggested that he borrow from the bank and had volunteered to be his security.

Mistaking naïveté for impudence, requiring money, increasingly suspicious that tenants were witholding rents in expectation of some measure which would wipe out arrears (an arrears bill was enacted as part of the understanding releasing Parnell from detention in Kilmainham), Gregory responded sharply to an appeal from the local priest. Timothy Shannon begged him to halt the process of ejectment served on the tenants of Coole and to reach a 'kindly' settlement with them. Father Shannon's intervention may well have been inspired by his own troubles. A group of parishioners were boycotting him, refusing to pay Easter dues following the appearance of notices denouncing him as the landlords' friend and suggesting that his support be left to them. Through the priest Gregory informed his tenantry that there would not be any general reduction of his 'acknowledged low rents', at least at this time, but he held out the prospect of later permanent adjustments. Anyone who thought the rents too high at Coole was invited to try his luck before the land court. Not that Gregory intended to wait patiently for a decision. 'I must now tell you with deep regret that I feel so deeply the way I have been treated that it is my intention no longer to reside at Coole,' he continued threateningly. 'I had hoped to have lived and died there, but I will certainly not expose my wife and child to the risk of vengeance and outrage.' He concluded with a melodramatic and heartfelt cry of anguish at what he regarded as the disloyalty of his tenantry. 'I mean to dismantle the house and to remove everything of value to a safe place, and if they blow up the residence I shall be very much obliged to them — I only regret that I have laid out very foolishly so much money upon it of late years which I did from the happiness of living among tenants who had I thought the affection for me which I had for them.' And in the aftermath of the Phoenix Park murders some of his fellow landlords took this threat seriously. 'I am very sorry to hear you talk of making your bow to this country,'' Clonbrock's son and heir wrote, 'but I'm sure I don't wonder at it — the prospect is gloomier and more sickening every day.'[27]

Alarmed, Sir William Gregory's tenants began in June to pay their rents in full. Most of them did so surreptitiously, sending payment through the mail, yet word of the settlement inevitably leaked out. The tenantry was roundly abused in the *Tuam News* and promised damnation in the next world if not punishment in this. The attack stopped the rents and Gregory was once again obliged to resort to the menace of 'extreme measures' in order to secure payment. When he appealed to Dublin Castle for action against this form of intimidation he learnt that the Viceroy did not think it desirable to take any action with respect to the newspaper article. His subsequent complaint that at a meeting in Loughrea the principal speaker 'characterized landlordism as a curse, said it should be banished root and branch from the island', brought a no more active response. One of the officials at the Castle noted that disparaging remarks about landlords in general had been accompanied by others directed at Gregory in particular. 'Landlords are not wanting in criticism generally hostile to this Government,' a member of the Chief Secretary's Office observed. 'This distinguished gentlemen is not a day in the country for shooting purposes, being at other times absent during the agitation, when he writes to the Chief Secretary. Their criticisms as a rule as well as newspaper reports are unworthy of consideration.'[28]

Returning to Coole in December 1882 to shoot or to be shot at, Gregory found himself involved in another tussle with his tenants. They expressed a desire for reconciliation but one founded on 'an immense reduction' of rents and the cutting of a large portion of his woods to supply them with fuel during this bitterly cold winter. 'The entente cordiale is therefore postponed,' he reported to Henry Layard. 'I do not think I am in danger at present but the Police think differently and patrol the place.' What did disturb him were small signs of a growing lack of respect, such as the failure of people to touch their hats as he passed. Uneasy about his personal safety, and suffering pain in the intense cold which had already driven off the woodcocks, he speedily beat a retreat to London. By the time the Gregorys returned to Britain from Portugal early in the summer of 1883 the reports from Galway were more reassuring, and when they arrived at Coole in August they found the area 'very quiet'. Sir William gave much of the credit to the 'young and vigorous' priest recently appointed to Gort – Jerome Fahy – and to his old electoral ally John McEvilly, who had in 1881 succeeded to the archiepiscopacy of Tuam. Another cheering sign was the miserly local response to a collection for Charles Parnell and the 'very nauseous' 'vials of indignation' poured on the residents of Gort by the outraged nationalist press. More satisfying still was the appearance of smiling tenants on rent day. 'This is a comfort,' he admitted to a friend, 'for I am experiencing the evil effects of a collapse in Ceylon and am a very much poorer man than I was when I returned from that Colony.' Yet as hard as his tenants struggled 'to make friends again', not only paying their rents but showing respect and coming as of old to request timber and old clothes, the experience of the past few years had made an indelible impression on Gregory and forever altered the relationship. He was never to trust them again. 'The disillusion I have undergone as to the character of the Irish peasant has been too painful, enough for one life,' he observed as much in sadness as anger. [29]

Distrust did not prevent Sir William Gregory from seeking an amicable understanding with his tenantry over rents, and may even have been an incentive to do so. Under the provisions of the Land Act rent might be judicially fixed either by the commission or by a voluntary agreement between landlord and tenant which was then lodged in the land court. The fact that Gregory settled all of his rents by agreement, and that in two thirds of the cases they remained unchanged, while in the remainder the reduction never exceeded 20%, has been offered as evidence that some landlord fears of the Land Act were groundless. What happened at Coole indicated that 'good' landlords did not suffer along with the 'bad', the argument runs, because rents were not reduced indiscriminately. Landlords on friendly terms with their tenants 'were able to conclude agreements with them fixing judicial rents at levels which meant very little loss of income. . . .' That was not Sir William Gregory's experience. Characteristically, a succession of miserable crop years in the middle of the decade saw him grant substantial abatements to tenants who were doing their best to pay but were 'undoubtedly very poor from the reverses of the last three or four years'. When the harvest on his lands proved to be 'splendid' in 1886, the potatoes good and plentiful, which meant ample supplies of food for families and pigs, and prices rose sharply, he expected to have an easier time. Instead, he discovered that many of his tenants had resolved not to 'disturb themselves about rents' until they were in funds. And that would not be, he caustically remarked, 'till they have ceased spending their profits on whiskey'. Over the objections of his agent he announced a 15% reduction on the judicial rents only to be informed that his tenants would settle for nothing less than an abatement of 28%. Infuriated, he again resolved to undertake a war 'to the knife' but the tenantry hastily accepted the smaller figure. However, a bad harvest in 1887 brought a 25% reduction and he tolerated large arrears on the part of those who could not pay. 'They seem to have shown a very friendly spirit, and I am much relieved at getting any settlement, as there is talk of no rent being paid,' he informed one friend. Evidently, Sir William Gregory's loss of income was substantial and painful. The rents on many holdings were barely half those paid four years earlier when they had already been 'notoriously low'. Here was a 'good' landlord who suffered along with the 'bad'.[30]

The fact that throughout this difficult period the country, and the area around Gort in particular, had remained surprisingly calm reinforced Gregory's somewhat reactionary faith in the efficacy of 'firm' government. 'Ours is an unfortunate country — but if ruled over by a benevolent despot it would be one of the most easily governed and most prosperous of countries,' he had instructed his young fiancée in 1882 harking back to the conservative lessons of his own youth. As soon as the people understood that the civil authority could not be frightened by 'cries and threats', and was determined to maintain the law, then they obeyed readily enough. 'Old Palmerston thoroughly understood them and the consequence was that never did a country advance more rapidly than did Ireland under his firm rule just as never did a country go to the devil more rapidly than has Ireland under the feebleness and sentimentality of Gladstone.' Fondly recalling a golden age of high land values and regular rent payments, he held Gladstone's policies responsible for unemployment, unpaid rents and unsaleable lands. 'Everyone is distressed and the only gainers are agitators, those in Parliament and the village ruffians who form the local National League Committees and levy blackmail on all around them,' he complained.

His disillusionment with Gladstone had long been smouldering but did not burst into flame until 1886. The Land Bill had been an unpleasant shock, as had the agitation by Radical members of the Government for elective county councils in Ireland. The relief which followed the Cabinet's rejection of this reform of local government was short-lived, for the Radicals did win a broadening of the county franchise without a redistribution of seats. Moreover, all of this time tenants were capturing control of Poor Law Boards from landlords. Gregory was appalled by what he regarded as a gallop 'helter skelter into Democracy', and he derided the belief, which seemed especially strong among English Radicals, that limited control over their own affairs would pacify Irish nationalists. Not that he derived any satisfaction from the evidence that another of his gloomy predictions in 1881 had come to pass. It was clear that the Radicals were motivated by a desire to end Irish obstruction of Parliament and thus of reform in the rest of Britain. 'There seems to be a kind of bamboozlement among our rulers, that Parnell and Company want a milk and water Home Rule,' Gregory noted in disbelief.[31]

That the government underestimated the reach of Parnellite ambition was the warning Gregory delivered personally when invited to the home of a junior member of the Irish Executive in August 1884 to discuss means of reinvigorating the Liberal Party in Ireland. He was one of 'a very small and select group', about sixteen in number, who gathered to plot strategy. Little came of the meeting, apart from an agreement to throw electoral support to those Tories who had a better chance than fellow Liberals of defeating nationalists. Gregory growled that if only the government would determine to strengthen the power of the British Constitution on every occasion it did not matter who got in. But dissatisfaction with Gladstone's course did not lead as yet to alienation. Parnellite attacks on John Bright held out hope that the Radicals would turn on the nationalists. Further, the Liberals had enacted a sweeping Crimes Act in 1882 which facilitated prosecutions. Finally, Gregory still had faith in Gladstone's inherent conservatism. They were members of the exclusive Grillion's Club, met socially, corresponded and argued about classical literature, and the Gladstones were among the fortunate recipients of Coole woodcocks. This personal contact appears to have reassured the nervous Irishman that from old traditions and discipline Gladstone could still be depended upon to resist violent changes and not to 'lend himself to anything more than moderate spoilations'. The Grand Old Man was indispensable as a check on the leading Radicals in the Government and Party, Joseph Chamberlain and Sir Charles Dilke. Moreover, where else politically were Irishmen such as Sir William Gregory to turn? They suspected the Tories, particularly the mercurial Lord Randolph Churchill, of being willing to outbid Radicals for the support of Parnell and his followers. 'Were there ever such a miserable lot of cripples as the Conservatives,' Gregory asked in 1884?[32]

The collapse of the Liberal Government in the summer of 1885 brought the minority Tories to power. They immediately abandoned coercion and in the general election at year's end were openly supported in England by Parnell. The result fully justified the nationalist leader's conduct, and another of Gregory's nightmare visions of 1881 was realized — the Parnellites held the balance of power in the Commons. The knowledge that the eighty-six Home Rulers were at last in a position to bring Parliament to a complete stand-still helped to convince Gladstone, whose followers in the House were exactly eighty-six more numerous than the Conservatives, that the Irish question now had to be confronted even at the risk of splitting his party. He would have preferred the Tories to introduce Home Rule and offered them his support but they elected to surrender office and leave the controversy to him.

Word of Gladstone's conversion to Home Rule reached the Gregorys while they were travelling across India. Both were stunned by what seemed to them to be the apostasy of a leader who had once described Parnell and his associates as men steeped to their lips in sedition and not ashamed to preach the doctrine of plunder. 'How little he knows my countrymen,' William Gregory remarked. But incredulity was fast replaced by much stronger emotions — anger, fear and hatred. Home Rule was a scheme 'fraught with disaster to England, ruin to every Irish proprietor and extermination of the reform religion in the three Provinces of Ireland.' A lurid scenario began to take shape in his mind. He fancied that within three months of the re-establishment of an Irish Parliament some 120,000 Irishmen would be under arms, drilled by Americans, commanded by Americans, and reinforced by Irish soldiers trained and presently serving with the British army. No English minister would risk conflict with this force to protect 'the flimsy paper safeguards' of Irish landlords and Protestants. Even the defeat of the Home Rule Bill in Parliament as a result of the defection of a significant minority of conservative Liberals, and of disenchanted Radicals led by Joseph Chamberlain, brought Gregory no immediate peace of mind. The Grand Old Man insisted on a dissolution and made the ensuing election a popular referendum on Home Rule. Gregory worried that the 'simple appeal for self government for Ireland strikes the ignorant as being a just and expedient one.' He respected and feared Gladstone's ambition and ability. 'His love of power and hatred of contradiction are so great that he will recoil from nothing in endeavouring to regain his despotic sway of the House of Commons.' For William Gregory the single overriding political consideration was the exclusion of this apostate from office. 'I am quite ready to welcome a Conservative Government much as I dislike the party to take the reins till Gladstone dies, or goes mad or becomes effete,' he fumed. 'His conduct is so outrageous and so caddish that I can only attribute it to mental derangement.' Nor did he relax when 'Demos' returned 'an emphatic No to Mr. Gladstone's proposal to dismember the Empire'.[33]

In the fight against Home Rule Sir William Gregory had long been willing to play the 'Orange card'. In 1883 he had privately urged that the Protestants of Ulster be roused and 'that speakers of no mealy-mouthed eloquence should be chosen to get up steam'. Their task was to drum into the ears of Ulster tenants the warning that once an Irish Parliament had been restored 'they will have to fight against overwhelming numbers who will not leave a heretic in the country, and whose religious zeal will be much whetted by the prospect of obtaining the heretics' farms'. Equally, he had recommended that the Protestant and non-conformist feeling of the rest of Britain be stirred up by speakers who would show that the Roman Catholic hierarchy adopted Home Rule because it would 'tend to the extirpation of Protestantism' in Ireland. Nevertheless, he did not accept the invitation extended by his remarkable and celebrated cousin Arthur MacMorrough Kavanagh — who had overcome the terrible handicap of being born without either arms or legs to become a proficient horseman, hunter and yachtsman — to join the Irish Loyal and Patriotic Union. This organization pledged 'to bring together and unite, all Irishmen, who considering that their country can best prosper as part of the Imperial system, desire to oppose by every form of legal combination, the spread of Socialist doctrine.' Gregory was sceptical of its prospects in electoral contests with the nationalists, fearing that its candidates might make laughing stocks of themselves yet stimulate American subscriptions to the National League. In fact this movement of bipartisan loyalist unity made a respectable showing in 1885, opposing Home Rulers in fifty-two southern constituencies. However, it averaged only 10% of the poll and all but eight of the candidates were Conservatives. Rather than throw himself into this quixotic activity Gregory staked his hopes of defeating Home Rule on the Liberal Unionists. He attended meetings of this group and helped to plot its strategy with the sole objective of maintaining the schism in Liberal ranks until nature did its work and took off Gladstone. The belief 'that the moment we get rid of Gladstone we get rid of Home Rule' became an idée fixé. Without him to lead there would be few to follow in Britain, the Irishman reasoned. Thus the maintenance of the Conservatives in power, and the avoidance of another general election in which the Liberal splinter group might go the the wall, were his constant aims. Moreover, as an advocate of firm government for Ireland, but by no means an opponent of 'very advanced measures' — 'We must progress with the age' — Gregory soon found much to admire in the Irish policy of Lord Salisbury and his nephew, Chief Secretary Arthur Balfour.[34]

The relative peace of the period following the passage of the Land Bill, which Gregory attributed to the Crimes Act, had been shattered with the launching of the 'Plan of Campaign' in 1886. Landlords who refused to lower rents were to receive none at all. Tenants contributed the monies instead to a fund which was used to aid those of them evicted for non-payment. In Galway, Clanricarde was again at the centre of controversy and the principal target of the renewed agitation. When he consulted Gregory about his plight he received the advice to sell his land to his tenants. Under the terms of the Ashbourne Act passed by the shortlived and conciliatory Tory Government in 1885 the state advanced the entire purchase price to tenants and allowed repayment to be made over forty-nine years. Clanricarde, in Gregory's words, was 'fool enough to refuse on the ground that his income would be diminished'. Frightened and confused, 'he talked a great deal of nonsense about England not allowing spoilation'. However, once Clanricarde was involved in a test of wills with the National League, Gregory reasoned that he had to be supported in order to 'show that the law of the land is stronger than that of the League'. Evictions had excited considerable resistance — enormous mobs assembled threateningly, roads were torn up and bridges pulled down — and a small army of police and soldiers had been required to protect the enforcing bailiffs. In Gort, those persons who took a surrendered holding were boycotted. They were unable to sell produce or purchase supplies. Consequently, Gregory applauded the government's decision 'to draw the sword' in 1887 with the passage of another Crimes Act which while less sweeping than the earlier measure was soon to be denounced as 'a savage law savagely administered'. The fact that most tenants, apart from Clanricarde's, subsequently paid their rents was interpreted by Gregory as additional proof that whenever the government 'show they do not mean to be beaten, they will not be beaten but find their task easy'. He might well have given at least a share of the credit for the quieting of the countryside to the other and more constructive measures introduced by the Conservative ministry — a Land Act which revised and reduced the judicial rents set by the commissioners appointed under Gladstone's bill; and the doubling in 1888 of the exhausted fund of £5 million originally provided to finance land purchases under the Ashbourne Act. Furthermore, on Clanricarde's estates the bitter struggle went on. Rents were not paid, evictions continued, and many were reduced to 'wretched poverty and distress'. Indeed, Gregory was tormented by the thought that Gladstone would be carried back into power on a wave of public sympathy in England for those suffering in Ireland. 'The speeches made by Irish members, the placards denouncing heartless evictions, the drawings representing old women dragged out of their cottages by fiendish bailiffs and old men lying by the roadside in the last state of emaciation have profoundly irritated and shocked the lower class of voter and no wonder,' he observed uneasily. Nor as a Unionist Irishman did he appreciate a speech by Lord Salisbury in which the Prime Minister ridicule the eighty-six Home Rulers in Parliament for uttering 'the same inanities in the same brogue'. 'Can anything be more odiously and wantonly offensive,' he remarked to an English friend. 'Argue with them and attack their acts and doctrines as much as you like in all cases where they outrage decency but it is his outrage on decency to assail the whole body of Irish Nationalist MPs in such scurrilous language.'[35]

In advising Clanricarde to sell to his tenantry Sir William Gregory was pointing to the avenue of escape from the miseries and tension of landownership which he had long been willing to take himself. More than once he had privately rued the nabob's decision to sell off his estates in England and keep that in Ireland. By the same token, neither he nor his young wife were prepared simply 'to give up to grasping hands the lands that had been bought and cultivated and worked by his great-grandfather'. Yet very few tenants had been able to take advantage of the provisions to facilitate purchase contained in the Land Act of 1881. With the passage of the Ashbourne Act Gregory began to hope that the sale of his estate might at last be possible. But after some debate he and Augusta resolved in the spring of 1886 at least to 'die game'. Besides 'the bribe is not big enough', she explained to their recent host in Madras, Grant Duff, 'and though for peace's sake we would gladly take any small sum and be sure of it — yet one has a feeling against selling one's child's birthright for a mess of hasty pudding.' That feeling did not long survive the opening of the 'Plan of Campaign', while Gladstone's refusal to retire or expire kept alive the danger of Home Rule and 'spoilation'. William Gregory was reminded of the fable of the beaver and the hunters, and though he had no desire to bite off his own tail and throw it to the National League he preferred to do that than run the risk of having to surrender his whole skin. So in October 1886 he offered his tenants the opportunity to buy their holdings for a sum equivalent to no more than twenty years rent. In fact, a price based on twenty-five years would have equalized the repayments and the existing rents over the forty-nine year life of the loan. 'The nominal sacrifice of income will be very great,' he admitted to Henry Layard, 'but at all events if they do buy, what I have will be secure for your godson whereas if Gladstone gets the upper hand the confiscation will be sweeping and universal.' Perhaps calculating that the Grand Old Man would return to power and carry Home Rule, and that from an Irish Parliament even better terms might be obtained (there was talk of the purchase price being set at twelve years rent), Gregory's tenants did not take up his generous offer. Despite this disappointment he opposed all schemes of compulsory purchase. 'It would at once give a pretext for subsequent repudiation,' he cautioned. Instead, he believed that the government should double again — raising to £20 millions — the fund to finance purchases under the Ashbourne Act. Actually, Balfour was planning to force recalcitrant landowners, such as Clanricarde, to sell but this was too radical a step for his party. The bill as finally passed in 1891 provided the enormous sum of £33 millions to assist purchases by tenants. Unfortunately, many tenants were frightened off by the requirement that they put down a substantial deposit and by the heavy annual repayments.[36]

Unable to sell and unwilling to leave, Sir William Gregory waited at Coole for the death or the return to power of the man he described with fearful respect as 'the Napoleon of English politics, worth 20,000 men in the field — After him comes no one.' Helplessly, he marked time and hoped. His confidence that the union would survive was bolstered by the difficulties of Charles Stewart Parnell, whom by implication he contrasted unfavourably with Daniel O'Connell in an article for *Nineteenth Century* (1889) which dwelt upon the Liberator's loyalty to the Crown and hatred of violence. However, Gregory deplored the government's response to the furore sparked by sensational accusations in *The Times* of Parnell's complicity in murder and intimidation. Instead of acceding to the nationalist's request for a select committee to investigate the authenticity of letters *The Times* had published to support the claim of a direct connection between 'Parnellism and Crime', letters Parnell had stigmatized in the Commons as forgeries, it set up a special commission to investigate the charges brought against him and his associates. Adroit, even cynically partisan, as this ploy appeared, Gregory labelled it inept. Far more artful and politic would have been an announcement that the government intended to keep its distance, and emphasising that it was under no obligation to brush dirt off the nationalists' clothes while those who claimed to have been libelled had recourse to the Law Courts. By establishing the commission the government was certain to be indentified in the public's mind with the conviction of Parnell and his associates, he immediately realized. 'If the inquiry washes them clean as I fully believe it will in spite of the Times and its documents, the Government will suffer severely and even if they the Parnellites do not get off scot free the Government will gain little in strength and reputation.' The collapse in February 1889 of this ill-conceived attempt to discredit Parnell vindicated Gregory's judgment and the results were all that he had feared. The leader of the Irish party was raised to new heights of popularity, which even extended to England. But within a year he had fallen to earth with crushing force.[37]

Charles Parnell's intimacy with Katherine O'Shea, the wife of the man he had forced upon local nationalists in the constituency of Galway borough in 1886, had long been known in society. Augusta Gregory reported to a friend that same year: 'The only scandal I hear is that Mr. Parnell is wheeling about Mrs. O'Shea's children in a perambulator.' But Captain O'Shea did not sue for divorce until year's end, 1889. Neither Parnell nor Mrs. O'Shea contested the action, for they wished to marry as soon as possible. Inevitably, the episode sent political shock waves through Britain and Ireland. 'It is not so much the intrigue with Mrs. O'Shea that condemns Parnell,' Henry Layard opined, 'other statesmen have, I fear, committed similar offences against the moral code — but it is the systematic lying and cold effrontery, which blasts his character'. The Court found that O'Shea was a cuckold but not a 'man debonnaire', and the verdict seemed certain to undermine Parnell's influence in Ireland. 'The R.C. clergy cannot adhere to him,' William Gregory excitedly concluded. He was convinced that the hierarchy would grasp this unexpected opportunity to recover the political influence which had slipped from their grasp over the past decade or so. Parnell he likened to an avalanche, which carries everything away and then melts. The Catholic hierarchy was like a glacier, which 'slowly, imperceptibly almost, but irresistibly forces its way by its enormous bulk and weight and steady continuous motion.'[38]

His faith in the conservative influence of a hierarchy restored to its former political eminence (and in letters to *The Times* he defended the Catholic clergy against the charge of hating Protestants as opposed to Protestantism) was not the sole reason William Gregory gave 'three cheers for Kitty O'Shea'. The Irish party had been rent, some members remaining loyal to the disgraced leader and others forming an anti-Parnellite faction. Even Parnell's premature death in October 1891 failed to reunite it. Moreover, Gladstone had been obliged to distance himself from the Irishman in order not to offend his own powerful non-conformist supporters. Not that these developments eased all of William Gregory's political worries. He sensed in 1891 a growing despondency among Conservatives about the next general election, if not a fatalistic concession of a Liberal victory. Even a short period in power would allow Gladstone to transform the Irish constabulary from a Loyal to a

Nationalist body, 'from the defenders of law and order into sympathizers with outrage', he charged hysterically. The present
magistrates and judges would all be replaced by separatists, thus
inviting another bout of anarchy. And while he remained confident that
the Grand Old Man would be unable to carry Home Rule he longed for
that assurance which only nature could provide. But Gregory died in the
knowledge that Gladstone still lived.[34]

Throughout the long decade of anxiety, as he worried about the future
of his country and his class, and under these pressures returned to the
first principles of firm government as taught and practised by his
grandfather a full biblical life span earlier, William Gregory drew
strength from the small family in which increasingly he took pride and
found joy. His relationship with his young wife underwent a subtle
change. Initially, he had been the instructor and she the student but
slowly he grew more dependent upon her. That dependence was
emotional rather than physical, despite his age. Writing to Augusta on
the eve of his departure for Ceylon in 1884, he observed that she knew
'well enough how deep is my affection for you, how steadfast my trust
in your honour and right judgment, how confident my expectation that
under your guidance our boy will grow up to be a credit to the name
which has not been wanting in men of some mark.' Nor was this simply
the conventional utterance of a man advanced in years who realized that
he might never return from a journey of such length. Augusta was his
'affectionate wife'. The great difference in their ages ceased to be quite
the embarrassment it had once been for him. Less sensitive, he came to
enjoy the gossip that he still pursued her ardently and he lightheartedly
informed friends that Augusta sent him away so often in order to gain
a respite from his 'importunate affection'.

The frequency and length of Gregory's absences from home during
the early years of their marriage thrust responsibilities upon Augusta,
both for the maintenance of Coole and the general supervision of the
estate. She had to confront and solve the tiresome problems created by
a long serving housekeeper of integrity and loyalty but volatile temperament. From a safe distance William counselled patience. 'I am so glad
that you have been toadying the servants,' he wrote after one eruption.
'It is the only way to make life go on smooth wheels.' More important
in building Augusta's self confidence to the point of asserting her
personality within the marriage was his evident respect for her
intelligence and abilities. In the many letters he wrote whenever they
were separated he discussed not only domestic matters, whether it be
the purchase of draperies or a carriage, but also the great national issues
of the day. He respected her 'remarkable political acuteness'. He
praised and supported her literary endeavours, which she continued
with the publication of 'The Philanthropist' in *Living Age* in 1891. 'I
wish you would flatter me sometimes as I flatter you,' he admitted. He
was full of admiration for her dedicated work among the poor. In
Galway she attempted to brighten the cheerless lives of the children in

the Gort Workhouse by inviting the young inmates to Coole for a day of play in the woods. At other times she took Robert to the forbidding institution to help her distribute fruit. In London she was tireless in her efforts to aid the under-privileged children of the parishes of St. George the Martyr, Holborn, and St. Stephen's, Southwark. Her husband tolerated without complaint the annual inconvenience of finding his tall house in St. George's Place crammed each December with clothes, toys and other paraphernalia she had collected in preparation for the children's Christmas party. Indeed, having studied closely the Layards' relationship, Gregory was struck by the contrast between Enid Layard's docility in the face of Sir Henry's strictures and Augusta's sharp replies to his own gentle criticisms. 'Is it not strange that instead of a deep and durable resentment my heart should yearn to a little "spiriting devil" who has so ill treated me that I should constantly miss her.'[40]

The bond between them also tightened as Gregory began to show greater interest ·in their son. Friends had long praised the child's 'vivacity and acuteness' and he soon demonstrated an aptitude for drawing which must have pleased his father. 'His letter to me with the design of a pig drinking out of a pot fully confirms his mother's prediction that he will turn out a Raphael if you permit him to devote himself to the fine arts,' Henry Layard laughingly remarked when Robert was six years old. However, it was the art of self defence in which William Gregory first instructed his son. Small and slight Robert fell victim to bullies at school, and so over the Christmas holidays, 1888, his father passed on to him the knowledge of boxing he had acquired from a professional pugilist while an Oxford undergraduate a half century earlier. Of course, he gave much time to his son's classical education but was sensibly wary of overtaxing him. 'I do not let him advance in Latin too quickly but go over rules and sentences and words again and again so that I think they will stick,' he reassured the child's godfather, 'as I am a little afraid of this progress on a very excitable little brain.' And if on occasion he complained of Robert's scatter-brained behaviour — trading a set of beautiful chessmen for a football which he kicked up the stairs of St. George's Place and had the French maid throw back down; almost setting fire to Coole as a result first of reading secretly in bed by candle-light, and later of experiments with combustible materials — William Gregory was transparently proud of his son's zest and intelligence. He was 'really an excellent boy', 'sharp', 'full of go, but obedient and strictly truthful'.[41]

The newly discovered joy of parenthood was tinged with the mournful knowledge that his life was ebbing away and Sir William willed himself to live 'for the sake of my boy and my dear good wife'. Although he and Augusta travelled to Spain in 1887, to Italy in 1889, and he went out to Ceylon alone in 1890 to complete the sale of the estate which had proven a financial 'drain and torment', Gregory discovered that his reserves of energy were now all too easily depleted. He found the regular trip from Gort to London exhausting, and tired of life in

London. 'The dim days of old age have cast their cloud over all that I used to enjoy,' he admitted to Augusta in 1887 at the age of seventy-one. It was in this mood that he copied out the lines written by Coleridge not long before his death:

> Where no hope is, life's a warning
> that only serves to make us grieve
> In our old age
> Whose bruised wings quarrel with the bars of the
> Still narrowing cage

Increasingly, he hungered for more time with his affectionate wife and enchanting son. He began to plant more trees at Coole and was conscious of the symbolism, remarking that this was 'rather a droll occupation' at his age. Yet there were constant reminders of the sparse foliage left on his own tree. Word came all too often of the death of friends of a life-time, and he was cursed with recurrent attacks of bronchial asthma. In July 1891 he consulted a leading London specialist who for a fee of two guineas informed him that his heart was weak but 'nothing much to signify', and placed him on a gentle regimen. He was to eat in the middle of the day, taking neither soup nor fruit, and to smoke no more than two cigars a day. No doubt he disregarded these restrictions when he attended the Harrow dinner at the Mansion House that year, but the final verse of the School's rousing song may have had more meaning than usual for him:

> Forty years on, growing older and older
> Shorter in wind, as in memory long
> Feeble of foot, and rheumatic of shoulder
> What will it help you that once you were strong

In August he consulted a second specialist, this one the rising man in Dublin. 'I am almost well during the day,' he explained to a concerned Henry Layard, 'but towards night the wheezing goes on and I am half suffocated.' Unable to sleep in bed he was obliged to prop himself up in a chair. Under the care of the Irish doctor he was able to breathe a little easier and sleep a little more soundly, but this improvement proved all too brief. He decided to pass the winter in London. Struck down by nausea, chills and diarrhoea in December he went to Bournemouth for ten days in January 1882, hoping to recuperate in the bracing sea air. 'I am as ill as a man can well be,' he acknowledged on his return. At their wits' end his doctors recommended warm sunshine and he and Augusta made plans to go to Marseilles. They never made the journey. Weakened by his debilitating illness, suffering painfully in the cold of that winter, frightened of the infirmities of old age, William Gregory's health finally collapsed in February. For nineteen days he lay in a state of delirium. Then, during a brief moment of clarity, he took his wife's hand in his, reaffirmed his love for her and their son, and 'said very solemnly "Remember I die believing in God. We are all God's children." ' He died on 6 March 1892. March thus continued as a month of particular meaning for Augusta. It had been the month of her birth, her marriage, her mother's death, and now the death of her husband.[42]

William Gregory had left a mark upon his age but not one of sufficient depth to impress posterity. His reputation was soon to be over-shadowed by that of his widow. She belonged to that vital group who inspired and sustained the Irish literary renaissance, and it is to honour her that visitors still drive through the arched avenue of ilex trees which once led to Coole but now lead only to the house's rebuilt foundations. Moreover, those who met William Gregory in his declining years and were unfamiliar with his career tended to dismiss him as a charming old gentleman and good raconteur. Augusta did attempt to keep his memory alive, editing and publishing his candid memoirs, which have long been mined by historians of the Nineteenth Century, but he eventually disappeared among the multitude of supporting players in the Victorian drama — the author of the 'exterminator clause', a champion of the Arts, an enemy of democracy whose opposition to sabbatarianism was inspired by a concern to enrich the lives of working people, and a successful colonial governor. His obscurity has naturally been attributed to his failure to win high political office. A contributor to the *Dictionary of National Biography* later observed: 'Gregory was a man of great natural abilities, real political talent, and marked personal charm, who, but for a certain instability, might easily have attained to the most eminent political positions.' More specifically, friends and obituarists pointed to his predilection for racehorses. William Gregory certainly squandered both income and career on the Turf. Had he worked diligently to secure re-election for Dublin in 1847, foregoing the excitement of a Goodwood race meeting, he might not have spent a decade in the political wilderness. Had he remained in Parliament throughout the 1850s he would certainly have been better placed to capitalize personally on the period of Peelite government and party realignments. However, this explanation of his ultimate lack of political success is at once too problematic and facile for it ignores the tension and difficulties inherent in his position as a Protestant representative of an Irish constituency. Therein lay the reason for his refusal to take office under Peel.

Following his defeat in Dublin William Gregory patiently constructed a coalition of supporters in Catholic Galway which was truly remarkable in its breadth. Whig and liberal Conservative landlords on one side were balanced by Roman Catholic clerics on the other. Thus were the two great electoral 'influences' employed on his behalf. Significantly, when he resigned his Commons seat to go off to Ceylon a bitter struggle ensued for dominance which resulted in a pyrrhic victory for the landlords. For a decade and a half Gregory had skilfully trod a fine line between these two allies and managed to avoid alienating either of them. But it was the fear of offending his backers in the county which governed his behaviour in 1859 during the last days of the brief Derby Government. The suspicion his conduct excited in the minds of leading Whig/Liberals hindered his chances of promotion. Questions about his political reliability discouraged first ministers from offering him posts worthy of his talents. Yet expediency in its crudest sense was by no means the sole determinant of his actions. His conservative objections to democracy were deep and heartfelt and they resulted in his break with his party in 1866. Conversely, it was distrust of his liberalism on Ireland which dissuaded the Tories from proffering the one office Gregory would have been sorely tempted to accept from them.

William Gregory dreamed of finally pacifying his native land, and he recognized that peace in Ireland was contingent on the passage of measures both just and generous. Central to his programme was an alliance between government and Roman Catholic Church. The waning political power of the landlords and the burgeoning influence of the clergy was a development to which he had been personally quick to respond in County Galway. His own understanding with the priesthood there appears to have convinced him that a much broader and far reaching arrangement in the name of order and stability was possible and essential. Of course, in order to make an ally of the conservative hierarchy it had first to be conciliated. Gregory envisaged sweeping concessions to the Roman Catholic Church on religious and educational issues, but just as opinion in Britain limited the rights granted to tenants in the Land Bill of 1870 so it also discouraged governments from meeting the demands of the hierarchy. The impracticability of Gregory's policies illustrated the intractability of the Irish question, as indeed did his life.

One of William Gregory's friends wrote of him: 'No man ever retrieved more honourably the errors of his youth; and to him more than any other man of my acquaintance might be applied the well-known French proverb "On ne revient pas de si loin pour peu de chose." ' This is an allusion to his redemption as a civilized and progressive Governor of Ceylon but the same observation might be made of his behaviour as an Irish landlord. Fears for the survival of his class had prompted him to introduce the infamous 'quarter-acre clause' which faciliatated the eviction of so many impoverished tenants during the Famine. Yet he managed to live down his notoriety as one of the most insensitive spokesmen of the landed interest and by his personal conduct at Coole well earned a reputation for generosity and compassion. If ever there was a 'good' landlord it was William Gregory, but at the end of his life he made the demoralizing and embittering discovery that this now counted for little. The land war was waged against landlordism. The conservatism of age and of fear hardened to the point of rigidity his attachment to the union, the fate of which he had been taught in childhood was inseparable from that of Protestant landowners and even of the Empire. Nor should his fears and those of many others like him be dismissed as hysteria. The Home Rule movement Charles Parnell led bore little resemblance to the conservative federalism of Isaac Butt. The fusion of the land and the constitutional questions, the violence, the links between the Parnellites and the Republican Irish-Americans, and the deliberate ambiguity of the nationalists on the matter of their ultimate goal, all of these considerations condemned men proud both of their British origins and Irish birth to fight to preserve the connection with the United Kingdom.

Notes

All references are to the Gregory Papers unless otherwise identified.

CHAPTER 1

1. For the lineage of the Gregory family see Vere R. T. Gregory, *The House of Gregory* (Dublin, 1943).
2. See J. G. Simms, *Jacobite Ireland 1685–1691* (London, 1969).
3. Gregory, *House of Gregory*, pp. 11–26; C. D. Milligan, *The Walls of Derry*, pt. II (Londonderry, 1959), p. 129.
4. Gregory, *House of Gregory*, pp. 21–30.
5. Simms, *Jacobite Ireland*, pp. 230–36; L. P. Curtis Jr., ed., W. E. H. Lecky, *A History of Ireland in the Eighteenth Century* (Chicago, 1972), pp. 91–99.
6. James M. Holzman, *The Nabobs in England: A Study of the Returned Anglo–Indian 1760–1785* (New York, 1926), pp. 28–61; R. B. McDowell, *Ireland in the Age of Imperialism and Revolution 1760–1801* (Oxford, 1979), pp. 43–44; W. L. Guttman, *The British Political Elite* (London, 1963), pp. 17–18.
7. Henry B. Wheatley, ed., *The Historical and Posthumous Memoir of Sir Nathaniel William Wraxall 1772–1784* (London, 1884), II, 106–8; *Parliamentary History of England from the Earliest Period to the Year 1803*, XXII, 125.
8. Gregory to Burke, March 3, 1786, Edmund Burke Papers, 1/2015, Sheffield Central Library.
9. T. G. P. Spear. *The Nabobs: A Study of the Social Life of the English in Eighteenth Century India* (London, 1932), pp. 82ff; C. Collin Davies, *Warren Hastings and Oudh* (London, 1939), p. 216.
10. Spear, *Nabobs*, p. 17; Paul Emden, *Regency Pageant* (London, 1936), pp. 212–13; Desmond Young, *Fountain of the Elephants* (London, 1959), p. 58.
11. Aram Bakshian, 'John Zoffany', *History Today*, XXIX (1979), 419–28; Gregory, *House of Gregory*, pp. 40–43; Lady Gregory, ed., *Autobiography of the Right Honourable Sir William Gregory K.C.M.G., F.R.S.* (London, 1894), pp. 2–4.
12. Gregory, *House of Gregory*, pp. 52–3; Gregory, *Autobiography*, pp. 6–7.
13. The Provisions of Robert Gregory's will are to be found among the Gregory Papers.
14. McDowell, *Ireland in the Age of Imperialism*, pp. 414–17; Lecky, *Ireland in the Eighteenth Century*, pp. 254–55.
15. McDowell, *Ireland in the Age of Imperialism*, pp. 233ff., 445; R. B. McDowell, 'The Fitzwilliam Episode', *Irish Historical Studies*, XV (1966), 115–30.
16. Gregory to Fitzwilliam, September 18, 1795, F 30/46, Fitzwilliam Papers, Sheffield Central Library; Gregory to Fitzwilliam, June 7, 1797, F 30/158.
17. Lecky, *Ireland in the Eighteenth Century*, pp. 355ff.
18. G. C. Bolton, *The Passing of the Irish Act of Union: A Study in Parliamentary Politics* (Oxford, 1966), pp. 169ff;. 144; C.J. Bartlett, *Castlereagh* (New York, 1966), p. 6.

19. Gregory, *House of Gregory,* pp. 32−5; Alfred Spencer, ed., *Memoirs of William Hickey,* 4 vols. (London, 1925), IV, 184−89.
20. Norman Gash, *Mr. Secretary Peel: The Life of Sir Robert Peel to 1830* (London, 1961); Charles Stuart Parker, ed., *Sir Robert Peel From His Private Papers,* 3 vols (reprint, New York, 1920), I, 35.
21. Lady Gregory, ed., *Mr. Gregory's Letter-Box 1813−1835* (London, 1898); Edward Bryn, *Crown and Castle: British Rule in Ireland 1800−1830* (Dublin, 1978), p. 70; Parker, *Peel,* I, 193.
22. R. B. McDowell, *Irish Public Opinion 1750−1800* (London, 1944), pp. 220ff; A. P. W. Malcomson, *John Foster: The Politics of Anglo-Irish Ascendancy* (Oxford, 1978), pp. 351ff; R. Barry O'Brien, *Dublin Castle and the Irish People* (London, 1909), pp. 52ff; Hereward Senior, *Orangeism in Ireland and Britain 1795−1836* (London, 1966); Gregory to Goulburn, March 19, 1822, Box C, Henry Goulburn Papers, Surrey Record Office, Kingston; Gregory, *Letter−Box,* p. 164.
23. Quoted in Galen Broeker, *Rural Disorder and Police Reform in Ireland 1812−1836* (London, 1970), p. 25.
24. Gregory to Peel, March 25, 1825, BM Add. Ms. 40334.
25. Gregory to Peel, May 22, 1813, BM Add. Ms. 40196; Gregory to Goulburn, March 6, 1825, Box C, Goulburn Papers.
26. Gregory to Goulburn, March 6, 1825.
27. Gregory to Peel, March 25, 1825, BM. Add. Ms. 40334; Gregory to Goulburn, April 24, 1825, Box C, Goulburn Papers; Gregory to Goulburn, May 22, 1825.
28. Gregory to Peel, June 27, 1813, BM. Add. Ms. 40197; Gregory to Peel, December 6, 1828, BM Add. Ms. 40334; Desmond Bowen, *The Protestant Crusade in Ireland 1800−1870* (Montreal, 1978), p. 138.
29. See James A. Reynolds, *The Catholic Emancipation Crisis in Ireland 1823−1829* (reprint, Westport, Conn., 1970).
30. Gregory to Peel, February 4, 1829, BM Add. Ms. 40334; Gregory to Goulburn, February 9, 1829, BM Add. Ms. 40334.
31. Lord Mahon and Edward Cardwell, *Memoirs by the Right Honourable Sir Robert Peel,* 2 vols (London, 1857), I, 19; Lloyd C. Sanders, ed., *Lord Melbourne's Papers* (reprint, New York, 1971), pp. 106, 169; Philip Ziegler, *Melbourne* (London, 1976), p. 92; R. Barry O'Brien, *Thomas Drummond Under Secretary in Ireland 1835−1840 Life and Letters* (London, 1889), p. 75; Maurice R. O'Connell, ed., *The Correspondence of Daniel O'Connell,* 8 vols. (Dublin, 1972−81), II, 47−49; III, 312−13, 341−42, 344; IV, 34, 38−9, 148, 237−38.

CHAPTER 2

1. McDowell, *Ireland in Age of Imperialism,* p. 143; Alexis de Tocqueville, *Journeys to England and Ireland,* ed. J. P. Mayer (New Haven, 1958), p. 122.
2. Gregory to Peel, February 14, 1816, BM Add. Ms. 40202; Peel to Gregory, February 26, 1816, BM Add. Ms. 40202; Gregory, *House of Gregory,* pp. 68−9.
3. See ms of Gregory Autobiography; certificate of baptism.

4. N. Parker Willis, *Famous Persona and Places* (Rochester, N. Y., 1854), p. 306; Harold Orel, ed., *Irish History and Culture: Aspects of a People's Heritage* (Lawrence, Kansas, 1976), p. 176; Gregory, *Autobiography*, pp. 17–8; Gregory, *House of Gregory*, pp. 60–1; see also Stephen Gwynn, *Dublin Old and New* (New York, 1938); Constantia Maxwell, *Dublin Under the Georges 1714–1830* (Dublin, 1946); Calvin Colton, *Four Years in Great Britain*, 2 vols. (New York, 1836); John Gamble, *Sketches of History, Politics, and Manners in Dublin and the North of England in 1810* (London, 1826).

5. O'Brien, *Drummond*, p. 211; Gwynn, *Dublin*, pp. 162ff; W. R. Le Fanu, *Seventy Years of Irish Life* (London, 1894), pp. 1–5; Francis B. Head, *A Fortnight in Ireland* (London, 1852), pp. 17–18.

6. See ms of Autobiography.

7. Gregory, *Autobiography*, pp. 12–14; Lady Gregory, *Coole* (Dublin, 1931), pp. 17–19; Talcott Parsons, *Social Structure and Personality* (New York, 1964); Sir William H. Gregory, 'Daniel O'Connell', *Nineteenth Century*, (1889), 583–4.

8. Gregory, *House of Gregory*, p. 62; C. Litton Falkiner, *Studies in Irish History and Biography* (London, 1902), p. 190; Denis Gwynn, *Daniel O'Connell The Irish Liberator* (London, 1929), pp. 159–62; Le Fanu, *Seventy Years*, pp. 175–6; Gregory to Goulburn, February 16, 1823, Box C, Goulburn Papers; Gregory to Peel, March 31, 1823, BM Add. Ms. 40334.

9. Gregory, *Autobiography*, pp. 22–4.

10. Falkiner, *Studies in Irish History*, pp. 194–8.

11. Gregory, *Autobiography*, p. 29.

12. Phyllis Grosskurth, *The Woeful Victorian A Biography of John Addington Symonds* (New York, 1964), p. 23; 'Harrow School', *Blackwood's Magazine*, XCIV (1863), 457.

13. Anthony Trollope, *An Autobiography*, introduction by Bradford Allen Booth (Berkeley, 1947), pp. 3–9; Thomas Adolphus Trollope, *What I Remember*, 2 vols. (London, 1887), I, 78; Edward Graham, *The Harrow Life of Henry Montagu Butler D. D.* (London, 1920); Richard Wellesley memoir, BM Add. Ms. 37416; the sense of crisis in Public School education is evident in the Reviews and Quarterlies of the period and is documented in the extensive secondary literature.

14. Thomas V. Short to Vicar of Harrow, March 20, 1829, ms. 1841, Charles Longley Papers, Lambeth Palace Library; see also the biographical sketch of Longley by Henry Longley; Aberdeen to Longley, May 23, 1829.

15. *Blackwood's Magazine*, XCIV, 471–2; Edmund W. Howson and George Townsend Warner, eds., *Harrow School* (London, 1898); Frederick Gale, *Life of Hon. Robert Grimston* (London, 1885).

16. See obituary of Kennedy in *The Classical Review*, III (1889), 226–7, 278–81; Gregory, *Autobiography*, p. 31.

17. Gregory, *Autobiography*, pp. 7, 31ff; W. H. Gregory to W. Gregory, June, 1833, April, 21; May 2, June/July, October 7, November 7, December 26, 29, 1834; May 18, June 23, 1835; Gregory, *Letter–Box*, pp. 345–6.

18. Leveson-Gower to Gregory, March 31, 1829, Leveson-Gower Papers, Public Record Office of Ireland, Dublin.

19. W. H. Gregory to W. Gregory, Speech Day, 1835, and summer, 1835.

20. 'Public Schools of England', *Edinburgh Review*, XVI (1810), 328; Gregory to Peel, June 7, 1835, BM Add. Ms. 40334.

21. W. H. Gregory to W. Gregory, January 9, 1836; Rev. W. Tuckwell,

Reminiscences of Oxford (London, 1907), pp. 114–5; 'Memorials of Oxford', *Quarterly Review*, CXXI (1838), 203ff; 'Universities of England — Oxford', *Edinburgh Review*, LIII (1831), 384–427; Rev. James Pycroft, *Oxford Memories*, 2 vols (London, 1886); Elizabeth Longford, *Wellington Pillar of State* (London, 1972), pp. 336–46; Colton, *Four Years in Britain*, II, 148–50; Lilian M Quiller Couch, *Reminiscences of Oxford by Oxford Men 1559–1850* (Oxford, 1892), pp. 302–4; E. G. W. Bill and J. F. A. Mason, *Christ Church and Reform 1850–1867* (Oxford, 1970); M. L. Clarke, *Classical Education in Britain 1500–1900* (Cambridge, 1959), pp. 98–105.

22. W. H. Gregory to W. Gregory, March 18, April 18, 1836; Tuckwell, *Reminiscences of Oxford*, p. 124; Gregory, *Autobiography*, pp. 44–46.

23. W. H. Gregory to W. Gregory, May 22, 1836; Rev. H. J. Torre, *Recollections of School Days at Harrow* (Manchester, 1890).

24. John Vincent, ed., *Disraeli, Derby and the Conservative Party: Journals and Memoirs of Edward Henry, Lord Stanley 1849–1869* (Hassocks, 1978), pp. 250–51.

CHAPTER 3

1. John Dodds, *The Age of Paradox: A Biography of England 1841–1851* (Westport, Conn., 1970), p. 45; Ziegler, *Melbourne*, p. 201; *Correspondence of O'Connell*, VII, 130; *Warder,* January 1, 1842.

2. Ziegler, *Melbourne*, p. 210; *Saunders's News–Letter*, January 5, 1842; *Dublin Evening Mail*, January 3, 1842; *Dublin Evening Mail*, January 7, 1842.

3. Gregory, *Autobiography*, p. 58; *Dublin Evening Mail*, January 10, 1842; *Warder*, January 8, 1842.

4. T. G. Wilson, *Victorian Doctor Being the Life of Sir William Wilde* (New York, 1946), pp. 70–74; M. C. Ferguson, *Sir Samuel Ferguson in the Ireland of His Day*, 2 vols (London, 1896), I, 268ff; Gwynn, *Dublin*, pp. 98–100.

5. K. Theodore Hoppen, 'Politics, the law, and the nature of the Irish electorate 1832–1850', *English Historical Review*, XCII (1977), 746–776; see also Norman Gash, *Politics in the Age of Peel* (London, 1953).

6. Gash, *Politics in Age of Peel*, pp. 105–35; Guttsman, *Elite*, p. 35.

7. Graham to Peel, January 1, 1842, BM Add. Ms. 40446; R. Barry O'Brien, *Fifty Years of Concessions to Ireland 1831–1881*, 2 vols. (London, 1881), I, 581ff.

8. Eliot to Peel, January 8, 1842, BM Add. Ms. 40480; Peel to Eliot, January 10, 1842, BM Add Ms. 40480; *Warder*, January 15, 1842; *Recollections of Jonah Barrington*, p. 157.

9. *Dublin Evening Mail*, January 14, 1842; *Warder*, January 22, 1842.

10. See Jacqueline Hill, 'The Protestant response to repeal: the case of the Dublin working class', in F. S. L. Lyons and R. A. J. Hawkins, *Ireland under the Union* (Oxford, 1980), pp. 35–68.

11. Gregory, *Autobiography*, p. 59; *Dublin Monitor*, January 18, 1842.

12. *Galway Vindicator*, January 15, 29, 1842; *Dublin Monitor*, January 18, 20, 22, 1842; Howard Jones, *To The Webster–Ashburton Treaty A Study in Anglo–American Relations 1783–1843* (Chapel Hill, 1977), p. 82; *Dublin Evening Mail*, January 24, 1842; *Dublin World*, January 29, 1842.

13. *Dublin Monitor*, January 25, 27, 29, 1842; *Galway Vindicator*, January 29, 1842; *Dublin Evening Mail*, January 31, February 23, 1842.

14. *Hansard's Parliamentary Debates*, 3rd ser., LXXXV, 1141–42; Gregg to Disraeli, March 24, 1846, B/XXI/9/327, Hughenden Coll., Bodleian Library.
15. Gregory, *Autobiography*, pp. 76–79, 82, 88, 95, 116–7; Gash, *Politics in Age of Peel*, pp. 393–99; Dodds, *Age of Paradox*, p. 183; Charles Whibley, *Lord John Manners and his Friends*, 2 vols. (Edinburgh, 1925), I, 137; Gregory to Layard, January 29, 1889.
16. Lawrence J. McCaffrey, *Daniel O'Connell and the Repeal Year* (Louisville, 1966); Kevin B. Nowlan, *The Politics of Repeal 1841–1850 A Study in the Relations between Great Britain and Ireland* (London, 1965), p. 5; Thomas Brown, *Politics of Irish Literature* (London, 1972), p. 46; *Quarterly Review*, LXXV (1842), 239.
17. Gregory, *Autobiography*, pp. 67–74; Michael Hurst, *Maria Edgeworth and the Public Scene: Intellect, Fine Feeling and Landlordism in the Age of Reform* (Coral Gables, 1969), p. 17; Gregory, *Nineteenth Century*; XXV (1889), 582–94; W. H. Gregory to W. Gregory, April 18, 1836; Gregory to Shaw Lefevre, July 27, 1887.
18. Dodds, *Age of Paradox*, p. 170; *Parl. Deb.*, 3rd ser., LXIII, 206–7; Gregory to Peel, May 24, 1842, BM Add. Ms. 40509; Peel to Gregory, May 25, 1842, BM Add. Ms. 40509; *Parl. Deb.*, 3rd ser., XCII, 375–6; Gregory, *Autobiography*, p. 66.
19. Lord Butler, ed., *The Conservatives* (London, 1977), pp. 54–65, 84–9.
20. 'Lord Alvanley on the State of Ireland', *Edinburgh Review*, LXXIV (1842), 474–93; Graham to Peel, December 1, 1841, BM Add. Ms. 40446; Eliot to Peel, January 20, 1842, BM Add. Ms. 40480; Graham to Gregory, November 28, 1842, BM Add. Ms. 40447.
21. Peel to De Grey, January 2, 1842, BM Add. Ms. 40446; *Greville Memoirs*, V, January 24, 1842; Butler, *Conservatives*, p. 73–80; *Quarterly Review,*LIII, 277; *Dublin Evening Mail*, August 4, 1843.
22. Nowlan, *Politics of Repeal*, pp. 56–7; *Greville Memoirs*, V, September 14, 1844.
23. Donal A. Kerr, *Peel, Priests and Politics* (Oxford, 1982), pp. 112; Brown, *Politics of Irish Literature*, pp. 81–2; Dodds, *Age of Paradox*, p. 155; McCaffrey, *Daniel O'Connell*, pp. 214ff.
24. *Parl. Deb.*, 3rd ser., LXXIII, 32–43.
25. Kerr, *Peel, Priests and Politics*, p. 108; William Makepeace Thackeray, *Irish Sketch Book for 1842* (London, 1843), p. 463.
26. E. R. Norman, 'The Maynooth Question of 1845', *Irish Historical Studies*, XV (1967), 407–437; Gilbert A. Cahill, 'The Protestant Association and the Anti-Maynooth Agitation of 1845', *Catholic Historical Review*, XLIII (1957), 273–308; G. I. T. Machin, 'The Maynooth Grant, the Dissenters and Disestablishment, 1845–1847', *English Historical Review*, LXXXII (1967), 61–85; E. R. Norman, *Anti-Catholicism in Victorian England* (London, 1968), p. 32; 61–85; *Greevey Papers*, II, 175.
27. Gregory, *Autobiography*, pp. 121–126; *Dublin University Magazine*, XXV (1845), 517–18; *Dublin Evening Mail*, April 7, 1845; *Warder,*March 29, 1845.
28. *Parl. Deb.*, 3rd ser., LXXIX, 58–63, 642–45.
29. *Warder*, September 9, 1843; see also April 15, May 20, 1843.
30. *Greville Memoirs*, V, April 22, 1845.
31. *Parl. Deb.*, 3rd ser., LXXXIII, 438–9.
32. Butler, *Conservatives*, pp. 94–106; William O. Aydelotte, 'The Country Gentlemen and the Repeal of the Corn Laws', *English Historical Review*, LXXXII (1967), 47–60.
33. *Parl. Deb.*, 3rd ser., LXXXIII, 680–95.

34. *Dublin Evening Mail,* February 13, 1846.
35. Gregory to Peel, March 6, 1846, BM Add. Ms. 40586
36. *Parl. Deb.,* 3rd ser., LXXXIII, 695.
37. Nowlan, *Politics of Repeal,* pp. 125–7; *Dublin Evening Mail,* January 5, 1846; J. C. Beckett, *The Making of Modern Ireland 1603–1923* (reprint, London, 1978), p. 338.
38. Dodds, *Age of Paradox,* pp. 227, 243ff; Brunel to ? February 10, 1847, 30/22/6B, Lord Russell Papers, Public Record Office (PRO), London; Nowlan, *Politics of Repeal,* pp. 131–33; see also R. Dudley Edwards and T. Desmond Williams, *The Great Famine: Studies in Irish History 1845–1852* (Dublin, 1956).
39. *Parl. Deb.,* 3rd ser., LXXXIX, 723–31.
40. *Parl. Deb.,* 3rd ser., XCI, 583–87.
41. *Parl. Deb.,* 3rd ser., XCII, 1415–21.
42. *Dublin Evening Herald,* April 3, 1847; *Nation,* April 3, 1847; *Galway Vindicator,* April 17, 1847.
43. *Tuam Herald,* March 11, November 4, 1854; see also September 8, 1855.
44. Fitzwilliam to Gregory, February 1 (?), 1848; Brown, *Politics of Irish Literature,* p. 117.
45. Jackson to Gregory, December 22, 1845, and January 7, 10, 16, 1846; Crampton to Gregory, February 13, 1846; Stanhope to Gregory, February, n.d., 1846.
46. *Warder,* June 29, December 21, 1844; Gregg to Gregory, May 24, 1846; Jackson to Gregory, October 15, 1846; Sheehan to Gregory, June 22, 1844; *Dublin Evening Mail,* March 31, 1847.
47. W. O'Connor Morris, *Memories and Thoughts of Life* (London, 1885), pp. 182–3; Clanricarde to Bessborough, March 16, 1847, PRO 30/22/6B; Bessborough to Clanricarde, March 19, 1847, PRO 30/22/6B.
48. Lord Lincoln to Gregory, August 18, 1847.
49. *Dublin Evening Mail,* August 2, 1847; *Saunders's News–Letter,* August 3, 1847; *Dublin Evening Herald,* August 9, 1847; Lyons and Hawkins, *Politics under the Union,* p. 51; John T. Gilbert, *A History of the City of Dublin,* 3 vols (reprint, Shannon, 1972), I, 185; *Warder,* August 14, 1847.
50. Gregory, *Autobiography,* p. 137; Lincoln to Gregory, August 18, 1847 and February 9, 1848.
51. Long to Gregory, August 12, 20, October 5, 1847, January 5, 1848; Hamilton to Gregory, August 18, October 22, 1847; Keatinge to Gregory, February 14, 1848; Clanricarde to Clarendon, February 25, 1848, A Box 9, Clarendon Papers, Bodleian.

CHAPTER 4

1. Ingram to Gregory, August 19, 1847; McDowell, *Ireland in Age of Imperialism,* pp. 108–9; Clanricarde to Clarendon, July 9, 1847, August 8, 1847, A Box 9, Clarendon Papers; *Galway Vindicator,* July 31, 1847.
2. *Galway Vindicator,* August 7, 1847; *Dublin Evening Mail,* August 16, 1847; Clanricarde to Clarendon, August 8, 1847, A Box 9, Clarendon Papers; *Galway Mercury,* August 14, 1847.

3. *Galway Vindicator,* August 14, 1847; Gregory to Clanricarde, September 1, 1847, Bdle 73, Clanricarde Papers, Leeds Public Library; Clanricarde to Gregory, September 8, 1847; Gregory, *Autobiography,* p. 138; *Tuam Herald,* August 14, 1847.
4. Horatio Sheafe Kraus, *Irish Life in Irish Fiction* (New York, 1903), pp. 80ff; Hugh B. Staples, *The Ireland of Sir Jonah Barrington* (Seattle, 1967), pp. 41ff; Gregory, *Autobiography,* pp. 40–3; Maurice George Moore, *An Irish Gentleman* (London, 1913), p. 85; *Galway Vindicator,* April 5, 1856.
5. F. V. Barry, *Maria Edgeworth Chosen Letters* (London, 1931), pp. 391–3; Thomas Campbell Foster, *Letters on the Condition of Ireland* (London, 1847), pp. 288ff.
6. E. H. Mikhail, ed., *Lady Gregory Interviews and Recollections* (London, 1977), p. 106; Thackeray, *Irish Sketches,* p. 204; Samuel Lewis, *A Topographical Dictionary of Ireland,* 2 vols. (London, 1837), I, 666–7; Jerome Fahy, *History and Antiquities of the Diocese of Kilmacduagh* (Dublin, 1893), p. 389; John O'Donovan, *OS Letters* (Galway), vol. 2, 247–48.
7. Fahy, *Kilmacduagh,* p. 352; McDowell, *Ireland in Age of Imperialism,* pp. 6ff; A. W. Hulton ed., *Arthur Young A Tour of Ireland 1776–1779,* 2 vols. (new ed., Shannon, 1970), I, 284.
8. Brian de Breffny and Rosemary ffoliott, *The Houses of Ireland: Domestic Architecture from the medieval castle to the Edwardian villa* (London, 1975), p. 137; Donald T. Torchiana, *W. B. Yeats and Georgian Ireland* (Evanston, 1966), p. 72; Orel, ed., *Irish History and Culture,* pp. 180–3; Ida Gantz, *Signpost to Eyrecourt* (Bath, 1975), p. 109; Colin Smythe, *A Guide to Coole Park, Co. Galway Home of Lady Gregory* (Gerrards Cross, 1973); Daniel Murphy, ed., *Lady Gregory's Journals Volume 1* (Gerrards Cross, 1978), 21, 283; W. B. Yeats, *Autobiographies* (London, 1966), pp. 389–91.
9. S. H. Cousens, 'The Regional Variations in Population Changes in Ireland, 1861–1881', *Economic History Review,* 2nd ser., XVII (1964–5), 311; Lecky, *Ireland in Eighteenth Century,* pp. 65–8; Michael Beames, 'Concepts and Terms Cottiers and Conacre in Pre-Famine Ireland', *Journal of Peasant Studies,* II (1975), 352–4; see also Edwards and Williams, *The Great Famine.*
10. R. B. McDowell, *Social Life in Ireland 1800–1845* (Dublin, 1957), pp. 43–56; Oliver Macdonagh, 'The Irish Famine Emigration to the United States', *Perspectives in American History,* X (1976), 366–68; Foster, *Letters on Ireland,* pp. 243–55.
11. *Dublin University Magazine,* XXV (1845), 471.
12. Report of Devon Commission, Part IV, 481–94.
13. *Galway Mercury,* April 4, 1845; S. H. Cousens, 'Regional Death Rates in Ireland during the Great Famine from 1846–1851', *Population Studies* XV (1960–1), 55–74; there is a great deal of information on conditions in the Gort area in the Irish University Press series of *British Parliamentary Papers Famine (Ireland),* 8 vols (Shannon, 1968).
14. Relief Commission Papers, II/2, 1A/50/69, Public Record Office of Ireland; *Tuam Herald,* October 10, 1846, April 10, 1847.
15. *Tuam Herald,* October 10, 1846.
16. A. R. G. Griffiths, 'The Irish Board of Works in the Famine Years', *Historical Journal,* XIII (1970), 634–52; *Galway Vindicator,* December 12, 1846.
17. *Galway Vindicator,* January 14, July 22, 1846; *Tuam Herald,* May 1, 1847.
18. Lord Clinton to Gregory, March 19, 1847; *Galway Vindicator,* December 8, 1847.

19. S. Godolphin Osborne, *Gleanings in the West of Ireland* (London, 1850), p. 39; see also *Parliamentary Papers Famine (Ireland)*.
20. Thomas Carlyle, *Reminiscences of My Irish Journey in 1849* (London, 1882), p. 185; *Parl. Deb.*, 3rd ser., XC, 1274–5; Gregory, *Autobiography*, p. 140; Gregory to Peel, February 11, 1846, BM Add. Ms. 40584.
21. Clarendon to Clanricarde, August 23, 1846, Bdle, 79, Clanricarde Papers; Clanricarde to Gregory, December 18, 1847.
22. *Tuam Herald,* February 26, June 3, 1848, June 16, 1849; Henry Coulter, *The West of Ireland* (Dublin, 1862), p. 146.
23. James S. Donnelly Jr., *The Land and the People of Nineteenth Century Cork: The Rural Economy and the Land Question* (London, 1975), pp. 98ff; *Tuam Herald,* June 16, 1849; *Galway Vindicator,* September 30, 1848; Torchiana, *Yeats,* p. 43; *Galway Vindicator,* March 26, 1849; *Tuam Herald* (citing *Limerick Examiner*), December 8, 1849.
24. See the ms of the *Autobiography* for Gregory's brief and candid discussion of his land agents.
25. Gregory, *Autobiography*, pp. 118–9.
26. For a brief account of Gregory's racing activities see John Kent, *Racing Life of Lord George Cavendish Bentinck MP* (London, 1892), pp. 366–425; *Sportsman's Almanack for 1847; Sportsmen's Magazine,* April 24, 1847; *Sporting Life,* November 20, 1847.
27. Corbett to Gregory, December 5, 1844; T.H. Bird, *Admiral Rous and the English Turf 1795–1877* (London, 1939), p. 66; T.A. Cook, *A History of the English Turf,* 2 divisions, 6 vols (London, n.d.), div. I, vol. III, 489; John Ashton, *The History of Gambling in England* (reprint, New York, 1968), pp. 194ff; James Christie Whyte, *History of the British Turf,* 2 vols. (London, 1840), II, 288; Richard Harris, ed., *The Reminiscences of Sir Henry Hawkins Baron Brampton,* 2 vols. (London, 1904), I, 84ff, II, 190–1; Louis Henry Curzon, *A Mirror of the Turf or The Machinery of Horse Racing revealed showing the Sport of Kings as it is To-Day* (London, 1892), pp. 258ff, 270; Robert Black, *Horse-Racing in England A Synoptical Review* (London, 1893), pp. 159ff, 180ff; Kellew Chesney, *Victorian Underworld* (London, 1970), pp. 279ff; 'Old Racing Times', *Gentlemen's Magazine,* CCXXVII (1869), 46–55; 'The Three Reports from the Select Committee of the House of Lords appointed to inquire into Laws Respecting Gaming', *Parliamentary Papers,* VI (1844), 281–486; 'Report from the Select Committee on Gaming', *Parliamentary Papers,* VI (1844), 3–279.
28. Gregory, *Autobiography*, p. 120; William Day, *Reminiscences of the Turf with Anecdotes and Recollections of its Principal Celebrities* (London, 1886), pp. 93, 115; Wray Vamplew, *The Turf A Social and Economic History of Horse Racing* (London, 1976), p. 31; Gregory, *Autobiography*, pp. 106ff; *Greville Memoirs,* November 25, 1843, September 28, 1848; Bentinck to Gregory, January 8, 1844.
29. Bentinck to Gregory, November 17, 21, 1843, January 8, 1844; Christie to Gregory, April 3, 1866.
30. John R. Reed, *Victorian Conventions* (Athens, Ohio, 1975), pp. 143–7; Gregory, *House of Gregory,* pp. 76–7.
31. Gregory, *Autobiography*, pp. 142–3; O'Flaherty to Gregory, January 7, 1853; *Tuam Herald,* September 2, 1854.
32. *Dublin Evening Mail,* June 29, July 2, 1855.
33. Lawley to Gregory, December 12, 1857.

34. Dunkellin to Gregory, November 23, 1855, Bdle 96, Clanricarde Papers.
35. The sale catalogue in the Gregory Papers describes the Coole Estate in some detail; a copy of a standard Gregory lease is to be found among Lady Gregory's Papers, Berg Collection, New York; for the operation of the Encumbered Estates Court see Padraig G. Lane, 'The Encumbered Estates Court, Ireland, 1848–49', *Economic and Social Review*, III (1972), 413–53; Foster, *Letters on Ireland*, p. 594; and L.P. Curtis Jr., 'Incumbered Wealth: Landed Indebtedness in Post Famine Ireland', *American Historical Review*, LXXXV (1980), 332–67.
36. Gregory, *Autobiography*, pp. 154–7; *Tuam Herald*, January 17, November 21, 1857.

CHAPTER 5

1. *Galway Vindicator*, March 14, 17, 24, 1849; William F. Bailey, *Local and Centralised Government in Ireland* (Dublin, 1888), pp. 14ff; Foster, *Letters on Ireland*, p. 450; Gregory to O'Flaherty, December 19, 1851, Gregory — O'Flaherty Correspondence.
2. *Tuam Herald*, March 22, 1845, March 24, 1849.
3. Correspondence and cuttings on the Carshalton affair are to be found in the Gregory Papers.
4. E. R. Norman, *Anti–Catholicism in Victorian England* (London, 1968), pp. 52ff, 159–61.
5. G. I. T. Machin, 'Lord John Russell and the Prelude to the Ecclesiastical Titles Bill, 1846–1851', *Journal of Ecclesiastical History*, XXV (1974), 277–95; D. G. Paz, 'Popular Anti–Catholicism in England, 1850–1851', *Albion*, XI (1979), 331–59.
6. *Greville Memoirs*, VI, November 26, 1850; Vincent, *Disraeli, Derby*, p. 38.
7. Vincent, *Disraeli, Derby*, pp. 57ff.
8. Vincent, *Disraeli, Derby*, pp. 17, 78–9; J. A. Whyte, 'Landlord Influence at Elections in Ireland, 1760–1885', *English Historical Review*, LXXX (1965), 740–60; P. L. Jupp, 'Irish Parliamentary Elections and the Influence of the Catholic Vote, 1801–1820', *Historical Journal*, X (1967), 183–96; Oliver MacDonagh, 'The Politicization of the Irish Catholic Bishops, 1800–1850', *Historical Journal*, XVIII (1975), 37–53; J. A. Whyte, 'The influence of the Catholic clergy on elections in nineteenth century Ireland', *English Historical Review*, LXXV (1960), 239–59; Emmet Larkin, 'The Devotional Revolution in Ireland, 1850–75', *American Historical Review*, LXXVII (1972), 625–52; Kerr, *Peel, Priests and Politics*, p. 51; *Parliamentary Papers: Bribery at Elections* (Shannon, 1968), vol. 1.
9. *Tuam Herald*, July 12, 1851.
10. Mahon to Clanricarde, March 23, 1852, Bdle 47, Clanricarde Papers; E. O'Flaherty to Gregory, n.d.
11. J. A. Whyte, 'The Appointment of Catholic Bishops in Nineteenth Century Ireland', *Catholic Historical Review*, XLVIII (1962), 12–32; Derry to Nelly, February 5, 1852.
12. *Galway Vindicator*, July 7, 1852.

13. Clanricarde to Clonbrock, July 15, 1852, Bdle 47, Clanricarde Papers.
14. E. O'Flaherty to Gregory, January 13, 1852; 'Report of the Commissioners appointed to investigate into the existence of Corrupt Practices in Elections of Members to serve in Parliament for the County of the Town of Galway', *Parliamentary Papers*, XXVI (1857–8), 307–531; *Tuam Herald*, July 10, 1852.
15. Dunkellin to Gregory, n.d. (July, 1852), Bdle 96, Clanricarde Papers; Newcastle to Clanricarde, July 10, 1852, Bdle 47, Clanricarde Papers; Newcastle to Gregory, July 10, 1852; Newcastle to Clanricarde, July 14, 1852, Bdle 47, Clanricarde Papers.
16. Clanricarde to Gregory, July 22, 1852; E. O'Flaherty to Gregory, January 7, 1853; *Tuam Herald*, January 8, 1853; Clarendon to Gregory, January 3, 1853.
17. See J. H. Whyte, *The Independent Irish Party 1850–59* (Oxford, 1958); *Galway Vindicator*, August 17, 27, 1853; Dunkellin to Gregory, n.d. (1854), Bdle 95, Clanricarde Papers.
18 Gregory, *Autobiography*, p. 141; W. W. Hunter, *Lord Naas, Life of the Earl of Mayo*, 2 vols (London, 1875), I, 78.
19 *Greville Memoirs*, V, June 6, 1843; Clanricarde to Gregory, December 29, 1845, also n.d. (1846) and December 6, 1846.
20. For the Handcock scandal see ms of *Autobiography* and Bdle 82, Clanricarde Papers; *Greville Memoirs*, VIII, February 20, 23, March 2, 17, 1858.
21. Gregory to Bess Gregory, November 13, December 16, 21, 25, 1855, and January 1, 1856.
22. Gregory to Bess Gregory, January 1, 22, 29, 1856.
23. Gregory to Bess Gregory, February 20, April 2, 19, 1856; see also ms of *Autobiography*.
24. For an extensive description of the Tunis expedition see ms of the *Autobiography*.
25. Clancarty to Bess Gregory, May 3, 1856; Gregory to Clancarty, March 25, 1857.
26. Gregory to Clanricarde, March 23, 1857, Bdle 9, Clanricarde Papers; *Galway Vindicator*, April 1, 1857; *Tuam Herald*, April 4, 1857.
27. *Tuam Herald*, November 25, 1854; Bermingham to Gregory, December 6, 1854; Gregory to Bermingham, December 19, 1854; Bermingham to Gregory, December 24, 1854.
28. *Galway Vindicator*, December 23, 1854.
29. Gregory to Clanricarde, March 16, 1857; Clanricarde to Gregory, March 18, 1857; Burke to Clanricarde, March 22, 1857; Gregory to Clanricarde, March 23, 1857; Redington to Clanricarde, March 26, 1857; Gregory to Clanricarde, April 3, 6, 8, 9, 1857; Clonbrock to Clanricarde, April 9, 10, 1857; all in Bdle 9, Clanricarde Papers.
30. *Tuam Herald*, April 11, 1857; *Galway Vindicator*, April 8, 1857.
31. *Galway Vindicator*, April 11, 1857; *Galway Mercury*, April 11, 1857; *Galway Express*, April 1, 1857; Gregory to Clanricarde, April 10, 1857, Bdle 9, Clanricarde Papers; Burke to Clanricarde, April 19, 1857, Bdle 9, Clanricarde Papers.
32 *Galway Vindicator*, April 11, 1857; Gregory to Clanricarde, April 11, 1857, Bdle 9, Clanricarde Papers; *Galway Mercury*, April 18, 1857; Crampton to Gregory, April 13, 1857.

CHAPTER 6

1. Sarah Agnes Wallace and Frances Elma Gillespie, eds., *Journal of Benjamin Moran 1857–1865*, 2 vols. (Chicago, 1948), II, 963; Lawley to Gregory, December 12, 1857.
2. *Tuam Herald*, May 15, 1858; see also June 12, July 3, 31, August 7, 1858; Gregory to Clanricarde, March 11, 1859, Bdle 80, Clanricarde Papers.
3. Election address; *Galway Vindicator*, May 23, 1857; *Parl. Deb.*, 3rd ser., CXLV, 622, 1943, 1956.
4. Derry to Gregory, February 17, 24, 1859; *Parl. Deb.*, 3rd ser., CLII, 1566; CLIII, 672–3; CLVI, 1244; Derry to Gregory, March 18, April 18, 1859.
5. Gregory to Clanricarde, April 18, 26, 1859, Bdle 80, Clanricarde Papers; K. Theodore Hoppen, 'Tories, Catholics and the General Election of 1859', *Historical Journal*, XXIII (1970), 48–67; K. Theodore Hoppen, 'Landlords, Society and Electoral Politics in mid-Nineteenth Century Ireland', *Past and Present*, LXXV (1977), 85; *Tuam Herald*, April 23, 1859; Gregory, *Autobiography*, p. 137.
6. *Tuam Herald*, May 14, 1859.
7. Clonbrock to Gregory, June 4, 1859; Clanricarde to Gregory, March 11, 1859, Bdle 80, Clanricarde Papers; Clanricarde to Gregory, June 9, 1859; Clonbrock to Gregory, June 10, 1859; Derry to Gregory, June 10, 1859.
8. Gregory to Bess Gregory, January 1, 1856, and November 6, 1859; Lawley to Gregory, July 14, 1858, and December 12, 1857; Gregory to Mrs J. Martin, August 28, 1859.
9. Gregory to Bess Gregory, September 1, 11, 1859.
10. Gregory to Bess Gregory, September 16, 26, 1859.
11. Gregory to Bess Gregory, September 26, October 2, 1859.
12. Gregory to Bess Gregory, October 2, November 6, 1859.
13. Martin Crawford, 'British Travellers and the Anglo–American Relationship in the 1850s', *Journal of American Studies*, XII (1978), 203; Gregory to Bess Gregory, October 15, November 26, 1859.
14. Gregory to Bess Gregory, October 15, 25, 1859.
15. Gregory to Bess Gregory, October 25, 1859.
16. Gregory to Bess Gregory, October 9, 25, December 14, 1859.
17. Gregory to Bess Gregory, December 14, 25, 1859.
18. Gregory to Bess Gregory, December 5, 25, 1859; see ms of *Autobiography*.
19. Gregory to Bess Gregory, December 14, 1859; Brian Jenkins, *Britain and the War for the Union* Volume 2 (Montreal, 1980), pp. 54–6; Miles to Gregory, May 14, 1861; Lawley to Gregory, November 24, 1861.
20. *Parl. Deb.*, 3rd ser., CLXII, 506, 564–5; CLXIII, 193, 631, 762; Martin to Gregory, July 11, 1861.
21. Mann to Gregory, May 1, 3, 6, July 6, October 10, 1861.
22. Mann to Gregory, August 7, 8, 19, October 12, 16, 17, 1861; Gregory to Layard, October 14, 1861, Layard Papers, BM Add. Ms. 39101.
23. Gregory to Layard, January 4, 1862, BM Add. Ms. 39102.
24. Mason to Hunter, February 7, 1862; Gregory to Mason, February 7, 1862; Mason to Hunter, February 22, 1862, *Official Records of Union and Confederate Navies* (ORN), 2nd ser., III, 331ff; Lawley to Gregory, January 21, 23, 1862.
25. Hotze to Hunter, March 11, 1862, *ORN*, ser., 2, III, 361; *Parl. Deb.*, 3rd ser., CLXV, 1158–81.
26. Jenkins, *Britain and War for the Union* Volume 2, 50–4, 56–7; *Parl. Deb.*, 3rd ser., CLXVII, 615.

27. Spence to Gregory, July 14, 1862; *Parl. Deb.*, 3rd ser., CLXVIII, 549–69; Brian Connell, *Regina v Palmerston* (London, 1962), p. 329; Earle to Disraeli, July 14, 1862, B/XX/E/253, Hughenden Papers.
28. Mann to Gregory, September 15, 1862.
29. Jenkins, *Britain and War for the Union* Volume 2, pp. 166–7; Gregory to Mason, September 16, 1862, James M. Mason Papers, Library of Congress.
30. Spence to Gregory, January 3, 15, 1863; Mann to Gregory, January 11, 1863; Gregory to Miles, April 7, 1863, William Porcher Miles Papers, Southern Historical Collection, Chapel Hill, North Carolina.
31. Adams to Everett, June 5, 1863, Charles Francis Adams Papers, Massachusetts Historical Society, microfilm, reel 169.
32. Gregory to Cozziris, January 10, 1864.
33. Gregory to Mason, November 5, 1862, Mason Papers.
34. Gregory to Kalopithakis, April 21, 1864.

CHAPTER 7

1. *Galway Vindicator*, March 25, 1865; Martin to Gregory, July 1, 11, 1861, March 21, 1863.
2. Clarendon to Bess Gregory, April 14, 1865; Clancarty to Dunkellin, June 29, 1865, Bdle 97, Clanricarde Papers; *Galway Vindicator*, June 28, 1865.
3. Russell to Gregory, December 2, 1865, PRO 30/22/15H; Vincent, *Disraeli, Derby*, p. 244; Dunkellin to Gregory, Xmas Day (1865), Bdle 96, Clanricarde Papers; James Winter, *Robert Lowe* (Toronto, 1976), pp. 203ff; Warwick to Gregory, January 17, 1866; Gregory to Clarendon, December 14, 1865, Clarendon Papers.
4. *Parl. Deb.*, 3rd ser., CLXXXI, 838; CLVIII, 574ff; wherever possible I have used Gregory's handwritten drafts of his speeches rather than rely exclusively upon the parliamentary recorder.
5. Brian Jenkins, *Britain and the War for the Union* Volume 1 (Montreal, 1974), pp. 78–9; Jenkins, *Britain and the War for the Union* Volume 2 pp. 339–40.
6. *Parl. Deb.*, 3rd ser., CLXXVII, 1616, 1622.
7. F. B. Smith, *The Making of the Second Reform Bill* (Cambridge, 1966) p. 63; *Parl. Deb.*, 3rd ser., CLXXXI, 832–38.
8. Smith, *Second Reform Bill*, pp. 66ff; Maurice Cowling, *1867 Disraeli, Gladstone and Revolution The Passing of the second Reform Bill* (Cambridge, 1967), pp. 88–9; 'The Reform Bill', *Quarterly Review*, CIX (1866), 530–59; "English Democracy and Irish Fenianism," *Quarterly Review*, CXXII (1867), 236–79; Elcho to Gregory, April 3, 1866.
9. Gervas Huxley, *Victorian Duke: The Life of Hugh Lupus Grosvenor First Duke of Westminster* (London, 1967), pp. 76–82; Smith, *Second Reform Bill*, pp. 102ff.
10. Lawley to Gregory, February 12, March 31, 1866; Brand to Gregory, April 1, 1866; McEvilly to Gregory, April 13, 1866.
11. Hankey to Gregory, April 19, 1866; Gregory to Layard, September 24, 1870; Winter, *Lowe*, pp. 225–6; Vincent, *Disraeli, Derby*, p. 254; Dunkellin to

Gregory, March 18, 1866; Dunkellin to Gregory, February 15, 1866, Bdle 96, Clanricarde Papers.

12. 'The Coming Session', *Quarterly Review*, CIX (1866), 250–80; Elcho to Gregory, January 17, 1866; Monsell to Gregory, June 15, 1866; Clanricarde to Gregory, June 26, 1866; *Galway Vindicator*, June 30, 1866; Hunter, *Life of Mayo*, I, 70; Cowling, *1867*, p. 413.

13. F. S. L. Lyons, *Ireland Since the Famine* (revised ed., London, 1978), p. 204; *Parl. Deb.*, 3rd ser., CLXIII, 1071–90.

14. Dunkellin to Gregory, November 9 (1863), Bdle 95, Clanricarde Papers; *Galway Vindicator*, October 24, 1860; *Galway Express*, April 14, October 20, 1860.

15. Vincent, *Disraeli, Derby*, p. 171; *Parl. Deb.*, 3rd ser., CLXIII, 614–16, 660, 1071–90.

16. *Galway Vindicator*, July 13, 1861; *Tuam Herald*, July 13, 17, 1861; *Parl. Deb.*, 3rd ser., CLXIV, 1735; CLXVII, 466; *Tuam Herald*, May 17, 1862; *Parl. Deb.*, 3rd ser., CLXIX, 187; *Tuam Herald*, October 24, December 19, 1863, March 5, June 11, August 6, 1864.

17. *Parl. Deb.*, 3rd ser., CLXIX, 1675; *Galway Vindicator*, August 17, 1861, March 30, 1864.

18. *Galway Vindicator*, September 28, October 16, 1861, April 19, 1862.

19. Coulter, *West of Ireland*, pp. 10ff; *Galway Vindicator*, April 9, 1862; *Tuam Herald*, December 14, 1861, March 12, 1864.

20. *Galway Vindicator*, October 23, 1861, October 15, 1862.

21. Robinson to Gregory, February 22, 24, 1862; *Parl. Deb.*, 3rd ser., CLXXIV, 1482; CLXXV, 761–63.

22. Geraghty to Gregory, March 26, 1862; Duggan to Gregory, April 3, 4, 1862; *Parl. Deb.*, 3rd ser., CLXVI, 1172; *Tuam Herald*, June 6, 1863; *Galway Vindicator*, January 21, 1863; Vincent, *Disraeli, Derby*, p. 196; *Parl. Deb.*, 3rd ser., CLXXI, 839–42.

23. See Brian Jenkins, *Fenians and Anglo–American Relations during Reconstruction* (Ithaca, 1969), and Leon O Broin, *Fenian Fever An Anglo–American Dilemma* (New York, 1971).

24. The Government's preoccupation with Fenianism is most easily followed in Vincent, *Disraeli, Derby*, pp. 275ff.

25. Dunkellin to Gregory, n.d., Bdle 96, Clanricarde Papers.

26. Carlisle to Gregory, October 16, 1861; McEvilly to Gregory, October 23, 1861, June 5, 1863, March 4, 1867; Gregory to Carlisle, October 24, 1861; *Parl. Deb.*, 3rd ser., CLXXXIII, 1017–26.

27. Derry to Gregory, March 18, 1862; *Parl. Deb.*, 3rd ser., CLXXIX, 1068–74.

28. Gregory to Bess Gregory, October 27, 1863; Duggan to Gregory, May 12, 1865; McEvilly to Gregory, January 22, 1867; *Tuam Herald*, September 10, 1864, and September 23, 30, October 14, November 4, 1865; *Galway Vindicator*, October 4, 1865; E.R. Norman, *Catholic Church in Ireland in the Age of Rebellion, 1859–1873* (London, 1965), pp. 150ff.

29. Gregory to Countess Dartrey, February 6, 1881; Gregory developed his proposals for Ireland in a series of parliamentary speeches, see *Parl. Deb.*, 3rd ser., CLXXXIV, 1168–81, 1456–58; CLXXXVI, 1710–26; CXC, 1703–22.

30. Vincent, *Disraeli, Derby*, p. 231.

31. Gregory's notes on the Viceroyalty in Gregory Papers.

32. Earle to Gregory, August 5, 1866; Brewster to Gregory, July 5, 1866; *Galway*

Vindicator, May 1, 1867; Clonbrock to Gregory, May 6, 1867; Derry to Gregory, March 13, 1867; McEvilly to Gregory, May 3, 1867.

33. Vincent, *Disraeli, Derby*, p. 286; Norman, *Catholic Church*, pp. 194–5, 121–3, 247, 265; Derry to Gregory, May 26, 1868.
34. Gregory to Layard, January 29, 1889; *Parl. Deb.*, 3rd ser., CLXXXV, 1231; Gregory to Disraeli, April 25 (1867).
35. *Day*, May 1, 1867; Gregory to Gladstone, March 1, 1867, Gladstone Papers, BM Add. Ms. 44412; Elcho to Gregory, April 26, 1866; *Parl. Deb.*, 3rd ser., CLXXXII, 1784–1803.
36. Norman, *Catholic Church*, pp. 340, 347ff.
37. *Tuam Herald*, December 5, 1868; *Galway Vindicator*, November 14, 1865; Layard to Gregory, September 6, 1868, BM Add. Ms. 38949; Gregory to Clarendon, December 5, 1868, BM Add. Ms. 44133.

CHAPTER 8

1. Vincent, *Disraeli, Derby*, p. 331; *Gentlemen's Magazine*, CCXXV (1868), 759; Reade to Gregory, April 16, 29, 1867.
2. Gregory to Bess Gregory, March 2, 1875, December 22, 1872, January 9, 1873; Gregory to Augusta Gregory, January 23, 1884.
3. Gregory to Bess Gregory, June 9, 1875, October 9, 1859.
4. Gregory, *Autobiography*, pp. 166–68; Clonbrock to Gregory, April 7, 1867; Derry to Gregory, January 21, 1869; Gregory to Chichester Fortescue, January 23, 1869.
5. Fortescue to Gregory, January 26, 1869; Gladstone to Fortescue, January 30, 1869, Strachie Mss., 324 CPI/26, Somerset Record Office, Taunton; Gregory to Fortescue, February 3, 1869.
6. *Parl. Deb.*, 3rd ser., CXCIV, 1694–1704.
7. *Parl. Deb.*, 3rd ser., CXCVIII, 61–2; Duggan to Gregory, March 13, 14, 24 and May 7, 1869.
8. For a recent discussion of the complicated land question see E. D. Steele, *Irish Land and British Politics: Tenant Right and Nationality 1865–1870* (Cambridge, 1970); Barbara Solow, *The Land Question and the Irish Economy 1870–1903* (Cambridge, Mass., 1971); Paul Bew, *Land and the National Question in Ireland 1858–1882* (Dublin, 1978); Samuel Clark, *Social Origins of the Irish Land War* (Princeton, 1979); T. W. Moody, *Davitt and Irish Revolution 1846–82* (Oxford, 1981); Cusack to Gregory, April 26, 1864.
9. Gregory to F. Waldegrave, September 17 (1869), Strachie Mss., 255 WW27/5; Duggan to Gregory, May 7, 1869; *Tuam Herald*, October 2, 1869; Duggan to Gregory, June 11 (1869); Clonbrock to Gregory, April 15, July 31, 1869; Vincent, *Disraeli, Derby*, p. 345.
10. Duggan to Gregory, July 26, 1869; Gregory to Kelley, July 5, 1869; Gregory to F. Waldegrave, September 17, 1869, Strachie Mss., 255 WW27/5; *Tuam Herald*, October 30, November 13, 1869.
11. Ussher to Gregory, September 23, 1869; *The Times*, October 2, 1869.
12. Bruce to Gregory, October 25, 1869; Steele, *Irish Land*, p. 120ff; Fortescue to Gregory, November 5, 1869.

13. Gregory to Layard, January 16, 1870; *Tuam Herald,* January 15, 1870; McEvilly to Gregory, January 23, 1870.
14. *Tuam Herald,* February 19, March 5, 1870; Duggan to Gregory, March 10, 1870; McEvilly to Gregory, n.d. (March, 1870); Derry to Gregory, March 3, 1870.
15. Lawley to Gregory, March 3, 1870; *The Times,* March 7, 1870.
16. *Parl. Deb.,* 3rd ser., CXCIX, 1745–60; CC, 756, 1303–4.
17. *Tuam Herald,* April 16, 1870; Gregory to Fortescue, (Feb), 1870, Strachie Mss., 322 CP3/100; *Tuam Herald,* May 28, 1870.
18. Duggan to Gregory, April 28, 1870; Longford to Gregory, Christmas, 1872.
19. *Parl. Deb.,* 3rd ser., CC, 90; CCIV, 1013–16; CCVI, 1784.
20. See Solow, *Land Question and Irish Economy.*
21. Derry to Gregory, September 23, 1869; McEvilly to Gregory, March 26, 1868, June 1, 1870; Gregory to F. Waldegrave, September 17 (1869), Strachie Mss., 255 WW 27/5; Gregory to F. Waldegrave, October 30, 1870, Strachie Mss., 255 WW 27/4; Donald H. Akenson, *The Irish Education Experiment The National System of Education in the Nineteenth Century* (London, 1970), p. 316; J. C. Beckett, *The Making of Modern Ireland 1603–1923* (London, 1966), p. 380.
22. *Tuam Herald,* June 10, 1865.
23. *Parl. Deb.,* 3rd ser., CLV, 442; CXCI, 383–96; CLVII, 2158; CLXIV, 1320–26; CLXVI, 1906–13; CLXXI, 913–24.
24. Layard to Gregory, September 27, 1860, BM Add. Ms. 38949; *Parl. Deb.,* 3rd ser., CLXXI, 913–24; CLXXII, 120–30; CLIII, 250–9.
25. Gregory, *Autobiography,* pp. 210–11, 221–2; *The Scotsman,* June 11, 1863; *Parl. Deb.,* 3rd ser., CLXXXIX, 346.
26. *Parl. Deb.,* 3rd ser., CLXXI, 525.
27. *Parl. Deb.,* 3rd ser., CXCVI, 1254–68; CCI, 343; *Day,* April 5, 1867.
28. See David Robertson, *Sir Charles Eastlake and the Victorian Art World* (Princeton, 1978); 'The National Gallery', *Gentlemen's Magazine,* CCII (1857), 50–54; 'National Gallery', *Quarterly Review,* CV (1859), 341–81; Eastlake to Gregory, June 13, 1864; *Parl. Deb.,* 3rd ser., CLXXV, 1315.
29. Gregory to Mason, November 5, 1862, Mason Papers; Gregory to Bess Gregory, October 27, November 3, 24, December 13, 1863; Gregory to Layard, August 31, November 28, 1872.
30. Robinson to Gregory, January 14, 24, 1866; Gregory, *Autobiography,* p. 98; Gregory to Layard, January 30, 1889.
31. Gregory wrote an account of the history and activities of the Arundel Society which was first published in *Nineteenth Century,* LXXXVI (1884) and subsequently issued by the society as a pamphlet (1887); Oldfield to Gregory, June 6, 1868; William N. Bruce, ed., *Sir A. Henry Layard Autobiography and Letters,* 2 vols. (London, 1903), II, 203; Gregory to Layard, November 26, 1870; Robinson to Gregory, January 14, 1867; Gregory to Layard, September 12, 1868.
32. Robinson to Gregory, January 14, 1869; Boxall to Gregory, September 9, 1870; Gregory to Layard, February 11, 18, March 9, 24, 1871; Peel to Gregory, March 7, 1871; *Parl. Deb.,* 3rd ser., CCV, 314.
33. Gregory, *Autobiography,* p. 254; Gregory to Layard, April 10, 16, May 14, 1870; Boxall to Gregory, August 6, 1870; Barry to Gregory, March 18, 1871.
34. *The Architect,* February 27, 1869.
35. Derek Hudson, ed., *Munby, Man of Two Worlds: The Life and Diaries of Arthur*

J. Munby 1828–1910 (London, 1972), p. 25; Gordon Waterfield, *Layard of Nineveh* (London, 1963), pp. 310, 453–4.

36. Trevelyan to Gregory, August 7, 1868; Gregory to Trevelyan, February 3, 1869; *Parl. Deb.*, 3rd ser., CLXCV, 1202–16; *The Architect*, February 27, 1869.
37. Arnold C. Brackman, *The Luck of Nineveh; Archaeology's Great Adventure* (New York, 1978), p. 293; Layard to Gregory, February 2, March 5, July 22, 1870; Gregory to Layard, February 27, 1870.
38. Gregory, *Autobiography*, pp. 255–56; Vincent, *Disraeli, Derby*, p. 199; F. Leveson Gower, *Bygone Years* (London, 1905), pp. 275–6.
39. F. Waldegrave to Gregory, October 26, 29, 31, 1869; Granville to F. Waldegrave, October 28, November 5, 1869; Fortescue to Gregory, November 5, 1869; Lawley to Gregory, June 28, 1870; Osbert Wyndham, *Strawberry Fair; A Biography of Frances, Countess Waldegrave 1821–1879* (London, 1956), p. 208; Gregory to F. Waldegrave, n.d. (1870), Strachie Mss., 255 WW27/2; Lawley to Gregory, n.d. (1870).
40. Gregory to Layard, August 8, 28, 1870, January 3, 1872, October 23, November 14, 26, December 12, 1870, January 12, 1871; Morris to Gregory, December 14, 1871.
41. *New York Tribune*, August 22, 1871; *Galway Vindicator*, December 2, 1871; Shannon to Gregory, December 27, 1871; Clanricarde to Gregory, August 28, 1872; *Galway Vindicator*, February 8, 1871.
42. McEvilly to Gregory, February 7, March 1, 1871; Roche to Gregory, February 22, 1871; *Galway Vindicator*, February 8, 1871; Lavelle to Gregory, July 11, 1871.
43. *Galway Vindicator*, July 29, 1871, January, 6, 10, 24, 1872; *Tuam Herald*, November 4, 1871, February 10, 1872; Gregory, *Autobiography*, p. 252; see also ms of *Autobiography*.
44. Clonbrock to Gregory, September 16, May 30, 1872; McEvilly to Gregory, November 28, 1872; Norman, *Catholic Church*, p. 424; *Tuam Herald*, June 1, 1872; Michael Hurst, 'Ireland and the Ballot Act of 1872', *Historical Journal*, VIII (1965), 326–52.
45. Doneraile to Gregory, August 1, 1872; Redington to Gregory, February 23, 1874; Norman, *Catholic Church*, pp. 428–30; Hutt to Bess Gregory, October 18, 1872.

CHAPTER 9

1. Clay to Gergory, February 12, 1863; Osborne to Gregory, February 8, 1863, January 21, 1866; Gregory to Layard, November 30, 1867.
2. Webb to Gregory, January 27, 1866; the state of Gregory's finances and his social life are documented in fragmentary form in a surviving engagement book for 1867.
3. Marriage settlement; Gregory to Layard, November 19, 1871.
4. Julia Bell to Gregory, October 26, 1872; Gregory to Layard, February 11, March 24, 1871; Sir James Emerson Tennent, *Ceylon*, 2 vols. 5th ed. (London, 1860); Ferguson, *Samuel Ferguson*, II, 115.
5. Gregory, *Autobiography*, p. 296; Lennox Mills, *Ceylon Under British Rule*

1795–1932 (London, 1933), pp. 168ff; Ferguson to Gregory, December 12, 1871.

6. Lord Spencer to Gregory, June 29, 1871; Gregory to Bess Gregory, January 26, February 9, 1872.
7. Ms. of *Autobiography*; Gregory to Bess Gregory, March 3, 1872.
8. Gregory, *Autobiography*, pp. 270ff; Gregory to Bess Gregory, March 5, 1872.
9. K. M. de Silva, ed., *Sri Lanka A Survey* (London, 1977), pp. 31ff; Gregory, *Autobiography*, pp. 278ff; see also ms of *Autobiography* for comments on Dunawilla.
10. Gregory, *Autobiography*, pp. 289–90; Gregory to Kimberley, October 15, 1872, Colonial Office (CO) 54/478; Gregory to Kimberley, February 3, 1873, CO 54/484.
11. Lizzie Gregory to Bess Gregory, April 6, 1872; Gregory to Layard, October 24, 1871; Gregory to Bess Gregory, June 21, 1872.
12. Gregory, *Autobiography*, pp. 312–13; see also ms of *Autobiography*; Gregory to Bess Gregory, September 30, 1872.
13. Gregory to Layard, June (1872).
14. Gregory to Layard, (June), 1872, August 31, November 28, 1872.
15. Robinson to Gregory, February 9, 1872; Gregory to Kimberley, March 30, 1872, CO 54/475; Gregory to Wall, July 25, 1872; Gregory to Carnarvon, June 19, 1875, CO 54/497.
16. Gregory to Kimberley, January 2, February 6, 1874; Gregory, *Autobiography*, p. 317.
17. Gregory's Address, September 25, 1872, CO 54/478; Gregory to Kimberley, March 21, 1872; Kimberley to Gregory, April 19, 1872; Hooker to Gregory, July 12, 1871; Gregory to Kimberley, August 3, 1872; Frederick Lewis, 'A Few Pioneer Estates and Early Pioneers in Ceylon', *Colombo Historical Association Papers*, X (1927).
18. Gregory to Herbert, June 10, 1872; Gregory to Kimberley, June 19, 1872, CO 54/476; Gregory to Kimberley, July 9, August 3, 1872, CO 54/477; Gregory to Kimberley, October 9, 1872, CO 54/478; Gregory to Kimberley, January 31, 1873, CO 54/484.
19. *Dublin University Magazine*, LXXXVIII (1876), 153; Gregory to Blunt, October 5, 1884, Berg Collection; Gregory to Kimberley, November 14, 1872, CO 54/479.
20. Gregory to Bess Gregory, March 31, 1872; Gregory, *Autobiography*, pp. 315–16; see also ms of *Autobiography*; Gregory to Kimberley, March 5, 1873, CO 54/484.
21. De Silva, *Sri Lanka*, pp. 32ff; Mills *Ceylon under British Rule*, pp. 132–3; Gregory to Bess Gregory, July 21, 1872; Gregory to Kimberley, January 31, 1873, CO 54/484.
22. Gregory to Kimberley, July 31, 1873, CO 54/487.
23. Gregory to Kimberley, June 7, 1872, CO 54/476; Gregory to Layard, June (1872); Kimberley to Gregory, September 19, 1872; Gregory to Kimberley, March 17, 1873, CO 54/484; Layard to Gregory, June 18, 1873, BM Add. Ms. 38949.
24. Gregory to Bess Gregory, May 8, 1873, October 14, 1872; Gregory to Layard, June (1872); Lizzie Gregory to Bess Gregory, May 24, 1872; Gregory to Bess Gregory, June 8, 1873.
25. Cameron to Gregory, April 30, 1873; Gregory to Bess Gregory, June 23, 1873; Constance Cummings to Gregory, n.d. (1873); Gregory to Bess Gregory, June

28, 1873; ms of *Autobiography.*
26. Gregory to Bess Gregory, June 28, 1873; Elizabeth (Lizzie) Gregory's will; Gregory to Bess Gregory, August 17, 1873.
27. Gregory to Layard, August 12, 1873; F. Waldegrave to Gregory, November 7, 1873; Gregory to Bess Gregory, October 13, 1873.
28. Gregory to Kimberley, June 24, 1873, CO 54/486; Gregory's address July 30, 1873, CO 54/487.
29. Gregory to Kimberley, January 8, 1874, CO 54/492; Gregory to Kimberley, February 15, 1874, CO 54/492.
30. Kimberley to Gregory, January 1, 1874, CO 54/489; Kimberley to Gregory, December 25, 1873; Gregory to Bess Gregory, December 8, 1873.

CHAPTER 10

1. Hamilton to Gregory, April 1, 1874; Gregory to Carnarvon, March 18, 1874, Carnarvon Papers, PRO 30/6/37; Gregory to Layard, December 8, 1877.
2. Gregory to Carnarvon, June 28, 1874, PRO 30/6/37; Gregory memorandum, June 2, 1874, PRO 30/6/37; Gregory to Carnarvon, CO 54/493; Gregory to Carnarvon, June 12, 1874.
3. Gregory to Bess Gregory, July 16, 20, 24, 30, August 5, 1874.
4. Gregory to Lady Dilke, October 14, 1874, Dilke Papers, BM Add. Ms. 43902; Gregory to Bess Gregory, February 12, 1875; Berwick to Gregory, February 18, 1884; Layard to Gregory, February 26, 1874, BM Add. Ms. 38949; Frederick Lewis, 'The Governorship of Sir W. H. Gregory', *Colombo Historical Association Papers*, XVI (1930).
5. Birch to Carnarvon, January 5, 1876, CO 54/500; Gregory to Carnarvon, March 28, 1876, CO 54/501; Gregory to Layard, February 16, 1875.
6. Gregory to Bess Gregory, March 2, 17, April 1, 1875; Cameron to Gregory, May 5, 1875; Gregory to Carnarvon, October 28, 1874, PRO 30/6/37; Carnarvon to Gregory, December 10, 1874.
7. Gregory to Bess Gregory, July 16, August 1, 19, September 2, 12, 29, October 23, November 10, 1875; Carnarvon to Gregory, September 20, October 25, 1875, PRO 30/6/37; Bartle Frere to Gregory, September 1, 1875; W. H. Russell to Gregory, November 12, 1875; see also W. H. Russell, *The Prince of Wales' Tour in India* (Montreal, 1877), pp. 221ff; Herbert to Gregory, May 12, 1876.
8. Gregory to Carnarvon, December 9, 1875, PRO 30/6/37; Gregory to Cambridge, December 17, 1875; Gregory to Bess Gregory, December 9, 1875; Gregory to Layard, n.d. (spring, 1876).
9. Gregory to Layard, n.d. (1875); Gregory to Bess Gregory, November 24, 1875; Gregory to Layard, February 16, 1875; Gregory to Carnarvon, September 26, 1876, PRO 30/6/37; Layard to Gregory, May 8, 1875, BM Add. Ms. 38949.
10. Ferguson to Gregory, March 29, 1875; Gregory to Carnarvon, March 3, 1875, CO 54/496; Gregory to Carnarvon, March 30, 1875, PRO 30/6/37; Carnarvon to Gregory, May 10, 1875; Gregory to Carnarvon, November 15, 1876.

11. Gregory to Carnarvon, June 21, 1875, PRO 30/6/37; Biship Bonjean to Gregory, December 9, 18, 1874, May 9, 1876, May 7, 1877.
12. Gregory to Carnarvon, November 18, 1877, July 4, 1876, PRO 30/6/37; Gregory to Layard, July 4, 1876; Layard to Gregory, August 13, 1876, BM Add. Ms. 38949.
13. Gregory to Layard, September 26, 1876; Gregory to Carnarvon November 10, 23, 1876, CO 54/504.
14. Gregory to Layard, April 10, 1877; Robinson to Gregory, September 21, 1877; Gregory to Leveson Gower, April 14, 1891.
15. *Lady Gregory's Journals*, I, 527–8, 534; Gregory to Bess Gregory, June 4, 1872, May 8, December 8, 1873, January 4, 1874, July 16, August 19, September 2, October 25, 1875; Gregory to Layard, December 8, 1877.
16. Gregory to Layard, September 27, October 17, 1877.
17. Gregory to Layard, April 6, December 15, 1873; Ferguson, *Samuel Ferguson*, I, 298; Wilson, *Victorian Doctor*, pp. 144–5; Gregory to Layard, April 25, 1874; Burton to Gregory, April 15, 1875, April 16, 1876; Layard to Gregory, August 13, 1876, BM Add. Ms. 38949.
18. Gregory to Layard, July 10, 1877, March 12, May 23, 1878, August 7, December 11, 1879; Hankey to Gregory, March 15, 1877.
19. Gregory to Layard, September 26, 1876; *Tuam Herald*, June 9, September 1, 1877; Redington to Gregory, June 16, August 1, 1877; Layard to Gregory, September 12, 1877, BM Add. MS. 38949; Gregory to Layard, September 27, 1877.
20. Gregory to Marlborough, November 9, 1878; Duggan to Gregory, January 15, 1879.
21. Gregory to Hankey, September 18, 1878; Shannon to Hogan, April 27, 1879; Gregory to Henry, November 7, 1879.
22. Gregory to Layard, August 7, December 11, 1879.
23. Gregory to Layard, August 7, 1879; Thomas to Gregory, August 20, 1879; Cayley to Gregory, June 27, 1879.
24. Duggan to Gregory, December 15, 16, 23, 1879.
25. Moody, *Davitt*, p. 315; Duggan to Gregory, December 23, 1879.
26. Gregory to Bess Gregory, October 29, 1873; Strandril to Gregory, September 3, 1878.
27. Lady Gregory, *Seventy Years: Being the Autobiography of Lady Gregory* (Gerrards Cross, 1974), pp. 1–28; Gregory to Augusta Persse, March 21, 1879.
28. Gregory to Augusta Persse, September 16, December 23, 1879, January 28, February 1, 1880.
29. O'Hara to Gregory, February 14, 1880; Redington to Gregory, February 15, 1880; Gregory to Layard, February 15, 1880; Gregory to Augusta Persse, February 16, 1880.
30. Gregory to Layard, March 9, 1880, May 17, 1883; Enid Layard Diary, May 7, 1880, BM Add. Ms. 46157; see also Lady Gregory's Diary for 1880; Gregory to Layard, January 6, 1883.
31. Gregory to Layard, October 26, 1880.

CHAPTER 11

1. See Lady Gregory's Diary; Gregory to Layard, September 3, 1881.
2. Gregory to Layard, October 9, November 27, 1881.
3. Gregory to Countess Dartrey, February 20, 1882; Gregory to Layard, May 4, January 2, 1882.
4. Gregory to Layard, November 27, 1881, February 20, 1882.
5. Gregory to Blunt, March (April) 4, 1882, May 2 (1882) Berg Coll.
6. Elizabeth Longford, *A Pilgrimage of Passion, The Life of Wilfrid Blunt* (London, 1979); Gregory to Layard, May 4, 1882; D. A. Farnie, *East and West of Suez The Suez Canal in History 1854–1956* (Oxford, 1969), p. 285.
7. Gregory to Augusta Gregory, January 17, 1884; Gregory to Layard, October 12, November 25, 1882.
8. Gregory to Layard, June 27, 1883; Gregory to Blunt, May 23 (1883), February 6, August 24, 1884, Berg Coll; Longford, *Pilgrimage of Passion*, pp. 191–2; Longden to Gregory, November 28, December 1, 1884; Gregory to Baring, May 20, 1890; Gregory, *Seventy Years*, pp. 33–55, 203–261.
9. Enid Layard Diary, April 24, 1882, BM Add. Ms. 46160; Gregory to Layard, April 16, August 31, 1882, May 17, 1883; Countess Dartrey to Gregory, April 24, 1883; Gregory to Augusta Gregory, April 8, 1884.
10. Gregory to Layard, October 26, December 26, 1880, March 21, August 5, 1881; Burton to Gregory, April 7, 1880; Gregory to Layard, June 22, 29, 1882.
11. Gregory to Layard, April 30, 1884; Gregory to Augusta Gregory, September 3, 1884.
12. Gregory to Layard, October 23, 1886; Layard to Gregory, January 12, 1889, BM Add. Ms. 38950; 'The National Gallery', *Quarterly Review*, CLXIII (1886), 396.
13. Gregory to Layard, July 31, 1888; Mansfield to Gregory, June 10, 1885; Roseberry to Gregory, June 11, 1885; Gregory to Augusta Gregory, June 12, 1885.
14. Gregory to Lee Childe, February 25, 1884; Gregory to Layard, February 22, 1884; Gregory to Gordon, October 11, 1886, Stanmore Papers, BM Add. Ms. 49207.
15. Gregory to Lee Childe, April 24, 1884, Berg Coll.
16. Gregory to Augusta Gregory, August 3, 1885; Gregory to Layard, January 5, 18, February 2, 19, 27, 1886; J. E. Tyler, *The Struggle for Imperial Unity 1868–1895* (London, 1938); G. C. Eldridge, *England's Mission The Imperial Idea in the Age of Gladstone and Disraeli 1868–1880* (Chapel Hill, 1975), pp. 120–141; Forster to Gregory, December 26, 1884; Gregory to Layard, December 2, 1884.
17. Gregory, *Autobiography*, p. 359; Fahy to Gregory, January 15, August 17, 1880.
18. See W. E. Vaughan, 'An Assessment of the economic performance of Irish landlords, 1851–1881', in Lyons and Hawkins, *Ireland under the Union*, pp. 173–199; although the estate records are fragmentary (Lady Gregory destroyed most of them) it is possible to compare rents in 1857 with those in 1880; Gregory to Shannon, May 1, 1882.
19. Gregory to Layard, August 27, October 10, December 5, 1880.
20. For the land war and British policy see Clark, *Social Origins*; Bew, *Land and the National Question*; and Thomas William Heyck, *The Dimensions of British Radicalism The Case of Ireland 1874–95* (Chicago, 1974); Gregory to Layard, October 10, 1880; Clonbrock to Gregory, October 2, 17, 1880; Countess

Dartrey to Gregory, November 16, December 10, 1880.
21. Monck to Gregory, November 4, 6, 16, 1880; Gregory to ? December 5, 1880.
22. Clonbrock to Gregory, January 13, March 28, April 23, 1881; Gregory to Augusta Gregory, March 31, February 25, 1881.
23. De Vere to Gregory, April 6, 1881; Morris to Gregory, March 29, April 13, 1881; Solow, *Land Question and Irish Economy*, p. 161; Dufferin to Gregory, January 31, 1882.
24. Gregory to Countess Dartrey, April 12, 1881.
25. Franks to Gregory, June 30, July 3, 1881.
26. Monck to Gregory, November 14, 1881; Countess Dartrey to Gregory, November 11, December 12, 1881, January 3, 1882; Dillon to Gregory, November 26, 1881; Gregory to Layard, September 3, October 9, 1881.
27. Gregory to Countess Dartrey, February 20, 1882; Constabulary Report, January 18, 1882, Chief Secretary's Office, Registered Papers (CSORP) 4024, State Paper Office, Dublin Castle; Franks to Gregory, January 29, 1882; Gregory to Shannon, May 1, 1882; Shannon to Gregory, April 21, 1882; Livie Franks to Gregory, April 18, 1882; Dillon to Gregory, May 10, 1882.
28. Gregory to Layard, June 2, 29, 1882; Gregory to Hamilton, n.d. (July/August), 1882; Gregory to Trevelyan, December 1, 1882, CSORP (1882), 45590.
29. Gregory to Layard, December 16, 1882; Gregory to Countess Dartrey, October 23, 1883; Gregory to Layard, November 8, 1883; Gregory to Countess Dartrey, May 2, 1885.
30. K. Buckley, 'The fixing of rents by agreement in co. Galway, 1881–5', *Irish Historical Studies*, VII (1951), 149–79; K. Buckley, 'The records of the Irish land commission as a source of historical evidence', *Irish Historical Studies*, VIII (1952), 28–36; Gregory to Layard, September 3, November 15, 1886, November 15, 1887.
31. Gregory to Augusta Gregory, February 13 (1882); Gregory to Layard, August 5, 1886; William L. Feingold, 'The Tenants' Movement to Capture the Irish Poor Law Boards, 1877–1886', *Albion*, VII (1975), 216–231; Countess Dartrey to Gregory, October 13, 1884; Gregory to Countess Dartrey, September 1, 1883.
32. Boyle to Gregory, August 5, 1884; Gregory to Countess Dartrey, August 17, 1884; Gregory to Augusta Gregory, July 29 (1884); Gregory to Layard, April 5, 1884; Gregory to Countess Dartrey, May 2, 17, 24, June 22, 1885.
33. D. A. Hamer, 'The Irish Question and Liberal Politics, 1886–1894', *Historical Journal*, XII (1969), 511–32; Gregory to Layard, February 2, 1886; Gregory to Countess Dartrey, May 1, 1886; Gregory to Layard, June 16, 1886; Gregory to Grant Duff, June 13, July 8, 1886; Gregory to Gordon, July 26, 1886, BM. Add. Ms. 49207.
34. Gregory to Countess Dartrey, October 12, 1883, April 8, 1886; Kavanagh to Gregory, August 17, 1885; Gregory to Layard, November 23, 1886; see also Patrick Buckland, *The Anglo–Irish and the New Ireland 1885–1922* (Dublin, 1972), pp. 1–18.
35. Gregory to Augusta Gregory, October 30, 1886; Gregory to Layard, December 4, 1886, July 11, November 27, 1887.
36. *Lady Gregory's Journals*, I, 332–3; Augusta Gregory to Grant Duff, May 7, 1886; Gregory to Augusta Gregory, October 30, 1886; Fahy to Gregory, October 24, 1886; Gregory to Layard, October 23, 1886; Solow, *Land Question and Irish Economy*, pp. 186–9; John P. Huttman, 'Fenians and

Farmers: The Merger of the Home–Rule and Owner–Occupancy Movements in Ireland, 1850–1915', *Albion*, III (1971), 189–90.

37. Gregory to Layard, January 8, 1891, January 27, October 28, 1888, February 24, May 9, 1889.
38. Augusta Gregory to Grant Duff, May 7, 1886; Layard to Gregory, December 18, 1890, BM Add. Ms. 38950; Gregory to Layard, November 18, December 12, 1890.
39. Gregory to Layard, February 22, 1891.
40. Gregory to Augusta Gregory, January 4, 12, 1884, October 4, 1885, October 3, 1883; Gregory to Layard, December 4, 1886; Gregory, *Autobiography*, pp. 80–95; Gregory to Layard, December 18, 1888; Gregory to Augusta Gregory, July 15, 1889.
41. Fanny Geary to Gregory, September 18, 1883; Layard to Gregory, October 17, 1887, BM Add. Ms. 38950; Gregory to Layard, December 18, 1883; *Lady Gregory's Journals*, I, 614; Gregory to Layard, August 23, December 7, 1889, October 20, 1890, January 10, 1892.
42. Gregory to Augusta Gregory, May 31, 1887; Gregory to Layard, October 18, 1889, October 20, 1890, August 12, 14, 1891; Gregory, *Autobiography*, pp. 262–3; Augusta Gregory to Basterot, March 17, 1892; *Lady Gregory's Journals*, I, 232.

Select Bibliography
Primary Sources

PRIVATE PAPERS

C. F. Adams. Massachusetts Historical Society. Microfilm.
Beaconsfield (Disraeli). Bodleian Library, Oxford.
Edmund Burke. Sheffield Central Library.
Carnarvon. Public Record Office, London.
Clarendon. Bodleian Library.
Clanricarde. Leeds Public Library.
Sir Charles Dilke. British Museum.
Fitzwilliam. Sheffield Central Library.
Philip Francis. India Office Library, London.
Lady Gregory. Berg Collection, New York Public Library.
Sir William Gregory.
Richard Gregory, National Library of Ireland.
W. H. Gregory — Edmund O'Flaherty Correspondence. National Library of Ireland.
William Gladstone. British Museum.
Henry Goulburn. Surrey Record Office, Kingston.
Warren Hastings. British Museum.
Sir A. Henry Layard. British Museum.
Lady Layard, Journals. British Museum.
F. Leveson – Gower. Irish Record Office, Dublin.
Charles Longley. Lambeth Palace Library and Harrow School.
J. M. Mason. Library of Congress, Washington D. C.
Mayo. National Library of Ireland.
W. P. Miles. Southern Historical Collection, Chapel Hill, North Carolina.
Newcastle. British Museum.
Palmerston. Historical Manuscripts Commission, London.
Sir Robert Peel. British Museum.
Rockingham. Sheffield Central Library.
Russell. Public Record Office.
Stanmore. British Museum.
Strachie (Waldegrave and Carlingford). Somerset Record Office, Taunton.
Wellesley. British Museum.

PUBLISHED PAPERS

The Correspondence of Edmund Burke, ed. by Thomas Copeland et al., 10 vols., Cambridge, 1958–78.
The Correspondence of Daniel O'Connell, ed. by Maurice R. O'Connell, 8 vols., Dublin, 1972-81.
Egypt in 1855 and 1856; Tunis in 1857 and 1858, by W. H. Gregory, 2 vols., London, privately printed, 1859.
Sir William Gregory, K.C.M.G,... An Autobiography, ed. by Lady Gregory, London, 1894. New edition Gerrards Cross, 1986.
Mr. Gregory's Letter-Box, ed. by Lady Gregory, London, 1898. New edition, Gerrards Cross, 1981.

PUBLIC PAPERS

Chief Secretary's Office, Registered Papers, State Paper Office, Dublin Castle.
Colonial Office, Ceylon Correspondence, Public Record Office, London.
Devon Commission, part 4, National Library of Ireland.
East India Company, Court Minutes and Ledger Books, India Office Library.
Hansard's Parliamentary Debates.
Parliamentary History of England from the Earliest Period to the Year 1803.
Parliamentary Papers: Bribery at Elections, vol. 1, Shannon, 1968.
Parliamentary Papers: Famine (Ireland), 8 vols., Shannon, 1968.
The Three Reports from the Select Committee of the House of Lords appointed to inquire into Laws Respecting Gaming, *Parliamentary Papers*, VI (1844), 281–486.
Report from the Select Committee on Gaming, *Parliamentary Papers*, VI (1844), 3–279.
Report of the Commissioners appointed to investigate into the existence of Corrupt Practices in Elections of Members to serve in Parliament for the County of the Town of Galway, *Parliamentary Papers*, XXVI (1857–8), 307–531.
Official Records of the Union and Confederate Navies in the War of Rebellion. 31 vols., Washington, 1894–1927.
Ordnance Survey Letters (Galway), National Library of Ireland.
Relief Commission Papers, Public Record Office, Ireland.

Newspapers and Periodicals

The Architect
Bell's Life in London
Blackwood's Magazine
The Classical Review
Day
Dublin Evening Herald
Dublin Evening Mail
Dublin Monitor
Dublin World
The Edinburgh Review
The Fortnightly Review
The Freeman's Journal
Galway American
Galway Express

Galway Mercury
Galway Vindicator
The Gentlemen's Magazine
The Nation
The Nineteenth Century
Quarterly Review
The Racing Calendar
Saunder's News–Letter
Sporting Life
Sportsman's Almanack
The Sportsman's Magazine
The Times
The Taum Herald
The Warder

Secondary Sources

Books

Akenson, Donald H. *The Irish Education Experiment The National System of Education in the Nineteenth Century.* Toronto, 1970.
Anglesey, *One–Leg The Life and Letters of Henry William Paget First Marquess of Anglesey K. G. 1768–1854.* London, 1961.
Ashton, John. *The History of Gambling in England.* reprint, New York, 1968.
Bailey, William F. *Local and Centralized Government in Ireland.* London, 1888.
Barrington, Jonah. *Recollections of Jonah Barrington.* Dublin.
Barry, F. V. *Maria Edgeworth Chosen Letters.* London, 1931.
Bartlett, C. J. *Castlereagh.* New York, 1966.
Beckett, J. C. *The Making of Modern Ireland 1603–1923.* London, 1966.

— *The Anglo-Irish Tradition.* London, 1976.

Bew, Paul. *Land and the National Question in Ireland 1858–1882.* Dublin, 1978.

Bill, E. G. W. and Mason, J. F. A. *Christ Church and Reform 1850–1867.* Oxford, 1970.

Bird, T. H. *Admiral Rous and the English Turf 1795–1877.* London, 1939.

Black, Robert. *Horse–Racing in England A Synoptical Review.* London, 1893.

Bolton, G. C. *The Passing of the Irish Act of Union A Study in Parliamentary Politics.* Oxford, 1966.

Bowen, Desmond. *The Protestant Crusade in Ireland 1800–1870.* Montreal, 1978.

Brackman, Arnold C. *The Luke of Nineveh: Archaeology's Great Adventure.* New York, 1978.

Breffny, Brian and ffoliott, Rosemary. *The Houses of Ireland: Domestic Architecture from the medieval castle to the Edwardian villa.* London, 1975.

Broeker, Galen. *Rural Disorder and Police Reform in Ireland 1812–1836.* London, 1970.

Brown, Thomas. *Politics of Irish Literature From Thomas Davis to W. B. Yeats.* London, 1972.

Bruce, William N. ed. *Sir Henry Layard Autobiography and Letters,* 2 vols. London, 1903.

Bryn, Edward. *Crown and Castle British Rule in Ireland 1800–1830.* Dublin, 1978.

Buckland, Patrick. *The Anglo–Irish and the New Ireland 1885–1922.* Dublin, 1972.

Burke, Oliver J. *Anecdotes of the Connaught Circuit.* Dublin, 1885.

Butler, Lord. ed. *The Conservatives A History from their Origins to 1965.* London, 1977.

Cannon, John. *The Fox–North Coalition Crisis of the Constitution 1782–1784.* Cambridge, 1969.

Carlyle, Thomas. *Reminiscences of My Irish Journey in 1849.* London, 1882.

Chaudhuri, Nirad C. *Clive of India: A Political and Psychological Essay.* London, 1975.

Chesney, Kellow. *Victorian Underworld.* London, 1970.

Christie, Ian R. *The End of North's Ministry 1780–1782.* London, 1958

Clarke, Samuel. *Social Origins of the Irish Land War.* Princeton, 1979.

Colton, Calvin. *Four Years in Great Britain.* 2 vols. New York, 1836.

Conacher, J. B. *The Peelites and the Party System 1846–1852.* Newton Abbot, 1972.

Connell, Brian. *Regina v. Palmerston.* London, 1962.

Cook, T. A. *A History of the English Turf.* Two divisions, 6 vols. London, n.d.

Cooke, A. B. and Vincent, J. R. *Lord Carlingford's Journal Reflections of a Cabinet Minister 1885.* Oxford, 1971.

Couch, Lilian M. Quiller. *Reminiscences of Oxford by Oxford Men 1559–1850.* Oxford, 1892.

Coulter, Henry. *The West of Ireland Its Existence Condition and Prospects.* Dublin, 1862.

Cowling, Maurice. *1867 Disraeli, Gladstone and Revolution The Passing of the second Reform Bill.* Cambridge, 1967.

Curtis, L. P. jr. *Anglo–Saxons and Celts: A Study of Anti–Irish Prejudice in Victorian England.* Bridgeport, 1968.

— *Coercion and Conciliation in Ireland, 1880–1892: A Study in Conservative Unionism.* Princeton, 1963.

Curzon, Louis Henry. *A Mirror of the Turf or The Machinery of Horse-Racing revealed showing the Sport of Kings as it is To–Day.* London, 1892.

Day, William. *Reminiscences of the Turf with Anecdotes and Recollections of its*

Principal Celebrities. London, 1886.

Danglish, M. G. and Stephenson, P. K. *Harrow School Register 1800–1911.* London, 1911.

Davies, C. Collin. *Warren Hastings and Oudh.* London, 1939.

De Silva, K. M. *Sri Lanka A Survey.* London, 1977.

Dodds, John W. *The Age of Paradox A Biography of England 1841–1851.*Westport, Conn., 1970.

Donnelly, James S. jr. *The Land and the People in Nineteenth Century Cork: The Rural Economy and the Land Question.* London, 1975.

Edwards, R. Dudley and Williams, T. Desmond. *The Great Famine: Studies in Irish History 1845–1852.* Dublin, 1956.

Eldridge, G. C. *England's Mission The Imperial Idea in the Age of Gladstone and Disraeli 1868–1880.* Chapel Hill, 1973.

Emden, Paul H. *Regency Pageant.* London, 1936.

Fahy, Jerome. *History and Antiquities of the Diocese of Kilmacduagh.* Dublin, 1893.

Falkiner, C. Litton. *Studies in Irish History and Biography.* London, 1902.

Farnie, D. A. *East and West of Suez The Suez Canal in History 1854–1956.* Oxford, 1969.

Feiling, Keith. *Warren Hastings.* Reprint, London, 1966.

Ferguson, M. C. *Sir Samuel Ferguson in the Ireland of His Day.* 2 vols., London, 1896.

Flanagan, Thomas. *The Irish Novelists 1800–1850.* New York, 1959.

Foster, Thomas Campbell. *Letters on the Condition of the People of Ireland.* London, 1847.

Gale, Frederick. *Life of Hon. Robert Grimston.* London, 1885.

Gamble, John. *Sketches of History, Politics, and Manners in Dublin and the North of England in 1810.* London, 1826.

Gardiner, Brian. *The East India Company: A History.* New York, 1972.

— *The Public Schools: An Historical Survey.* London, 1973.

Gash, Norman. *Mr. Secretary Peel The Life of Sir Robert Peel to 1830.*London, 1961.

— *Politics in the Age of Peel.* London, 1953.

Gantz, Ida. *Signpost to Eyrecourt.* Bath, 1975.

Gilbert, John T. *A History of the City of Dublin.* 3 vols., reprint, Shannon, 1972.

Graham, Edward. *The Harrow Life of Henry Montagu Butler D. D.* London, 1920.

Graham, Gerald S. *Great Britain and the Indian Ocean.* Oxford, 1967.

Gregory, Augusta, Lady. *Coole.* Dublin, 1931. Enlarged ed., Dublin, 1971.

— *Autobiography of the Right Honourable Sir William Gregory K.C.M.G., F.R.S.* London, 1894.

— *Seventy Years: Being the Autobiography of Lady Gregory.* Gerrards Cross, 1974, New York, 1976.

Gregory, Vere R. T. *The House of Gregory.* Dublin, 1943.

Greville, Charles C. F. *The Greville Memoirs.* London, 1887.

Grosskurth, Phyllis. *The Woeful Victorian A Biography of John Addington Symonds* New York, 1964.

Gun, W. T. J. *Harrow School Register 1571–1800.* London, 1934.

Gupta, Brijen K. *Sirajaddaullah and the East India Company, 1756–1757 Background to the Foundation of British Power in India.* Leiden, 1966.

Guttsman, W. L. *The British Political Elite.* London, 1963.

Gwynn, Denis. *Daniel O'Connell The Irish Liberator.* London, 1929.

Gwynn, Stephen, *Dublin Old and New.* New York, 1938.

Gathorne-Hardy, Jonathan. *The Public School Phenomenon 1597–1977.* London, 1977.

Harris, Richard. ed. *The Reminiscences of Sir Henry Hawkins Baron Brampton.* 2 vols., London, 1904.

Head, Francis B. *A Fortnight in Ireland.* London, 1852.

Hewett, O. W. *Strawberry Fair: A Biography of Frances, Countess Waldegrave.* London, 1956.

Heyck, Thomas William. *The Dimensions of British Radicalism The Case of Ireland 1874–95.* Chicago, 1974.

Holzman, James M. *The Nabobs in England A Study of the Returned Anglo-Indian 1760–1785.* New York, 1926.

Howson, Edmund W. and Warner, George Townsend. *Harrow School.* London, 1898.

Hudson, Derek. ed. *Munby Man of Two Worlds: The Life and Diaries of Arthur J. Munby 1828–1910.* London, 1972.

Hulton, A. W. ed. Arthur Young's *A Tour of Ireland 1776–1779.* 2 vols. new edition, Shannon, 1970.

Hunter, W. W. *Lord Naas, Life of the Earl of Mayo.* 2 vols. London, 1875.

Hurst, Michael. *Maria Edgeworth and the Public Scene: Intellect, Fine Feeling and Landlordism in the Age of Reform.* Coral Gables, 1969.

Huxley, Gervas. *Victorian Duke: The Life of Hugh Lupas Grosvenor First Duke of Westminster.* London, 1967.

Huxley, Michael. ed. *Irish Anglicanism 1869–1969.* Dublin, 1970

Jenkins, Brian. *Fenians and Anglo-American Relations during Reconstruction.* Ithaca, 1969.

— *Britain and the war for the Union Volume 1.* Montreal, 1974.

— *Britain and the war for the Union Volume 2.* Montreal, 1980.

Bence-Jones, Mark. *Clive of India.* London, 1974.

Jenkyns, Richard. *The Victorians and Ancient Greece.* Oxford, 1980.

Jones, Wilbur Devereux and Erickson, Arvel B. *The Peelites 1846–1857.* Columbus, Ohio, 1972.

Jones, Howard. *To The Webster-Ashburton Treaty A Study in Anglo-American Relations 1783–1843.* Chapel Hill, 1977.

Kent, John. *Racing Life of Lord George Cavendish Bentinck.* London, 1892.

Khan, Abdul Majed. *The Transition of Bengal A Study of Saiyid Muhammad Reza Khan.* Cambridge, 1969.

Kraus, Horatio Sheafe. *Irish Life in Irish Fiction.* New York, 1903.

Larkin, Emmet. *The Roman Catholic Church in Ireland and the Fall of Parnell 1888–1891.* Chapel Hill, 1979.

Lecky, W. E. H. *A History of Ireland in the Eighteenth Century.* ed. by L. P. Curtis jr.

Le Fanu, W. R. *Seventy Years of Irish Life.* London, 1894.

Leveson–Gower, F. *Bygone Years.* London 1905.

Lewis, Samuel. *A Topographical Dictionary of Ireland.* 2 vols. London, 1837.

Longford, Elizabeth. *Wellington Pillar of State.* London, 1972.

— *Pilgrimage of Passion The Life of Wilfrid Scawen Blunt.* London, 1979.

Lyons, F. S. L. *Ireland since the Famine.* rev. ed. London, 1978.

Lyons, F. S. L. and Hawkins, R. A. J. *Ireland under the Union.* Oxford, 1980.

Mack, Edward C. *Public Schools and British Opinion 1780–1860 An Examination of the Relationship Between Contemporary Ideas and the Evolution of an English Institution.* London, 1938.

Mahon, Lord and Cardwell, Edward. *Memoirs by the Right Honourable Sir Robert Peel.* 2 vols. London, 1857.

Malcomson, A. P. W. *John Foster The Politics of the Anglo-Irish Ascendancy.* Oxford, 1978.

Maxwell, Constantia. *Dublin Under the Georges 1714–1830.* Dublin, 1946.

Maxwell, William H. *Wild Sports of the West.* London, 1832.

Mikhail, E. H. ed. *Lady Gregory Interviews and Recollections.* London, 1977.

Milligan, C. D. *The Siege of Londonderry 1689.* Londonderry, 1951.

— *The Walls of Derry: Their Building, Defending and Preserving,* pt. II. Londonderry, 1959.

Mills, Lennox A. *Ceylon under British Rule 1795–1932.* Oxford, 1933.

Minchin, J. G. Cotton. *Old Harrow Days.* London, 1898.

Moody, J. W. *Davitt and Irish Revolution 1846–82.* Oxford, 1981.

Moore, Maurice George. *An Irish Gentleman: George Henry Moore.* London, 1913.

Morris, W. O'Conner. *Memories and Thoughts of Life.* London, 1895.

Murphy, Daniel. ed. *Lady Gregory's Journals Volume 1.* Gerrards Cross, 1978.

McCaffrey, Lawrence J. *Daniel O'Connell and the Repeal Year.* Louisville, 1966.

McDowell, R. B. ed. *Social Life in Ireland 1800–1845.* Dublin, 1957.

— *Irish Public Opinion 1750–1800.* London, 1944.

— *Ireland in the Age of Imperialism and Revolution 1760–1801.* Oxford, 1979.

Macrory, Patrick. *The Seige of Derry.* London, 1980.

Namier, Sir Lewis. *England in the Age of the American Revolution.* 2nd ed. reprint, London, 1963.

— and Brooke, John. *The House of Commons 1754–1790.* 3 vols. London, 1964.

Norman, E. R. *Anti–Catholicism in Victorian England.* London, 1968.

— *Catholic Church in Ireland in the Age of Rebellion, 1859–1873.* London, 1965.

Nowlan, Kevin B. *The Politics of Repeal 1841–1850 A Study in the Relations between Great Britain and Ireland.* London, 1965.

O'Brien, R. Barry. *Dublin Castle and the Irish People.* London, 1909.

— *Fifty Years of Concessions to Ireland 1831–1881.* 2 vols. London, 1881.

— *Thomas Drummond Under Secretary in Ireland 1835–1840 Life and Letters.* London, 1889.

Ó Broin, Leon. *Fenian Fever An Anglo-American Dilemma.* New York, 1971.

O'Farrell, Patrick. *Ireland's English Question Anglo-Irish Relations 1534–1970.* London, 1971.

Orel, Harold. ed. *Irish History and Culture: Aspects of a People's Heritage.* Lawrence, Kansas, 1976.

Osborne, S. Godolphin. *Gleanings in the West of Ireland.* London, 1850.

Overton, John Henry and Wordsworth, Elizabeth. *Christopher Wordsworth Bishop of Lincoln 1807–1885.* London, 1888.

Pakenham, Thomas. *The Year of Liberty The story of the great Irish Rebellion of 1798.* London, 1969.

Parker, Charles Stuart. ed. *Sir Robert Peel from His Private Papers.* 3 vols. reprint, New York, 1920.

Parsons, Talcott. *Social Structure and Personality.* New York, 1964.

Philips, C. H. *The East India Company 1784–1834.* Manchester, 1961.

Pomfret, J. E. *The Struggle for Land in Ireland 1800–1923.* Princeton, 1930.

Probyn, J. W. ed. *Local Government and Taxation in the United Kingdom.* London, 1882.

Pycroft, Rev. James. *Oxford Memories.* 2 vols., London, 1886.

Reed, John R. *Victorian Conventions.* Athens, Ohio, 1975.

— *Old School Ties The Public Schools in British Literature* Syracuse, 1964.

Reynolds, James A. *The Catholic Emancipation Crisis in Ireland, 1823 – 1829.* reprint, Westport, Conn., 1970.

Richardson, Joanna. *George 1V A Portrait.* London, 1966.

Robertson, David. *Sir Charls Eastlake and the Victorian Art World.* Princeton, 1978.

Robson, Robert. *Ideas and Institutions of Victorian Britain.* New York, 1967.

Rugoff, Milton. *Prudery and Passion Sexuality and Victorian America.* New York, 1971.

Russell, W. H. *The Prince of Wales' Tour in India.* Montreal, 1877.

Saunders Lloyd C. ed. *Lord Melbourne's Papers.* reprint, New York, 1971.

Senior, Hereward. *Orangeism in Ireland and Britain 1795 – 1836.* London, 1966.

Seward, Frederick. *The Life of William H. Seward.* New York, 1877.

Simms, J. G. *Jacobite Ireland 1685 – 1691.* London, 1969.

Smith, E. A. *Whig Principles and Party Politics Earl Fitzwilliam and the Whig Party 1748 – 1833.* Manchester, 1975.

Smith, F. B. *The Making of the Second Reform Bill.* Cambridge, 1966.

Smythe, Colin. *A Guide to Coole Park, Co. Galway Home of Lady Gregory.* Gerrards Cross, 1973.

Solow, Barbara. *The Land Question and the Irish Economy 1870 – 1903.* Cambridge, Mass., 1971.

Somerville, E and Ross, Martin. *An Incorruptible Irishman.* London, 1932.

Spear, T. G. P. *The Nabobs A Study of the Social Life of the English in Eighteenth Century India.* London, 1932.

Spencer, Alfred. ed. *Memoirs of William Hickey.* 4 vols., London, 1925.

Staples, Hugh B. *The Ireland of Sir Jonah Barrington.* Seattle, 1967.

Steele, E. D. *Irish Land and British Politics Tenant Right and Nationality 1865 – 1870.* Cambridge, 1970.

Sutherland, Lucy S. *The East India Company in Eighteenth Century Politics.* Oxford, 1962.

Tennent, Sir James Emerson. *Ceylon An Account of the Island Physical, Historical and Topographical with notices of its Natural History, Antiquities and Productions.* 2 vols. 5th ed., London, 1860.

Thackeray, William M. *Irish Sketch Book for 1842.* London, 1843.

Thornton, Percy M. *Harrow School and its Surroundings.* London, 1885.

Tocqueville, Alexis de. *Journeys to England and Ireland.* ed. by J. P. Mayer. New Haven, Conn., 1958.

Torchiana, Donald. *W. B. Yeats and Georgian Ireland.* Evanston, Ill., 1966.

Torre, Rev. H. J. *Recollections of School Days at Harrow.* Manchester, 1890.

Trollope, Anthony. *An Autobiography.* Introduction by Bradford Allen Booth, Berkeley, 1947.

Trollope, Thomas Adolphus. *What I Remember.* 2 vols., London, 1887.

Tuckwell, Rev. W. *Reminiscences of Oxford.* London, 1907.

Tyler, J. E. *The Struggle for Imperial Unity 1868 – 1895.* London, 1938.

Vamplew, Wray. *The Turf. A Social and Economic History of Horse Racing.* London, 1976.

Vincent, John. ed. *Disraeli, Derby and the Conservative Party Journals and Memoirs of Edward Henry, Lord Stanley 1849 – 1869.* Hassocks, Sussex, 1978.

Wallace, Sarah Agnes and Gillespie, Frances Elma. *Journal of Benjamin Moran 1857 – 1865.* 2 vols., Chicago, 1948.

Waterfield, Gordon. *Layard of Nineveh.* London, 1963.

Wheatley, Henry B. ed. *The Historical and the Posthumous Memoir of Sir Nathaniel*

William Wraxall 1772–1784. 5 vols., London, 1884.

Wheeler, J. Talboys. *Early Records of British India: A History of the English Settlements of India.* London, 1878.

Whibley, Charles. *Lord John Manners and his friends.* 2 vols., Edinburgh, 1925.

Whyte, James Christie. *History of the British Turf.* 2 vols., London, 1840.

Whyte, J. H. *The Independent Irish Party 1850–59.* Oxford, 1958.

Wilcocke, S. H. trans. *Voyages to the East Indies by J. S. Stavoriuus.* 3 vols., reprint London, 1903.

Willis, N. Parker. *Famous Persona and Places.* Rochester, N. Y., 1854.

Willson, Beckles. *Ledger and Sword or The Honourable Company of Merchants of England Trading to the East Indies (1599–1874).* 2 vols., London, 1903.

Wilson, T. G. *Victorian Doctor Being the Life of Sir William Wilde.* New York, 1946.

Winter, James. *Robert Lowe.* Toronto, 1976.

Woodham-Smith, Cecil. *The Great Hunger* (New York, 1962).

Yeats, W. B. *Autobiographies.* London, 1966.

Young, Desmond. *Fountain of the Elephants.* London, 1959.

Ziegler, Philip. *Melbourne.* London, 1976.

Articles

Allen, Edward A. 'Public School Elites in Early Victorian England: The Boys at Harrow and Merchant Taylors' schools from 1825 to 1850', *Journal of British Studies*, XXI (1982), 87–117.

Aydelotte, W. O. 'The House of Commons of the 1840s', *History*, (1954), 248–262.

— 'The Country Gentlemen and the Repeal of the Corn Laws', *English Historical Review*, LXXXII (1967), 47–60.

Bakshian, Aran. 'John Zoffany', *History Today*, XXIX (1979), 419–428.

Beames, Michael. 'Concepts and Terms Cottiers and Conacre in Pre–Famine Ireland', *Journal of Peasant Studies*, II (1975), 352–54.

Buckley, K. 'The fixing of rents by agreement in co. Galway, 1881–5', *Irish Historical Studies*, VII (1951), 149–79.

— 'The records of the Irish land commission as a source of historical evidence', *Irish Historical Studies*, VIII (1952), 28–36.

Cahill, Gilbert A. 'The Protestant Association and the Anti-Maynooth Agitation of 1845', *Catholic Historical Review*, XLIII (1957), 273–308.

Caplan, Maurice. 'The New Poor Law and the Struggle for Union Chargeability', *International Review of Social History*, XXIII, pt. 2 (1978), 267–300.

Christianson, Cale E. 'Secret Societies and Agrarian Violence in Ireland', *Agricultural History*, XLVI (1972), 369–84.

Conacher, J. B. 'Peel and the Peelites 1846–50', *English Historical Review*, LXXIV (1958), 431–52.

Cousens, S. H. 'Emigration and Demographic Change in Ireland, 1851–61', *Economic History Review*, ser. 2, XIV (1961–2), 275–87.

— 'The Regional Variations in Population Changes in Ireland, 1861–81', *Economic History Review*, ser. 2, XVII (1964–5), 301–21.

— 'Regional Death Rates in Ireland during the Great Famine from 1846 to 1851', *Population Studies*, XV (1960–1), 55–74.

Crawford, Martin. 'British Travellers and the Anglo-American Relationship in the 1850s', *Journal of American Studies*, XII (1978), 203–19.

Cullop, Charles P. 'English Reaction to Stonewall Jackson's Death', *West*

History, XXIX (1967), 1–5.

Curtis, L. P. jr. 'Incumbered Wealth: Landed Indebtedness in Post–Famine Ireland', *American Historical Review*, XCV (1980), 332–67.

Davis, Richard W. 'Toryism to Tamworth: The Triumph of Reform, 1827–35', *Albion*, XII (1980), 132–46.

Derrett, J. Duncan M. 'Nandakumar's Forgery', *English Historical Review*, LXXV (1960), 223–38.

Escott, T. H. S. 'Egyptian Policy: A Retrospect', *Fortnightly Review*, XXXVIII (1882), 94–123.

Feingold, William L. 'The Tenants' Movement to capture the Irish Poor Law Boards, 1877–86', *Albion*, VII (1975), 216–31.

Goldsmid, Sir F. J. 'Non Political Control in Egypt', *Fortnightly Review*, XL (1883), 27–38.

Gregory, Sir W. H. 'Daniel O'Connell', *Nineteenth Century*, XXV (1889), 582–94.
— 'The Arundel Society', revised edition published by Arundel Society, 1887.

Griffiths, A. R. G. 'The Irish Board of Works in the Famine Years', *Historical Journal*, XIII (1970), 634–52.

Hamer, D. A. 'The Irish Question and Liberal Politics, 1886–94', *Historical Journal*, XII (1969), 511–32.

Hoppen, K. Theodore.',Landlords, Society and Electoral Politics in mid Nineteenth Century Ireland', *Past and Present*, LXXV (1977), 62–93.
— 'Tories, Catholics and the General Election of 1859', *Historical Journal*, XIII (1970), 48–67.
— 'Politics, the law and the nature of the Irish electorate', *English Historical Review*, XCII (1977), 746–76.

Jenkins, Brian. 'William Gregory Champion of the Confederacy',*History Today*, XXVIII (1978), 322–30.
— 'Frank Lawley and the Confederacy', *Civil War History*, XXIII (1977), 144–60.

Jupp, P. J. 'Irish Parliamentary Elections and the Influence of the Catholic Vote, 1801–20', *Historical Journal*, X (1967), 183–96.

Huttman, John P. 'Fenians and Farmers: The Merger of the Home–Rule and Owner–Occupancy Movements in Ireland, 1850–1915', *Albion*, III (1971), 182–93.

Keswani, Dhan. 'Private Commercial Dealings of the Servants of the East India Company from 1757–67', *Indian Historical Quarterly*, XXXVI (1960), 128–40.

Kriegel, A. D. 'The Irish Policy of Lord Grey's Government', *English Historical Review*, LXXXVI (1971), 22–45.

Lane, Padraig G. 'The Encumbered Estates Court', *Economic and Social Review*, III (1972), 413–53.

Larkin, Emmet. 'The Devotional Revolution in Ireland, 1850–75', *American Historical Review*, LXXVII (1972), 625–52.

Lewis, Frederick. 'The Governorship of Sir W. H. Gregory', *Colombo Historical Association*, Papers, XVI (1930).
— 'A Few Pioneer Estates and Early Pioneers in Ceylon', *Colombo Historical Association*, Papers, X (1927).

Macdonagh, Oliver. 'The politicization of the Irish Catholic Bishops, 1800–1850', *Historical Journal*, XVIII (1975), 37–53.
— 'The Irish Famine Emigration to the United States', *Perspectives in American History*, X (1976), 357–448.

McDowell, R. B. 'The Fitzwilliam Episode', *Irish Historical Studies*, XV (1966), 115–30

Machin, G. I. T. 'Lord John Russell and the Prelude to the Ecclesiastical Titles Bill, 1846–51', *Journal of Ecclesiastical History*, XXV (1974), 277–95.

— 'The Maynooth Grant, the Dissenters and Disestablishment, 1845–47', *English Historical Review*, LXXXII (1967), 61–85.

McCaffrey, Lawrence J. 'Irish Federalism in the 1870s: A Study in Conservative Nationalism', *Transactions of the American Philosophical Society*, LII (1962).

Miller, David W. 'Irish Catholicism and the Great Famine', *Journal of Social History*, IX (1975), 81–98.

Mukherji, Tarit Kumar. 'Aldermen and Attorneys — Mayor's Court Calcutta', *Indian Historical Quarterley*, XXVI (1950), 51–66.

Norman, E. R. 'The Maynooth Question of 1845', *Irish Historical Studies*, XV (1967), 407–37.

Paz, D. G. 'Popular Anti–Catholicism in England, 1850–51', *Albion*, XI (1979), 331–59.

Shipkey, Robert. 'The Problems of Irish Patronage during the Chief Secretaryship of Robert Peel, 1812–1818', *Historical Journal*, X (1967), 41–56.

Steele, E. D. 'Gladstone and Ireland', *Irish Historical Studies*, XVII (1970–71), 58–88.

Whyte, J. H. 'Landlord Influence at Elections in Ireland, 1760–1885', *English Historical Review*, LXXX (1965), 740–60.

— 'The Appointment of Catholic Bishops in Nineteenth Century Ireland', *Catholic Historical Review*, XLVIII (1962), 12–32.

— 'The Influence of the Catholic Clergy on Elections in Nineteenth Century Ireland', *English Historical Review*, LXXV (1960), 239–59 .

Index

333

England, 15, 16, 27, 43, 45, 61, 77, 94,
    113, 124, 151, 163, 195
Epsom, 43
Established Church, 9, 15, 17, 19, 21,
    55, 58–61, 63, 64, 69, 72, 175, 176,
    179, 184, 186–89, 198
    and the Protestant crusade, 17
    and disestablishment, 179, 183, 184,
    186–89, 198
Exeter Hall, 63

Fahy, Father Jerome, 277, 286
Fallon, Patrick, Bishop of Kilmacduagh
    and Kilfenora, 129, 130, 132,
Famine, 65, 69, 71, 72, 74, 75, 90–6,
    108, 114, 170, 239, 256, 257
Fenians, 172–77, 183, 186, 191, 194
Ferguson, A. M., 220, 249, 274
Fitzgerald, Vesey, 18
Fitzwilliam, Lord, 9–11
Fortescue, Chichester, 185, 187, 188,
    190, 193, 197, 199, 211, 213
Fortnightly Review, 271, 281
Fox, Charles James, 7, 85
Freeman's Journal, 69, 190
French Revolution, 9, 11, 15, 62
Gaisford, Dean, 38, 40
Galle, 221, 223, 228, 251
Galway, 3, 4, 6, 9, 10, 11, 16, 22, 46,
    53, 58, 66, 72, 80, 82, 83, 90, 91, 94,
    100, 103, 108, 114, 122, 129, 137, 139,
    159, 165, 170–72, 186, 194, 242, 258,
    260, 264, 279, 290, 294, 298
    and politics, 80, 81, 88, 101, 109,
    115–20, 129, 131–33, 137, 138, 165,
    174, 184, 185, 214–17, 255–57
Galway Mercury, 134
Galway Packet Line, 135, 138, 146,
    167–70
Galway packet station, 135, 168–70, 194
Galway Vindicator, 109, 130, 133, 170,
    171, 177, 185,
Gambling, 7, 8, 43, 44, 46, 54, 79
Garbally, 47, 82
Gentleman's Magazine, 205
Germany, 43, 44
Gladstone, William Ewart, 62, 68, 105,
    139, 155, 157, 162, 163, 165, 182–85,
    188, 193–95, 197, 199, 202, 209, 210,
    237, 241, 257, 263, 264, 270, 272, 273,
    277, 279, 281, 287–94
Gort, 82, 83, 88–90, 93, 117, 118, 130,
    256, 275, 282, 283, 286, 287, 290, 295
Gort Poor Law Union, 85, 87, 90–92,
    238
    and Board of Guardians, 90–94, 109,
    191, 278

    and workhouse, 91–93, 295
Gort Relief Fund, 89
Graham, Sir James, 57, 105
Graham, Sandford, 125–27
Granville, Earl, 211, 213
Gray, Sir John, 190, 197
Greece, 156–58
Gregg, Rev. Tresham Dames, 49, 50,
    57, 63, 75, 77–80, 116, 132
Gregory, Anne, 21, 22
Gregory, Lady Anne (Trench), 9, 21,
    22, 36
Gregory, Lady (Augusta Persse), 259,
    260, 263–66, 270–72, 274, 275, 277,
    281, 282, 285, 291, 29–97
Gregory, Charles, 252, 278, 283
Gregory, Elizabeth "Bess," 22, 27, 36,
    55, 96, 107, 108, 126, 128, 129, 205,
    218, 219, 224, 225, 242, 247, 252
Gregory, Elizabeth "Lizzie," 218–221,
    223–25, 235–37, 239, 241, 258, 259
Gregory, George, 1–3
Gregory, Henry, 3, 4
Gregory, Richard, 8, 9, 12, 21, 22, 34,
    40, 46, 84, 85, 89, 105, 205
Gregory, Robert, the nabob, 3–9, 11,
    12, 21, 83–85, 95, 125, 291
Gregory, Robert, senior merchant, 6–8,
    97
Gregory, Robert, 21, 22, 27, 36, 44, 46,
    48, 58, 68, 81, 85, 97, 105, 110, 205
    and Coole, 85, 87–89, 129
    and the Famine, 89–91, 96
Gregory, William, 9, 22, 25, 26, 28,
    34–38, 40, 41, 44, 46, 50, 54–56, 61,
    64, 85, 95, 97, 108
    as Under Secretary, 11–14, 19, 21, 22,
    24
    conservatism, 9, 13, 14
    and opposition to Catholic claims,
    14–18, 20, 27
Gregory, Rev. William, 21, 96
Gregory, William Henry, 20, 24, 36–38,
    46, 54, 60, 70, 79, 121, 124, 134, 158,
    210, 213, 241, 253–57, 266, 297
    and Americans, 125, 139, 143
    and American Civil War, 146–48,
    150–56, 158
    and *Autobiography*, 43, 53, 63, 68, 94, 97
    and British Museum, 200, 201, 208,
    209
    and Canada, 140–42
    and Ceylon, 211, 214, 220–45,
    247–51, 253, 274, 277, 298
    and childhood, 24–28
    and democracy, 61, 143, 160, 161,
    163, 165, 252, 287, 298